英语词汇学

| 第二版 |

主编◎汪榕培 王春荣

English
Lexicology:
A Coursebook

华东师范大学出版社
·上海·

图书在版编目(CIP)数据

英语词汇学/汪榕培,王春荣主编. —2版. —上海:华东师范大学出版社,2022
 ISBN 978-7-5760-3479-0

Ⅰ.①英⋯　Ⅱ.①汪⋯②王⋯　Ⅲ.①英语—词汇　Ⅳ.①H313

中国版本图书馆 CIP 数据核字(2022)第 226857 号

英语词汇学　第二版

主　　编　汪榕培　王春荣
责任编辑　李恒平
责任校对　林小慧　时东明
装帧设计　俞　越

出版发行　华东师范大学出版社
社　　址　上海市中山北路3663号　邮编 200062
网　　址　www.ecnupress.com.cn
电　　话　021-60821666　行政传真 021-62572105
客服电话　021-62865537　门市(邮购)电话 021-62869887
地　　址　上海市中山北路3663号华东师范大学校内先锋路口
网　　店　http://ecnup.taobao.com/

印 刷 者　常熟高专印刷有限公司
开　　本　787毫米×1092毫米　1/16
印　　张　21
字　　数　507千字
版　　次　2023年1月第2版
印　　次　2024年7月第3次
书　　号　ISBN 978-7-5760-3479-0
定　　价　59.00元

出 版 人　王　焰

(如发现本版图书有印订质量问题,请寄回本社客服中心调换或电话 021-62865537 联系)

主　编（第二版）　汪榕培　　王春荣

主　编（第一版）　汪榕培　　王之江　　朱越峰

副主编　沈昌洪　　吴晓维　　汪学磊　　俞霞君

编　委　汪榕培　　王之江　　朱越峰　　沈昌洪

　　　　吴晓维　　汪学磊　　俞霞君　　王春荣

Preface
(Second Edition)

The first edition of this coursebook has been used in the classroom for over ten years. Since its first publication, there has been considerable progress in linguistic studies. So some chapters had to be revised or modified. The authors found it necessary to modify the first chapter to provide such fundamentals as the definition of lexis, lexicon, lexicalization, lexicology, methods and the latest development in lexicology. Other chapters have been reviewed and revised as necessary and in response to reviewers of the second edition, to whom I would like to express my gratitude for their suggestions. The URLs for websites cited in the text have all been checked and updated and quite a few figures and tables have been updated where required.

This coursebook is aimed at students of English language or linguistics, taking courses in the analysis and description of the English language, possibly with little prior knowledge of linguistics. In order to encourage interaction with the material discussed in the book, each chapter is interspersed with tasks, some of which require dictionary consultation. It is therefore advised that students should have a good up-to-date dictionary at hand, preferably of the desk-size or collegiate type. A key to the exercises is provided at the end.

I am pleased that the book continues to be used in teaching about English words and vocabulary, and I trust that this further edition will provide students of the English language with a useful introduction to the lexicology of English.

Wang Chunrong
August 10, 2022 in Shanghai

Foreword
(First Edition)

    Vocabulary, as an integral component of language, comprises an important part of language teaching and learning. Lexicology, the science of the study of vocabulary, is an indispensable part of linguistics. However, the mainstream of twentieth-century linguistics has largely ignored this discipline and thus hindered the development of language research and education. Thanks to the growth of the computational science and the cognitive science, people have again realized the significance of vocabulary and paid more attention to the study of it. Lexicology has revived and provided a new impetus to language teaching and learning.

    English Lexicology is one of the core courses for English majors. *English Lexicology: A Coursebook* gives a concise account of the basic concepts of the discipline, providing insights into the growth, mechanism, structure, employment and learning strategies of the English vocabulary for undergraduate students of the English major and other learners of the English language.

    The present book is compiled with joint efforts with the colleagues of Hangzhou Normal University. I cherish a pleasant memory of the six years of cooperation with them and hope that the young teachers will make rapid progress in their research and teaching. I also hope that the readers will benefit from this book.

Wang Rongpei
March 3, 2011 in Suzhou

Contents

Chapter 1 English Words and Lexicology — Basic Concepts 1
  1.1 Understanding Words 1
  1.2 Understanding Lexicology 7

Chapter 2 The Growth of the English Vocabulary (1) — Sources 16
  2.1 The Language Family of English 16
  2.2 From Old English to Modern English 18
  2.3 The Origins of English Words 22

Chapter 3 The Growth of the English Vocabulary (2) — British & American 36
  3.1 World Englishes 36
  3.2 British English 39
  3.3 American English 41
  3.4 The Future of English 47

Chapter 4 The Growth of the English Vocabulary (3) — New Words 53
  4.1 Neologisms 53
  4.2 The Study of New Words 55
  4.3 Reasons of the Growth 58
  4.4 Sources for New Words 62

Chapter 5 The Formation of English Words (1) — Major Types 69
  5.1 Notions of Morphological Formation 69
  5.2 Derivation 73
  5.3 Conversion 77
  5.4 Compounding 80

Chapter 6 The Formation of English Words (2) — Minor Types 89
  6.1 Abbreviation 89
  6.2 Back-formation 97
  6.3 Onomatopoeia 98
  6.4 Reduplication 99

Chapter 7   The Meanings of English Words (1) — Aspects of Meaning; Change of Meaning 106
   7.1   Aspects of Meaning 106
   7.2   Change of Meaning 110
   7.3   Mechanisms for Meaning Change 120

Chapter 8   The Meanings of English Words (2) — Sense Relations 126
   8.1   Synonymy 126
   8.2   Antonymy 129
   8.3   Polysemy 131
   8.4   Homonymy 132
   8.5   Hierarchical Relations 134

Chapter 9   Lexical Chunks (1) — Collocations 143
   9.1   Lexical Chunking 143
   9.2   Definition of Collocation 145
   9.3   The Features of Collocation 148
   9.4   Characteristics, Classifications and Categories of Collocations 150
   9.5   Basic Types of Collocations 153
   9.6   The Significance of Learning Collocations 158

Chapter 10   Lexical Chunks (2) — Idioms 163
   10.1   Definition of Idiom 163
   10.2   Classifications of Idioms 165
   10.3   Figurative Idioms 174

Chapter 11   The Use of English Words (1) — Words in Context 181
   11.1   Words and Their Meanings in Use 181
   11.2   The Meanings of Words: "Mean" and "Meaning" 182
   11.3   Lexical Semantics 183
   11.4   Lexical Semantics and Lexical Pragmatics 189
   11.5   Lexical Meaning and the Context 192
   11.6   Meanings of English Words in Lexical Pragmatics 195

Chapter 12   The Use of English Words (2) — Metaphor, Metonymy, etc. 203
   12.1   An Introduction to Figures of Speech: the Figurative Uses of Words 203
   12.2   English Words in Metaphor 204
   12.3   English Words in Metonymy 212
   12.4   Other Figurative Uses of English Words 214

Chapter 13   The Dictionaries of English Words (1) — Types of Dictionaries 224
   13.1   The Development of Dictionaries 225
   13.2   The Contents of Dictionaries 230
   13.3   The Types of Dictionaries 235

Chapter 14　The Dictionaries of English Words (2) — How to Use Dictionaries ······ 246
 14.1　How to Use Dictionaries ·· 246
 14.2　Corpus and Lexicography ··· 250
 14.3　Electronic Dictionaries ·· 256

Chapter 15　The Learning of English Words (1) — The Mental Lexicon ··············· 268
 15.1　Memory in the Language-Processing System ······························· 268
 15.2　The Mental Lexicon and Its Organization ·································· 275
 15.3　Variables Influencing Lexical Access ·· 279

Chapter 16　The Learning of English Words (2) — Learning Strategies and Tactics ······ 287
 16.1　The Vocabulary Size ·· 287
 16.2　Vocabulary Acquisition ·· 289
 16.3　Vocabulary Learning Strategies ·· 294

References ·· 308

Key ··· 318

Chapter 1
English Words and Lexicology
— Basic Concepts

Points for Thinking
1. How do you define "word"?
2. What are the differences between the physical and semantic structures of the word?
3. What is vocabulary?
4. How large do you think your vocabulary is as a college student of English?
5. Give examples to illustrate the development of lexicology.

When Ali Baba used the magic words to swing open the door of the robbers' cave, he was dazzled by the array of precious jewels and gold piled inside. Just learning the words "Open sesame!" made him rich beyond his dreams. In a sense, all words are magic, and like the treasure in Ali Baba's cave, a good vocabulary including the usage of words — their forms, pronunciations, histories, meanings, etc. can be an "open sesame" to success in education, professional work, and social life.

1.1 Understanding Words

Words, which help people to know the language and use the language to exchange their thoughts, are an important part of the linguistic knowledge. Every language learner may agree that we can learn thousands of words in a language but still do not know what the word is. We use words every day, yet, we find it very difficult to state explicitly what a word is. Leonard Bloomfield, one of the greatest linguists in the 20th century, gave a definition in 1933 that "a minimum free form is a word". This can be viewed as one of the classical definitions of the word, by which Bloomfield means that the word is the smallest meaningful linguistic unit that can be used on its own. Its physical form cannot be divided into smaller units that can be used independently to convey the same meaning. For instance, *book* is a word. We cannot divide it up into smaller units that can convey meanings when they stand alone. On the other hand, the word *bookish* can be further divided into *book-* and *-ish*. While the *book* bit of *bookish* is meaningful when used independently, the same is not true with *-ish* which cannot be used on its own, though it means something like "having the (objectionable) qualities of" (as in *childish, devilish, impish, mannish, sheepish, womanish*, etc.).

There is a great need to understand what a word is in an explicit and systematic manner. In order to do this, we should have an awareness of the "nature" of words. Words should be seen in terms of the physical or morphological structure and the internal or semantic structure, and not simply as isolated entities, each carrying one fixed "meaning".

1.1.1 The morphological structure of the word

By the morphological structure of a word, we mean the word's external structure from a morphological point of view. If we look at the word *revitalized*, we can see that it can be analyzed into several units of meaning: *re-vital-ize-d*. These smaller elements can be recognized as parts of other words in which they have the same meaning. For instance, the element *re* occurs in *repossess* and *retake* with the meaning of *again*. *Vital* occurs by itself as a word and in *vitality* with the meaning of *life* or *liveliness*. The element *ize* occurs in *nationalize* and *pluralize*, with the function of *change this adjective into a verb*. Finally, the element *(e)d* occurs in *tied* and *turned* with the meaning of *past tense or past participle*. These smaller units of meaning are called *morphemes* and may be defined as the minimal units of meaning in a language. All these morphemes constitute the physical structure of the word *revitalized*. It should be borne in mind that the knowledge of the word's morphological structure helps us decode words and acquire their morphologically related forms, e.g.

kind — *kindly, kindness, kindliness, unkind, unkindly*;
like — *likely, unlike, unlikely, alike, likelihood*;
live — *alive, lively, liven, enliven, liveliness, livelihood*;
pure — *impure, impurity, purify, purification*;
response — *responsive, responsible, irresponsible, responsibility*.

The above groupings of word families or "paradigms" are useful in making us aware of the morphological rules of the word.

In a word which is composed of more than one morpheme there is a central one which contains the principal meaning, and a peripheral one or peripheral ones attached to the central morpheme. For example, in *undecided*, the morpheme *decide* is central, while *un-* and *-ed* are peripheral. The central morpheme is called the *root* while the peripheral morphemes are called *affixes*. Compounding, which involves the combination of more than one root to form a new word (e.g. *babysit*, *teapot*), and conversion, which involves a change in the word class of a word without the addition of affixes (e.g. ˈobject n. — obˈject v.), are two more major morphological types in the physical structure of a word.

The morphological structure of a word is also concerned with various word-formation patterns which will be further discussed in Chapters 5 and 6.

> **Task**
> Many English words are formed from combinations of words and prefixes or suffixes, or from combinations of other words. It is plausible to be able to find a connection between the meaning of a combination and the meanings of its parts. So if you find a new word, you may be able to guess what it means.
> Match the items in Column I to those in Column II.
> Column I   Column II
> 1. biopic   A. a place where scientists look at stars, etc.
> 2. point of view   B. to say the opposite of a statement, opinion, etc.
> 3. contradict   C. an idea or opinion
> 4. pro-education   D. a film based on the events of someone's life
> 5. observatory   E. in favor of education
> Key: 1. D   2. C   3. B   4. E   5. A

1.1.2 The semantic structure of the word

A word's semantic or internal structure, is commonly referred to as its meaning. Words can serve the purposeful communication of human beings solely due to their meanings. So it is certain that the semantic structure is one of the word's main aspects. Among the word's various characteristics, *meaning* is definitely the most important, for the very function of the word in a language is made by its possessing of a meaning. Only through the meaning can a concept be communicated. A word has the ability of denoting concrete objects, real qualities, actual actions and abstract notions.

Denotation refers to the conceptual meaning of the word. When we want to know the meaning of a word, it is its denotation that we ask for. For example, we may define *great* as *big, large, huge* and *grand*; therefore we may say that *great* denotes *big, large, huge* and *grand*. However, *great* may have other meanings or denotations: *more than usual, important / powerful, enthusiastic about something or someone, able to do something very well, for expressing pleasure or agreement, very good / enjoyable / attractive, showing relationships between previous generations of family members, very well* (adv.), *someone who is admired by a lot of people, especially someone famous* (n.), etc.

For example,

China is a *great* country with a population of more than 1.3 billion people.

Albert Einstein was one of the *greatest* scientists in the 20th century.

A huge earthquake hit Wenchuan in Sichuan Province on May 12, 2008, causing the *greatest* environmental disaster in decades in China.

The representatives of the NPC are entering the *Great* Hall of the People in Beijing.

The really *great* thing about this computer is its speed.

She is *great* at mathematics and physics.

Isn't she *great* with the children?

I have never been a *great* one for spiders and snakes.

She's a *great* reader of biographies.

Your *great*-aunt is the sister of one of your grandparents.

I don't think that we played *great*.

Fred Perry is one of the all-time *greats* of tennis.

Great Britain is used for referring to the unity of England, Scotland and Wales. It is often simply called Britain.

Generally speaking, the different denotations of a word are not unrelated, but they are closely related to the basic meaning of the word. Let's take *father* and *head* for example.

Table 1.1 Different Denotations of *Father*

Denotations	Examples
one's make parent	People often call their *father* Dad, or especially if they are young children, Daddy.
a title of respect for a priest, especially a Roman Catholic priest	*Father* Peter said that wasn't a sin.
used for talking to or about God in the Christian religion	Heavenly *Father*, please hear our prayers.
Santa Claus: an imaginary old man with a long white beard and a red suit who brings presents for children at Christmas	A primary school teacher left a class of 25 pupils in tears when she told them *Father* Christmas does not exist.
the man who started something or first did it successfully	Albert Einstein was the *father* of modern physics.

Table 1.2　Different denotations of *head*

Denotations	Examples
the upper part of a human body	I saw a bruise on the side of her *head*.
the leader or most important person in a group (company, school, etc.)	The ceremony was attended by *heads* of government from 27 countries.
the top or front part of something (a bed, a table, etc.)	He walked straight to the *head* of the queue. / When we have dinner, my grandfather always sits at the *head* of the table.

However, the different denotations can sometimes be unrelated. Let's take *order* and *row* for example.

Table 1.3　Different denotations of *order*

Denotations	Examples
an instruction given by someone in a position of authority	Try to persuade your employees, and don't just give *orders*.
a request for a product to be made or delivered to someone	A major *order* for 100,000 cars will guarantee the company's future.
the way in which a set of things is arranged or done	Please try to keep the pictures in *order*.
a situation in which people obey the law and follow the accepted rules of social behavior	The police's most urgent task will be to maintain *order*.

Table 1.4　Different denotations of *row*

Denotations	Examples
a series of people or things arranged in a straight line	We can see a *row* of new houses by the river. / The soldiers stood in a *row* against the wall.
a short journey in a rowing boat	Let's go for a *row* on the lake on Sunday.
to move a boat through water or move a boat as a sport	The young people *rowed* past the docks. / As an athlete, he used to *row* for his college.

Words do not exist in isolation and their meanings are defined by contexts and by their relations with each other. Most words have several denotations. Only by knowing the context in which the particular word occurs can we understand what the word means or which specific denotation is intended.

Another type of meaning of a word is its connotative or affective meaning called connotation. Connotation refers to a meaning that is implied by a word apart from the thing which it describes explicitly. Words carry cultural and emotional associations or meanings, in addition to their literal meanings or denotations. For instance, *Wall Street* literally means a street situated in Lower Manhattan, but connotatively it refers to wealth and power. Below are a few common connotation examples. Their suggested meanings are shaped by cultural and emotional associations:

● "He's such a dog." — In this sense, the word *dog* connotes shamelessness, or

ugliness.
- "That woman is a dove at heart." — Here, the *dove* implies peace or gentility.
- "There's no place like home." — While *home* may refer to the actual building someone lives in, connotatively, it most often refers to family, comfort, and security.
- "What do you expect from a politician?" — *Politician* has a negative connotation of wickedness and insincerity. To imply sincerity, the word *statesperson* might be used.
- "That woman is so pushy!" — *Pushy* refers to someone who is loud-mouthed, insisting, and irritating.
- "My mom and dad worked hard to put me through college." — The words *mom* and *dad*, when used in place of *mother* and *father*, connote loving parents, rather than simply biological parents.

While some words may have similar denotations, they may have different connotations and thus they may not be used interchangeably. These connotations may be positive or negative, e. g.

lean, slim, skinny, slender, thin;
obstinate, tenacious, stubborn, determined, resolute, hard-headed;
complacent, content, satisfied, easy-going, resigned.

It is obvious that contexts and clearly defined meanings are vital in knowing words. Only by seeing words in clear, meaningful contexts can we understand different denotations and connotations. One good contextualized example of a word may be more effective than a long definition or explanation. For example, "*It was so stifling in the room that I could hardly breathe.*" is a better illustration of the meaning of *stifling* than "*It was stifling in the room.*" because it actually defines the meaning of *stifling* with the help of "*that I could hardly breathe*". We should look closely to contexts when trying to understand words or looking up words in the dictionary. (See further discussions about the meanings of English words in Chapters 7 & 8)

Task

We may say that *dawn* denotes "daybreak" or "sunrise". However, *dawn* may have other meanings or denotations, e. g.
    It was the *dawn* of a new era.
    The solution began to *dawn* on him.
Write the different denotations of the word *branch*:
    branch — of a tree, of a company, of knowledge, ...
Can you write some gradable words in between?
    enormous — very big — ... — ... — ... — very small — tiny

---

So far we have highlighted the word's major characteristics — the morphological structure or the form and the semantic structure or the meaning, which, of course, do not suffice to give a detailed definition of the word. However, all that we have talked about can help us understand how *The New Oxford Dictionary of English* (2003) defines *word: a single distinct meaningful element of speech or writing, used with others (or sometimes alone) to form a sentence and typically shown with a space on either side when written or printed.* From the relatively authoritative definition of *word*, we understand the fundamental nature of the word:

Firstly, the word is a unit of speech or writing, which serves the purposeful human communication;

Secondly, the word can be perceived as the total of the sounds that comprise it;

Thirdly, the word, in writing, is seen as a sequence of letters bounded on either side by a blank space;

Fourthly, the word, viewed linguistically, possesses its physical structure (form) and semantic structure (meaning).

1.1.3 Vocabulary

Vocabulary, generally speaking, refers to all the words used in a particular kind of work, business, etc. or known to a particular person. *The New Oxford Dictionary of English* (2003) gives the definition of *vocabulary*: (i) a part of such a body of words used on a particular occasion or in a particular sphere: *the vocabulary of law*/ [mass noun] *The term became part of business vocabulary;* (ii) the body of words known to an individual person: *He had a wide vocabulary;* (iii) a list of difficult or unfamiliar words with an explanation of their meanings, accompanying a piece of specialist or foreign-language text; (iv) a range of artistic or stylistic forms, techniques, or movements: *Dance companies have their own vocabularies of movements.*

Penny Ur says in his book *A Course in Language Teaching: Practice and Theory* (2000):

> Vocabulary can be defined, roughly, as the words we teach in the foreign language. However, a new item of vocabulary may be more than a single word: for example, *post office* and *mother-in-law*, which are made up of two or three words but express a single idea. There are also multi-word idioms such as *call it a day*, where the meaning of the phrase cannot be deduced from an analysis of the component words. A useful convention is to cover all such cases by talking about vocabulary "items" rather than "words".

In terms of what is said above, Ur continues to point out that in order to help language learners enlarge their vocabulary, *form* (*pronunciation and spelling*), *grammar* and *collocation* need to be taught. It is implied that these three aspects are supposed to be the most important in vocabulary. Vocabulary is central to the learning and the use of the language. As D. A. Wilkins says, "without grammar very little can be conveyed; without vocabulary nothing can be conveyed."

A typical example of the vocabulary size of English native speakers is shown in *Teaching and Learning Vocabulary* by I. S. P. Nation (1990):

VOCABULARY SIZE OF NATIVE SPEAKERS

Age in years	Vocabulary size	Age in years	Vocabulary size
1.3	235	10.7	7020
2.8	405	11.7	7860
3.8	700	12.8	8700
5.5	1528	13.9	10660
6.5	2500	15.0	12000
8.5	4480	18.0	17600
9.6	6620		

In thinking about the size of the English vocabulary, we should be careful about what sort of vocabulary we are referring to: "the words used by almost every English speaker, the words used by an average person, the words understood by an average person, all the words used by any

English speaker, all possible words, whether actually attested or not, the words most often used by many persons, and so on" (Romaine, 1997). It is estimated by English experts that in Britain an average user of English may have a vocabulary of 50 thousand words, compared with those without higher education whose working vocabulary is about 35 thousand words. However, the well-educated people may need to have a vocabulary size of over 75 thousand words before they could be called "the social elite".

English and globalization have spread hand in hand throughout the world since the last decades of the 20th century. The process started with the rapid development of the world's politics, economics, culture, science and technology and continues with the new virtual empire of the Internet. By most common estimates, at the end of the third decade in the 21st century, about 450 million people will speak English as a first language, another 300 to 500 million as a fluent second language, and perhaps more than 800 million as a foreign language. Thus the English language no longer "belongs" to its native speakers in the English-speaking countries and regions but to the whole world. As a phenomenon never seen before, English is spoken in some form by three times as many nonnative speakers as native speakers. Not only Caribbean English, South African English, etc. but also Chinese English, Indian English, etc. are rapidly increasing their share of the English language. The change that is ongoing in present-day English is the easiest to see in its vocabulary, which has grown so much in size. At present, new English words are being coined at the rate of 14.7 words per day, that is, a new word appears every 98 minutes. As expected by Global Language Monitor (GLM), Texas U.S.A., English crossed the 1,000,000 word threshold on June 10, 2009 at 10:22 a.m. GMT. Consider the age of William Shakespeare when there were said to be only about 100 thousand words in the English vocabulary that were used by only about 2 million people.

Task
Choose an intensive reading passage, either from a textbook or from other sources. How would you deal with the vocabulary in the passage in order to concentrate upon understanding the content and gradually enlarge your vocabulary?
    Firstly, if an unknown word is not essential to understanding the text, nor useful, ignore it.
    Secondly, if an unknown word is essential to understanding the text, but not useful, use a synonym or translate it.
    Thirdly, if an unknown word is both essential to understanding the text and useful, translate it or give a synonym and later try to learn it by heart.
    ...

1.2 Understanding Lexicology

1.2.1 What is lexis, lexicon and lexicalization

Lexis is a term in linguistics referring to the vocabulary of a language. Lexis is a Greek term meaning "word" or "speech". We will often use the word *vocabulary* interchangeably with *lexis*. But it should be noted that *lexis* and *vocabulary* are non-count nouns; if it is the individual items that are referred to, we should talk about *lexical items* or *vocabulary items*. We might also encounter the term lexicon, which unfortunately can be used in a couple of ways: firstly, it can be used as a more technical version of lexis; many people use it synonymously with *dictionary*. What must be remembered is that any dictionary can never be comprehensive in its listing of the lexis of a particular language. The process of adding words and word patterns to the lexicon of a language is called lexicalization.

> **Information Box**
> *lexis*: all the words in a language;　　*lexicon*: the vocabulary of a language;
> *lexico-*: of lexis or lexicon;　　　　　　*-logy*: the science or study of.
> Combine "lexico-" and "-logy", and you can have the form of the word "lexicology" and you can also get the meaning of it.

1.2.2　What is lexicology

Lexicology might be defined as the study of the lexicon or lexis (specified as the vocabulary or total stock of words of a language). *The New Oxford Dictionary of English* (2003) defines *lexicology* as *the study of form, meaning, and behavior of words*. There are other prevalent views on this term. *Lexicology is a branch of linguistics, inquiring into the origins and meanings of words* (Webster's new world dictionary). *Lexicology is an area of a language study concerned with the nature, meaning, history, and use of words and word elements and often also with the critical description of lexicography* (Oxford Concise Companion to the English Language). To briefly sum up, lexicology aims at investigating and studying the morphological structures of words, their semantic structures, relations, historical development, formation and usages. However, lexicology must not be confused with lexicography, the writing or compilation of dictionaries, which is a special technique rather than a level of language studies.

Lexicology must include both the study of individual words and their structure and of the overall structure of the vocabulary as a whole. In other words, lexicology deals not only with simple words in all their aspects but also with complex and compound words, the meaningful units of language. Since these units must be analyzed in respect of both their form and their meaning, lexicology relies on information derived from morphology, the study of the forms of words and their components, and semantics, the study of their meanings (Jackson and Amvela, 2007). It may be thought at first sight that phonology does not interact with lexicology in any significant manner. However, if we compare, for instance, the pair of *toy* and *boy*, *feet* and *fit*, *pill* and *pin*, they differ only in one sound unit and yet the difference has serious consequences at the level of lexicology (Amvela, 2000). The position of lexicology can be illustrated in the following classical structuralist model in Ullmann's *Principles of Semantics* (1957).

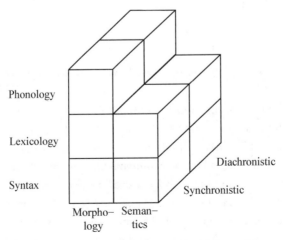

Fig. 1.1　Classical structuralist linguistic model

In this three-dimensional linguistic model, lexicology, as the discipline concerned with the lexicon, is represented as a level in between phonology and syntax. All three levels, phonology, lexicology and syntax, are subsystems of the entire language system. They may be described at a particular point in time, i.e. synchronically, or in their historical evolution, i.e. diachronically. Phonology, which is concerned with the sound system of the language, has a formal but no semantic aspect. Lexicology has both a morphological and a semantic dimension, and both may be regarded from a diachronic or a synchronic point of view. The same holds for syntax, which is concerned with larger linguistic units.

1.2.3 Methods in lexicology

In M. A. K. Halliday's eyes, there are two principal methods for describing lexical items. One is by writing a dictionary; the other is by writing a thesaurus. In a dictionary, words are arranged in alphabetical order, so the place where a word occurs shows nothing about what it means. On the other hand, words that are similar in meaning are grouped together in a thesaurus (e.g. all the words that are species of fish or all the words for emotion).

In a dictionary, each entry stands by itself as an independent piece of work. There may be some cross-referencing to save repetition; but it plays only a relatively small part. Here is a typical entry from a fairly detailed dictionary of English, the *New Shorter Oxford English Dictionary* (2007).

cut/kʌt/ *v*. Infl. **-tt-**. Pa. t. & pple **cut**. See also CUT. CUTTED *ppl adjs*. ME [Rel. to Norw. *kutte*, Icel. *kuta* cut with a little knife, *kuti* little blunt knife. Prob. already in OE.]

I *v. t.* Penetrate or wound with a sharp-edged thing; make an incision in. ME.

b *fig.* Wound the feelings of (a person), hurt deeply.

(...)

1 N. MOSLEY The edge of the pipe cut his mouth, which bled. *fig.* : ADDISON Tormenting thought! it cuts into my soul.

b F. BURNEY He says something so painful that it cuts us to the soul.

(...)

Phrases: (...)

cut both ways have a good and bad effect; (of an argument) support both sides.

cut corners *fig.* scamp work, do nothing inessential. (...)

Fig. 1.2 The entry "cut" in the *New Shorter Oxford English Dictionary* (2007)

Generally speaking, entries in a dictionary are organized as follows:
1. the headword or lemma, often in bold or some other special font;
2. its pronunciation, in some form of alphabetic notation;
3. its word class (part of speech)
4. its etymology (historical origin and derivation)
5. its definition
6. citations (examples of its use)

In a thesaurus, by contrast, there is no separate entry for each word. The word occurs simply as part of a list; and it is the place of a word in the whole construction of the book that tells you what it means.

Thus if we look for the same word *cut* in Roget's *Thesaurus of English Words and Phrases*, we will find it in the middle of a paragraph as follows:

v. **cultivate**; till (the soil); farm, garden; sow, plant; reap, mow, cut; manure, dress the ground, dig, delve, dibble, hoe, plough, plow, harrow, rake, weed, lap and top, force, transplant, thin out, bed out, prune, graft.

This may not seem to have very much organization in it; but it is actually the final layer in a comprehensive lexical taxonomy, an organization of words into classes and sub-classes and sub-sub-classes (etc.). Many of us might organize our shopping around taxonomies such as the one for *fruit* shown in the following figure.

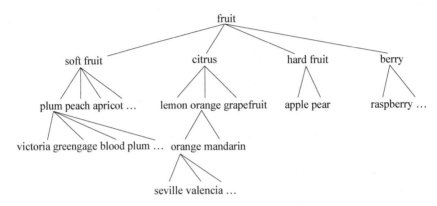

Fig. 1.3 The taxonomy for fruit

1.2.4 Development of English lexicology

Leonard Bloomfield made a successful attempt last century to define the word according to formal rather than semantic criteria, the main concern of which is the relation of the word to the sentence. S. Ullmann pointed out in 1979 in his academic book *Semantics: An Introduction to the Science of Meaning* that the word plays such a crucial part in the structure of language that it is necessary to have a special branch of linguistics to examine it in all its aspects, and that lexicology deals not only with words but also with all types of morphemes entering into the composition of words. S. Ullmann summarized what he had explored: "Lexicology deals by definition with words and word-forming morphemes, that is to say with significant units. It follows that these elements must be investigated both in their form and in their meaning. Lexicology will therefore have two subdivisions: *morphology*, the study of the forms of words and their components, and *semantics*, the study of their meanings." Since then, the studies of lexicology have been developing steadily with the dimensions of linguistic profundity and scope.

It is the common understanding now that lexicology is concerned with the study of vocabulary of a language and deals with words, their origin, development, history, structure, meaning and application. More comprehensively and precisely, T. McArthur writes in *Oxford Concise Companion to the English Language* (2001): Lexicology is "an area of language study concerned with the nature, meaning, history, and use of words and word elements and often also with the critical description of LEXICOGRAPHY. Although formerly a branch of PHILOLOGY, lexicology is increasingly treated as a branch of LINGUISTICS, associated with such terms as LEXEME, lexical field, lexical item, LEXICON and LEXIS, on the premise that they offer (or could offer, if tightly defined and widely adopted) a more precise and useful basis for the study of language than imprecise terms such as WORD and VOCABULARY".

At the turn of the 21st century, significant changes took place in the theory and practice of lexicology. Since then, more works of lexicology have come off the press and the journal *Lexicology* has started to be released, which evidently demonstrates the achievement in the lexicological researches throughout the world.

> **Reading Task**
> At the beginning of the 20th century, Leonard Bloomfield said that vocabulary was "really an appendix of the grammar, a list of basic irregularities". Decades later, Anna Wierzbicka, however, pointed out that syntax was "no more than the glue that is used to paste words together", emphasizing the importance of lexis in the linguistic studies. We can find the following remarks in *The Linguistics Encyclopedia* (1991) compiled by Kirsten Malmkjaer: "The study of lexis is the study of the vocabulary of languages in all its aspects: words and their meanings, how words relate to one another, how they may combine with one another, and the relationships between vocabulary and other areas of the description of languages, the phonology, morphology, and syntax."

1.2.5 Recommended works of lexicology

There are three classic works of lexicology to be recommended here.

The first one is *Lexicology: An International Handbook on the Nature and Structure of Words and Vocabulary*, edited by D. A. Cruse, F. Hundsnurscher, M. Job & P. R. Lutzeier, published by Walter de Gruyter in Berlin, Germany in 2002 (Volume I) and 2005 (Volume II). The handbook contains 214 essays contributed by more than 200 senior linguists. The book intends to present the fact that words, as an indispensable component of the linguistic system — a combination of sound, form and meaning — are a most direct and perfect semiotic system reflecting the realistic world.

The second one is *Lexicology: A Short Introduction* by M. A. K. Halliday and Colin Yallop, published in 2007 by YHT Ltd. London. This readable introductory textbook presents a concise survey of lexicology. The first section of the book is a survey of the study of words, providing students with an overview of basic issues in defining and understanding the word as a unit of language. This section also examines the history of lexicology, the evolution of dictionaries and recent developments in the field. The second section extends this study of lexicology into the relationship between words and meanings, etymology, prescription, language as social phenomenon and translation. In short, this book will be of interest to undergraduate students of linguistics.

The third one is *Lexicology: Critical Concepts in Linguists*, edited by Patrick Hanks, published by London/New York Routledge in 2008. The whole book, a paper collection of XXVI+2,723 pages, consists of 6 volumes. The book is a remarkably comprehensive selection of papers and book extracts on different aspects of the lexicon — by philosophers, anthropologists, computational linguists, and others, ranging from the 4th century BC (Aristotle) to important contemporary lexicologists (such as Sinclair, Wierzbicka, Mel'čuk and Pustejovsky). The collection is not confined to the English-speaking world, and some of the contributors express incompatible points of view. As editor, Patrick Hanks is not trying to argue a case or develop a single, coherent point of view, but rather to present a broad spectrum of stimulating and thought-provoking reading, enabling readers to make up their own minds about what is good and what is bad. The papers and extracts in this collection provide essential reading for any worthwhile university course in lexicology, while Hanks's "General Introduction" offers a lively and readable overview of the whole field.

This chapter offers a brief survey of the basic concepts of English words and lexicology, including their definitions, implications and functions. Each English word has its morphological and semantic structure. By the morphological structure, we mean the external structure of the word's morphological formation and the rules by which words are formed. Morpheme, the smallest unit of meaning in the English language, is supposed to constitute the morphological structure of the word. The semantic structure, also called the word's internal structure, is generally referred to as the word's meaning, including its denotation (conceptual meaning) and connotation (connotative or affective meaning). Vocabulary refers to all the words in a language or used in a particular kind of work, business, etc. or known to a particular person. The English vocabulary, central to the learning and use of the language, is becoming larger and larger in size. As the study of the word's structure, meaning and behavior, English lexicology is a sub-discipline of English linguistics, concerned with the English vocabulary and the properties of words as the main units of the English languge. English words are always changing, so English lexicology is developing simultaneously. This chapter also attempts to make clear the development of lexicology by offering various achievements of lexicological researches from the latest international publications concerned. Recommended are three meticulously chosen books: (1) *Lexicology: An International Handbook on the Nature and Structure of Words and Vocabulary* (2002/2005) by D. A. Cruse, F. Hundsnurscher, M. Job and P. R. Lutzeier; (2) *Lexicology: A Short Introduction* (2007) by M. A. K. Halliday and Colin Yallop; (3) *Lexicology: Critical Concepts in Linguistics* (2008) by Patrick Hanks.

> **Reading Task**
>
> After writing that *beauty is truth, truth beauty*, John Keats concluded: *That is all ye know on earth, and all ye need to know.* Naturally the poet's romantic philosophy must be appreciated on a lofty level while at the same time we concede that there are more specific things on this earth that we *need to know*.
>
> To really come to grips with the question, we should be aware of our purposes, our aims in life. It is obvious that there are vital facts which a surgeon needs to know, just as there are essential knowledges and skills for butchers, bakers, and the manufacturers of candlesticks. The individual's life-style ultimately determines just how much he/she needs to know. There is a discipline, however, which cuts across every mode of living, and the mastery of it can bring all types of rewards. We are referring to the study of vocabulary.
>
> — Bromberg, M. & Gordon, M.

Further Reading

1. Finch, G. (2000). *Linguistic Terms and Concepts*. New York: St. Martin's Press.
2. Jackson, H. and Ze Amvela, E. (2000). *Words, Meaning and Vocabulary: An Introduction to Modern English Lexicology*. London: Cassell.
3. Schmitt, N. (2000). *Vocabulary in Language Teaching*. Cambridge: Cambridge University Press.

● Extended Reading

■ What is a word?

To many people the most obvious feature of a language is that it consists of words. If we write English, we recognize words on the page — they have a space on either side; we learn to spell them, play games with them like Scrabble, and look them up in dictionaries. It ought not to be difficult to know what a word is and how to describe it.

Yet when we look a little more closely, a word turns out to be far from the simple and obvious matter we imagine it to be. Even if we are literate English-speaking adults, we are often unsure where a word begins and ends. Is *English-speaking* one word or two? How do we decide about sequences like *lunchtime* (*lunch-time*, *lunch time*), *dinner-time*, *breakfast time*? How many words are there in *isn't*, *pick-me-up*, *CD*? Children who cannot yet read have little awareness of word boundaries, and often learn about them through word games, like "I'm thinking of a word that rhymes with . . . "

Even more problematic is whether two forms are, or are not, instances of the same word. Presumably if they sound alike but are spelled differently, like *horse* and *hoarse*, they are two different words. But how about pairs such as:

like "similar to"   like "be fond of"
part "portion"   part "to separate"
shape "the outline of"   shape "to mould"
content "happy"   content "that which is contained"

— not to mention *shape* as the old name for a kind of solid custard pudding.

We know that there is no single right answer to these questions, because different dictionaries take different decisions about what to do with them.

Then, what about variants like *take*, *takes*, *took*, *taking*, *taken*? Are these five different words, or is there just one word *take* with many forms? Or *go*, *goes*, *went*, *going*, *gone*? Are *book* and *books*, *friend* and *friendly* one word or two? Are *big*, *bigger*, *biggest* three forms of a single word *big*? If so, what about *good*, *better*, *best*? Or *four* and *fourth*, *three* and *third*, *two* and *second*?

All these are problems within English, a language where the words are fairly clearly bounded. In Chinese it is much harder, because words are not marked off in writing; Chinese characters stand for morphemes, which are components of words. (For example, if English was written in Chinese characters, then a word like *freedom* would be written with two characters, one for *free* and one for *dom*.) The Chinese are very conscious of morphemes, even before they are literate, because each one is pronounced as one syllable and hardly ever varies; but they have much less intuition about what a word is. Many other writing systems, such as Japanese, Thai, Arabic and Hindi, also give not very consistent indication of word boundaries. When Ancient Greek was first written down, all the words were joined together without any spaces, and it was a few centuries before the word emerged as a clearly distinct unit.

So writing systems do not always identify words: partly because there are different kinds of writing system, but partly also because the languages themselves are different. There is no universal entity, found in every language, that we can equate with what in English is called a "word". And in unwritten languages the "word" can be a very elusive thing.

Nevertheless there is a general concept underlying all this diversity; that is the lexical item. Every language has a vocabulary, or "lexicon", which forms one part of its grammar — or, to use a more accurate term, one part of its lexicogrammar. The lexicogrammar of a language consists of a vast network of choices, through which the language construes its meanings: like the choices, in English, between "positive" and "negative", or "singular" and "plural", or "past", "present" and "future"; or between "always", "sometimes" and "never", or "on top of" and "underneath"; or between "hot" and "cold", or "rain", "snow" and "hail", or "walk" and "run". Some of these choices are very general, applying to almost everything we say: we always have to choose between positive and negative whenever we make a proposition or a proposal (*It's raining / It isn't raining*; *Run! / Don't run!*). Others are very specific, belonging to just one domain of meaning; these arise only when we are concerned with that particular domain. The choice between rain and snow, for example, arises only if we are talking about the weather. Choices of this second kind are expressed as lexical items: e. g. *hot / cold*; *rain / snow / hail*; *walk / run*.

If we are using the term "word" to mean a unit of the written language, i. e. "that which (in English) is written between two spaces", then ultimately all these choices are pressed as strings of words, or wordings, as in *it always snows on top of the mountain*. But teachers of English have customarily distinguished between content words, like *snow* and *mountain*, and function words, like *it*, *on*, *of* and *the*; and it is the notion of a content word that corresponds to our lexical item. Lexicology is the study of content words, or lexical items.

The example sentence in the last paragraph shows that the line between content words and function words is not a sharp one: rather, the two form a continuum or cline, and words like *always* and *top* lie somewhere along the middle of the cline. Thus there is no exact point where the lexicologist stops and the grammarian takes over; each one can readily enter into the territory of the other. So dictionaries traditionally deal with words like *the* and *and*, even though there is hardly anything to say about them in strictly lexicological terms, while grammars go on classifying words into smaller and smaller classes as far as they can go — again, with always diminishing returns.

This gives us yet a third sense of the term "word", namely the element that is assigned to a word class ("part of speech") by grammar. So the reason "word" turns out to be such a complicated notion, even in English, is that we are trying to define it simultaneously in three different ways. For ordinary everyday discussion this does not matter; the three concepts do not in fact coincide, but they are near enough for most purposes. In studying language systematically, however, we do need to recognize the underlying principles, and keep these three senses apart. The reason our lexicogrammar is divided into "grammar" and "lexicology" (as in traditional foreign language textbooks, which had their section of the grammar and then a vocabulary added separately at the end) is that we need different models — different theories and techniques — for investigating these two kinds of phenomena, lexical items on the one hand and grammatical categories on the other. This is why lexicology forms a different sub-discipline within linguistics.

— Halliday, M. A. K. & Yallop, C.

Exercises

I. Match the following words to their definitions.

1. word   a. a list of words used in a piece of writing or subject, with explanations of their meanings
2. lexis   b. a group of words that form a unit within a clause
3. lexicon   c. unclassified linguistic unit of any length: words, phrases, sentences, paragraphs, etc.
4. vocabulary   d. the choice of words used in a speech or piece of writing

5. glossary
6. phrase
7. expression
8. diction
9. collocation
10. phraseology
11. morphology
12. lexicology
13. etymology
14. lexicography
15. lexical semantics

e. words in general known, learnt, used, etc. or a list of words, usually in alphabetical order and with explanations of their meanings
f. all the words and phrases in a language or a dictionary
g. all the words in a language
h. the smallest unit of spoken or written language which has meanings and can stand alone
i. the study of origins and development of words
j. the writing and making of dictionaries
k. the study of words and their meanings
l. the study of meaning and uses of words
m. the study of how words are formed in a language
n. the words and phrases used in a particular profession or activity, or a particular way of putting words together to express something
o. a grouping of words which "naturally" go together through common usage

II. What are the Chinese for the following?

1. acronym
2. antonym
3. synonym
4. hyponym
5. affix
6. morpheme
7. lexeme
8. idiom
9. collocate
10. function word
11. content word
12. corpus
13. corpus linguistics
14. lexical chunk
15. polysemy
16. wording
17. word class
18. headword
19. 3C(信息产品)
20. 5G(手机)
21. GSM
22. SIM(卡)
23. TDMA
24. CDMA
25. LCD
26. UMPC
27. SUV
28. CD-ROM
29. IT
30. DVD
31. HTML
32. LAN
33. RAM
34. CRH

III. Do you know the following names of linguistic experts? Surf the Internet and try to find their academic background and achievements in lexicological studies.

Leonard Bloomfield   P. H. Matthews   James R. Hurford
Randolph Quirk   D. A. Cruse   M. A. K. Halliday
George Lakoff   Patrick Hanks   Colin Yallop

IV. The Internet will help you learn words, learn about words and learn through words. The following are ready for you to choose for your individual purposes.

ESL Podcast: http://www.eslpod.com
English-at-home: http://www.english-at-home.com
Englishpage: http://www.englishpage.com
ESL Partyland: http://www.eslpartyland.com
Today's Podcast: http://www.todayspodcast.com

Chapter 2
The Growth of the English Vocabulary (1)
— Sources

> **Points for Thinking**
> 1. How should English be positioned in the language family?
> 2. How did French affect the growth of the English vocabulary?
> 3. How did Latin affect the English vocabulary?
> 4. What sources are most common to the English vocabulary?
> 5. How many Chinese words have been borrowed into English? Give examples.

How far back do we have to go in order to find the origins of global English? In a sense, the language has always been on the move.

— Crystal, D. (1941 -)

English was first brought to Britain in the 5th century. Before the 1600s it was almost exclusively spoken in England and sporadically in Wales, Ireland and Scotland. But today it has grown into a lingua franca, a common language used by speakers of different languages, and earned many compliments attached to itself including "world", "global" and "international".

Understanding the growth of the English language should not be isolated from its history. As an indispensable aspect of the English language, its word inventory, under centuries of political, cultural and economic influence, serves as a mirror of the English speaking peoples in the world history, whether of hostility, isolation, colonization or of openness, cooperation and harmony. Such a historical view of English words allows us to see the vivid development of an international language. It also prepares us to find answers to such questions as where it is from and what the origins are.

2.1   The Language Family of English

Languages are usually classified metaphorically into "families" like the "tree diagram". These families are phylogenetic units with their members deriving from a common ancestor, conventionally known as the protolanguage. A language family can be subdivided into smaller "branches", showing the genetical relation to each other. These "daughter languages" usually share similarities in their basic lexis and grammar, proving the features of their common "parent language".

English is classified into the Indo-European family. It is a superfamily of eight language families, the others being Sino-Tibetan, Semito-Hamitic, Bantu, Uralic, Altaic, Malayo-Polynesian and Indian. According to Stockwell and Minkova (2001), the name of the superfamily is attributed to two facts: first, "many of the daughter languages from the earliest recorded times were spoken on the Indian subcontinent", and second, "from equally early times most of the languages of Europe are descended from that common ancestor too".

The branches of Indo-European are as follows:

Indo-Iranian includes Persian, Sanskrit, Urdu, Bengali and the language of the Gypsies.

Armenian, spoken in the Caucasus Mountains and also used by the Armenian diaspora, has two major dialects, Eastern and Western.

The Slavic languages are spoken in most of Eastern Europe, much of the Balkans, some areas of central Europe and the northern part of Asia. They include Russian and Polish.

The Hellenic, which has developed into today's Greek, rivals Latin as an important source of influence on the English language.

The Italic includes Latin, and Romance languages spread by the Roman Empire, such as French, Spanish, Italian, Portuguese and Romanian. It is considered to have had the biggest effect on the composition of the English language.

Celtic includes Gaelic, Welsh, Briton, etc. Celtic, Hellenic and Italic are more directly responsible for the shape of the modern English language.

Albanian is the ancestor of the modern Albanian. Like Armenian, it is regarded as having an independent nonbranching lineage too.

One of the branches that English has come from is Germanic. Also from this branch are German, Dutch, Yiddish and the Scandinavian languages. They have become the closest relatives of English.

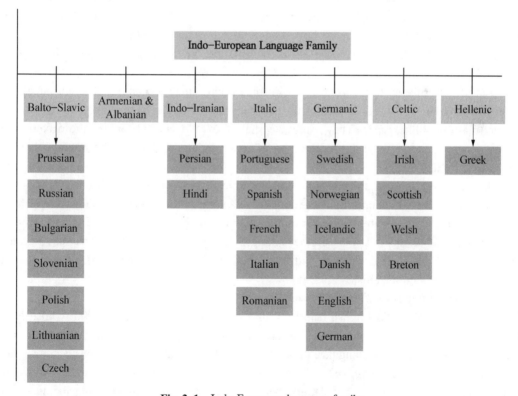

Fig. 2.1 Indo-European language family

Linguists usually divide the history of the English language into three periods, Old English (450 – 1100), Middle English (1100 – 1500) and Modern English (1500 –   ).

> **Task**
> Can you find connections among the following columns?
>
> | | | |
> |---|---|---|
> | Sino-Tibetan | Indian | Celtic |
> | Semito-Hamitic | Indo-Iranian Group | Albanian |
> | Bantu | Slavic | Dutch |
> | Uralic | Armenian | German |
> | Indo-European | Germanic | English |
> | Altaic | Hellenic (Greek) | Yiddish |
> | Malayo-Polynesian | Italic | the Scandinavian languages |

2.2 From Old English to Modern English

The first inhabitants in Britain were known as the Celts. In 55 BC, the Romans led by Julius Caesar invaded the islands but without an immediate occupation. By AD 43, when Claudius ruled the area, most of Britain had come under permanent Roman occupation and military control. The Celts had to take refuge in the woods between Wales and Scotland. Britain did not become a province of the Roman Empire until AD 400. After all the Romans pulled out of the island that year, the Celts in the south of the island found themselves exposed relatively defenseless to the invasions of the Vikings, the Picts and the Scots. So they resorted to the Germanic mercenary soldiers, mainly the Angles, the Saxons and the Jutes. But they never expected that the allies would finally become conquerors. The Germanic tribes took permanent control of the land that was later to be called England, known as the *Land of Angles*. The language spoken by the Angles, *Angle-ish*, became the predominant language, from which today's *English* is derived.

After the Germanic tribes settled down in Britain, they occupied different areas and established kingdoms. By AD 830 England had been united under King Alfred the Great. But different dialects still existed. They were the dialect of Wessex spoken by the Saxons, the Kentish dialect spoken by the Jutes, and the Mercian dialects and the Northumbrian dialects, both spoken by the Angles.

Still, not to be ignored are two influential historic events during this period. The first was the introduction of Christianity by Augustine of Canterbury from Rome. Together with the founding of the English Church came the introduction of the Roman culture to England. And the second was the raids and invasions of the Vikings. Since AD 790 the Scandinavians began to settle in England and their exchanges with the Anglo-Saxons largely increased, bringing many Scandinavian words into English.

2.2.1 Old English's Germanic words

It is estimated that Old English had a vocabulary of about 25,000 to 30,000 words. Many of them came down from the Indo-European parent language. The words, assumed to have come from the earliest times of the language family, are related to nature and the basic human life, such as *be*, *brother*, *do*, *long*, *me*, *mine*, *that*, *two*. The other early Germanic words that entered the vocabulary later are also found to have a connection with the same theme: *boat*, *earth*, *fox*, *house*, *meat*, *rain*, *starve*, *thief*, *wife*, etc.

Though the majority of the vocabulary of Old English was homogeneous in origin, loan words did come into the language through communications. Celtic, Latin, and Scandinavian were the three major contributors.

2.2.2 Middle English

A symbolic event marking the beginning of Middle English was the Norman Conquest in 1066. The victory of the Duke of Normandy made him the king of England, and his followers the overlords of the Anglo-Saxons. In the following 200 years England became a bilingual country, with French as the ruling language for the nobility and English as the everyday language for the ordinary public. A typical picture then could be English-speaking peasants working in the fields or doing manual jobs around the French-speaking noblemen's estates.

The Middle English period is traditionally known as a period of tremendous change. More extensive and fundamental changes took place than any other time in the English history. They affected English in its grammar and vocabulary. The inflections became greatly reduced, making the period known as the period of leveled inflections. In the English vocabulary French words were borrowed especially in the fields related to the government of the ruling class, such as *indict*, *jury*, *verdict*. It actually started the trend for English to borrow from other languages. The gradual adoption of loan words from outside languages altered English's etymological features.

Middle English is usually subdivided by the year of 1204, when King Philip of France took Normandy from England. Central France then became the new interest for England's military affairs, economy and culture. Naturally, an increasing number of French words spoken in and around Paris began to be borrowed into English. Many old English words began to be replaced by new borrowings, such as *army*, *assembly*, *defense*, *mayor*, *navy*, *parliament*, *state*. Words from the fields of literature, art, science and medicine came into English in large numbers, such as *literature*, *art*, *science*, *medicine*, *logic*, *pain*, *poet*, though many of them originated from classical Greek and Latin.

At the same time English began to gain increasing attention and application in England. In 1362, the Parliament opened with English as the language of choice. Also in that year English replaced French as the official language in the law courts of England. After the fourteenth century the dominance of the English language extended into other fields including administration, commerce, art and education. As an extremely important period of language changes in English history, Middle English witnessed a rapid growth of vocabulary which permanently changed the English lexicon.

Reading Task

The Middle English Period was marked by great changes in the English language, more extensive and fundamental changes than those that had taken place at any time before or since. The changes in grammar reduced English from a highly inflected language to an extremely analytic one, as you can see from the following indications: (SEE: *Albert C. Baugh & Thomas Cable*, *A History of the English Language*, 1993)

    1. Inflections decayed and the elimination of grammatical gender followed;

    2. Grammar inflections were generally reduced;

    3. Endings of the noun and adjectives marking distinctions of number and case and often of gender were altered in pronunciation as to lose their distinctive form;

    4. The universal sign of plural became *-(e)s*;

    5. The verbs lost their inflectional ending, and a lot of strong verbs disappeared, while others became weak;

    6. The "*to*" and final *-e* infinitive form of the verb replaced the *-an* form of the Old English (for example: OE *drīfan*→*drīven*→*drive*);

7. The vowels *-a*, *-o*, *-u*, *-e* in inflectional endings were obscured to a sound, the so-called "indeterminate vowel", which came to be written *e* (less often *i*, *y*, *u*, depending on place and date). As a result, a number of originally distinct endings such as *-a*, *-u*, *-e*, *-an*, *-um* were reduced generally to a uniform *-e*, and such grammatical distinctions as they formerly expressed were no longer conveyed;

8. The forms of the adjectives were levelled;

9. The pronouns lost their inflections; word order and the use of prepositions made clear the relations of words in a sentence; the personal pronouns retained most of their distinctions; the fixed forms for the demonstratives became: *the*, *this*, *that*, *these*, *those*; the second person singular *thou*, *thee*, *thy* (*you*, *your*) were abandoned, and *ye* was replaced by "you", pre-vocalic *mine* by "my", the third person singular verb ending *-th* by *-s*;

10. The changes in the vocabulary involved the loss of a large part of the Old English word-stock and the addition of thousands of words from French and Latin.

2.2.3 Modern English

By the end of the Middle English period, English had established itself as a national language. Geoffrey Chaucer's works showed English to be a well-developed language. By this time a large part of the original inflectional system had completely disappeared, furthering the evolution of English.

Also pushing forward the English evolution were several historical and social changes. Around the time of the transition from Middle English to Modern English, the history-making printing press was introduced by Sir William Caxton in 1476, marking a turning point in the production and accessibility of books. And in 1492, the New World was discovered, causing extraordinary consequences for the composition of the English lexicon. What affected the English vocabulary most in the Early Modern English period (1476 – 1776) was the Renaissance. It brought an intellectual ardor for reinvention and reinterpretation of classical models. As a result, English turned gradually away from French borrowings to Latin and Greek words. During this period, using Greek and Latin was often taken to be evidence of being well-educated. The Renaissance led to a great amount of research into the cultures of ancient Greece and Rome. Great success was made in the development of science, art, religion, and so on. New words in these fields were directly borrowed into English as a result when their equivalents in English were not immediately found for translating. They include *climax*, *appendix*, *exterior*, *consult*, *exotic*, *curriculum*, *abdomen*, *compute*, *larva*, *species*, *asterisk*, *catastrophe* and *lexicon*.

Besides the Renaissance, Shakespeare and his works also had a significant impact on the English vocabulary. Thousands of new words were created and many became so popular that they still exist today, such as *critical*, *majestic*, *dwindle*, *pendant*. The *King James Bible*, widely read in churches, was written in conservative language without many new words, but it has become a great source for English idioms today: *an eye for eye*, *new wine in old bottles*, *the straight and narrow*, etc.

Near the end of the Early Modern English period, two other important events took place which, different from the previous ones, tried to set down a norm for the English language. In 1755, Samuel Johnson's *Dictionary of the English Language* was published. The dictionary is recognized by many as the first really influential dictionary of English. After that came a large wave of English lexicographical research. The second demarcation point was witnessed around the time of the American Revolution in 1776. After the Americans won their political independence, they started a pursuit of linguistic independence with American characteristics.

Chapter 2 The Growth of the English Vocabulary (1)

The period following 1776 is known as the Late Modern English. Many historic events left their marks on the English vocabulary: *world trade*, *liberation movements in colonies*, *world wars* and *the rapid rise of America*. Lexically the new changes in this period are associated with the sharp increase of words for the development of science and technology, the establishment of American English and the formation of new Englishes throughout the world as a result of the spread of English as a national and international language.

As new technology developed at an unimaginable rate, many new words were brought into use, such as *SARS-CoV, coronavirus, Ebola, diabetes, transgenosis* in medical science; *nuclear weapons, meltdown* in physical science; *extrovert, behaviorism, defense mechanism* in psychology; *automobile, petrol, garage* in auto industry. The two world wars gave rise to the use of *air raid, tank, gas mask, blackout, evacuate, roadblock*, etc. The rise of American English as an independent English variety proved in some sense its predominant role in the world. The new image of the United States was forged with the spread of the words such as *emancipation, feminist, liberty, materialism, freedom of speech*, and *puritan*. But the globalization of English never stopped at American English. As one result of the British colonization, many new English varieties with local cultural and ethnic characteristics were formed and became independent after their speakers won independence from colonization: Australian English, Indian English, African English, etc.

In word formation, Late Modern English has expanded its vocabulary through self-explaining compounds, affixation or inventing new words. Compounds have examples of *skydiving, greenhouse effect, acid rain, junk food*, etc.; affixation has examples of *postwar, preschool, counterattack, subirrigate*, etc.; invented new words include *Alt-right, Snowmageddon, Monstration, Kleenex, xerox, Doggo-Lingo*, etc.

Today English is one of the most important languages in the world in terms of either its speaking population or its uses for international communication. With 400 million native speakers, English is the largest of the Western languages.

Task

With the help of the following figure, tell in your own words the history of the English language and explain its three periods.

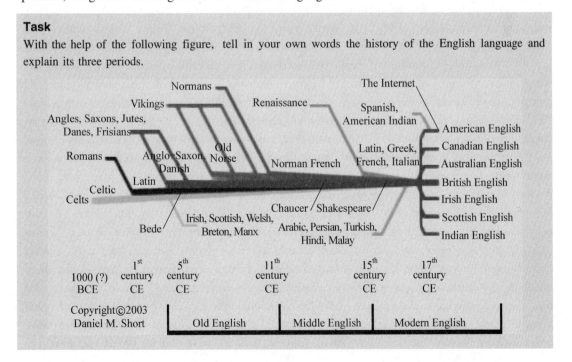

2.3 The Origins of English Words

Generally speaking, the great size and mixed character of the English vocabulary are attributed to three components: native words, loan words and neologisms. Most of the native words have a strong Anglo-Saxon character, while loan words and neologisms are the two powerful sources of new English words. Together they have made the English vocabulary cosmopolitan.

As a Germanic language, English shares many common words with its cousin languages, such as German, Dutch, Flemish, Danish, Swedish and Norwegian. In contributing loan words to English, Latin has played a major role. Over half of the English vocabulary is derived from the latter. Other languages that are derived from Latin also contributed their words to English, such as French, Italian, Spanish and Portuguese.

2.3.1 Anglo-Saxon elements

When the Angles, Saxons and Jutes crossed the Channel to Britain in the 5th and 6th centuries, they brought with them a mutually intelligible set of dialects, which came to be the basis of what is now known as Old English. Though their dialects displayed obvious geographical features of where they had settled down, they were generally homogeneous. As language changed, many grammatical rules, for example, the noun case system, were eroded. Till now most of the old English words died out as a large number of words from French and Latin were borrowed. Those kept in use today account for only a very small proportion in the entire English word stock, but their role as the core vocabulary in English enjoys a disproportionate position in use. And this core retains a strong Anglo-Saxon character.

Old English words represent the most common root words in perhaps the most basic areas of human life, e. g. description of the human body: *hand, foot, arm, eye, ear, chin, hear, bone, back, beard, belly, body, breast, breech, chest, finger, hair, heart, hip, bosom, brain, head, heel, knee, mouth, nostril*; date, month and time: *month, morning, evening, midday, midnight, night, sun, spring, summer, Sunday, today, year, yesterday, day, time, winter*; weather: *cloudy, cold, cool, frost, heat, ice-cold, storm, warm, wind, windy, hail, snow*; clothing: *cloth, clothes, sock;* transportation: *keel, sea-boat, boat, board, ship*; one's identity: *earl, father, goldsmith, husband, monk, mother, nephew, priest, queen, shoemaker, ward, widow, wife, alderman, king, knight, shepherd, sister, son, daughter*; plants and animals: *corn, cock, wolf, bear, bee, beetle, berry, bitch, boar, cat, chicken, cow, crow, fish, fox, hare, hawk, hawthorn, lobster, sheep, ox, roe, shellfish, shoat, sparrow, studhorse, worm, wort, adder, ant, ape, bird, calf, bull, clover, cod, cuttle, deer, fowl, gar, hart, hound, mare, moth, ram, whale, buck, beaver, beech*. The following is a list of other Anglo-Saxon words grouped into word-classes, e. g. common nouns: *acre, ale, alms, answer, anthem, apple, ark, arrow, ash, barn, bath, beacon, beat, bellows, belt, bench, bill, binder, bishop, bit, bite, bladder, blade, blast, blaze, bliss, blood, bloom, bolster, book, borough, bottom, box, brass, breadth, breath, bride, bridge, brother, brown, butter, burden, candle, canon, cap, care, chaff, chalk, cheese, child, church, clew, cliff, clothes, cluster, coal, comb, cook, copper, cradle, cripple, cross, cup, daughter, day, death, deal, deed, devil, dish, door, doom, dream, drink, dust, earth, edge, end, errand, feather, field, file, fire, flight, flood, floor, food, folk, friend, game, gang, gate, gem, ghost, God, gold, ground, guest, hall, ham, hammer, harm, harvest, hat, haven, health, heat, hell, hill, hive, hole, holiday, honey, hook, hope, horn, hunger, island, iron, ladder, land, leather, life, light, love, mail, master, man, mankind, murder, name, needle, offspring, path, salt, shade, shadow, shrine, side, sin, site, soul, spark, spear, song, speed, star, steam, stone, sun, sweat, temple, thing, threat, tide, tile, tool, tree, verse, weapon, wine, wire, wisdom, wish, wall, ward, water, wonder, wood, word, work, wound*; common adjectives: *alive, all, almighty, any, bare, best, better, bitter, black, blind, blithe, bold, bridal, bright, broad, busy, callow, clean, crisp, dark, dead, deep, dim, dizzy, dreary, dumb, fair, fast, fat, free, full, further, good, green, half, hard, heavy, hoarse, high, hollow, holy, hot, idle, keen, kind, least, like, mild, narrow, new, old, open, quick, red, steep, strong, sweet, swift, tame, true, young*; common adverbs: *about, above, again, along, always, beneath, east, even, ever, far, gladly, here, hereafter, how, less, long, near, now, out, seldom, soon, then, there, thereof, thereto, though, thus, together, too, toward, up, west, where, yet*; common verbs: *abide, allay, allow, answer, are, arise, ask, awaken, bake, bark, bathe, bear, become, befall, begin, behold, bell, bend, bequeath, beset, bid, bite, bleach, bless, blow, blush, borrow, break, breathe, breed, brew, bring, bruise, build, burn, burst, bury, buy, can, chew, choose, cleanse, climb, cling, clip, clothe, come, cough, crack, dive, do, drink, drive, earn, eat, fall, fasten, feed, feel, fight, find, flow, fly, follow, forgive, gather, give, greet, hate, have, heed, hide, hold, hit, hop, hunt, know, last, laugh, lay, lead, leap, learn, leave, let, like, listen, loan, look, make, meet, melt, mourn, offer, open, reach, read, ride, sail, see, seek, sell, send, shake, shape, shear, shoot, show, sleep, steal, swear, swim, teach, tease, teem, tell, thank, unlock, wake, warn, wax, withstand, write, yell*; common prepositions: *amid, among, at, before, beside, between, beyond, but, by, for, in, on, over, under, with*; and conjunctives: *and, but, or*.

The common feature of the Anglo-Saxon words can still be viewed from another perspective. According to the list of the most frequent items in the 100-million-word British National Corpus, all the most commonly occurring words have Anglo-Saxon origins. Taking a closer look at the top 100 English words, we can only find two words, *people* and *use*, which are outside the Germanic origin.

Besides the high frequency with which these words are used, their length is another noticeable character. Most of them are "four-letter words" or shorter. The following is the top 20 words on the above-mentioned list: *the, be, of, and, a, in* (preposition, as in *in town*), *to* (infinitive-maker, as in *to go*), *have, it, to* (preposition, as in *to town*), *for* (preposition, as in *for hours*), *I, that* (relative pronoun, as in *the car that I saw*), *you, he, on* (preposition, as in *on time*), *with* (preposition, as in *with ease*), *do* (verb, as in *I do*), *at* (preposition, as in *at times*), *by* (preposition, as in *by bus*).

2. 3. 2 Loan words

However Germanic the English language is, the vast majority of English words in dictionaries do not have such an origin. Only about 20 percent of words are probably descended from Old English. Of the estimated one million English words, most were borrowed from other languages. English has borrowed words from more than 350 languages around the world. The major contributors include French, Latin, Greek, etc.

1. French

It was before the Norman Conquest that English started its borrowing of words from French. But the substantial flow of French words into English was seen after that, when the French language started its significant influence on the British politics and society. The unprecedented borrowing of foreign words immediately altered the composition of the English lexicon, changing the percentage of foreign elements in English from 5% in Old English to 25% in Middle English. An estimated number of over 10,000 French words were adopted during the Middle English period and 75% of them are still in use today. The adoption never stopped. Modern English keeps such a tendency of borrowing words from French. Today 30% of the English lexicon have French origin.

1) The Middle English period

The year of 1250 can be considered the dividing line for this period. The words borrowed into English before 1250 can be called Norman French, as the Normans brought with them the language and culture of medieval France. Assimilation happened in their contact with the English locals. The loan words of this early post-conquest period were not large in number and were mostly associated with a phonetic style of Anglo-Norman character. Records show that about 900 words were borrowed into English during this period. Many of them were reflections of the communication between the lower English class and the ruling French nobles, e.g. *baron*, *noble*, *dame*, *servant*, *messenger*, *fest*, *minstrel*, *juggler*, *largess*. Other borrowings that entered English at this stage include *air*, *beast*, *beauty*, *color*, *dangerous*, *diet*, *feast*, *flower*, *jealous*, *journey*, *judge*, *liquor*, *oil*, *part*, *peace*, *soil*, *story*, *tender*.

New changes took place after 1250 which gave English back its official status. English was taught at school again and made popular across the whole nation. However, this English comeback did not hinder, but promoted, the borrowing of French words, especially when insufficiency of expression was met in the use of the English vocabulary. The borrowed words mainly belonged to the areas of governmental and administrative affairs, fashion, food, art, learning, medicine and social life: *army*, *assembly*, *council*, *defense*, *empire*, *mayor*, *navy*, *parliament*, *record*, *soldier*, *state*, *statute*, *tax*, *science*, *medicine*, *number*, *figure*, *grammar*, *image*, *logic*, *music*, *pain*, *physician*, *poet*, *remedy*, *romance*, *study*, *surgeon*, *tragedy*.

Fig. 2.2 The Norman Conquest, the (Le Roux's) Bretton Knights formed a very important element in the left flank of William the Conqueror at the Battle of Hastings in 1066.

2) The Modern English period

Great historic events in the Modern English period, such as colonization and the industrial revolution, gave reasons for the introduction of French words to the English vocabulary. In this process the original sounds of the loan words were likely borrowed as well as their spelling forms. This kind of borrowing was heated in the latter half of the seventeenth century. *Soup*, *naïve*, *rapport*, *chandelier*, *jaunty*, *champagne*, *envoy*, *ballet*, *aide-de-camp*, *penchant*, *beau*, *commandant*, *tête-à-tête*, *ménage* and *salon* were all borrowed in this century.

In the 18th century, a great number of words about military and foreign affairs and the French Revolution entered the English vocabulary: *brochure*, *bureau*, *canteen*, *corps*, *critique*, *depot*, *espionage*, *nuance*, *picnic*, *police*, *rouge*.

The 19th century witnessed the most French loan words since the Middle English period. They were predominantly seen in art, literature, diplomacy and food: *baton*, *matinée*, *premier*, *attaché*, *chargé d'affaires*, *prestige*, *menu*, *chef*. Other words borrowed in this period include *café*, *surveillance*, *liaison*, *de luxe*, *coupon*, *laissez-faire*, *restaurant*, *coupé*, *lingerie*, *chic*, *cigarette*, *fines herbes*, *impasse*, *foyer*, *suede*, *risqué*, *revue*, *décor* and *chauffeur*.

Since the 20th century, the borrowing tendency of English has continued: *camouflage*, *fuselage*, *déjà vu*, *haute couture*, *collage*, *courgette* and *rotisserie*.

Over the centuries the number of French loan words has been rising steadily. The reason for this varies: whether to project a positive image of France with high culture on the part of the speakers or the objects they talk about, or to express speakers' admiration of the French contribution to civilization. Whatever it is, English is hooked on French words.

2. Latin

Latin had been a language of great power for at least a thousand years before it declined and lost ground to English. The influence of Latin on the English language has been profound and is reflected in the great number of words borrowed from Latin in a variety of spheres.

In general, Latin loan words have some common features in word formation. For instance, word endings of *-er* and *-or* are identity indicators, as in *arbiter* and *creditor*; *-um* at the end of a singular noun is changed to *-a* in its plural form, as in *stadium* and *stadia*; the *-a* singulars will end in *-ae* in their plural, as in *formula* and *formulae*; and the *-us* singulars change their end to *-i* in their plural as in *fungus* and *fungi*. Many prefixes in English are Latinate in origin, such as *ab-*, *af-*, *dis-*, *extra-*, *im-*, *inter-*, *multi-*, *op-*, *post-*, *pre-*, *re-*, *semi-*, *suf-*, *super-*; and so are some suffixes, such as *-able*, *-al*, *-ar*, *-ary*, *-cide*, *-ent*, *-er*, *-idle*, *-ic*, *-ify*, *-ile*, *-ism*, *-ive*, *-ize*, *-ment*, *-ous*, *-sion*, *-ure*, *-tion*, *-tude*, *-ule*.

The Latin influence on English is seen in four periods: the Germanic period, the Old English period, the Middle English period and the Modern English period.

1) The Germanic period

The Latinate influence can date back to the times before the Anglo-Saxons left the European continent for England. In their contact and trade with the Romans, they borrowed their words. This kind of borrowing was a manifestation of their relations with the Romans in trade, household crafts and religion, etc. The following is such a list: *pear*, *turnip*, *kettle*, *cup*, *dish*, *oil*, *wall*, *street*, *mile*, *cheap*, *monger*, *pound*, *mint*, *wine*, *kitchen*, *cheese*, *cherry*, *butter*, *plum*, *pea*, *pitch*, *pipe*, *tile*, *church*, *bishop*.

2) The Old English period

After the Roman troops withdrew from their occupation of the British Isles, many Latin names of places were kept in use, such as *Chester*, *Manchester*, *Lancaster*, *Dorchester*, *Colchester*, *Doncaster*, *Sloucester* and *Worcester*.

But the wholesale borrowing of Latin words in this period did not appear until the Christianization of England which began from the south at the end of the 6th century (There was already a presence in Scotland and the north of England due to Christianization in Ireland.). By the end of the 7th century, the Anglo-Saxons had started constructing monasteries in Wearmouth and Jarrow, to collect Latin documents from Rome. Of the Latin words borrowed in the Christianization period many were religious terms, such as *altar*, *abbot*, *alms*, *anthem*, *candle*, *creed, disciple, epistle, hymn, litany, mass, nun, shrine, pope, priest, shrive, stole, temple.*

3) The Middle English period

After the Norman Conquest, Latin words were also directly borrowed into English as well as indirectly absorbed through French. Latin words did not go into popular use but mainly remained in written texts. A relatively small number of spoken Latin words could have been introduced into English through the speeches of the ecclesiastics and men of learning.

Directly borrowed words in this period are found in different spheres including law, medicine, theology, science and literature: *abject, adjacent, allegory, conflagration, conspiracy, contempt, custody, distract, equivalent, frustrate, genius, gesture, history, homicide, immune, incarnate, include, incredible, incubus, incumbent, index, individual, infant, inferior, infinite, innumerable, intellect, interrogate, interrupt, juniper, legal, legitimate, limbo, lucrative, lunatic, magnify, malefactor, mechanical, mediator, minor, missal, moderate, necessary, nervous, notary, ornate, pauper, picture, polite, popular, prevent, private, project, promote, prosecute, prosody, quiet, rational, reject, remit, script, scripture, secular, simile, solar, solitary, spacious, submit, subscribe, substitute, summary, supplicate, suppress, temperate, temporal, testify, testimony, tract, tributary, ulcer, zenith, zephyr.* Of them, the suffixes *-able, -ible, -ent, -al, -ous, -ive* are in popular use in Modern English.

4) The Modern English period

Renaissance, as a historic incident in this period, exerted great influence on the development of the English vocabulary. During the Renaissance, the English people started to study ancient Greek and Roman cultures to counterwork the medieval feudal practices. A lot of Latinate literature was translated into English, giving rise to its borrowing from Latin words. Latin was also a popular language used, between the 16th and 18th centuries, by the scientists and litterateurs such as Francis Bacon and Isaac Newton. This kind of borrowing continued in the later centuries. So far, Latin has still been the first and most consistent of the many languages English has borrowed from in the history of the English language.

Here is a selection of such borrowings in this period: *abdomen, acumen, advocate, agile, anatomy, angina, arbitrator, area, axis, benevolent, capsule, census, civil, compensate, complex, curriculum, decorum, dedicate, dexterity, discus, education, enterprise, esteem, excavate, executer, expensive, fictitious, focus, furuncle, gradual, habitual, insane, janitor, jurist, ignoramus, impetus, item, lens, malignity, meditate, minimum, momentum, notorious, omen, orbit, pendulum, peninsula, physician, pollen, premium, specimen, studious, superintendent, terminus, tuberculosis, ultimate, veto, vindicate.*

3. Greek

As a precedent of Roman culture, the ancient Greek culture once had an important influence on Latin. Many Latin words originated from Greek, as did some French words. So the Greek loan words in English were mainly borrowed through Latin or possibly through French, such as *atheism, atmosphere, chaos, dogma, economy, ecstasy, drama, irony, pneumonia, scheme* and *syllable*. However, during the Renaissance, many Greek words were directly borrowed especially for terminology, e. g. *hepatitis, neurology, phlebotomy*. Other directly borrowed Greek words in English today are *asterisk, catastrophe, crypt, criterion, dialysis, lexicon, polyglot, rhythm, syllabus*. It is noteworthy that Modern Greek is still one of the foreign sources for the English borrowings, which finds evidence in the words like *bouzouki, moussaka, ouzo,*

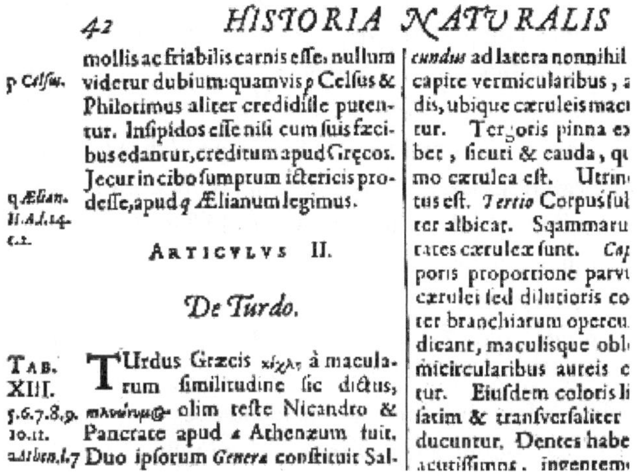
42 HISTORIA NATURALIS

mollis ac friabilis carnis esse, nullum videtur dubium: quamvis p Celsus & Philotimus aliter credidisse putentur. Insipidos esse nisi cum suis fæcibus edantur, creditum apud Græcos. Iecur in cibo sumptum ictericis prodesse, apud q Ælianum legimus.

ARTICVLVS II.

De Turdo.

TURdus Græcis κίχλη, à macularum similitudine sic dictus, olim teste Nicandro & Pancrace apud Athenæum fuit. Duo ipsorum Genera constituit Sal-

Fig. 2.3 Extract from Jan Jonston's *Historia Naturalis De Piscibus Et Cetis Libri V.*

sirtaki and *souvlaki*.

There are four types of Greek loan words or word forms in English. The first is of an inflectional ending retained but spelt in the Latin style: *aegis*, *analysis*, *antithesis*, *automaton*, *charisma*, *cytokinesis*, *diagnosis*, *dogma*, *enigma*, *genesis*, *gnosis*, *hoi polloi*, *kerygma*, *lalophobia*, *magma*, *phenomenon*, *rhinoceros*, *rhododendron*, *synthesis* and *thesis*. The second type has a Latin ending: *brontosaurus*, *chrysanthemum*, *diplodocus*, *hippopotamus*, *pliohippus*. The third type has a dropped or adapted ending: *agnostic*, *agnosticism*, *alphabet*, *alphabetic*, *analytic*, *anthocyanin*, *astrobleme*, *automatic*, *biologist*, *blasphemy*, *charismatic*, *chemotherapy*, *chronobiology*, *cinematography*, *critic*, *criticism*, *dramatic*, *dramatist*, *electric*, *electronic*, *enigmatic*, *epistemic*, *gene*, *genetic*, *herpetology*, *narcolepsy*, *odyssey*, *oligarchy*, *patriarch*, *phenomenology*, *pterodactyl*, *sympathomimetic*. And the most common borrowing is with Greek roots and affixes, e. g. roots: *-anthrop-*, *-chron-*, *-dem-*, *-morph-*, *-path-*, *-ped-*, *-philo-/-phil-*, *-phon-*; prefixes: *a-/an-*, *anti-/ant-*, *auto-*, *bio-/bi-*, *geo-*, *hyper-*, *micro-*, *mono-*, *neo-*, *pan-*, *thermo-/therm-*; suffixes: *-ism*, *-ist*, *-ize*, *-gram*, *-graph*, *-logue/-log*, *-logy*, *-meter/-metry*, *-oid*, *-phile*, *-phobe/-phobia*, *-phone*.

Task

The following is a list of 12 Greek words you should know. Do you happen to know them?

1. acme	2. acropolis	3. agora	4. anathema
5. anemia	6. ethos	7. dogma	8. eureka
9. genesis	10. phobia	11. plethora	12. kudos

4. Scandinavian

Most of the Scandinavian loan words in English were borrowed during the Old English period. After the Scandinavians invaded England in AD 790, they kept little communication with the Anglo-Saxons. The Scandinavian loan words were small in number and mainly related to attacks and invasions by the seafarers, such as *cnearr*, *dreng*, *batswegen*, *orrest*, *ran*. But later, when more and more of the invaders, many of whom traveled without womenfolk, settled down in England, they started intermarriages with the local people. This development created a favorable ground for the transfer of vocabulary from Scandinavian to Old English. As many as

1,400 Scandinavian words are found as names of places in the northern and eastern parts of England, recognizable with endings like *-by*: *Carnaby*, *Ellerby*, *Rugby*, *Thirtleby*; *-thorpe*: *Barleythorpe*, *Grimsthorpe*, *Hamthorpe*, *Hilderthorpe*, *Low Claythorpe*, *Fridathorpe*; or *-thwaite*: *Hampsthwaite*, *Hunderthwaite*, *Husthwaite*. They can be the results of the earliest linguistic encounter between the Scandinavians and the Anglo-Saxons. Thanks to their linguistic closeness, more Scandinavian words were quickly borrowed. They settled into the spoken Old English and were carried into the written Middle English in the 13th century. The following words all appeared in the Middle English texts: *anger*, *blight*, *by-law*, *cake*, *clumsy*, *doze*, *egg*, *fellow*, *gear*, *hale*, *hit*, *husband*, *kick*, *kill*, *kilt*, *kindle*, *law*, *low*, *lump*, *rag*, *raise*, *scathe*, *scorch*, *score*, *scowl*, *scrape*, *scrub*, *seat*, *skill*, *skin*, *skirt*, *sky*, *they*, *them*, *their*, *thrall*, *thrust*, *ugly*, *want*, *wing*.

Modern English has taken in only a small number of Scandinavian words. *Fjord*, *maelstrom*, *ombudsman*, *ski*, *slalom* and *smorgasbord* are typical ones. Altogether, an estimated number of 900 Scandinavian words or word forms are found in Modern English.

5. Other European elements

Enlightened by the Renaissance spirit of intellectual renewal and discovery, the English people started their adventurous travels to other European countries. The heightened cultural and commercial ties prepared a very good condition for the borrowing of other European words. The adoption of these non-classical words set a trend to absorb words from both past and contemporary languages, though the amount of them is not comparable to classical borrowings. This trend still goes on today.

1) Italian

The Italian's influence on the English vocabulary was mainly seen during the Renaissance period. The English visitors to Italy brought back Italian words as well as Italian costumes and customs. In the 16th and 17th centuries, the borrowed Italian words were found in the areas of everyday life, military activities, architecture and arts, such as *artichoke*, *gondola*, *squadron*, *stanza*, *fresco*, *bazaar*, *balcony*, *opera*, *vermicelli*, *rotunda*. The 18th century witnessed an explosion of new English words on music, which were borrowed from Italian as a result of the wide spread of Italian music and opera in England. The English were just unable to talk about Western music without resort to Italian words, such as *allegretto*, *aria*, *bravo*, *coda*, *concerto*, *duet*, *falsetto*, *impresario*, *lento*, *maestro*, *mezzo-soprano*, *oratorio*, *pianissimo*, *soprano*, *tempo* and *violoncello*.

Other Italian loan words in English are *cannon*, *colonel*, *attack*, *partisan*, *cornice*, *colonnade*, *corridor*, *grotto*, *niche*, *piazza*, *portico*, *bank*, *bankrupt*, *manager*, *broccoli*, *macaroni*, *ballot*, *fascist*, *Mafia*, and so on.

2) Celtic

Celtic is the language spoken by the earliest inhabitants on the British Isles. After the invasion of the Angles and Saxons, the Celts were pushed into Wales, Cornwall and Scotland. In their contact with the Celts, the Angles and Saxons adopted some of their words, such as *bald*, *down*, *glen*, *bard*, *cradle*. There are also some Celtic words borrowed after the Norman Conquest: *bucket*, *crockery*, *noggin*, *gob*, *slogan*, *flannel*, *truant* and *gaol*.

Research has shown only a meager amount of Celtic words in the English vocabulary. Of them many are names of rivers, hills and places, such as *Avon*, *Exe*, *Esk*, *Thames*, *Wye*, *York* and *London*. This feature, however, is not difficult to understand. Conquerors as they were, the Angles and Saxons successfully forced their own language after their invasion but saw no reason to abandon the original Celtic names of places.

3) German

Though German and English are cousins in the same langage family, the number of German words in English is small. These words were generally borrowed through American English.

Many German words are kept in the same spelling form in English, such as *lederhosen*, *zeitgeist*, *fasching* in culture; *schnitzel*, *sauerkraut*, *wiener* in cooking; and *blitzkrieg*, *lebensraum* in military terminology.

The fruitful chemical studies in the 19th and 20th centuries led to the ultimate adoption of *bismuth*, *quartz*, *cobalt*, *zinc*, *nickel*, etc. The Second World War's influence on English is also reflected in the borrowing of *Gestapo*, *Nazi*, *rocket*, etc. Many German words that reach the average speakers of English are mainly related to food and drink: *lager*, *frankfurter*, *muffin*, *noodle*, *pretzel*, *strudel*. Other German loan words in English are *abseil*, *angst*, *blitz*, *brake*, *clock*, *dollar*, *flak*, *hamburger*, *heroin*, *hinterland*, *kindergarten*, *poodle*, *rucksack*, *schadenfreude*, *shirk*, *sod*, *swindle*, *vandal*, *waltz*, *waylay*, *wrangle*, *yodel*, and *zeppelin*.

4) Dutch

Different from the Italian borrowings which relied mainly on paper transmission, the Dutch words in English were adopted through direct contact between speakers of the two languages. This is evidenced in the word classes of the loans. While Italian loan words are almost all nouns, the Dutch borrowings are a good blend of both nouns and verbs. A selection of these words can be *foist* (v.), *rant* (v.), *drill* (v.), *cookie* (n.), *crap* (n.), *gin* (n.), *kid* (n.), *kit* (v.), *roster* (n.), *scoop* (n.), *snuffle* (n.), and *track* (v.).

5) Spanish and Portuguese

Spanish and Portuguese borrowings in English are attributed to the fact that Spain and Portugal led Europe in the colonization of the New World. Some of the Spanish loan words have been borrowed into English from the American-Indian languages. Selections of Spanish words in English are *cockroach*, *adobe*, *alligator*, *armada*, *barricade*, *bravado*, *cask*, *embargo*, *grenade*, *hoosegow*, *mosquito*, *negro*, *ranch*, *sarsaparilla* and *vamoose*. The following can be samples of the Portuguese borrowings: *albino*, *banana*, *caste*, *marmalade*, *molasses*, *pagoda*, *veranda*, *zebra*.

6. Chinese

Mary S. Serjeantson (1935) recorded in her *A History of Foreign Words in English* 28 Chinese words borrowed into English by the end of the 19th century, through translation of non-English works or by travelers and traders. The earliest loan word is *silk*, followed by *galingale*, *li*, *litchi*, *ginseng*, *cha*, from the 17th century onwards, *sampan*, *japan*, *bohea*, *tea*, *pongee*, *sycee*, *ketchup*, *pekoe*, *congou*, *hong*, *kaolin*, *hyson*, *souchong*, *chin-chin*, *kowtow*, *whangee*, *loquat*, *yamun (yamen)*, *wampee*, *oolong*, *kylin*, *tong*. In addition, three Tibetan words were recorded in the 17th and 18th centuries: *lama*, *Dalai-lama* and *yak*.

Some dictionaries also try to identify Chinese loan words in English. *An Etymological Dictionary of the English Language* by Walter W. Skeat (2005) recognizes 10 directly borrowed Chinese words: *bohea*, *China*, *congou*, *hyson*, *nankeen*, *pekoe*, *souching*, *tea*, *kowtow*, *oolong*, and 5 indirect ones: *galingale*, *silk*, *serge*, *sampan*, *bonze*; while *9,000 Words: A Supplement to Webster's Third New International Dictionary* collects 21 Chinese loan words: *bok choy*, *cheongsam*, *chiao*, *Chien ware*, *renminbi*, *running dog*, *kungfu*, *Lantian man*, *Mao*, *Maoism*, *mao-tai*, *Peking duck*, *Pekingology*, *pinyin*, *Shih Tzu*, *tai chi chuan*, *wok*, *Wu-ts'ai*, *Yi-hsing ware*.

Besides loan words, another type of Chinese borrowings in English is loan translations. Loan translations involve "rearranging words in the base language along patterns provided by the other and thus create a new meaning" (Romaine, 1995: 57). In other words, loan translation is a special type of borrowing, in which "each morpheme or word is translated in the equivalent morpheme or word in another language" (Hu, 2001: 102).

This is also called calque, which may be a word, a phrase, or even a short sentence. For this kind of loan to English, there are: *spring rolls*, *bean curd*, *dragon boat*, *Chinese herbal medicine*, *running dog*, *the Great Leap Forward*, *yellow jacket*, *moon cake*, *gold fish*, *Long March*, *Paper Tiger*, etc.

This chapter clears up the track of the English language development, and discusses its association with other genetic relatives in the language family. In the evolution of the English vocabulary, its historical context plays the most important role. As a reflection of history, the growth of the English vocabulary proves a gradual cultural continuation, though the history of English is usually known through three main divisions: Old English, Middle English and Modern English. As a result of racial and national contacts of all kinds, together with social and cultural development, loan words were often adopted from other languages, which transformed the English language mainly with Anglo-Saxon words to an international language with borrowings from over 350 languages. French, Latin and Greek have left the most obvious marks in the growth of the English vocabulary. Other languages including Scandinavian languages, Italian, Celtic, German, Dutch, Spanish, Portuguese and Chinese have become significant supplements as well.

Further Reading

1. Freeborn, D. (2006). *From Old English to Standard English.* Basingstock: Palgrave Macmillan.
2. Crystal, D. (2003). *English as a Global Language.* Cambridge: Cambridge University Press.
3. Stockwell, R. and Minkova, D. (2001). *English Words: History and Structure.* Cambridge: Cambridge University Press.

● Extended Reading

■ How the English language came to Britain?

By AD 443, the Roman legions had withdrawn from Britain to defend Rome itself. So when the Romano-British leader Vortigern invited the Angles Hengest and Horsa to help defend Britain, they found the country undefended, and open not only for raid and plunder but for invasion and settlement.

The coming of the Angles, Saxons and Jutes

This was not a peaceful process. Bede (673 – 735) described what happened in his *Historia Ecclesiastica Gentis Anglorum* (*History of the English Church and People*), written in Latin and completed in AD 731.

It was not long before such hordes of these alien peoples crowded into the island that the natives who had invited them began to live in terror. [...] They began by demanding a greater supply of provisions; then, seeking to provoke a quarrel, threatened that unless larger supplies were forthcoming, they would terminate the treaty and ravage the whole island. [...] These heathen conquerors devastated the surrounding cities and countryside, extended the conflagration from the eastern to the western shores without opposition. [...] A few wretched survivors captured in the hills were butchered wholesale, and others, desperate with hunger, came out and surrendered to the enemy for food, although they were doomed to lifelong slavery even if they escaped instant massacre. Some fled overseas in their misery; others, clinging to their homeland, eked out a wretched and fearful existence among the mountains, forests and crags, ever on the alert for danger.

(Translation from the Latin by Leo Sherley-Price, Penguin, 1955)

— Freeborn, D.

Origins of global English

How far back do we have to go in order to find the origins of global English? In a sense, the language has always been on the move. As soon as it arrived in England from northern Europe, in the fifth century, it began to spread around the British Isles. It entered parts of Wales, Cornwall, Cumbria and southern Scotland, traditionally the strongholds of the Celtic languages. After the Norman invasion of 1066, many nobles from England fled north to Scotland, where they were made welcome, and eventually the language (in a distinctive Scots variety) spread throughout the Scottish lowlands. From the twelfth century, Anglo-Norman knights were sent across the Irish Sea, and Ireland gradually fell under English rule.

But, compared with later events, these were movements on a very local scale — within the British Isles. The first significant step in the progress of English towards its status as a global language did not take place for another 300 years, towards the end of the sixteenth century. At that time, the number of mother-tongue English speakers in the world is thought to have been between 5 and 7 million, almost all of them living in the British Isles. Between the end of the reign of Elizabeth I (1603) and the beginning of the reign of Elizabeth II (1952), this figure increased almost fiftyfold, to some 250 million, the vast majority living outside the British Isles. Most of these people were, and continue to be, Americans, and it is in sixteenth-century North America that we first find a fresh dimension being added to the history of the language.

— Crystal, D.

Why English is so rich?

Modern English is the product of a long and complex process of historical development. Consequently, we can expect to find clues to its character in the past. Indeed, English has a history as rich as its vocabulary. The most important historical factor in the growth of the English vocabulary has been the ease with which it has borrowed words from other languages and adapted them to its own uses. The word *clique*, for example, was taken into English from French around the year 1700. Since that time, *clique* has become a familiar English word. It has been incorporated into the language to such an extent that it participates in processes that originally applied only to native vocabulary, resulting in the new words *cliquish*, *cliquishness*, *cliquey*, *cliqueless*, the verb *to clique* and others. In fact, English now has many more words derived from *clique* than French does.

English has been so ready to take words from foreign sources that the greater part of the modern English vocabulary has either been borrowed or formed from borrowed elements. Understanding why English vocabulary is as rich and diverse as it is gives us an important aid in learning to master it. The reason why English has two words with such similar meanings as *fatherly* and *paternal* is that it retained a native word (*fatherly*) while borrowing from Medieval Latin a near synonym (*paternal*). In a sense, this allowed *fatherly* to "share" its duties with *paternal*. This is the general pattern with native and borrowed synonyms: the native word is more familiar or more basic and usually shorter, while the borrowed word is more formal or more technical and longer. A few additional synonym pairs serve to illustrate this point.

Native   **Borrowed**
tell   *inform*
spin   *rotate*
pretty   *attractive*

In each of these pairs the first member is more appropriate for everyday use, more conversational, and less formal or technical than the second. But the choice between familiar and formal words is only one small part of the picture. With its wealth of native and foreign resources, English vocabulary has tremendous freedom to expand. Specialized and technical terminology, which generally involve the use of elements borrowed from Latin and Greek, are the most frequent sites of vocabulary innovation.

...

The history hidden in words

English words encode interesting and useful historical information. For example, compare the following three words:

captain
chief
chef

All of them derive historically from *cap*, a Latin word element meaning "head", which is also found in the words *capital*, *decapitate*, *capitulate*, and others. It is easy to see the connection in meaning between them if you think of them as "the **head** of a vessel or military unit", "the leader or **head** of a group", and "the **head** of a kitchen", respectively. Furthermore, English borrowed all the three words from French, which in turn borrowed or inherited them from Latin. Why then is the word element spelled and pronounced differently in the three words?

The first word, *captain*, has a simple story: the word was borrowed from Latin with minimal change. French adapted it from Latin in the thirteenth century, and English borrowed it from French in the fourteenth. The sounds /k/ and /p/ have not changed in English since that time, and so the Latin element *cap-* /kap/ remains substantially intact in that word.

French did not borrow the next two words from Latin. As mentioned earlier, French developed from Latin, with the grammar and vocabulary being passed down from speaker to speaker with small, cumulative changes. Words passed down in this way are said to be **inherited**, not borrowed. English borrowed the word *chief* from French in the thirteenth century, even earlier than it borrowed *captain*. But because *chief* was an inherited word in French, it had undergone many centuries of sound changes by that time. Across the vocabulary, certain /k/ sounds and /p/ sounds became /tʃ/ and /f/ sounds, respectively, so that *cap-* became *chief*. It was this form that English borrowed from French. After English borrowed the word *chief*, further changes took place in French.

Among these changes, /tʃ/ sounds changed to become /ʃ/ sounds, without changing the <ch> spelling, so that *chief* became *chef*. Subsequently English also borrowed the word in this form. Thanks to the linguistic evolution of French and the English propensity to borrow words from that language, a single Latin word element, *cap-*, which was always pronounced /kap/ in Roman times, now appears in English in three very different guises.

Two other word triplets that follow the same /k/ to /tʃ/ to /ʃ/ pattern are *candle*, *chandler* (candle maker), *chandelier* (originally an elaborate candle holder) and *cant* (singsong intonation, jargon; also visible in *incantation*), *chant*, *chantey* (as in *sea chantey*).

The history and relationship are diagrammed in table 2.1. Old French refers to that earlier stage of French, up to about 1300, when English borrowed a great many words. Modern French began in 1500. (The intermediate period was known as Middle French.)

Table 2.1 Changes in Sound in Latin and French and Their Results in Borrowings

Source	*Sounds*	*English borrowings with these sounds*		
Latin	/k/, /p/	*ca*ptain	*ca*ndle	*ca*nt
↓	↓			
Old French	/tʃ/, /f/	*chi*ef	*cha*ndler	*cha*nt
↓	↓			
Modern French	/ʃ/, /f/	*che*f	*cha*ndelier	*cha*ntey

Another example of a historical correspondence of sounds can be seen by comparing the originally Latin element *semi-* (as in *semicircle*) with the Greek element *hemi-* (as in *hemisphere*). Both *semi-* and *hemi-* mean "half". This correspondence of /h/ in one to /s/ in the other results from the fact that Greek and Latin are **related** languages, that is, they share a common ancient vocabulary, including the element *semi-* "half". Over a long period of time, the two languages came to differ in certain respects, including the pronunciation of the first sound of this element. We discuss the nature of language relationships and sound changes in detail in later chapters.

Such correspondences between the sounds of words borrowed from related languages such as French, Latin and Greek give us a way to organize information about English words. Knowing something about their historical development can provide useful clues to meanings and word relationships. In later chapters we show exactly how to use sound correspondences to learn new word elements.

— Denning, K., Kessler, B. & Leben, W. R.

Brief history of the Chinese loan words in English

Words loaning as a historic-linguistic phenomenon has existed between Chinese and English for more than one thousand years. The earliest direct contact between China and Britain dated back to 1637 when the British ship reached and dealt with tea. Previous to 1637, Chinese and British contact was mainly conducted through third countries, and Chinese language influence on English was limited. According to *the Oxford English Dictionary*, "silk" entered English in 888 via Latin and Greek, through the Silk Road. The entrance of china (porcelain) tells a similar story of indirect loaning. Comparing the loans silk and china with their models in Chinese ("si" and "ci"), we can find influentially formal and phonological changes which make them more like English than Chinese.

Increasingly, Chinese loans found their way into English during the Ming Dynasty (1268 – 1644). The loaning rate sped up during the Qing Dynasty (1644 – 1911), and we can find many loans dated in this time in the *Oxford English Dictionary*, such as "ginseng" (1654), "bohea" (1711) and "Taoism" (1639). The Chinese loans such as "bohea" (1711) and "kaoline" (1727) indicate that trade was one carrier of Chinese loans. Cultural terms like "kowtow", "Taoism", "pailou" and governmental terms such as "yamen" and "taotai" were also introduced into English through direct contacts and translation. In the 20th century, as the world wars affected the lives of everyone, many words concerning politics, culture and business entered into English. The historical changes after 1949 in China influence English with loans, such as "Great Leap Forward", "*Gang of Four*", "Four Modernizations", "Maoism", etc. Some of these loans are recorded in the dictionaries while some only appear in the mass media.

In general, all the Chinese words borrowed by the English language at different periods of time reflect the Chinese cultural and linguistic influences on the English language. They concern wide fields such as Chinese products, customs, economics, arts, politics, botany, etc.

(On Chinese Loanwords in English, 2011)

— Liu, X. & Zhang, L.

Exercises

I. True or False decisions.
1. Indo-European refers to the family languages spoken originally in Europe. (　　)
2. English, in origin, is closer to French than German. (　　)
3. Latin and French belong to different language groups. (　　)
4. English belongs to the Germanic language group of Indo-European language family. (　　)
5. The first people in England about whose language we have definite knowledge are the Celts. (　　)
6. Certain Germanic tribes, Angles, Saxons and Jutes, were the founders of the English nation. (　　)
7. Inflection is the most typical in the Middle English period. (　　)
8. About 95 percent of Old English are no longer in use. (　　)
9. Old English is characterized by the frequent use of compounds which in turn is an important linguistic feature of the Germanic language. (　　)
10. Old English has much less loan words compared with Modern English. (　　)
11. The early material of Middle English is of limited value, because it is largely written in Latin or French. (　　)
12. The Norman Conquest virtually introduced French-English bilingualism into England. (　　)
13. The increase in foreign borrowing is the most distinctive feature of the Renaissance for English. (　　)
14. Modern English is a language of leveled endings. (　　)
15. From the point of view of lexis, Modern English may be characterized by three main features: the unprecedented growth of scientific vocabulary, the assertion of American English as a dominant variety of the language, and the emergence of other varieties known as "New Englishes". (　　)

Chapter 2 The Growth of the English Vocabulary (1)

II. Choose the best choice to answer the following questions.

1. The following terms were taken by the Anglo-Saxons from the Romans. Which of them did not refer to a building material but to their system of currency?
   A. Poteus.　　　　B. Calx.　　　　C. Moneta.　　　　D. Tegula.

2. Which of these statements may be a partial explanation for the Roman words *vallis* (valley) and *vallum* (wall)?
   A. Romans usually built a wall around the fertile valleys.
   B. Romans built their defensive walls in fertile valleys mostly.
   C. "Vallum" was also the word for a "ditch" along a "wall".
   D. Romans used clay from valleys to make bricks for their walls.

3. The Latin word *discus* did not only mean the thing used in disc-throwing, but also the plate used by Romans for eating. But now the word means both the vessel and the food served in it. Thus it has come into Modern English as "_____".
   A. dish　　　　B. plate　　　　C. disc　　　　D. bowl

4. What word did the Anglo-Saxons derive from the very Mediterranean word *vinum*?
   A. Alcohol.　　　　B. Tequila.　　　　C. Brandy.　　　　D. Wine.

5. Many foodstuffs such as fruits, nuts and vegetables were "imported" into the cooking style of the Anglo-Saxons via contact with the Romans. Which of these was a NUT?
   A. Pisum.　　　　B. Castanea.　　　　C. Prunum.　　　　D. Cerasca.

6. *Caseum, furca, butyrum, cerefolium* were all culinary terms. Which of them did not refer to a dairy-product, vegetable or herb, but to a kitchen utensil?
   A. Cerefolium.　　　　B. Butyrum.　　　　C. Furca.　　　　D. Caseum.

7. The Anglo-Saxons also took over church terms of Latin, especially when they had settled in Britain and had been Christianized. The church (Greek kyrika) put *episcopoi* (inspectors) at the head of its "regional entities". What is the modern word for such an *epi-scopos* (controller)?
   A. Bishop.　　　　B. Teacher.　　　　C. Professor.　　　　D. Preacher.

8. The Church brought "good news". Those "good tidings" were originally called *god-spell*, or "good prophecy, good message for the future". What is the word that derived from *god-spell*?
   A. Gospel.　　　　B. Gory.　　　　C. Godliness.　　　　D. Godship.

9. Many borrowings happened during the Renaissance. New words were coined especially in scholarly and scientific language. What was the Latin-Greek word created by scholars to describe "a general course of instruction" or "the full circle of knowledge children had to learn"?
   A. Encyclopedia.　　　　B. Comprehension.　　　　C. Dictionary.　　　　D. Omniscience.

10. Some English words derive from Latin and some others may derive from bastardized forms of Latin, such as Italian, Spanish or French. They are often very close in appearance. Which of these is the only word of truly Latin origin?
    A. Fresco.　　　　B. Sonnet.　　　　C. Peninsula.　　　　D. Belvedere.

Chapter 3
The Growth of the English Vocabulary (2)
— British & American

> **Points for Thinking**
> 1. How did English spread in the world?
> 2. How do you comment on the similarities and disparities among the English varieties in the world?
> 3. What lexical differences are found between British English and American English?
> 4. How do British English and American English affect each other?
> 5. How will the English language develop in the future?

The spread of English in recent years is, by any criterion, a remarkable phenomenon. But the closer one examines the historical causes and current trends, the more it becomes apparent that the future of English will be more complex, more demanding of understanding and more challenging for the position of native-speaking countries than has hitherto been supposed.

— Graddol, D. (1953 –)

3.1 World Englishes

The status of the English language as the lingua franca in the world is beyond doubt. Thus, a Chinese can understand and be understood by, for example, a German through the medium of English. But such a role for English, seemingly a result of globalization, is not complete in itself, as we do find obvious disparities among its speakers from different regions, reflecting characteristics of their home regions. A better word to describe the development of the English language can probably be "glocalization", the blending of "globalization" and "localization", which is already in good use in financial and social sciences. The glocalized English implies that English today has been engaged in two simultaneous forces of evolution: becoming more global and common in use for international communication, and absorbing local characteristics from the region that it comes to.

3.1.1 The spread of English

The outbound spread of English temporally falls into four stages. The first stage started from the late 17th century to the 18th century during which America, Canada, Australia and New Zealand were established as English colonies. English settled into these areas with the new inhabitants. The second stage features the Industrial Revolution of the 18th and 19th centuries. Advances in technology brought a great amount of new English words into being. In exchanges with Britain, other nations had to learn English well in order to grasp the advanced technology imported from England. From the late 19th century to the early 20th century is the third stage, highlighted by the two World Wars. The major force in internationalizing English came from America, which leaped to a super power in both economy and politics. At present the country holds 70% of the English native speakers in the world. Since the late 20th century, English has entered the fourth stage of expansion. The driving force in this period was the American innovation of information technology, especially the advanced computer technology and the rapid development of the Internet.

According to David Crystal (2003), the UK's most popular language scholar, there are some 75 territories in which English is spoken as a mother tongue or an important second language. The numbers of these speakers are respectively 329 million and 430 million, while another 750 million speak English as a foreign language. Globally, 75% of the written information is conveyed in English; 80% of the data stored in computers is English; and 90% of the web pages are written in English. The American linguist Braj Kachru (1988) has suggested a helpful approach to recognize the divisions of countries according to how English is acquired and used. He puts forward three concentric circles: the *inner circle* refers to the traditional bases of English, including the USA, the UK, Ireland, Canada, Australia, New Zealand, using English as the primary language; the *outer circle* refers to the non-English countries including India, Nigeria, Pakistan, Singapore, South Africa, Zambia and other territories, where the language is used as a "second language" for institutional practices especially in education, government and culture; and the *expanding circle* involving the nations where English is taught as a foreign language, mainly for some specific purposes. China, Japan, South Korea, Indonesia, Iran, Russia, Greece, Poland and a steadily increasing number of other nations all belong to this circle.

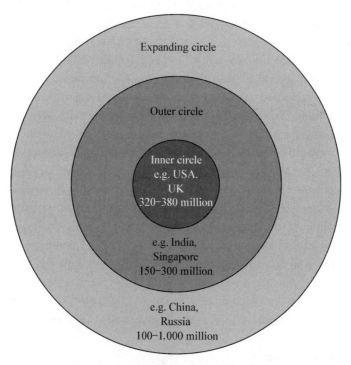

Fig. 3.1 Kachru's three circles of English

Task

1. What are the positive and negative consequences of the spread of English to an expanding circle country like China?
2. What is the latest trend of the spread of English in the 21st century?

Viewed generally from its application purposes, English has come to be a must-to-have medium not only for international politics, trade and finance, but also for entertainment, travel, sports and global information exchanges. It is no longer tied to one place, culture or people, but is increasingly used to communicate across regional boundaries.

3.1.2 Features of English as a global language

The enormous vocabulary coming from a good variety of sources makes English outstanding amongst today's world of languages. Even before its world-wide expansion, English had grown into a language of diverse words. Sharing a common ancestor with German, Danish, Dutch, Swedish and Norwegian, English keeps many cognates with them. In addition, over half of the words in the English vocabulary have their origins in Latin. Since its spread outside the British Isles, English has been the most ready to borrow words from other languages as well. Words such as *chipmunk*, *hominy*, *moose*, *raccoon*, *skunk* come from the American Indian languages; *brandy*, *cruller*, *landscape*, *measles*, *uproar*, *wagon* from Dutch; *alligator*, *cargo*, *contraband*, *cork*, *hammock*, *mosquito*, *sherry*, *stampede*, *tornado*, *vanilla* from Spanish; *acme*, *acrobat*, *anthology*, *barometer*, *catarrh*, *catastrophe*, *elastic*, *magic*, *tactics*, *tantalize* from Greek; *steppe*, *vodka*, *ruble*, *troika*, *glasnost*, *perestroika* from Russian; and *caravan*, *dervish*, *divan*, *khaki*, *mogul*, *shawl*, *sherbet*, *jasmine*, *paradise*, *lemon*, *lilac*, *turban* from Persian, and so on. However, the origins of the borrowings in English are usually ignored by most of the language learners and users. Together with that negligence is their lack of awareness that the borrowings should have a connection to the cultures they come from — a manifestation of the borderless identity of the English language.

An example of the growing interest in the research of English as a global language is some websites, which list "Top 500 English Words", "Top 100 English Verbs", "Top 100 Misspelt English Words" and even "World English Slang", etc. To understand the street English spoken around the world, it is considered essential to know *airhead* (stupid person), *ace* (excellent), *apples and pears* (rhyming slang for "stairs"), *barbie* (barbecue), *beans* (money), *biggie* (something important), *bird* (woman/girl/girlfriend), *cakehole* (mouth), *cheesy* (cheap), *dickhead* (an idiot), *dinosaur* (something out of date or old fashioned), *French kiss* (kissing with the tongue), *grass* (marijuana), *guts* (courage), *in* (fashionable), *ivories* (teeth), *knock* (condemn), *kook* (peculiar person), *mickey-mouse* (unimportant, time-wasting), *neat* (cool, great), *party animal* (someone that loves parties), *peanuts* (very little money), *screw up* (to make a mistake), *yabber* (talk), *zero* (an unimportant person). To impress educated native speakers or examiners in examinations like IELTS, TOFEL and Cambridge CAE and CPE, you are supposed to know *aberration* (irregularity), *alacrity* (smartness), *brusque* (impolite), *callous* (cruel), *cajole* (coax), *deferential* (respectful), *deride* (mock), *eloquent* (silver-tongued/fluent), *embezzle* (misappropriate), *erudite* (learned), *fractious* (angry), *furtive* (stealthy), *gratuitous* (unnecessary), *haughty* (arrogant), *impertinent* (rude), *impeccable* (perfect), etc.

3.1.3 English nativization

However, the English expansion does not simply mean the assimilation of the world. In its contact with other local cultures and languages, English keeps a two-way communication with them, having an effect on both sides. Globally, English is forming a universal standard; while locally, it interacts with other languages and transforms into a regional dialect. For instance, English in China has been significantly affected by the Chinese language. China English, as a regional dialect of English, seems firmly verified by an increasing number of Chinese loan words and loan translation. Its vocabulary vividly depicts the Chinese culture, such as the early borrowed words, *chopstick*, *chow mein*, *coolie*, *dim sum*, *feng shui*, *ginkgo*, *ginseng*, *kanji*, *kowtow*, *longan*, *lychee*, *mahjong*, *sampan*, *silk*, *Tai Chi*, *tea*, *tofu*, *typhoon*, *wushu*, *yin yang*, and relatively recent ones, *loving care project*, *comfortable housing project*, *eight-treasure rice pudding*, *vegetable basket program*, *issue IOU*, *return students*, *kungfu film*, *new year's film*, *Golden Rooster Awards*, *Chinese Peasants' and Workers' Democratic Party*, *National People's Congress (NPC)*, *three represents theory*, *Three Gorges Project*, *Shanghai Cooperation Organization (SCO)*, *tube-shaped apartment*, *Western Development*, *Hope Project*, *Hong Kong Special Administrative Region*, *crosstalk*, *little smart*, *Spark Program*, *vanity project*, *"One country, two systems"*, *One Belt One Road*, *Community of Shared Future for Mankind*, *Chinese knot*, *China Compulsory Certification*.

In David Crystal's words (Burns and Coffin, 2001: 55), "the unprecedented scale of the growth in the usage (approaching a quarter of the world's population) has resulted in an unprecedented growth in regional varieties". In the 1980s and 1990s, a series of regional English dictionaries were published, such as *The Australian National Dictionary* (1988), *A Dictionary of South African English on Historical Principles* (1996), *A Dictionary of Caribbean Usage* (1996), *The Canadian Oxford Dictionary* (2004), and *The Dictionary of New Zealand English* (1997). Of all the regional Englishes, Indian English is a steadily and rapidly growing variety. 76 percent of the Indian speakers (of various first languages) "used indirect questions involving permission, ability, or willingness, much like native speakers would use … However, as many as 20 percent used imperatives or desideratives, reflecting Indian language conventions" (quoted in Burns and Coffin, 2001: 19). In terms of the differences in vocabulary, many words from Indian native languages have been introduced, some notable examples being *jungle*, *bungalow*, *punch*, *shawl*, *veranda*, etc. Two examples of Indian English words that non-Indian English speakers probably never encounter include *airdash*, which is used for someone who is in a hurry, and *badmash*, another word for a hooligan. Sometimes speakers of English in India add a new level of meaning to existing words. For instance, if a person wears a *hi-tech outfit*, it does not mean that they are equipped with the latest digital gadgets. Instead, a *hi-tech outfit* stands for being fashionable and modern. This kind of growth of the English language outside its conventional native speakers has also pressed them to overturn their traditional belief that wherever the English of its non-native speakers differs from native English varieties, it shall be considered "erroneous".

We have to be careful, though, when making claims about the positions of the regional English varieties. In the future, Indian English may be very highly looked upon, while at present we do not take our eyes off the two leading English varieties in the world, British and American, each a source of fascination for lexicologists.

3.2 British English

British English has a broad sense and a narrow sense. In its broad use, it refers to the language of the entirety of the United Kingdom, including all the varieties of the language, temporal or regional, standard or non-standard, formal or informal. The narrow use refers to the form of Standard English used in Britain, or the medium of the upper and (especially the professional) middle class. The standards cover its pronunciation and vocabulary and came into being during the 15th century. This form of English mainly follows the accent of Received Pronunciation (RP), though a number of other accents can be involved as well. Today Standard

English is widely taught at school and to foreign students. It has been associated with the phrases of the *Queen's English*, the *King's English*, *Oxford English* or *BBC English*.

3.2.1 Dialects and accents

Inside the British Isles, the diversity of dialects draws up another picture of British English. The dialects generally fall into four classes: Southern English dialects, Midlands English dialects, Northern English dialects and Scottish English and the closely related dialects of Scots and Ulster Scots. Due to the different sources the dialects have turned to for borrowing, they vary greatly from one another in their vocabulary.

In terms of accents, RP is the best known one to the world. It is not related to a specific locality but turns out to be generally more southern rather than northern in character. Until the Second World War, it was the exclusive language used by the BBC, for its reputation of being more educated than other accents. But in recent decades, regional accents have rivaled and won a seat at the BBC. Since the 1990s Estuary English, a new dialect, has spread through south-east England. It combines Cockney and RP in character. Researchers believe that it is the result of compromise between two social movements: an upward one of some Cockney speakers and a downward one of some middle-class speakers. Its recent spread has influenced the accents throughout the southeast.

The past decades have witnessed a wave of immigration to Britain, particularly from Commonwealth countries, with speakers bringing fresh dialects and accents that further enrich the linguistic landscape. Especially in urban areas, speakers of Asian and Caribbean descent have blended their mother tongue speech patterns with existing local dialects to produce wonderful new varieties of English, such as London Jamaican or Bradford Asian English.

3.2.2 The changing British English vocabulary

Modern English consists of three main elements. At the very core of its vocabulary lie the Anglo-Saxon elements, almost commonly used in life, such as *father*, *mother*, *brother*, *hand*, *heart*, *bone*, *year*, *month*, *day*. The second powerful source is French, which brought to English a great number of words involving administration, religion, military, fashion and art, especially after the Norman Conquest, such as *government*, *state*, *authority*, *religion*, *confession*, *communion*, *army*, *navy*, *enemy*, *fashion*, *robe*, *veil*, *etiquette*, *literature*, *critique*. While in areas of medicine, law, theology, science and literature, Latin has contributed the most: *education*, *tuberculosis*, *civil*, *history*, *technology*, and *crisis*.

As English expanded into non-English regions and met with non-native speakers, changes occurred to itself. In the British colonial period, the British Empire opened to a wider world by sending out its poor, criminals and middle classes to the new settlements, and then its better-off administrators. All their contact with non-English peoples, cultures and languages created chances for English to borrow words from other languages. It is in this period that some Indian words, for example, *verandah*, *pukka* and *palanquin*, entered the English vocabulary. Immigration is another reason for the borrowing of words from non-English languages. The 20th century witnessed a wave of immigrants to Britain, such as Indians, Pakistanis, Cypriots, the Caribbeans, East and West Africans. They brought from their native cultures new words to refer to new things. Today the Britons will not find words like *dashikis*, *saris*, *tandoor*, *feta* and *pita* exotic to them.

3.3 American English

American English or US English is the largest regional English variety. According to David Crystal (2003), English is spoken by about 241 million people in the United States, compared with 59 million in Great Britain. According to the 2018 survey by the Census Bureau, 78.1% of the US population speak American English, followed by Spanish (13.5%), other Indo-European languages (3.7%), Asian and Pacific languages (3.6%) and other languages (1.2%).

3.3.1 History

Historically the growth of the English language in the United States falls into three periods corresponding to the country's social and political changes.

English was first brought to America by an expedition commissioned by Walter Raleigh in 1584. In 1585, he sponsored the first English colony in America on Roanoke Island (now North Carolina). The colony failed and another attempt at colonisation also failed in 1587. Raleigh has been credited with bringing potatoes and tobacco back to Britain, although both of these were already known via the Spanish.

The first permanent English settlement, called Jamestown, was set up by the British immigrants in 1607. Two years later, they established the first colony Virginia. From here, the English language took its root. Its speakers included soldiers, adventurers, well-to-do merchants, devout Puritans and deported convicts. But the best-known expedition in American history was in November of 1620, when *Mayflower* reached the American continent in an area later called Massachusetts. The ship was loaded with the first group of English Puritans, or strictly speaking Separatists, who had separated from the Church of England. Obstructed and diverted by bad weather, they drifted north from their planned direction to Virginia. They finally established the second permanent English settlement Plymouth. By 1732, 13 English colonies had been established along the Atlantic seaboard. At the end of this colonial period the population reached four million, most living along the east coast.

1607 Jamestown (Virginia)

1620 Pilgrim Fathers' Plymouth Plantation

Fig. 3.2 The earliest British settlements in America.

The immigrants came from a diversity of linguistic backgrounds, such as the Midlands, north England, Germany and Northern Ireland. But their originally sharp divisions were gradually blurred as communications among them increased. Generally, the colonists spoke Elizabethan English, similar to what we read in Shakespeare's works, a form of Early Modern

English.

In 1756, the term "American dialect" was coined by Samuel Johnson, author of the *Dictionary of the English Language*, intended only as an insult. The official proclamation of the linguistic independence was made in *The American Spelling Book* by Noah Webster in 1783. The American lexicographer, who has been called "Father of American Scholarship and Education", intended to set up a standard for American spelling. His pursuit of American independence in language was clearly made in his *Dissertations on the English Language* in 1789, saying "as an independent nation, our honor requires us to have a system of our own, in language as well as government" (http://www.bartleby.com/185/7.html).

The second period is known as the National Expansion Period, extending from 1790 to 1865, characterized by the expansion to the south and the west. After the American Revolution, the newly established government encouraged expansion into "the Old Northwest", and pushed its frontiers to the Pacific Ocean through annexation, diplomacy, technology and war, including the Louisiana Purchase in 1803, the War of 1812, and so on. This period also saw great waves of immigrants, especially the influx of the Irish, following the potato famine in Ireland in the 1840s, and the Italians and the Germans, escaping the consequences of the failed 1848 Revolution.

In this period Noah Webster showed his concern over the establishment of schools and of a uniform standard of spelling. In 1828, at the age of 70, he published *An American Dictionary of the English Language*, containing 70,000 entries. He introduced many spelling forms with American characteristics, such as *honor*, *favor*, *center*, in contrast with the British *honour*, *favour* and *centre*. These changes were quickly accepted and were popular in use among the immigrants.

After the Civil War, which ended in 1865, started the third period. Great changes took place in terms of the sources of the immigrants. A great number of Nordics, southern Europeans and Slavs rushed in. In the first two decades of the 20th century, about 750,000 immigrants settled in America. By 1950, the population in the country had risen to more than 150 million, twice the 1900 population. Together with the growth of the population was the massive increase of mother-tongue use of English. The 1990 census showed that 198 million people of five years of age and above only speak English at home. The figure far surpasses that of any other English-speaking country in the world.

Another noteworthy factor that has accelerated the growth of American English in this period is the two World Wars. They substantially weakened Great Britain and finally contributed to the decline of the "sun-never-set" empire; while at the same time, the United States rose to the leading power in the West. Its fast developments in economy, politics, culture and modern communications thrust the country to the front of the world stage. Together with all the above-mentioned came an unprecedented recognition of the American English variety, which had been mocked by the British but now deeply affected by the British. In fact, an increasing number of American words have been accepted by the British: *teenager*, *commuter*, *babysitter*, *striptease*, *brain drain*, *brainwash*, *streamline*, *miniskirt*, *hovercraft*, *campus*, *kickback*, *the Establishment*, *egghead*, *stagflation*, *bluff*, *blizzard*, *grapevine*, *Yuppie*.

3.3.2 The differences between American English and British English

Although British English and American English share commonality in the majority of linguistic forms in English, they do diverge at a great number of points. The most obvious differences between them are perhaps found in vocabulary.

Several reasons have made American English words differ from the British English ones. The first is obviously the necessity to name the things or experiences that were unknown to the English settlers when they first encountered them in America. Adapting existing words or creating new words are two helpful ways for this purpose. A well-known example is the word "corn", which, as the general English term for grain, denotes the most common grain crop *wheat* in England but *maize* in America. The second cause is the technological and cultural developments. Thus we find that Americans use *trunk*, instead of the British use of *boot*, to refer to the compartment at the rear of an automobile, and that the American *private school* and the British *public school* actually refer to the same kind of school. The influences of other languages also make American English diverge from its British counterpart. Many languages have contributed words to American English, but not necessarily to British English: *hickory*, *hooch*, *muskie* from American Indians; *mesa*, *tornado*, *tortilla* from Spanish; *schmaltz*, *schlep*, *schlock* from Yiddish. And linguistic changes within one or both of them have become the last cause for their lexical differences. A typical example is the use of *gotten* as the past participle of *get* in 17th century England. This usage has been kept in American English but has been changed to *got* in modern British English.

1. Differences in word choice

The major differences between the two varieties are in the choice of words, though both share most of them.

1) Different words, same meaning

The Americans and the British sometimes use different words to express the same idea. This is perhaps the most outstanding difference of all lexical differences. *Emcee, faucet, muffler, rookie, sophomore* and *washcloth* are only familiar to the Americans, but they do have equivalents in British English: *compere, tap, silencer, first year member, second year student* and *face-flannel*. *Dynamo, hire, purchase, nought, queue, spanner, lorry* and *treacle* are mostly found in British English; they are comparable with *generator, installment, buying, zero, line, monkey wrench, truck* and *molasses* in American English. Some synonymous words originally belonging to one variety have already earned much reputation in the other, such as the American *call, couch, game* and *gas* and the British *ring* or *phone, sofa, match* and *petrol*.

Other words of this category are numerous. An *apartment* in America is called a *flat* in Britain. A "building containing several individual apartments" is known as *apartment house* in America but *block of flats* in Britain. While the Americans *brush teeth*, the British *clean teeth*. In America pedestrians are supposed to walk on the *sidewalk*, but in Britain, on the *pavement*. You may buy a *home* for residence in America, and grow some *corn* in your own *land*, but in the UK you will find them called *house*, *maize* and *field*.

2) Same word, different meanings

In the process of independent development of the two varieties, some words gradually gained new meanings. In this category the two varieties share a word or a phrase, but with an entirely different meaning. The word *vest* is such a case in point. The American English *vest* is called *waistcoat* in British English, and the British English *vest* means *undershirt* in American English. As the original meaning of *subway* — a passage under something — weakened, the word gained different concepts in the two varieties. It means in American English *underground urban railroad*, while in British English *underground pedestrian tunnel*. *Creek* is, to the Americans, a *small stream*, but to the British, a *small inlet in a shoreline*. A *pressman* in Britain is a *newspaper reporter*, but in America is a *man who operates a printing press*. Indeed, the differences in the meaning of a word in the two varieties can be huge, thus deserving our full attention. A *billion*, for example, means a *thousand million* to the Americans, but to the British, a *million million*, a thousand times in difference.

3) Words cross-matching in meaning

A more confusing picture of the lexical differences between the two varieties is the fact that the same word can mean different things in the varieties but in each variety its meaning is echoed by another word in the other variety. It is a special kind of word phenomenon between the above-mentioned categories. Take *biscuit* for example. In British English it refers to what is called *cookie* in American English, but the American English *biscuit* is synonymous to *scone* in British English. In another case *pudding* is common to both the varieties, but has different meanings. The British refer it to what Americans call *dessert*, while the Americans use it for the British English *custard*. Other similar words include *suspender*, used by the British for what the Americans call *garter* and by the Americans for British English *braces*. Similarly, *knickers* means the same to the British as *women's underpants* to the Americans, and in the American context means what the British call the *knickerbockers*.

4) Same word, additional meaning in one variety

In this group both varieties share a word and a good part of its meaning(s). The differences are only seen in part, where additional meaning is attached to the word. Both the Americans and the British use *tube* to refer to a *hollow cylinder*, but it additionally means *television* in America, and *underground* in Britain. Likewise, *sleeper*, besides the common meaning in the varieties, means in American English a *sleeping car* or *one that achieves unexpected recognition or success* and in British English a *small earring used to keep the hole in a pierced ear open*.

Sometimes the development of the new meaning of a word is not balanced and equally seen in both varieties. The additional meaning in one variety may be not known or used in the other. Though both the varieties share the common meaning of *leader*, in British English it can additionally refer to what is called *editorial* in American English. Similarly American English *fall* has the additional meaning of the season of a year or *autumn* in British English. The extra meaning of *dumb* is found in American English: *stupid*. *Cute* has earned an American meaning, *attractive and charming*. And *to mind* means additionally in British English *to look after*, as in the sentence "She stayed at home and minded the baby".

5) Words unique to one variety

Some words are only used in one of the two varieties. This is often true because they refer to something only known in one of the Englishes. This category is different from the first one in that no corresponding synonyms can be found from the other. When words are used to refer to the unique environment in America, they are found absent from British English, such as *prairie*, *canyon*, *Everglades*, *caribou*, *bayou*, *sagebrush*. In referring to social and political institutions, *succotash*, *favorite son* are unique terms in American English while *Yorkshire pudding*, *back bench* are only in British English. While *bankroll* and *interstate* remain only American English, *wicket*, *bowler*, *prince*, *duke*, *marquis*, *count*, *viscount*, *baron* and *knight* adhere to the British sphere.

Table 3.1 The naming of school years in British (except Scotland) and American English

Age range	British English			American English	
	Name	Alternative name	Syllabus	Name	Alternative name
	Preschool (optional)				
1 – 4	Nursery	Playgroup	Foundation stage 1		
	Primary school			Preschool	
4 – 5	Reception	Infants reception	Foundation stage 2	Pre-kindergarten	
5 – 6	Year 1	Infants year 1	Key stage 1	Kindergarten	
				Elementary school	
6 – 7	Year 2	Infants year 2		1st grade	
7 – 8	Year 3	Junior year 3		2nd grade	
8 – 9	Year 4	Junior year 4	Key stage 2	3rd grade	
9 – 10	Year 5	Junior year 5		4th grade	
10 – 11	Year 6	Junior year 6		5th grade	
	Secondary school			Middle school	Junior high school
11 – 12	Year 7	First form		6th grade	
12 – 13	Year 8	Second form	Key stage 3	7th grade	
13 – 14	Year 9	Third form		8th grade	
14 – 15	Year 10	Fourth form	Key stage 4	High school	
				9th grade	Freshman year
15 – 16	Year 11	Fifth form		10th grade	Sophomore year
	Sixth form (optional)				
16 – 17	Year 12	Lower sixth	Key stage 5, A level	11th grade	Junior year
17 – 18	Year 13	Upper sixth		12th grade	Senior year

2. Differences in spelling forms

Though American English and British English share a common spelling form for the majority of their vocabulary, some words do take on a little difference in spelling. This is largely due to their different choices of word forms in their independent development processes. However, it is almost unlikely that these spelling differences would hinder the readers of one variety from understanding the other. What is more meaningful to notice is that we should try to cling to one systemic form of either of the varieties within the same article, though often their spelling forms are borrowed between each other.

According to Gramley and Patzold (2004), there are five categories of spelling differences between the two varieties. The first principle, *simplification*, is common to both but comparatively more reputed in American English. *-ae/oe-* in British English words may be shortened into *-e-* in their American forms: *anaesthetic/anesthetic*, *amoeba/ameba* and *foetus/fetus*. Likewise, British English *faggot* and *waggon* are found next to American English *fagot* and *wagon*. Concerning the changes of words' endings, *regularization* is also more completely employed in American English. Typical examples are the regularization of the British English endings *-our* to *-or* in American English: *colour/color*, *favour/favor*, *honour/honor*; and of

-re to -er: *centre / center*, *fibre / fiber*, *metre / meter*. The third principle is *derivational uniformity*. While British English writes *defence*, *licence*, *offence*, *pretence*, *connexion*, *deflexion* and *inflexion*, American English has *defense*, *license*, *offense*, *pretense*, *connection*, *deflection* and *inflection*. The fourth principle, *reflection of pronunciation*, explains why the American forms of *analyze* and *paralyze*, ending in *-ize*, may seemingly violate the principle of derivational principle, as some may have already questioned. They really conform to the requirements of pronunciation. Similar examples in American English are *apologize*, *capitalize*, *dramatize* and *naturalize*. In American English, -l at the end of multi-syllabic word is doubled if it is followed by an ending beginning with a vowel, and if the final syllable of the root is stressed and is spelled with a single-letter vowel: *rebel / rebelling*, *compel / compelling*, *patrol / patroller*. If the final syllable is not stressed, -l is not doubled such as *traveled*, *quarreling* and *counselor*. Also to indicate end stress, American English favours *fulfill* and *distill* over British English *fulfil* and *distil*. Such comparison of British English words with American ones release disparity of choices in *-en / -in* forms: *ensure / insure*, *enclose / inclose* and *endorse / indorse*; hyphenated / unhyphenated words: *ash-tray / ashtray*, *book-keeper / bookkeeper*, *flower-pot / flower pot*, *note-paper / note paper*, *co-operate / cooperate*, *anti-aircraft / antiaircraft* and *make-up / makeup*; and words with / without French diacritics: *café / cafe*, *élite / elite*, *entrée / entree*, *fête / fete* and *fiancée / fiancee*.

Table 3.2 Differences in spelling forms

Letter groupings (AmE/BrE)	American spelling	British spelling
-ter/-tre	center	centre
	liter	litre
	theater	theatre
-or/-our	color	colour
	neighbor	neighbour
	honor	honour
-ense/-ence	defense	defence
	offense	offence
	expense	expence
-ize/-ise	civilize	civilise
	organize	organise
	modernize	modernise
-ll/-l	skillful	skilful
	fulfill	fulfil
others	gray	grey
	program	programme
	tire	tyre
	cafe	café
	bookkeeper	book-keeper

3.4 The Future of English

As a fact of life, American English is just one of the "New Englishes" that followed the course of British exploration and empire building. New forms of "Englishes" are swiftly evolving. The first permanent English settlement in Canada was established in the late 16th century. Australian English, New Zealand English and Indian English began at the end of the 18th century. And South African English started to develop at the beginning of the 19th century. The two World Wars of the 20th century fundamentally shook the British Empire and the following independence movements across the world brought to life the new varieties of English in the former British colonies such as Ghana, Nigeria, Kenya, Zambia and Singapore. The growth of all these international Englishes was quick, as was their regional lexical development. This is perhaps why, as David Crystal (2006) argues, "The global perspective is the future of English dialectology" (p. 106).

But should we worry about the fragmentation of the English language into unintelligible varieties? Indian English, for example, is a mixture of English and Hindu. And Singlish, spoken in Singapore, is a mixture of English and Chinese. Their spoken forms may appear incomprehensible to an English speaker if he does not know the linguistic background involved. But in the more formal uses of English, like newspaper articles and school teaching, the English language employed has no big difference from those of the Unites States, Britain and Australia.

At another level, disputes can be still heard on whether English will drop in dominance by the middle of the century, though probably not in terms of the number of its speakers. However, all the signs today suggest that English is the global language. Non-English nations, who are caught in the struggle for identity and internationalism, have to ponder carefully as they make political decisions and allocate resources for language planning. Long-term views and provision plans are needed to guarantee that they play their role in the future linguistic world. But English-speaking nations are not a bit released at all. When the non-English nations become more bilingual and multilingual, those who speak only English will be put at a competitive disadvantage. In the new linguistic world order, as Mr. Graddol puts in VOA's *Coast to Coast* on *Future of English* (March 18, 2004), most people will switch between languages for routine tasks but monolingual English speakers will have difficulty in fully participating in society. Finally he suggests job seekers in the next decade to learn modern Chinese.

As this chapter reveals, the growth of the English vocabulary is connected to the spread of the English language outside the British Isles. The four stages of its history marked respectively the English colonization, the Industrial Revolution, the two World Wars and the American technology innovation, all driving forward the expansion of the language. Under the influence of "glocalization", the English vocabulary has taken on a diverse look. It has borrowed words from a diversity of languages. Many of the words have been made familiar or common in use to all the peoples who speak English. Still, the English expansion does not simply mean assimilation of the world. While English may well take a word from another language and use it internationally, it does often retain a regional characteristic of the local language and culture that the borrowed word comes from. This explains the course of the formation of regional English varieties. As the comparison of the most important varieties of the English language — British English and American English — shows, their differences are obviously seen in word choice and spelling forms. The two varieties can use different words for the same idea, or the same word for different meanings. Some of their words are cross-matching in meaning, or have additional meaning found in one variety but not in the other. And there are still some others whose meaning is unique to only one variety. But such regional character in Englishes should not be pushed too far. Though they might take on clear marks of the local culture and language in the spoken form, in more formal uses of English the language employed is often similar to each other. It is in such an integrated force of both globalization and localization that English as a lingua franca is recognized, and its dominance in the linguistic world guaranteed.

Further Reading

1. Gramley, S. and Patzold, K. (2004). *A Survey of Modern English*. London and New York: Routledge.
2. Jenkins, J. (2003). *World Englishes*. London and New York: Routledge.
3. Tottie, G. (2002). *An Introduction to American English*. Oxford: Blackwell.

● Extended Reading

■ A Typology of American English and British English

If we want to characterize British/American lexical differences in a systematic fashion, we need some kind of typology. Such a typology can be based either on form or on meaning. We can either start with a particular form and ask questions like "What does this word or expression mean in American English?" or "How is this word or expression used in American English compared with British English?" Or we can start from a semantic point of view and ask "How does one express this concept in American English compared with British English?".

Let's start with the form-based classification, where it is possible to distinguish four different types. Although our goal is to give a characterization that works for present-day American English and British English, we also need some historical perspective here — see types 3 and 4 below.

1. A form-based classification

Type 1: Words with the same basic meaning in British English and American English but with differences in style, connotation, or frequency

Good examples here, with the American variant given first, would be the words just discussed in 5.3.2 — *vacation / holiday* and *maybe / perhaps*. Another interesting pair is *post / mail*. Although the British have their Royal Mail, they seem to prefer the word *post*, except of course in *e-mail*, which is everywhere. Americans go to the *post office*, but prefer to use *mail* in *mailbox* or *to mail a letter*, and *mailman* is certainly as common as *postman*. (Both of the latter are now considered politically incorrect and should be replaced by *postal worker* in official contexts.)

Type 2: Words that share a basic meaning but which have developed additional meanings in one or both varieties

Bathroom and *tube* are good examples in this category. We have already seen in chapter 3 that *bathroom* has developed an additional meaning in American English, where it also means "toilet". Tube has the same basic meaning in both varieties: "a long hollow cylindrical object". In British English it is frequently used to refer to the London underground, "underground railway". It has a different additional meaning in American English, "television". Thus if an American says I saw this movie star on the tube, it does not mean that he or she saw a movie star on the subway, but on TV.

Another example is *concession*, whose basic meaning is "giving up something, or something that is given up", as in "He made no concessions to their demands". In American English the meaning "a small business", as in *ice cream concession*, has developed from the meaning "privilege of maintaining a business within certain premises"; there are thus *concessions at a baseball park*, for instance, selling hot dogs, hamburgers and the like. In British English this lexeme can now also be used in this way, but it has another meaning, unknown to the Americans, namely, a reduced entrance fee to museums or theaters, *conceded* (given) to students, the elderly, the disabled, etc. The Americans would use *senior discount* or some similar expression for this concept.

Obviously, not only nouns belong to this category. The verb *ship*, for example, which normally means "send by ship" in British English, is used to mean "send by any means of conveyance, by road or by air" in American English. The original meaning of *momentarily* in both British and American English is "for a moment or an instant", and it is still often used in this sense, as in "A rainbow momentarily lightened the skies". However, in American English, *momentarily* is also often used to mean "in a moment; very soon", as in "The doctor will be with you momentarily". This usage is sometimes criticized by purists. *Presently* is normally used to mean "soon, in a minute" in British English but in American English it is more frequently used to mean "just now, at the moment".

Type 3: Words that used to have a common meaning but which now have different meanings in the two varieties

The type of semantic development seen in type 2 is what underlies the third category: In chapter 4 I mentioned *subway* and *pavement*, which used to mean "a passage under something" and "paving", respectively, but whose common meanings were lost or became obsolete, and which now have different meanings in American and British English. Other examples include *creek*, which in British English usually means "a small inlet in a coastal shoreline, going further inland than a cove", but in American English denotes "any small stream, usually a tributary to a river". *Football* now denotes very different kinds of games in American and British English; the Americans always (and Britons sometimes) say *soccer* when referring to the same game, as "American football is a totally different game". *Clerk* used to mean "clergyman" or "scholar" but now means "office worker" in British English and "salesperson" or "hotel receptionist" in American English (In British English a salesperson is called a shop assistant.).

The phrasal verb *wash up* has acquired different meanings in the two varieties; thus in British English *wash up* means "wash the dishes" but in American English it means "wash oneself". Thus if you say "Peter washed up after dinner" a British person will think that Peter took care of the dirty dishes, but an American will think that Peter just washed (himself). For washing dishes, the Americans prefer the expressions *wash or do the dishes*, and most would probably say "Peter did the dishes after dinner" or "Peter washed the dishes".

Somewhere between categories 2 and 3 are words like *shop*, where some meanings are shared and others are not. When *shop* is used as a verb, as in *He went shopping*, there are great similarities between British and American usage, but when it is used as a noun, there are major differences. For places where you buy things, the Americans generally use *store*, and *shop* is more frequent in such collocations as *coffee shop* "simple restaurant", or *body shop* "garage where bodies of cars are repaired". In American English *shop* is also used to mean "woodwork, metalwork", etc. , as taught in schools, or the classroom where this is done.

Type 4: Words, collocations and idioms that are used only or predominantly in one variety

In this category there are several subclasses:

(a) English words that have disappeared from one variety, such as *lorry*, which is a typically British word (the Americans use *truck*).

(b) Coinages and compounds based on English material, or foreign words which have been anglicized, but which are used only or mostly in one variety. Examples of this type abound. Some examples follow:

American English	**British English**
band-aid	(sticking-) plaster
cell(ular) phone	mobile (phone)
corral	paddock
envision	envisage
funeral director, mortician (as well as undertaker)	undertaker
line	queue
realtor	estate agent
stroller	push chair

(c) Sometimes only one variety uses a particular word but there exists: synonym that works in both varieties; thus only British English uses the informal form *telly* for TV. Only the Americans tend to use *ornery* (from ordinary) to mean "mean-spirited, disagreeable".

2. A classification based on semantic categories

Sometimes it is easier or more natural to start with a concept and look at how it is expressed in either variety. In this case it seems possible to manage with two categories:

(1) Phenomena or concepts that exist in both America and Britain but where different words are used, such as *truck/lorry*, *cell/mobile phone*, etc. If we take the semantic field "man" and look for informal expressions, an Englishman might talk of a *bloke*, a *chap*, a *lad*, or sometimes a *guy*, whereas an American would definitely prefer the word *guy*. The Americans are not likely to recognize the British expressions *jacket potatoes* "baked potatoes with their skins on", *soft fruit* "red berries", or *Wellingtons* "rubber boots", although the concepts themselves are well known to them.

(2) Phenomena or concepts that exist only on either side of the Atlantic, such as North American trees and plants (live *oak*, *poison ivy*, *cottonwood*, etc.) and animals (*skunk*, *raccoon*, *moose*), or certain phenomena in society, such as the *surgeon general*, *sororities*, *fraternities*. Similarly, there are many British phenomena that have no counterparts or are rare in the United States, e.g. *elevenses* (a late morning snack) or *eggcups* (The Americans don't normally use them.) or the somewhat old-fashioned *high tea* (an evening meal at which the drink is tea and meat is served).

— Tottie, G.

■ The semantic approach

Perhaps the most common way to deal with the lexis of the two varieties is what may be called the semantic approach. This method compares words and phrases with their referents or meanings in terms of sameness and difference. Despite varying approaches with sometimes numerous groupings, five different groups may conveniently be recognized.

First of all, most words and their meanings are the same, which explains the fact that British and American speakers rarely experience any difficulty in understanding each other. As a result this first group is seldom mentioned. The second group comprises words which are present in only one variety because they refer to something unknown in the other culture. This can be words for things in the natural environment such as BrE *moor* or *heath* and AmE *prairie* and *canyon*. It also may include social and political institutions, e. g. BrE *Yorkshire pudding* or *back bench* and AmE *succotash* or *favorite son*. Although cases in the second category make linguistic help necessary, they do not cause misunderstandings. A variant on this type of distinction involves lexical gaps. Here the referent or concept is known in the other variety but not lexicalized, i. e. only paraphrases are available, e. g. BrE *chapel* "a local (branch) of a printers' union" or BrE (slang) *to tart up* "to dress up in a garish manner".

The third group covers those cases where different words and phrases are used to express the same meaning. BrE *petrol* is AmE *gas* (*oline*) and AmE *truck* is BrE *lorry*. In the fourth category the two varieties share a word/phrase, but with a fully different meaning, as with *vest*, which in AmE is what is called a *waistcoat* in BrE, but in BrE is what is called an *undershirt* in AmE. A variation on this is the case in which the two varieties agree in the meanings, but one variety has an additional meaning not known or used in the other. For example, both agree in the meaning of *leader* "someone who leads", but BrE also uses it in the sense of AmE (and shared) *editorial*. Conversely, both understand the noun *fall* as "downward movement", but AmE also uses this word in the sense of BrE (and shared) *autumn*. In many cases special words and meanings arise only in certain contexts. Examples in BrE are *sit* or *enter for* when they collocate with *exam*, while *freshen* has the extra meaning "add more liquid etc. to a drink" in AmE only in collocation with *drink*. BrE *set an exercise* is *assign an exercise* in AmE. The final, fifth grouping is the very common instance in which both varieties share an expression and its meaning(s), but where one or both have a further expression for the same thing not shared by the other. Both AmE and BrE have *taxi*, while *cab* is AmE. Likewise, both share *raincoast*, but only BrE has *mac*(*intosh*); *pharmacy* is common, while *chemist's* is BrE only and *drug store* is typically AmE.

— Gramley, S. and Patzold, K.

Exercises

I. Give the British English equivalents of the following American English words.

1. apartment _____
2. argument _____
3. baby carriage _____
4. band-aid _____
5. bathroom _____
6. can _____
7. chopped beef _____
8. cookie _____
9. corn _____
10. diaper _____
11. elevator _____
12. eraser _____
13. flashlight _____
14. fries _____
15. gas _____
16. guy _____
17. highway _____
18. hood (car) _____
19. jello _____
20. jelly _____

II. Give the American English equivalents of the following British English words.

1. paraffin _____
2. solicitor _____
3. number plate _____
4. queue _____
5. post _____
6. caravan _____

7. cinema _____ 8. silencer _____ 9. serviette _____
10. nought _____ 11. flyover _____ 12. dummy _____
13. trousers _____ 14. car park _____ 15. full stop _____
16. chemist _____ 17. crisps _____ 18. hire _____
19. banger _____ 20. pavement _____

III. Give the American English equivalents of the following British English words, and put them into Chinese.

1. accumulator _____ 2. aerial _____ 3. bed-sitter _____
4. bespoke _____ 5. cloakroom _____ 6. cot _____
7. cotton wool _____ 8. crisps _____ 9. drawing pin _____
10. dressing gown _____ 11. primary school _____ 12. estate agent _____
13. estate car _____ 14. flat tyre _____ 15. goods wagon _____
16. hairgrip _____ 17. handbag _____ 18. hire purchase _____
19. ironmongery _____ 20. off-the-peg _____ 21. petrol station _____
22. plaits _____ 23. public convenience _____
24. sideboards _____ 25. single/return (ticket) _____
26. spanner _____ 27. sweet _____ 28. tap _____
29. trunk call _____ 30. underdone _____

IV. Choose the best choice to answer the following questions.

1. In British English we say "to queue", in American English that is to _____ .
   A. stand in line　　B. stand in a row　　C. stand in a crowd　　D. stand in a string
2. In American English the "fall" refers to which season?
   A. Spring.　　B. Summer.　　C. Autumn.　　D. Winter.
3. The British people say "a tap". What is that in American English?
   A. Hose.　　B. Faucet.　　C. Pipeline.　　D. Garbage.
4. The British say "tyre puncture" or "flat tyre"; the Americans say: _____ .
   A. a blow up　　B. a blow out　　C. a blow down　　D. a blow
5. Answer true or false. "Lift" is British English for "elevator".
   A. True.　　B. False.
6. Where would people be embarrassed if someone saw their pants?
   A. England because "pants" in England is "underwear".
   B. The USA because "pants" means "underwear".
7. "The underground is about two minutes from here".
   A. American.　　B. British.

Chapter 4
The Growth of the English Vocabulary (3)
— New Words

> **Points for Thinking**
> 1. Why do we need to study new words?
> 2. What are the main causes for the growth of the English vocabulary?
> 3. How has the English vocabulary been affected by Chinese? Give examples.
> 4. How has the Internet changed the English vocabulary?
> 5. How is the English vocabulary going to develop?

New words are the cutting edge of language. They carve sounds into new shapes and give form to new aspects of experience.

— Gozzi, R.

4.1 Neologisms

In linguistics, a *neologism* is a recently coined word, phrase or usage. It can also be an existing word or phrase which has been assigned a new meaning. The term itself was coined around 1800.

The most important job of a language is to help us describe our world, which is different today in a thousand ways from yesterday. The growth of the English vocabulary is actually a result of the social and historical changes that the language has gone through. The 20th century saw rapid glocalization of the English language, with new ideas, new inventions and new phenomena continually arising. When English failed to express them, new words were created. Neologisms, or new words, are often found in association with those new things or old ideas taking on a new connotation. The Oxford English Dictionary Online adds at least 1,000 new words every three months. New words and usages are now created everywhere English is spoken. This trend today is being accelerated by the rapid advances in science, technology, and the Internet.

Below are some of the new words to enter a recently published dictionary of current English: *The Concise Oxford English Dictionary* (12th Edition, 2011). Check how many of them come to your knowledge:

abdominoplasty n. a surgical operation involving the removal of excess flesh from the abdomen

aerobicized or *aerobicised* adj. (of a person's body) toned by aerobic exercise: aerobicized Hollywood women

agroterrorism n. terrorist acts intended to disrupt or damage a country's agriculture

bahookie n. (Scottish) a person's buttocks

best of breed any item or product considered to be the best of its kind

blowback n. (chiefly US) the unintended adverse results of a political action or situation

celebutante n. a celebrity who is well known in fashionable society

crunk n. (chiefly US black slang) a type of hip-hop or rap music characterized by repeated shouted catchphrases and elements typical of electronic dance music, such as prominent bass

the elephant in the room a major problem or controversial issue which is obviously present but avoided as a subject for discussion because it is more comfortable to do so

emulsion n. a fine dispersion of one liquid or puréed food substance in another: ravioli with pea and ginger emulsion

hardscape n. (chiefly US) the man-made features used in landscape architecture, e.g. paths or walls, as contrasted with vegetation

hoody (also *hoodie*) n. (informal) a person, especially a youth, wearing a hooded top

mentee n. a person who is advised, trained or counselled by a mentor

mesotherapy n. (in cosmetic surgery) a procedure in which multiple tiny injections of pharmaceuticals, vitamins, etc. are delivered into the mesodermal layer of tissue under the skin, to promote the loss of fat or cellulite

mzee n. (in East Africa) an older person; an elder

obesogenic adj. tending to cause obesity

plank n. (Brit. informal) a stupid person

ponzu n. (in Japanese cookery) a sauce or dip made with soy sauce and citrus juice

radge n. (Scottish informal) a wild, crazy or violent person
  adj. wild, crazy or violent

rendition n. (also extraordinary rendition) (especially in the US) the practice of sending a foreign criminal or terrorist suspect covertly to be interrogated in a country with less rigorous regulations for the humane treatment of prisoners

retronym n. a new term created from an existing word in order to distinguish the original referent of the existing word from a later one that is the product of progress or technological development (e.g. acoustic guitar for guitar)

riffage n. (informal) guitar riffs, especially in rock music

shoulder-surfing n. the practice of spying on the user of a cash-dispensing machine or other electronic device in order to obtain their personal identification number, password, etc.

SIPP n. (in the UK) a self-invested personal pension, a pension plan that enables the holder to choose and manage the investments made

therapize or *therapise* v. subject to psychological therapy: you don't need to therapize or fix each other

tri-band adj. (of a mobile phone) having three frequencies, enabling it to be used in different regions (typically Europe and the US)

twonk n. (Brit. informal) a stupid or foolish person

upskill v. [often as noun *upskilling*] teach (an employee) additional skills

wedge issue n. (US) a very divisive political issue, regarded as a basis for drawing voters away from an opposing party whose supporters have diverging opinions on it

Yogalates (also trademark *Yogilates*) n. a fitness routine that combines Pilates exercises with the postures and breathing techniques of yoga

zombie n. a computer controlled by a hacker without the owner's knowledge, which is made to send large quantities of data to a website, making it inaccessible to other users

4.2 The Study of New Words

A great number of new words have entered the English vocabulary, either as loan words from other languages or through productive word formation processes from existing items in the language.

The Oxford English Dictionary has been constantly updating new words to its revised versions of the latest edition, which bear testimony to the fact that new words are springing up like mushroom. The following is taken from the new words list of January 2020 included in *The Oxford English Dictionary*.

(https://public.oed.com/updates/new-words-list-march-2019/)

Argonautical, adj.: "Of, relating to, or likened to the Argonauts. Cf. Argonautic adj."

baggataway, n.: "The game of lacrosse, esp. as played by certain indigenous peoples of eastern Canada and the midwestern and northeastern United States, using sticks ... "

chipmunky, adj.: "Resembling or characteristic of a chipmunk, typically with reference to a person having prominent cheeks or a perky, mischievous character."

dof, adj.: "Stupid, dim-witted; uninformed, clueless."

eeksie-peeksie, adj.: "Evenly balanced; equal."

fantysheeny, adj.: "Showy, fancy, or ostentatious."

grassy knoll, n.: "With reference or allusion to the conspiracy theory that a second gunman (positioned on a grass verge) was involved in the assassination of U.S ... "

hir, pron.: "Used as a gender-neutral third person singular objective pronoun; cf. hir adj. In later use often corresponding to the subjective pronoun ze (see ze ... "

Koevoet, n.: "A paramilitary counter-insurgency unit of the South African police force, deployed in South West Africa (now Namibia) from 1979 until 1989."

neurostimulator, n.: "Any of various devices used to stimulate nerves or neural tissue by means of electrical current, for experimental or therapeutic purposes."

presser, n. 2: "A press conference."

rooked, adj.: "Originally: deprived of money through fraudulent or underhand means; swindled, fleeced. In later use also (chiefly Scottish): without money ... "

sewist, n.: "A person who sews, esp. as a hobby. Cf. sewer n. 3"

situatedness, n.: "The quality of being situated (in various senses)."

spritzer, n. 1: "Any of various implements used to spray or squirt a liquid; esp. a spray bottle or atomizer. Frequently attributive or as the second element in ... "

titless, adj.: "Of a girl or woman: having small breasts; = flat-chested adj. at flat adj. adv. n. 3 compounds 3a."

weedily, adv.: "With many weeds (weed n.11); in a manner characterized by an abundance of weeds."

yebo, adv. and n.: "Used to express affirmation, assent, or agreement: 'yes'. Also occasionally as n.: an utterance of 'yebo'. Frequently in representations of South ... "

The study of new words in English, however, did not really start until the late 20th century, though the term *hard words* did appear as early as in the 17th century. The study is mainly associated with lexicography. From 1972 to 1987, the first edition of *The Oxford English Dictionary* had four supplementary volumes published. They are probably the most complete inventory of new words in English, but they are not the only ones. *Barnhart Dictionary of New English*, with three editions published successively in 1973, 1980 and 1990, had a timely collection of new words used in everyday life. Other dictionaries of new words include Susan Butler's *The Macquarie Dictionary of New Words* (1990), Sarah Tulloch's *The Oxford Dictionary of New Words* (1991), and John Ayto's *Twentieth Century Words* (1999). Of all the dictionary makers, "Random House Webster's" is considered the quickest to absorb new words. *Random House Webster's College Dictionary*, for example, is the first general dictionary to take in *Internet* and *World Wide Web*. In recent years the second edition of *Cambridge Advanced Learners' Dictionary*, published in 2005, collected new words like *website*, *text message*, *reality TV*, and more recent creations such as *blog*, *whiteboard* and *graphics card*.

The reasons to study new words are diverse. For instance, learning new words is to keep pace with the times, to express oneself with more precision, to read between the lines, to achieve occupational success, etc. But the main one is for its reflection of the culture the language is spoken in. McFedries (2004) has more specific explanation on the cultural association of new words.

> New words both reflect and illuminate not only the subcultures that coin them, but also our culture as a whole. New words give us insight into the way things are even as they act as linguistic harbingers (or canaries in the cultural coal mine), giving us a glimpse of (or a warning about) what's to come. (p. 4)

Similarly, Gozzi (1990: 1) believes that "new words are markers of cultural attention", and that "by studying new words we can tell where the culture has newly focused its attention, what it has been talking about".

As the anonymous pieces of human creativity, and condensed and codified bits of life experience, new words in history retain memories of those who have lived through the changes in it. So they are a mirror of their times. When we read *Twentieth Century Words*, we feel like surfing in review of the entire history of the 20th century, encoded in words such as *accelerator* (1900), *airbus* (1910), *Balkanize* (1920), *electric blanket* (1930), *pool* (1940), *summit* (1950), *bunny* (1960), *Big Mac* (1970), *boot* (1980), *Java* (1990). The American Dialect Society, a learned society founded in 1889, dedicates itself to the study of the English language. It has selected *web* as its "Word of the 1990s", *jazz* "Word of the 20th Century" and *she* "Word of the Past Millennium". Since 1990, the society has also selected a word featuring each year, forming a list of *Word of the Year*: *bushlips* (1990), *the mother of all* (1991), *not!* (1992), *information superhighway* (1993), *cyber* and *morph* (1994), *web* (1995), *mom* (1996), *millennium bug* (1997), *e-* (1998), *Y2K* (1999), *chad* (2000), *9–11* (2001), *weapons of mass destruction* (WMD) (2002), *metrosexual* (2003), *red state/blue state/purple state* (2004), *truthiness* (2005), *plutoed* (2006), *subprime* (2007), *bailout* (2008), *tweet* (2009), *app* (2010), *occupy* (2011), *hashtag* (2012), *because* (2013), *columbusing* (2014), *they* (2015), *dumpster fire* (2016), *fake news* (2017), *nomination* (2018), *my* (2019). Even *China Daily* has come up with "Top 10 New Words in Year 2009": *sockpuppet* (online identity used for purposes of deception within an online community), *downshifting* (a social behavior or trend in which individuals live simpler lives to escape from the rat race of obsessive materialism and to reduce the "stress, overtime and psychological expense that may accompany it"), *ringxiety* (the sensation and the false belief that one can hear his or her mobile phone ringing or feel it vibrating, when in fact the telephone is not doing so), *staycation* (a period of time in which an individual or family stays at home and relaxes at home or takes day trips from their home to area attractions), *Scene kid* (a person who adopts an unconventional style of dress), *sexting* (the act of sending sexually explicit text messages — or pictures of oneself — instantly over a mobile phone), *chick lit* (a literary genre that features books written by women and marketed to young women, especially single, working women in their twenties and thirties), *flash mob* (a large group of people who gather in a usually predetermined location, perform an unusual action for a brief time, and then quickly disperse), *NEET* (16-to 18-year-olds, "not in education, employment or training") and *strawberry generation* (young workers, of only child families, who have been active in the workforce for just a year or two, generally well-educated but self-centered and give too much importance to appearance and material comforts), and *carbon footprint* (the total amount of greenhouse gases produced to directly and indirectly support human activities, usually expressed in equivalent tons of carbon dioxide). Generally speaking, the new words in the past told us stories of a culture becoming more complex, contentious and confusing.

Fig. 4.1 An example of neologism, "staycation". A staycation (staycation or stacation) is a neologism for a period of time in which an individual or family stays at home and relaxes at home or takes day trips from their home to area attractions. Staycations have achieved high popularity in the financial crisis of 2007 – 2009 in which unemployment levels and gas prices are high.

Even in one single year the most used words tend to be new and reflect a particular cultural phenomenon. The most looked-up words in the online *Merriam-Webster Dictionary* in 2019 is *they*. It reflects a surprising fact: even a basic term — a personal pronoun — can show gender identity is nonbinary. The shifting use of *they* has been the subject of increasing study and commentary in recent years. Lookups for *they* increased by 313% in 2019 over the previous year. English famously lacks a gender-neutral singular pronoun to correspond neatly with singular pronouns like everyone or someone, and as a consequence they has been used for this purpose for over 600 years.

However, new words do not simply reflect culture, but enable us to predict a future. New words suggest a trend of the development of a language and a preview of the social reality.

Goldman Sachs, a bank holding company that engages in investment banking, securities services and investment management, created *BRICs*, an acronym that refers to the fast growing developing economies of Brazil, Russia, India and China. It argued that by 2050 the combined economies of these countries could eclipse the combined economies of the current richest countries of the world. And later a newer term, *BRIICS*, was created by Organization for Economic Cooperation and Development, adding two more countries, Indonesia and South Africa, to BRICs. In both cases, the new words present an economic future. R. Gozzi (1990: 2) has given his support for the study of new words as follows:

> And so a study of new words becomes a study in prediction. Using this view of language as a reality-constructor, we can ask ourselves just what labels and what interpretations our vocabulary provides us with to face the newness of the future. What is the reality going to be like that we are constructing with our language, and within which we will all live?

4.3　Reasons of the Growth

4.3.1　Influence of other languages

A genetically "pure" language is hard to imagine. English has taken in a great number of words from other languages. Those loans were "new words", at least for the time they were borrowed. The most grand process of borrowing happens when English is brought to other regions meeting with other languages and getting glocalized. Like other languages, English travels with the people who speak it.

In history, English has never stopped borrowing words from other languages. As the British established Jamestown in America, English began its borrowing of words from the American Indian languages, such as *raccoon*, *totem*, *caribou*, *opossum*. One of the recent examples is the adoption of Chinese words on space explorations. Right after China's success in its first manned space travel went popular, the Chinese loan word *taikonaut* came into English. It is synonymous to *astronaut*, but particularly refers to the Chinese. It was then followed by other new words in the same area, including *taikonautics* and *taikonausea*. Actually, many borrowings in English finally settled into dictionaries of local English varieties. For example, the first edition of *Dictionary of South African English* collected 3,000 local English entries; *Dictionary of New Zealand English* has 6,000 and *The Concise Australian National Dictionary* has 10,000, to mention only a few.

4.3.2　Social and cultural reasons

From the above discussion it is not surprising to argue that social and cultural changes nourish the English vocabulary. Many new words are created in response to the changes in different sectors of human life. The typical lexical growth areas are science and technology, politics and finance, education and sports, and media and the Internet.

1. Science and technology

Science and technology have provided the most striking force for the creation of new English words, to describe the great amount of new inventions and findings made in history. The big story in this area is the growth in electronics and digital techniques. It has pushed forward *moletronics*, *mechatronics* and *photonics*; our life has been made more convenient and comfortable with *instant camera*, *instant photo*, *CD writer*, *camcorder*, *flatscreen television*, *cordless telephone with caller ID*, *liquid crystal display* (*LCD*), and *e-edition* of books instead of *dead tree edition*.

As a promising subject in the 21st century, biology has greatly affected and continues to affect our life. The following words may appear incomprehensible at the first sight but most of them have actually come so close to us: *gene, genome, genetic fingerprinting, clone, DNA, RNA, artificial insemination, test-tube baby, transgene, genetic code, codon, transfer RNA, messenger RNA* and *transcription*.

The development in psychology has aroused scientists' interest in *affective computing* and *affective forecasting*. They are both related to one's emotion, which is considered an important factor for his work performance. *Emotional correctness* is thought to be able to increase his success rate. As demanded by the modern society, *soul proprietor* and *emotional labor* are becoming more and more popular. While *hoplophobia, school refusal* and *lottery mentality* appeared as new psychological diseases, special treatments have been created as well, such as *bibliotherapy, therapy through reading* and *cinematherapy*, therapy through watching films.

The heavy expansion of medical sectors has contributed another group of new words. New threats to life have been discovered, such as *HIV, karoshi, dioxin, anthrax* and new diseases: *AIDS, Mad Cow Disease* or *BSE, SARS, avian flu* or *bird flu, swine flu* or *A(H1N1) flu*. Some "diseases" are related to the excessive use, for example, of emails: *direct mail fatigue* or *junk mail fatigue*; of phone calls: *telephonitis* or *phone neck*, of the *mouse* of a computer: *mouse wrist*; of *SMS* of cell phones: *text message injury* (*TMI*); or of electronic games: *Repetitive Strain Injuries* (*RSI*).

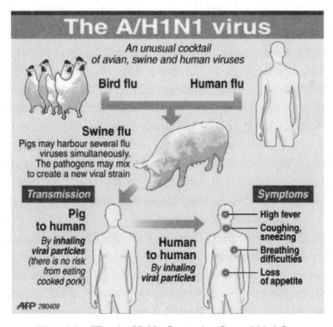

Fig. 4.2 The A/H1N1 flu, swine flu and bird flu.

Of the vocabulary of the environment the forms *bio-* (*biodiversity, bio-gas, bio-sphere*) and *eco-* (*ecoclimate, eco-labelling, ecosphere, ecosystem*) are frequently used. One of the most frequently used words is *green*, to mean "concerned with or supporting the protection of the environment" or to replace *environmentally friendly*. The word is found in countless combinations: *green consumer, green equities, green ideas, green issues, green lobbyists, green management*, *green policies*, *green products*, *green protein*, *green regulation*, *green reputation*, *green revolution*, *green shoppers*, *green standards*, *green technology*, *green voters*, etc. Today one of the urgent problems we face is the *greenhouse effect* or *global warming*, caused by various *greenhouse gases*, including *carbon dioxide*, *methane*, *nitrous oxide*, *tropospheric ozone*, and *chlorofluorocarbons*. In energy, *fossil fuels* have been proved polluting, so *alternative energy* or *renewable energy sources* are being looked for as cleaner ways of producing power. *Wind farms*, *photovoltaic* or *solar cells*, *solar panels* and *hydroelectric plants* have been established. The *environmentally conscious* governments are rethinking better transport policies, by building more *pedestrianized areas* and replacing *gas guzzlers* with *gas sippers*. And *intensive farming* using all kinds of *pesticides*, *insecticides*, *fungicides* and *herbicides* should be banned as well.

2. Politics and finance

The American Dialect Society's list of *Word of the Year* has sufficiently explained the influence of politics and finance on the growth of the English vocabulary.

Some minority and oppressed groups have become active in the US. Spanish-Americans developed *Chicanismo*, their own ethnic pride. Homosexuals protested for *gay liberation*. *Women's liberation* criticized *sexism* in a *male-chauvinist* society and called for *sisterhood* of all women.

Such protests have helped to form a *counterculture*, contributed by a series of *anti*-words: *anti-authoritarian*, *anti-nuke*, *anti-war* and *against technology* that was *anti-human*. However the excess of the *counterculture* in general was also objected by *neoconservatives*, who were also *anti-radical, anti-feminis*t and *anti-obscenity*.

In the American administration *hawks* and other *hardliners* usually oppose *doves* and *peaceniks*, and in the middle are *dawks*.

Of all the combining forms, -*gate*, implying "scandal", is a powerful one. Since the first-*gate* word, *Watergate*, appeared in 1972, many have been created: *Debategate* (1983), *Iraqgate* (1992), *Whitewatergate* (1994), *torturegate* (2003) and *huntgate* (2006). -*ism* is a popular suffix in English. It means a type of doctrine, theory or system represented by the word to the end of which the suffix is added, e.g. *Clintonism, Bushism, Blairism, Kerryism* and *Majorism.*

Whenever a war or a historical event happens, new words are created. The terrorist attacks on the American soil in 2001 not only changed the mind of the American people, but also influenced their language. *9/11* or *September 11* is no longer a mere date, but a new word to mark the historic event. *Ground Zero* has become an incurable wound left not on the original site of the twin towers but on the entire American nation. "*Let's Roll*", therefore, has naturally become a call for action against *Evil Doers*, while the *Terrible Tuesday* is going to be remembered always in the *Post-September 11* US.

In finance, *Clintonomics* was created to refer to the economic policy adopted by the Clinton administration. Other similar new words include *Enronomics* and *Katrinanomics*. As China's economy continued to grow, many new English words or phrases with Chinese characteristics have enriched its vocabulary, such as *plunge into the commercial sea*, *laid-off workers* and *courtyard economy.*

With the administrative advances of modern enterprises, the leading positions in different sectors are named *CEO* (Chief Executive Officer), *CFO* (Chief Finance Officer), *CBO* (Chief Brand Officer), *CCO* (Chief Cultural Officer), *CDO* (Chief Development Officer), *CHO* (Chief Human Resource Officer), *CIO* (Chief Information Officer), *CKO* (Chief Knowledge Officer), *CMO* (Chief Marketing Officer), *CNO* (Chief Negotiation Officer), *COO* (Chief

Operation Officer), *CPO* (Chief Public Relation Officer), *CQO* (Chief Quality Officer), *CSO* (Chief Sales Officer), *CTO* (Chief Technology Officer) and *CVO* (Chief Valuation Officer).

3. Education and sports

The development in education is first seen in new forms of classes and schools, such as *Open University*, *open classroom*, *alternative school*, *coedism* and *megaversity*. The new phenomena seen in the area of education are also of fascination: *car-schooling*, *dormcest*, *education mortgage*, *equity education*, *freshman 15*, *novelty degree*, *paraeducator*, *studentification*, *text literacy* and *yeardisc*.

Sports are always of shining glamor. *Yoga* and *taekwondo* have gone popular in the world, while *skateboarding*, *skydive*, *land yacht*, *sand yacht*, *hang glider*, *surfriding*, *cyclo-cross*, *roller hockey*, *demolition derby*, *slimnastics*, *isometrics*, *parkour*, *dancesport*, *black water rafting*, *zorbing* and *sky-riding* have started to attract more public attention. Even in the traditional area of soccer, new words are created to name new things or phenomena: *golden goal*, *silver goal*, *clogger*, *onion bag*, *chocolate wrists*, *smash-mouth*, *tonk*, *socks-around-the-ankles* and *ham-and-egging*.

4. Media and the Internet

Today television and radio are paying increasing attention to *audience rating*. They have set up a *hot line* to allow more communication with their audience; they have made different types of programs, ranging from *call-in* and *talk show* to *sitcom* and *soap opera*. Even the same type of program can be furthered in classification, such as *mockumentary*, *rockumentary*, *shockumentary*, *stalkumentary* and *jokumenatry*, all of documentary.

An increasingly applied medium today is the computer. Its wide use also brought into English many names. For example, the *hardware* consists of *mouse*, *monitor*, *keyboard*, *CPU* (*Central Processing Unit*), *ROM* (*Read-Only Memory*) and *RAM* (*Random Access Memory*). But computers have to be supported by a series of *software*, such as *Windows*, *COBOL*, *ALGOL* and *BASIC*. The *digital revolution* has advanced far beyond *PC*, with information becoming more *digitized*. Some people worry that while the West gets *wired*, or hooked up to the *Internet*, the poor countries are to be in danger of falling even further behind, or the so-called *digital divide*.

However, the new medium has already become an indispensable part of *netizens*' life. It allows them to *browse*, *surf*, talk with *net friends* on *MSN*, *QQ* or *WeChat* and *blog* online. Blogs are seen in such a variety as *warblog*, *journal blog*, *knowledge blog* or *k-blog*, *news blog*, *video blog*, *tech blog*, *group blog*, *moblog* and *digest blog*. After blog came *podcast* in 2005. Other new words related to the Internet are *iPod*, *iPeople*, *virtual bank*, *e-retail*, *online publishing*, *e-customer*, *cybereconomy*, *online love affair*, etc.

Task
Tell the names of the online talking tools in the following.

4.4 Sources for New Words

There are many ways of expanding the vocabulary: forming new words from existing words, borrowing from other languages, coining new words and expressions, and extending the meaning of existing words.

1. Word formation

Most new words are simply additions to existing words or recombinations of their components. Chapter 5 and 6 will discuss in details the formations of English words. To be more specific, they can be called the formations of new words.

One of the most frequent and perhaps the most important mechanism for creating new words is *derivation*, a process of adding affixes and suffixes to existing words. Powerful affixes and suffixes of this category include *anti-*, as in *antivirus, antinuclear*; *cyber-*, as in *cyberspace, cyberpunk, cybernaut*; *info-*, as in *infodump, infocentres, infosystem, infosphere, infotainment, infomercial, infotech*; *hyper-*, as in *hypertension, hypersensitive, hypersuspicious, hyperactive, hypersonic, hyperslow* and *hyperverbal*; *-ee*, as in *abscondee, affectee, vendee, evacuee, goatee*; and *-teria*, as in *chocolateria, restauranteria, candyteria, fruiteria* and *washateria*. Other common prefixes and suffixes for this purpose are *un-, pre-, dis-, re-, non-, con-, mini-, ex-, de-, step-, proto-, counter-, -ness, -ful, -ity, -less, -ly, -al, -ian, -esque, -ese* and *-ize*.

Without any change in form, a word can also become new if its lexical category, or part of speech, is changed. This way to coin a new word is called *conversion*. For example, the adjective *brown* becomes a verb in *brown the meat*; and the noun *sign* is moved to a verb in *signed*. Changing of word class is also seen in *leafleting* a neighborhood, *networking* a computer and to have a long *commute* to work. Other words of conversion from adjectives to nouns are *faithfuls, abnormals, affluents, antisocials, blinds, deads* and *absolutes*; and from nouns to verbs: to *aircraft*, to *airline*, to *arson*, to *charge*, to *sheet*, etc.

English has a tradition of combining words to make new ones, known as *compounding*. At various times, English speakers have created such compounds as *go-cart, sailboat, diet pill, easy meat, acid jazz, hard science, hard disk, soft disk, top gun, head time, camel kid, bushbaby, dustproof, war weary, fat-free, flying squad, wading pool, wading bird, baking powder, lodging house, chewing gum, glowworm, tugboat, drift ice, frostbite, airdash, bottlefeed, cashflow, boombox, brain-dead, knee-jerk, motormouth, meltdown, red-eye, scumbucket, stargaze* and *underhanded*.

Clipping is another process for the formation of a new word-form, keeping the same meaning as the original lexical item and working as an extracted word from it. For example, *flu* is a clipping from *influenza*, *shrink* from *head-shrinker*, *show biz* from *show business*, *fast* from *fast food*, *ciggy* from *cigarette*, *nightie* from *night gown*, *ammo* from *ammunition*, *umpy* from *umpire*, *hyp* from *hypochondria*, *rep* from *reputation*, *ult* from *ultimate*, *penult* from *penultimate*, *incog* from *incognito*, *hyper* from *hypercritic*, *extra* from *extraordinary*, *mob* from *mobile crowd*.

Sometimes a new word is formed by combining pieces of existing words. This sort of combination of both compounding and clipping is called *blending*. Typical examples are *motel* (motor+hotel), *brunch* (breakfast+lunch) and *Oxbridge* (Oxford+Cambridge). Like clippings, blends are usually not apparently new to most speakers. In recent decades blends are growing popular. The following is a list of blends well established in the English language: *heliport* (helicopter+airport), *Eurovision* (Europe+television), *breathalyser* (breath+analyser), *Chunnel* (Channel+tunnel), *sexsational* (sex+sensational), *infotisement* (information+advertisement), *rockumentary* (rock+documentary), *sit tragedy* (situation+tragedy), *camcorder* (camera+recorder), *psywar* (psychological+warfare), *sexploiter* (sex+exploiter), *autocide* (automobile+suicide), *telelecture* (telephone+lecture), *airtel* (airplane+hotel), *fruice* (fruit+juice), *botel* (boat+hotel), *medevac* (medical+evacuation), *comsat* (communication+satellite), *telex* (teletype+exchange), *autoanalyzer* (automatic+analyzer).

A very interesting device for coining words is *reanalysis*, gaining a new morpheme for use in creating words through false interpretation of a word's formation. Take *bikini*. It was the name of a Pacific atoll known as the location of some of the earliest nuclear bomb tests, but is later used to name the newly invented scanty bathing suits, stressing their stunning impact when other traditional ones cover a lot more skin than they do. "Unfortunately", the word was mistaken in the analysis of its formation to be formed on *bi-+kini*, since *bi-* does exist in English to mean "two". So when a newer bathing suit with only the bottom part of a *bikini* appeared, it was immediately named *monokini*, making use of the prefix *mono-*, meaning "one".

A similar but simpler form of reanalysis is *back-formation*, the creation of a word by removing actual or supposed affixes from another word. Back-formation changes part of speech. In this sense it is distinguished from clipping, which also creates shortened words from longer words, but does *not* change the part of speech. It is also opposite to derivation. Back-formation removes affixes to create a new word, while derivation adds an affix to an existing word to create a new one. For example, the noun *resurrection* was borrowed from Latin, and the verb *resurrect* was then back-formed from it hundreds of years later by removing the suffix *-ion*. This segmentation of *resurrection* into *resurrect+ -ion* was acceptable because English speakers know the fact that Latinate words had verb and verb+-*ion* pairs and that in these cases the *-ion* suffix is added to verb forms in order to create nouns. A recent example of back-formation is the verb *self-destruct*, back-formed from the compound *self-destruction*. Other back-formed words are *peddle* from *pedlar*, *edit* from *editor*, *sculpt* from *sculptor*, *burgle* from *burglar* and *lech* from *lecher*.

Reduplication is a morphological process by which the root or stem of a word, or part of it, is repeated to create a new word. There are two types: full reduplication, reduplication of the entire word, and partial reduplication, reduplication of only part of a word. For the former the examples are *go-go* and *slow-slow*, while for the latter the examples are *fuddy-duddy*, *walkie-lookie*, *dillydally* and *niddle-noddle*. A reduplication can be based on sound immitation, like *pooh-pooh*, *dingdong*, or a product name, like *Coca-Cola*, *ping-pong*, and acronyms, like *hi-fi*, *huff-duff*, and so on.

Initialism and *acronym* are recently becoming more and more popular in coining words. They reduce a long phrase or name to a few important letters. The coinages that can only be pronounced letter by letter are called initialism, such as *BBQ* (barbecue), *CEO* (Chief Executive Officer), *CPU* (Central Processing Unit), *DJ* (disc jockey), *DVI* (Digital Video Interactive), *DVD* (Digital Video Disk). If such a coinage can be pronounced as a word, it is called an acronym, such as *DINK* (double income, no kids), *DOS* (Disk Operating System), *AIDS* (acquired immune deficiency syndrome) and *laser* (light amplification by the stimulated emission of radiation). The advantages of initialisms and acronyms are obvious, i. e. they are more convenient to use and easier to remember than their full names.

2. Borrowing

Languages are always borrowing words from one another, even if they change the pronunciation and spelling a little. Many times a new word comes along with a new item, such as *spaghetti* (Italian), *camel* (Hebrew) and *chocolate* (Mexican-Indian by way of Spanish). *Ketchup* (sometimes spelled *catsup*), *Maotai*, *jiaozi*, *feng shui*, *guanxi*, *yin* and *yang* all come from Chinese and have been in wide use in English. Most recent Chinese borrowings found in English newspapers are *Gaokao*, *buzheteng*, and *shanzhai*. Some more words from other languages are *westpolitik*, *kindergarten*, *blitz*, *poodle* from German; *salad*, *restaurant*, *garage* from French; *autopista*, *rodeo*, *tornado*, *potato* from Spanish; *piano*, *carnival*, *studio*, *autostrada* from Italian; *sputnik*, *samizdat*, *perestroika*, *glasnost* from Russian; *sushi*, *judo*, *karaoke*, *hibakusha* from Japanese; and *algebra*, *hamam*, *safari*, *sugar* from Arabic.

3. New coinage

A few of the new English words are created from nothing. Though the number of them is small, putative examples do exist. *Blur* was coined by Gelett Burgess, an American humorist, in 1907; *paraffin* was invented by Reichenbach in 1830 based on Latin *parum* (too little, barely) plus *affinis* (having affinity), and even *gas* was a coined word, by Dutch chemist Jan Baptista van Helmont in 1632, who was inspired by Greek *khāos*. Other coinages of this type are *dweeb*, *Prozac*, *periapsis*, *cladistics*, *penetralium*, *ekistics*, *isomorphism* and *quark*.

However, if we make a further study, we may find many of the "root creations" are not really created out of thin air. This claim is supported by the above-mentioned *paraffin* and *gas*; the famous Chinese IT company, *Lenovo*, is based on *le-* clipped from *legend* plus Latin *novo* meaning innovation; and the famous website *Yahoo* comes from Jonathan Swift's *Gulliver's Travels* for an imaginary race of brutes with human form.

4. Semantic shift

Sometimes an old word takes on a new meaning, while its form keeps unchanged. In this type of new-word creation metaphors play an important role. For example, *kite* was originally a hawk-like bird. Since the English speakers invented the light wooden frames with cloth or paper stretched across them, they called it *kite*, certainly because they found some similarity between the flying object and that bird. Today the computer technicians call a programming problem a *bug*, but the story was that when computers were first being developed, some programmers, searching the causes for computer failure, finally traced it to a moth that landed on the circuitry. The intriguing word *gay* originally meant "lighthearted" and "joyous" in the 13th century or "bright and showy" in the 14th century, and it also came to mean "happy". It acquired connotations of immorality as early as 1637, either e. g. *gay woman* "prostitute", *gay man* "womanizer", *gay house* "brothel", or otherwise, e. g. *gay dog* "over-indulgent man" and *gay deceiver* "deceitful and lecherous". In the United States by 1897 the expression *gay cat* had referred to a hobo, especially a younger hobo in the company of an older one; by 1935, it had been used in prison slang for a homosexual boy; and by 1951, and clipped to *gay*, had referred to homosexuals. George Chauncey, in his book *Gay New York*, would put this shift as early as the late 19th century among a certain "in crowd" knowledgeable of *gay night-life*. In the modern day, it is most often used to refer to homosexuals or as a synonym for "stupid", "lame", or "boring".

This chapter discusses the causes for the increasing number of new words in English. The expansion of the English vocabulary should be first attributed to the glocalization of the language. As English spreads to the other regions it takes in words from other languages. The second reason of the vocabulary growth is the social and cultural developments in such areas as science, technology, politics, finance, education, sports, media and the Internet. But the final process in creating new words involves lexical changes, through word formations like derivation, conversion, compounding, clipping, blending, reanalysis, back-formation, reduplication, initialism and acronym, or through borrowing from other languages, or creations from nothing, or semantic shifts, where an old word takes on a new meaning. Many of the creations have become more frequent and conventionalized over time. The growth of new words has been accelerated by the rapid advances in science, technology and the Internet. Looking at those new words, we are able to get a glimpse of lexical changes in history, and in addition, to understand how the world has evolved, and even to predict how the world is going to change.

Further Reading

1. Gozzi, R. (1990). *New Words and a Changing American Culture.* Columbia: University of South Carolina Press.
2. Gramley, S. and Ptzold, K. (2004). *A Survey of Modern English.* London and New York: Routledge.
3. Aitchison, J. (2003). *Words in the Mind.* Malden: Blackwell Publishing.

● Extended Reading

■ Why study new words

New words are the cutting edge of language. They carve sounds into new shapes and give form to new aspects of experience.

New words are mysterious anonymous pieces of human creativity. They bubble up through the cultural conversation at unpredictable moments. They begin life as outlaws, unsanctioned by the guardians of cultural propriety. They struggle for acceptance through an inherently democratic process of choice — will they catch on or will they slip into alphabetic oblivion? Will they take the country by storm, only to disappear as quickly as yesterday's news? Or will they quietly take their place in the working vocabulary of the culture, competently encoding some new shard of experience?

New words tend to slip into our conversation without our paying too much attention. Simply recalling and pointing out the new words that have entered the vocabulary between 1961 and 1986 serves a useful purpose — particularly for young people who accept their received vocabulary as a given. New vocabulary can also be interesting for those who have lived through the period studied, as a way to look back and imagine what life was like before we had the word *yuppie*, for example. Somehow, we managed to get along without it, as we did without *microwave ovens*, *microcomputers* and *micrographics*.

A new word is a condensed, codified bit of experience. It exists because people have noticed something new. Therefore new words are markers of cultural attention. By studying new words, we can tell where the culture has newly focused its attention, what it has been talking about. New words answer the eternal question: what's new?

For those of us looking back, new words encode memories: what was new back in the 1960s? The term *Black Power* reminds us of a militant stage of the Civil Rights movement; the term *counterproductive* brings back the techno-jargon of the Vietnam War.

This book puts new words together to tell stories, to gain perspectives on the changes of the times. The stories composed of new words highlight changes in the culture's attention. Certainly, older words continue to be used. This study does not measure constancy of language use. Instead, it maps the distinctively new areas of experience in the culture during the quarter century from 1961 to 1986.

But a study of new words is more than a stroll down *memory lane*, pleasant though that may be. The new words that have "made it" into *12,000 Words* (Merriam-Webster, 1986) are largely part of the working vocabulary of the culture. They are in use, doing what language does — carving out an interpreted reality, within which we live, think and act. We think with these new words, we communicate with them, to some extent we follow where their implications lead us.

And so a study of new words becomes a study in prediction. Using this view of language as a reality-constructor, we can ask ourselves just what labels and what interpretations our vocabulary provides us with to face the newness of the future. What is the reality going to be like that we are constructing with our language, and within which we will all live?

— Gozzi, R.

■ New words reflect our culture

Language wears many hats, but its most important job is to help us name or describe what's in the world. As the American writer and editor, Howard Rheingold says, "Finding a name for something is a way of conjuring its existence, of making it possible for people to see a pattern where they didn't see anything before." So we have nouns for things, verbs for actions, and adjectives and adverbs for describing those things and actions. But the world changes, constantly. New things are created; old things are modified; light bulbs are appearing over people's heads all the time, signaling new ideas and theories; people do things differently; they look at existing things from new perspectives. Today's world is different in a thousand ways from yesterday's world.

So if language describes the world, and if the world changes, then language must also change as a way of keeping up with the world. We're compelled to create new words to name and describe our new inventions and ideas and institutions; we're driven to create new meanings for existing words to accommodate our newly modified things and actions.

It follows then — and this is the central premise of this book — that you can understand the culture by examining its new words, by going out to what one linguist calls the "vibrant edges" of language. However, it's not enough just to note the existence of a neologism and move on to the next one. Each new word reflects something about the culture, but you have to examine the word closely to see the details of that reflection. How is the word being used? Who is using it? What are the cultural factors that gave rise to and nourished the word's existence? Each new word opens a door (One writer likened them to "the doorbells of the mind".) that leads you to a room with various cultural and sociological artifacts. The Czech playwright Daniela Fischerova said it best: "Every new word is a new reality."

New words both reflect and illuminate not only the subcultures that coin them, but also our culture as a whole. New words give us insight into the way things are even as they act as linguistic harbingers (or canaries in the cultural coal mine), giving us a glimpse of (or a warning about) what's to come. Here's the lexicographer Victoria Neufeldt on this neologism-as-cultural-reflection idea:

The neologisms that especially capture our attention are indeed often remarkable; some with their metaphorical baggage can constitute miniature sociological studies in themselves like *McJob*, for instance, which for comprehension depends on all the associations and connotations of the name McDonald's, as well as an awareness of the difficulties of the current employment situation, in particular for new graduates wanting to enter the workforce.

— McFedries, P.

Exercises

I. Fill in the blanks by using the following new words with the appropriate forms.

don't ask, don't tell	pukka	consensualist	hot desking	du jour
ethnic cleansing	Euroland	internots	boot	off-message
marketization	roadkills	slacker	gabbers	SoHo
bad hair days	twigloo	informericals	goodfellas	zorbing
black Monday	stalked	domains	dragons	eco-friendly
feel good factors	gnarly	personal stereo	canyoning	luvvies

1. Soon you will notice how much less complaining you do, even on _____. (*Post*, 1994)
2. _____ is another thrilling sport where you are carried along by the power of a waterfall. (*Daily Mail Holiday Action*, 1995)
3. Under the listening regime of Mr. Mandelson, in a _____ age, there's no good reason why that shouldn't happen. (*Guardian*, 1997)
4. Soldiers accused of homosexuality often become the focus of investigations and may be discharged from the military if they are found to have violated the military's "_____, don't pursue" policy on gays. (*San Diego Union-Tribune*, 1997)
5. The area has a large number of towns and villages, many emptied of Muslims and Croats in three years of _____. (*Times*, 1995)
6. The launch of the euro makes it much cheaper to convert between the national currencies in _____. The exchange rate is legally fixed to six decimal figures, and it is illegal to offer different buy and sell rates. (*Observer*, 1999)
7. "It's the fastest dancing you've ever seen," said DJ Curley, a veteran of the Dutch scene. "_____ really bounce, kicking alternate legs forward while sticking out their bums." (*Observer*, 1997)
8. Like the _____ who become gangsters so they don't have to stand in line to buy bread, Scorsese can get his hands on any film he has a passion for. (*Village Voice*, 1990)
9. The new trend, "_____" is that desks are shared between several people who use them at different times. This has been made possible because more people are now working from home or with customer. (*Sunday Times*, 1991)
10. In the world of wide-area computer networking, the "haves" and the "have nots" could be called the "internauts" and the "_____". (*Computers in Libraries*, 1992)
11. The 43rd Gannes International Festival of Cinema ... It's a rough deal for the poor

being paid to watch movies and party. (*Guardian*, 1998)

12. The president essentially went "_____". He moved from topic to topic and promoted his economic plan only in passing. (*Washington Post*, 1993)

13. If you want your children to keep their music to themselves during the holidays a _____ is the ideal gift. (*Which?*, 1992)

14. I'm going to France soon, so I'll look well _____ trendy. (*Independent*, 1991)

15. We all know any number of men who can cook a virtuoso dish or two, but outside of this they are strictly _____ in the kitchen. (*Esquire*, 1993)

16. "It's certainly a reaction to the _____ thing, which was so 'anti-style'" says Paul Tunkin, promoter of the London club Blow Up. (*Guardian*, 1995)

17. It has been unable to completely fulfill orders from any of its chosen sectors, from _____ to corporates, over the past nine months. (*Computing*, 1994)

18. For five years, she was _____ by a man who would taunt and threaten her, hiding in the shadows in restaurants and shops, never showing his face. (*Guardian*, 1995)

19. She lives in a tree house, known as a "_____", at Slyward Camp. (*Daily Telegraph*, 1995)

20. Bungee jumping and the latest tourist craze, _____ — climbing into a large ball and rolling down a hill — have prompted the hasty introduction of a safety code for adventure-tour operators in New Zealand. (*Guardian*, 1996)

21. The Dow Jones, once up 712 points for the year, drops 508 points on _____. Paper losses total $500 billion. (*Life*, 1988)

22. If you _____ up your system without the keyboard being plugged in, you will see an error message. (*Courier-Mail*, 1986)

23. In 1991, the Internet boasted about 9,000 commercial "_____", the electronic equivalent of a storefront address. Today, more than 21,700 different commercial domains are registered. (*Economic*, 1995)

24. One of Asia's four rapidly developing "Little _____" — along with South Korea, China's Taiwan region and China's Hong Kong SAR, Singapore is the smallest and in some ways most successful. (*Times.*, 1993)

25. Religiously oriented swindles have become the "fraud _____" of the investment world. (*Christianity Today*, 1989)

26. The only way that _____ products are going to take off is for them to be presented by manufacturers and retailers as high tech and modern. (*Daily Telegraph*, 1989)

27. The _____ are the same in Japan as in the United States because human nature is inherently the same East and West. (*Industry Week*, 1984)

28. This to me is _____ Cool. Radical. Intense. It makes a statement. (*Tulsa World*, 1991)

29. Educational commercials, or so-called _____ are attracting much interest. J. Walter Thompson has been producing several at its own expense. (*Christian*, 1981)

30. Does it advance or slow the _____ of the Russian economy? (*New Republic*, 1993)

Chapter 5
The Formation of English Words (1)
— Major Types

Points for Thinking
1. Is the morpheme a minimal unit in a word? Give examples to illustrate your judgment.
2. What are the relations among stems, roots and affixes?
3. Do you think there is something in common between inflectional and derivational morphemes? Why or why not?
4. Give examples to state the characteristics of conversion.
5. Why do we say that compounds are usually easy to understand in meaning?

"I never heard of 'Uglification'," Alice ventured to say. "What is it?" The Gryphon lifted up both its paws in surprise. "Never heard of uglifying!" it exclaimed. "You know what to beautify is, I suppose?" "Yes," said Alice doubtfully, "it means — to make — anything — prettier." "Well, then," the Gryphon went on, "if you don't know what to uglify is, you are a simpleton." (*Alice in Wonderland*)
— Lewis Carroll (1832 – 1898)

In the passage above, we find out that *-ify* is added to the adjective *ugly* and the verb *uglify* is formed; *-cation* is added to *uglify* and a noun, *uglification* is formed. Many verbs and nouns in English have been formed in this way: adjective + *-ify* — verb (to make adjective); verb + *-cation* — noun (the process of making adjective).

By using rules of word formation, such as derivation, conversion and compounding, the English people, with only twenty-six letters, have created so many new words as to more than one million.

5.1 Notions of Morphological Formation

There exist in every language rules which relate to the formation of new words, morphological rules, which determine how words are formed. For example, *unhappy*, *unadvisable* and *undesirable*, which are morphologically rule-governed, are words in English, but *happyun, *doneun and *advisedun are not. The study of the morphological rules, which are used in the processes of word-formation, is morphology. Part of knowing a language is knowing its morphology. Like most linguistic knowledge, this is generally unconscious knowledge. If we want to know the formation of English words, we must learn about some notions of morphological structures in the English language.

5.1.1 Morpheme

We can notice that *un-* in the three words *unhappy*, *unadvisable* and *undesirable* means the same thing — "not". *Unhappy* means "not happy"; *unadvisable* means "not advisable"; *undesirable* means "not desirable". If we assume that the basic unit of meaning is the word, what do we say about parts of words like *un-* which has a fixed meaning? The linguistic term for the most elemental unit of grammatical form is morpheme which is derived from the Greek word *morphe* meaning "form".

A single word may consist of one or more morphemes, e. g.

one morpheme	nation
two morphemes	nation+al
three morphemes	nation+al+ize
four morphemes	de+nation+al+ize
more than four	de+nation+al+iz+ation

A morpheme may be represented by a single sound, such as the morpheme *a* meaning "without" as in *amoral* or *asexual*, or by a single syllable, such as *child* and *-ish* in *childish*. A morpheme may also consist of more than one syllable: by two syllables, as in *camel* and *water*; or by three syllables, as in *Hackensack* or *crocodile*; or by four or more syllables, as in *elevator*.

Therefore, a morpheme is the minimal linguistic unit — an arbitrary union of a sound and a meaning that cannot be further analyzed. That is to say, a morpheme, the smallest unit of meaning in a language, may be a word or part of a word which has meaning; it cannot be divided into smaller meaningful parts without violation of the original meaning; and it may recur in different verbal environments with a relatively stable meaning.

5.1.2 Free and bound morphemes

Morphemes can be classified into two types, namely, free morphemes and bound morphemes. In English it can be seen that some morphemes may stand alone as words in their own right and enter into the structure of other words. For instance, morphemes like *interest*, *map* and *vital* may stand by themselves as words, or be part of other words such as *interesting*, *mapping*, *revitalize*. These morphemes have been traditionally called free morphemes. Other morphemes like *-s* in *dogs*, *-al* in *national*, and *dis-* in *disclose* may occur only if they combine with at least another morpheme, i. e. they cannot appear "unattached". These morphemes are called bound morphemes. Simply put, free morphemes may occur alone, that is, they may constitute words by themselves; bound morphemes cannot be used by themselves, but must be combined with other morphemes to form words.

5.1.3 Content and function morphemes

Morphemes can also be divided into content morphemes and function morphemes. Content morphemes express some general sort of content, while function morphemes are heavily tied to a grammatical function, expressing syntactic relationships between units in a sentence, or categories such as number or tense. Briefly speaking, content morphemes are those morphemes that carry meaning. They are generally contrasted with function morphemes which signal the relations among words. This distinction is conceptually different from the free-bound distinction but partially overlaps with it in practice.

Thus nouns, verbs and adjectives like *sand*, *throw* and *green* are all English content morphemes. Content morphemes are also often called open-class morphemes, because they belong to categories that are open to the invention of arbitrary new items. By contrast, prepositions (*to*, *by*), articles (*the*, *a*), and conjunctions (*and*, *or*) are typically function morphemes. Function morphemes are also called closed-class morphemes, because they belong to categories that are essentially closed to invention or borrowing — it is very difficult to add a new preposition, article or conjunction to the English language.

5.1.4 Derivational and inflectional morphemes

Derivational morphemes can be added to a word to create another word. This type of morphemes changes the meaning of the word or part of speech or both. Therefore, they carry semantic information. For example, the derivational morpheme *un-* added to *invited* changes the meaning of the word; the addition of *-ness* to *happy* creates *happiness* which is a noun turned from the adjective *happy*.

Derivational morphemes generally have the following characteristics:

1) They change the part of speech or the basic meaning of a word. Thus *-ment* added to a verb *judge* forms a noun *judgment*. *Re-activate* means "activate again".

2) They are not required by syntactic relations outside the word. Thus *un+kind* combines *un-* and *kind* into a single word, but has no particular syntactic connections outside the word — we can say he is *unkind* or he is *kind* or they are *unkind* or they are *kind*, depending on what we mean.

3) Some of them are often not productive — derivational morphemes can be selective about what they will combine with and may have different effects on meaning. Thus the suffix *-hood* occurs with just a few nouns such as *brother*, *neighbor* and *knight*, but not with most others, e.g. *friendhood, *daughterhood or *candlehood. Besides, *brotherhood* can mean "the state or relationship of being brothers", but *neighborhood* cannot mean "the state or relationship of being neighbors".

An inflectional morpheme creates a change in the function of the word, and it modifies a word's tense, number, aspect, and so on. The plural marker morpheme *-s* in *cats* is an inflectional morpheme; the *-d* in *invited* indicates past tense. English has eight inflectional morphemes, as is shown in the following table:

	Morpheme	Grammatical function	Examples
Nouns	Plural	Marks as more than one	Regular: *dogs, cats, horses*
			Irregular: *sheep, phenomena, children*
	Possessive	Marks for ownership	*Bart's, Homer's, My sister's*
Adjectives	Comparative	Marks for comparison	*closer, whiter, quicker*
	Superlative	Marks as superlative	*closest, whitest, quickest*
Verbs	3rd-singular Present Agreement	Marks to agree with singular third person in the present tense	*runs, waits, pushes, tries, hisses*
	Past Tense	Marks (roughly) for past action	Regular: *dragged, backed*
			Irregular: *hit, ran, sat, spread*
	Past Participle	Marks past participle; Indicates passive voice	Regular: *chosen, proven, woken*
			Irregular: *drunk, hung, spread*
	Present Participle	Marks present participle	*walking, jumping, swinging, hitting*

The main features of the inflectional morphemes are as follows:

1) They do not change the basic meaning or part of speech, e.g. *big, bigger, biggest* are adjectives which share the same meaning of "more than average size, amount or importance".

2) They express grammatically-required features or indicate relations between different words in the sentence. Thus in *Joan loves Kim*, *-s* marks the third person singular present form of the verb, and relates it to the third person singular subject *Joan*.

3) They are productive. Inflectional morphemes typically combine freely with all members of some large class of morphemes, with predictable effects on usage or meaning. Thus the plural morpheme can be combined with nearly any noun, usually in the same form and with the same effect on meaning.

4) They occur outside any derivational morphemes. Thus in *rationalizations* the final *-s* is inflectional, and appears at the very end of the word, outside the derivational morphemes *-al*, *-iz* and *-ation*.

5.1.5 Roots, stems and affixes

In a word which is composed of more than one morpheme, there is one morpheme that is central and contains the principal lexical meaning and one or more others that are peripheral and are attached to the central morpheme. For example, in *undecided*, the morpheme *decide* is central, while *un-* and *-ed* are peripheral. The central morpheme in a word is often a free morpheme and is called the root. Some other examples of English roots are *paint* in *painter*, *read* in *reader* and *ceive* in *conceive*. The peripheral morphemes that are attached to the root are always bound morphemes and are called affixes.

In English, some roots may stand alone as words, such as *moon*, *boy* and *paint*. These roots are free roots. It is the free roots that provide the English language with a basis for the formation of new words. Many roots in English are bound roots. Many bound roots derived from foreign languages, especially from Greek and Latin. For example, *tain* in words like *contain*, *detain* or *retain*, and *ceive* in *conceive*, *deceive* or *receive* were once words in Latin: *tain* from Latin *tenere* "to hold", and *ceive* from Latin *capere* "to take". Yet in modern English, they are not words, and so are not free morphemes; they cannot stand alone as words.

When a root morpheme is combined with an affix, it forms a stem, which may or may not be a word (*painter* is both a word and a stem; *-ceive+er* is only a stem). A stem can also be morphologically complex, as shown in the following:

root	*believe*
stem	*believe+able*
word	*un+believe+able*
root	*system*
stem	*system+atic*
stem	*un+system+atic*
stem	*un+system+atic+al*
word	*un+system+atic+al+ly*

An affix is a morpheme that is attached to a root to form a word. They are bound morphemes by definition. Affixes are divided into several categories. Depending on their position with reference to the root, prefixes and suffixes are extremely common terms. Affixes which come before the root (e.g. *dis-*, *un-*, *in-*) are called prefixes, and those coming after the root (e.g. *-able*, *-ize*, *-al*) are suffixes. According to the functions, affixes may be divided into inflectional and derivational affixes.

An inflectional affix is often a suffix in English that performs a grammatical function and does not change the word class of its root. English plural *-s* and past tense *-ed* are inflectional suffixes, which have the following characteristics:

1) They do not change the part of speech of the word, e. g. cold, colder (adjectives); cough, coughed (verbs).
2) They go with all stems of a given part of speech, e. g. He eats, drinks, dreams, runs, thinks, works, etc.
3) They do not "pile up", only one ends a word, e. g. unverbalized.
4) They come last in a word, e. g. nationalized.

A derivational affix is an affix by means of which one word is formed from another. The derived word is often of a different word class from the original. In English, derivational affixes may be prefixes or suffixes. They have a lexical function, that is, they create new words out of existing words or morphemes by their addition. In English *-ness* and *pre-* belong to the derivational affixes. Derivational and inflectional affixes are identical with derivational and inflectional morphemes.

Task

I. What do the following definitions refer to?
1. a smallest unit of meaning in a language _____
2. a bound morpheme attached to a base _____
3. an affix attached to the beginning of a base _____
4. an affix attached to the end of a base _____
Key: 1. a morpheme   2. a combining form   3. a prefix   4. a suffix

II. Give more examples.

ROOT	MEANING	EXAMPLES
-auto-	self	automation, autonomy, ...
-bio-	life	amphibious, biology, ...
-form-	form, shape	formative, transform, ...
-port-	carry	transport, importation, ...
-sol-	alone	solitude, solitaire, ...

5.2 Derivation

Bound morphemes like *-ify* and *-cation* are called derivational morphemes. When they are added to a root morpheme or stem, a new word with a new meaning is derived. The addition of *-ify* to *pure* makes *purify* which means "to make pure" and *purification* derives from the addition of *-ation* to *purify* meaning *the process of making pure*. If we invent an adjective, *pouzy*, to describe the effect of static electricity on hair, you will immediately understand the sentences "Walking on that carpet really *pouzified* my hair." and "The best method of *pouzification* is to rub a balloon on your head.". This means that we must have a list of the derivational morphemes as well as the rules that determine how they are added to a root or stem.

Derivation is the morphological process whereby a derivational morpheme is attached to a *root* or *stem*. This process is also known as affixation, by which new words are derived from old ones. The form that results from the addition of a derivational morpheme is called a derived word. Derivational morphemes have clear semantic contents. In this sense they are like content words, except that they are not words. As we have seen, when a derivational morpheme is added to a root or stem, it adds meaning. The derived word may also be of a different grammatical class from the original word.

In English derivational morphemes are mainly *prefixes* and *suffixes*. Affixes are referred to as prefixes when they are attached to the beginning of another morpheme (like *re-* in words such as *redo*, *rewrite*, *rethink*) and as suffixes when they are attached to the end of another morpheme (like *-ize* in words such as *modernize*, *equalize*, *centralize*).

5.2.1 Features of prefixes and suffixes

There is usually only one prefix in a word in English, and prefixes do not change the word class of the word to which they are attached, e.g.

a+moral   *re+print*
auto+biography   *sub+prime*
dis+agree   *un+important*

However, recent changes take place that some prefixes in current English do alter words into different classes, e.g.

anti-+aircraft → anti-aircraft   *be-+little → belittle*
en-+rich → enrich   *inter-+state → inter-state*
pre-+plant → preplant   *un-+leash → unleash*

According to Quirk *et al* (1972), major living prefixes can be classified by their meaning into the following classes: negative prefixes (*a-*, *dis-*, *in-*, *non-*, *un-*); reversative or privative prefixes (*de-*, *dis-*, *un-*); pejorative prefixes (*mal-*, *mis-*, *pseudo-*); prefixes of degree or size (*arch-*, *hyper-*, *mini-*, *out-*, *over-*, *sub-*, *super-*, *ultra-*, *under-*); prefixes of attitude (*anti-*, *co-*, *counter-*, *pro-*); locative prefixes (*inter-*, *sub-*, *super-*, *trans-*); prefixes of time and order (*fore-*, *ex-*, *post-*, *pre-*, *un-*); number prefixes (*bi-*, *di-*, *mono-*, *multi-*, *poly-*, *tri-*, *uni-*); conversation prefixes (*a-*, *be-*, *en-*); prefixes of a miscellaneous category (*auto-*, *neo-*, *pan-*, *proto-*, *semi-*, *vice-*).

A very important characteristic of derivational suffixes is that they can often change the word class of the word to which they are attached, as shown by suffixes such as *-able* and *-ly*. When a verb is suffixed with *-able*, the result is an adjective, as in *desire+able = desirable* and *adore+able = adorable*. When the suffix *-en* is added to an adjective, a verb is derived, as in *dark+en = darken* and *ripe+en = ripen*. One may form a noun from an adjective, as in *sweet +ie = sweetie* and *short+y = shorty*. Below are other examples:

Noun to Adjective   Noun to Verb
boy+ish   *class+ify*
virtue+ous   *moral+ize*
life+like   *vaccine+ate*
history+ic
trust+ful

Verb to Noun   Verb to Adjective
collect+ion   *accept+able*
act+or   *select+ive*
acquit+al   *require+ed*
pay+ment   *care+less*

Adjective to Verb   Adjective to Adverb
pure+ify   *exact+ly*

ample+ify　　　　　　*quiet+ly*
putrid+fy (*putrefy*)　　*interesting+ly*

Not all suffixes cause a change in grammatical class, such as:
vicar+age　　　　　　*old+ish*
fad+ist　　　　　　　*Paul+ine*
music+ian　　　　　　*America+n*
pun+ster

Unlike prefixes, there can be several derivational suffixes in a word, e. g.
interest+ing+ly　　　　*familiar+iz+ation*
trust+ee+ship　　　　　*nation+al+ist+ic*

When a new word enters the lexicon by the application of morphological rules, other complex derivations may be blocked. For example, when *Commun+ist* entered the language, words such as *Commun+ite* (as in *Trotsky+ite*) or *Commun+ian* (as in *grammar+ian*) were not needed and were not formed. Sometimes, however, alternative forms coexist, for example, *Chomskyan* and *Chomskyist* and perhaps even *Chomskyite* (all meaning "follower of Chomsky's views of linguistics"). *Linguist* and *linguistician* are both used, but the possible word *linguite* is not.

5.2.2　Types of prefixes and suffixes

There are many types of prefixes and suffixes in English. Some of them are productive, others are not. Here are some groups of prefixes and suffixes that are used to create particular types of meaning.

1) Prefixes containing ideas to do with information technology or aspects of life, material and environment, e. g.
　audio-, *bio-*, *cyber-*, *e-*, *eco-*, *geo-*, *nano-*, *radio-*, *techno-*, *tele-*, *video-*
　audiovisual: using both recorded sounds and images;
　biochemistry: the study of chemical processes that occur in living things;
　cyber-crime: crime involving the use of computers;
　nanosecond: a unit for measuring time; there are one billion (= one thousand million) *nanoseconds* in a second;
　nanotechnology: the skill of building very small machines by using computer technology;
　technobabble: confusing technical language.

2) Prefixes used to create words that suggest something is partly true, or that something seems to be one thing but is actually something else, e. g.
　crypto-, *demi-*, *half-*, *mock-*, *near-*, *neo-*, *part-*, *pseudo-*, *quasi-*, *semi-*
　cryptogram: a secret message written in code;
　half-truth: a statement that is only partly true or gives only some of the facts;
　near-certainty: It's a *near-certainty* (meaning "It will almost certainly happen.");
　pseudoexperts: not real, but pretending to be real experts;
　quasi-legal: The agreement has a sort of *quasi-legal* (partly lawful) status;
　semi-independent: a *semi-independent* (partly but not completely independent) region.

3) Suffixes used in words to indicate that something is done in a particular way or with a particular thing, e. g.

-fashion, *-like*, *-ly*, *-shaped*, *-style*, *-wise*

moving *spider-fashion* (moving the way a spider moves);

a *heart-shaped* (in the shape of a heart) box of chocolate;

An *old-style* (traditional) building is being renovated;

lengthwise: (from one end to another; in the direction of the longest side of something) Slice the pears in half *lengthwise* or *lengthways*.

4) Suffixes used to refer to persons and actors, e. g.

-ain, *-aire*, *-ian*, *-ese*, *-ant*, *-ary*, *-ate*, *-ee*, *-eer*, *-er*, *-ar*, *-or*, *-ier*, *-eur*, *-ess*, *-ician*, *-ist*, *-ite*, *-ive*, *-sman*, *-on*, *-ster*

captain, millionaire, barbarian, Chinese, applicant, secretary, candidate, referee, engineer, manufacturer, scholar, dictator, premier, entrepreneur, hostess, musician, dogmatist, Israelite, captive, spokesman, companion, gangster.

5) Suffixes used in adjectives that describe someone's clothes, appearance, or personality. New adjectives are often created by combining a word with a participle, or with a noun and *-ed*, e. g.

-boned, *-cheeked*, *-chested*, *-clad*, *-coated*, *-eyed*, *-faced*, *-haired*, *-handed*, *-hatted*, *-headed*, *-hearted*, *-legged*, *-limbed*, *-lipped*, *-minded*, *-necked*, *-skinned*, *-sleeved*, *-tongued*, *-waisted*

The *pink-cheeked* fashion model (the fashion model with a pink color on her cheeks) was warmly welcomed by the audience;

pictures of a *denim-clad* president (the type of clothing that the president is wearing) relaxing on the ranch;

The *brown-eyed* girl (the girl with a particular eye color) is dancing with a handsome young man;

straw-hatted (wearing straw hat) girls;

a *conservation-minded* country;

an *innovation-minded* nation.

6) Suffixes referring to those who really want or like a particular thing, or are trying hard to get it, e. g.

-aholic, *-crazy*, *-hungry*, *-loving*, *-mad*, *-mania*, *-phile*, *-seeking*

Soccer-crazy youngsters are young people who are extremely enthusiastic about football games;

She's *sports-mad* (very much interested in and excited by sports);

Obamamania: a tsunami of excitement about US President Barak Obama's 2008 presidential race;

Attention-seeking children are kids who are trying to get special interest in doing something.

7) Suffixes of nouns meaning "small or little", e. g.

-cle, *-cule*, *-el*, *-le*, *-en*, *-in*, *-et*, *-ette*, *-ie*, *-y*, *-kin*, *-let*, *-ling*

particle, molecule, kitten, bulletin, islet, gazette, birdie, kitty, napkin, leaflet, seedling.

8) Suffixes popular in present-day English, e. g.

-friendly, *-gate*, *-impaired*, *-ista*, *-meister*

a lot of *environment-friendly* automobiles, an *environment-friendly* society, *computer-friendly*, *consumer-friendly*, *family-friendly*, *iPod-friendly*, *reader-friendly*, *user-friendly*;

Watergate, Irangate, Hurricanegate, Nannygate, Camilla-gate, Donorgate, Travelgate, Whitewatergate, zippergate;

Her husband is an *entertainment-meister* (meaning, her husband is an expert in entertaining people).

9) Prefixes and suffixes used to make words negative or to make words with opposite meanings, e. g.

a-, contra-, counter-, de-, dis-, il-/ im-/ in-/ ir-, mis-, non-, un-; *-free, -less*

There must be some effective ways to *counteract* global warming;

decentralize: to take power from a central government or organization and give it to several smaller and more local ones;

non-toxic (that are not poisonous or harmful) chemicals;

unsmiling: seeming very serious and *unfriendly*.

10) Prefixes and suffixes containing meanings such as "having a lot of something", "to a large degree", or "always", e. g.

all-, arch-, ever-, extra-, hyper-, mega-, mul-, oft-, pall-, poly-, super-, ultra-; *-infested, -intensive, -rich, -ridden*

The visit left an *everlasting* (keeping on for a very long time) impression on me;

an *ultra-successful* (one that is extremely successful) product;

A *labor-intensive* industry or process needs a lot of people to do the work.

Task

I. Do you know another form of the following prefixes?
1. semi- (in *semicircle*) —
2. uni- (in *uniform*) —
3. quadr- (in *quadruped*) —
4. cent- (in *centennial*) —

Key: 1. hemi- (in *hemisphere*)   2. mono- (in *monologue*)   3. tetra- (in *tetrahedron*)   4. hecto- (in *hectogram*)

II. Do you know the meanings of the following suffixes?
1. -dom (in *serfdom, wisdom*) — _____;
2. -some (in *tiresome, meddlesome*) — _____;
3. -ism (in *baptism, barbarism*) — _____;
4. -tude (in *fortitude, certitude*) — _____.

Key: 1. state/condition/rank;   2. tending to/apt to/showing;   3. act/manner/state/doctrine;   4. quality/state/condition.

5.3 Conversion

Lexical items in English are very often created not by affixation but by conversion or zero derivation, i. e. without any affixes being attached to the root or stem. Conversion involves a change in the word class of a word. The word-form remains the same, but it realizes a different lexical item. For example, the lexical items *bail, net, plan, skin* may be both nouns and verbs. Words such as *conflict, object, subject* can be distinguished as noun or verb by their stress patterns, e. g.

'*conflict* (noun)   con'*flict* (verb)
'*object* (noun)   ob'*ject* (verb)

ˈsubject (noun)   subˈject (verb)

Conversion in English is a fairly productive process.

5.3.1 Properties of conversion

Often a word of one part of speech is converted to a word of another part of speech. Conversion of verbs into nouns and nouns into verbs is extremely productive in English. Usually the same word-form can be used as a verb or a noun, with only the grammatical context enabling us to know which category it belongs to. Thus, *jump* in the two sentences below is exactly the same in form but it belongs to two different lexemes: *jump* in "The pig will jump over the stile." is the non-finite form of the verb, while *jump* in "What a jump!" is the singular form of the noun *jump*. In "What a jump!", the verb is converted into a noun by conversion, i.e. without using any affix. What enables us to know whether the word is a noun or a verb is the position that it occupies in the sentence. If we see the subject the *pig* and the auxiliary verb *will* before the word *jump*, we know it must be a verb. But when *jump* occurs after the indefinite article *a* we know it must be a noun.

Conversion is not restricted to nouns and verbs. Adjectives too can undergo conversion. Conversion from adjectives to nouns is very common in English. For instance, the word-form *green* realizes an adjective in the first sentence and a noun in the second one:

The *Green* Party had political clout in the 1980s.

The *Greens* had political clout in the 1980s.

The widespread use of conversion shows the value of syntactic function in determining word-class membership in English. Very often it is by its function rather than by its morphological form that we tell the word-class to which a word belongs.

The boundary between conversion and functional shift is not grammatically well-defined. In linguistics, functional shift occurs when an existing word takes on a new syntactic function. For example, the word *like*, formerly only used as a preposition in comparisons (as in *eats like a pig*), is now also used in the same way as the subordinating conjunction as in many dialects of English (as in *sounds like he means it*).

Reading Task

Some words can be used as different parts of speech in different constructions: *study* may be a verb, as it is in the sentence, *I study*; it may be a noun, as in the sentence, *Study made him an expert*; it may be an adjective, as in the sentence, *Go to the study hall*. Dictionaries usually do not list uncommon uses with separate part of speech labels. Often they also do not notice adjective uses of nouns, as in *an automobile tire*, if they are so simple and common that they may be taken for granted.

5.3.2 Types of conversion

1) Conversion to nouns

 A) Verb to noun

  a) Nouns meaning "state" (generally "state of mind" or "state of sensation")
   desire, doubt, love, taste, want, smell

  b) Nouns meaning "event/activity" (from verbs used dynamically)
   attempt, fall, hit, laugh, release

  c) Nouns which are the objects
   answer ("*that which answers*"), *bet, catch, find, hand-out*

  d) Nouns which are the subjects
   bore ("*someone who or that which bores/is boring*"), *cheat, coach, stand-in*

e) Nouns which are instruments of verbs
   cover ("*something with which to cover things*"), *paper, wrap*
f) Nouns referring to the manner of verb-ing
   walk ("*manner of walking*"), *throw, lie*
g) Nouns referring to the place of verb
   divide, retreat, rise, turn, drive-in

B) Nouns from other sources
   There are a few nouns from other sources, for example:
   They're running in the *final* ("*the final race*").
   to have a *down* ("*grudge*") on someone

2) Conversion to verbs
   A) Noun to verb
      The conversion of noun to verb may be subdivided into the following groups and most of the verbs in this category are transitive.
      a) "to put in/on noun"
         bottle ("*to put into a bottle*"), *corner, position, garage*
      b) "to give noun, to provide with noun"
         butter ("*bread*"), *coat, mask, oil, muzzle*
      c) "to deprive of noun"
         core ("*remove the core from*"), *gut, peel, skin*
      d) "to ... with noun"
         brake ("*to stop by means of brake*"), *elbow, hand, finger, glue*
      e) "to be/act as noun with respect to ..."
         chaperon ("*to act as chaperon to*"), *father, nurse, parrot, pilot*
      f) "to make/change ... into noun"
         cash ("*to change into cash*"), *cripple, group*
      g) "to send/go by noun"
         mail ("*to send by mail*"), *ship, telegraph*
         bicycle ("*to go by bicycle*"), *boat, canoe, motor*
   B) Adjective to verb
      a) (transitive verbs) "to make adjective" or "to make more adjective"
         calm ("*to make calm*"), *dirty, dry, humble, lower, soundproof*
      b) (intransitive verbs) "to become adjective"; generally adjectives in Type a) can also have this function, and it may be seen as a secondary conversion
         dry ("*to become dry*"), *empty, narrow, yellow*
      c) The phrasal verb derived from the adjective by the addition of a participle
         smooth out ("*to make smooth*"), *sober up, calm down*

3) Conversion to adjectives
   Conversion to adjectives is much less productive than the other two types of conversions. This type of adjectives is mostly derived from nouns. For example:
   a gold ring, a chalk board, production manager, world population, a log cabin

4) Change of secondary word class
   The notion of conversion may be extended to changes of secondary word class, within the same major word category.
   A) Uncountable nouns are used as countable nouns, or vice versa. For example:

Some *paints* are more lasting than others.

a few square feet of *floor*

B) The conversion between intransitive verbs and transitive verbs

run the water ("cause the water to run"), *march* the prisoners

C) Nongradable adjectives can be converted to gradable ones

He's more *English* than the English.

I have a very *legal* turn of mind.

5) Other conversions

In English, there are some other conversions, which do not frequently occur. For example:

Tom went *home* early. (noun to adverb)

I will take a *through* train. (preposition to adjective)

The company has had its share of *ups* and *downs*, but it seems to be doing well now. (adverb to noun)

This dictionary is a *must* for the students of English. (auxiliary verb to noun)

Task

I. Pay attention to the changes of the parts of speech of the italicized word "*smoke*" in the following sentences.
1. Watch the *smoke* from the chimney.
2. The tall chimney *smokes*, polluting the air around.
3. John used to *smoke* a pipe after supper.
4. — Let's have a *smoke*. — No, it is not allowed here.

Key: 1. (noun);   2. (verb);   3. (verb with a new meaning);   4. (noun with a new meaning)

II. Pay attention to the changes of the final consonants of the following nouns and verbs.
1. house (*n.*) — house (*v.*);   2. use (*n.*) — use (*v.*);   3. belief (*n.*) — believe (*v.*);
4. half (*n.*) — halve (*v.*);   5. mouth (*n.*) — mouth (*v.*);   6. wreath (*n.*) — wreathe (*v.*)

Key: 1. /-s/—/-z/;   2. /-s/—/-z/;   3. /-f/—/-v/;   4. /-f/—/-v/;   5. /-θ/—/-ð/;
6. /-θ/—/-ð/

5.4 Compounding

While affixation involves the addition of a bound morpheme to a root morpheme, compounding is concerned with the combination of two or more words to form a new word — a compound word or a compound. The combinations that occur in English are nearly limitless, as the following table of compounds shows.

greenhouse	*bittersweet*	*whitewash*	*download*
homework	*babysitter*	*spoonfeed*	*bandwidth*
pickpocket	*raindrop*	*sleepwalk*	*netspeak*

Besides, *frigidaire* is a compound formed by combining the adjective *frigid* with the noun *air*. Very recently, some compounds have been introduced into English, such as *carjack*, *computer geeks*, *mall rat*, *mouse potato*, *snail mail*, *road rage*, *palm pilot*, *user-friendliness*, *web page*, *web traffic*, *iPad*, *iPhone* and *slow-speed chase*.

5.4.1 Characteristics of compounds

1. Compounds can be distinguished from grammatical structures

1) When the two words are in the same grammatical category, the compound will be in this category:

noun+noun: *girlfriend, fighter-bomber, paper clip, elevator-operator, landlord, mailman, cell/cellular/mobile phone, search engine.*

adjective+adjective: *bittersweet, icy-cold, red-hot, worldly-wise.*

2) In many cases, two words in a compound fall into different categories. In such cases, the class of the rightmost word will be the grammatical category of the compound. And that rightmost word in English is the head of the compound, which is usually the part of a word or phrase that determines its broad meaning and grammatical category. For example:

noun+adjective=adjective: *headstrong, watertight, lifelong.*

verb+noun=noun: *pickpocket, pinchpenny, dare-devil, sawbones.*

3) Compounds formed with a preposition are in the category of the non-prepositional part of the compound, such as *overtake, hanger-on, undertake, sundown.*

4) Compound words cannot be divided by inserting intervening material, unlike grammatical structure, e.g.

a. She is a *sweetheart*.

b. She has a *sweet heart*.

Whereas in (a.) *sweetheart* is indivisible and one cannot insert another word between *sweet* and *heart*, in (b.) one can say "She has a sweet, kind heart".

5) A member of the compound word cannot participate in a grammatical structure, e.g. a *hard ball*; a *baseball* (compound). We can say "It was a very hard ball". But the sentence "It was a very baseball." is not grammatically acceptable.

2. Compound words have their own ways of spelling and stress patterns

1) Compounds can be quite lengthy. Consider *three-time loser, four-dimensional space time, sergeant-at-arms, mother-of-pearl, man about town, master of ceremonies*, and *daughter-in-law*. Though two-word compounds — two nouns combined to create a meaning which differs from that of each are the most common in English, it would be difficult to state an upper limit.

2) Spelling does not tell us what sequence of words constitutes a compound; whether a compound is spelled with a space between the two words, with a hyphen, or with no separation at all depends on the idiosyncrasies of the particular compound, as shown, for example, in *blackbird, gold-tail* and *smoke screen*.

3) Compounds often have different stress patterns from noncompounded word sequences. When we pronounce a compound, the stress is usually put on the first word, which is different from the way a noun phrase is pronounced. In a noun phrase, the second word is often stressed. The primary stresses in *redcoat, greenhouse* and *lighthouse keeper* are on the first words of the compounds, while in *red coat, green house* and *light house keeper* the stresses fall on the second words.

3. The meaning of compound words cannot be taken for granted

1) Many compounds have obvious meanings, e.g. *a computer game* is a game played on a computer. Yet, the meaning of a compound is not always the sum of the meanings of its parts: a *greenhouse* is not green; *heavy metal* is not metal that is heavy, but a type of rock music; a *darkroom* refers to "a room for photographic processing" which does not necessarily need to be in darkness and there are many *dark rooms* which are not *darkrooms*.

2) Some compounds reveal some meaning relations between the parts, but the meaning relations are not entirely consistent because many compounds in English are idiomatic. *Big-ticket* items are expensive. A *boathouse* is a house for boats, but a *cathouse* is slang for a house of prostitution, which has nothing to do with cats. A *jumping bean* is a bean that jumps, a *falling star* is a star that falls, and a *magnifying glass* is a glass that magnifies; but *looking glass* is not a glass that looks, nor is an *eating apple* an apple that eats, and *laughing gas* does not laugh.

3) Many compounds must be learned as if they were individual simple words because they do not seem to relate to the meanings of the individual parts at all. A *Redcoat* refers to a soldier during the American Revolutionary War and a *jack-in-a-box* is a tropical tree. A *highbrow* does not necessarily have a high brow, nor does a *big-wig* have a big wig, nor does an *egghead* have an egg-shaped head.

5.4.2 Classification of compounds

As mentioned above, all types of combinations are possible. *Killjoy* combines a verb and a noun. *Windbreak* is combined by a noun and a verb. An adverb *down* and a noun *grade* can form a verb compound *downgrade*. Two verbs can be combined, as in *make-believe*. And *red-hot* combines two adjectives. It appears that compounding can take place within any of the word classes, but the most productive ones in English are nouns, adjectives and verbs. According to parts of speech of the compounds, this section will focus on three major classes of compounds.

1. Noun compounds

The majority of English compounds are nouns. There are many productive patterns of noun compounds such as noun + noun (*bathroom*), adjective + noun (*greenfly*), adverb + verb (*newlywed*), adjective + verb (*highlight*) and verb + noun (*tell-tale*). Although the patterns themselves are simple, there are very complicated internal semantic and grammatical relationships between the compounding elements, which will be described in the following:

1) Subject+verb

This pattern of compounds are usually composed of a noun and a verb or a verbal element, and the noun is normally analyzed as the agent of the action (the subject of the verb/the verbal element). For example:

headache, sunshine, daybreak, dancing girl, play boy, motion picture

2) Verb+object

This pattern of compounds are usually composed of a noun and a verb or a verbal element, and the noun is normally analyzed as the patient of the action (the object of the verb/the verbal element). For example:

chewing gum, passport, cease-fire, tongue-twister

3) Verb+adverbial

In this pattern of compounds, the adverbial can be further classified as that of time, place, instrument and others. e.g.

Place: *hiding-place* (hide in a place), *sun-bathing* (bathe in the sun)

Time: *sleep-walking* (walk in one's sleep), *night flight* (fly during the night)

Instrument: *handwriting* (write by hand), *gunfight* (fight with a gun)

Others: *shadow boxing* (box against a shadow), *telephone call* (call by the telephone)

4) Subject+object

In this pattern of compounds, both the agent and the patient of the action will be present. The following compounds belong to this pattern:

steamboat, power plant, gaslight, honey bee, etc.

5) Restrictive relation

The first element in this pattern of compounds restricts the meaning of the second: *girlfriend*, *longboat*, *chocolate bar*, *etc.*

6) Appositive relation

The first element in this pattern of compounds is in apposition to the second: *a pine tree*, *prison camp*, *a peasant girl*, etc.

2. Adjective compounds

Adjective compounds are also productive compounds. The term *subprime* has become all too familiar as a result of the current credit crisis (2007 – 2009 in the US), which is attributed in part to the proliferation of *subprime* loans — loans made on unfavorable terms to borrowers unable to qualify for conventional loans. Of many patterns of adjective compounds, *noun+v-ing* (*record-breaking*), *noun + adjective* (*thread-bare*) and *noun + verb-ed* (*custom-built*) are very productive. According to their internal grammatical relationship, adjective compounds fall into the following subclasses:

1) Subject+verb

The verb is usually in the form of past participle: *thunder-struck*, *weather-beaten*, *suntanned*.

2) Verb+object

The verb is usually in the form of present participle: *breath-taking* (take breath), *fault-finding* (find fault).

3) Verb+adverbial

The verb is usually in the form of present participle or past participle: *everlasting*, *well-meant*.

4) Noun adverbial+adjective

homesick (sick because of missing home), *war-weary* (weary of war).

5) Coordinating relation

The two elements are in a coordinating relationship: *bittersweet*, *Anglo-French*, *Sino-American*.

Adjective compounds can also be formed by other patterns, such as *win-win* (*adj.* denoting a situation in which each party benefits). Those mentioned above are some major ones.

3. Verb compounds

Among the three major patterns of compounds, verb compounds are not so productive as noun compounds and adjective compounds. Verb compounds can be formed in two ways: by back-formation and by conversion (zero derivation) from noun compounds.

1) By back-formation

Back-formation is a "reversal" of derivation. For example, *house-keep* is formed by deleting *-ing* and *-er* from *housekeeping* and *housekeeper*. Here are some other examples: *lip-read* (from *lip reading*), *mass-produce* (from *mass-production*), *chain-smoke* (from *chain-smoker*).

2) By conversion

nickname n.   to *nickname*
honeymoon n.   to *honeymoon*
moonlight n.   to *moonlight*
first-name n.   to *first-name*

The above classification of compounds is restricted to two-word compounds. As stated already, compounds can also be composed of phrases or clauses. We can use the rules that produce sentences to produce compound words. The compounds formed by phrases and clauses such as *heart-to-heart*, *wait-and-see*, *at-the-first-sight*, *state-of-the-art-technology*, *stay-at-home*, *forget-me-not*, *ahead-of-schedule*, *an I-told-you-so air*, *jump-on-the-chair-at-the-sight-of-mouse* are usually hyphenated.

Compounding is a useful way of condensing information and adds a variation to the way we refer to concepts in discourse. Therefore, compounding is an important type of word formation.

Task

I. Take a look at the following compounds. Can you say their structure types?
1. daybreak   2. self-control   3. sun-bathing   4. windmill   5. girlfriend
Key: 1. The day breaks. (subject+verb)   2. to control the self (verb+object)
3. to bathe in the sun (verb+adverbial)   4. The wind powers the mill. (subject+object)
5. The friend is a girl. (subject+complement)

II. What is the common feature of the following compounds?
1. footsore   2. camera-ready   3. dustproof   4. airsick   5. watertight
Key: They are all adjective compounds, which are called "verbless". For example, *footsore* means sore in respect to (one's) feet.

This chapter is concerned with morphology, by the principles and practice of which English words are made. Just as knowledge of a language implies knowledge of its phonology, so it implies knowledge of its morphology. Although a distinction has traditionally been made between morphology and syntax, there are certain aspects of morphology which have syntactic implications. In the first part of the chapter, some basic concepts are introduced. Morphemes, free and bound morphemes, content and function morphemes, derivational and inflectional morphemes, roots, stems and affixes are all absolutely necessary notions and indispensable elements in the English word-formation processes. The reason why morphemes can be combined into words is that there exist, in English as well as in other languages, morphological rules, which determine how morphemes are combined to form new words.

There are three main types of word-formation, the first of which can be referred to as derivation / affixation (prefixation and suffixation). Prefixation is the way of putting a prefix in front of the base of a word, sometimes with, but more usually without, a change of word class (e. g. *pre + determine* — *predetermine*), while suffixation puts a suffix after the base of a word, sometimes without, but more usually with, a change of word class (e. g. *friend+ship* — *friendship*). Conversion is the second type of word-formation, which assigns the base of a word to a different word class with no change of form [e. g. (*We're going to*) *carpet* (*the room.*) — verb from noun]. Compounding, the third type of word-formation, involves the combination of more than one root to form a new word. It is something like adding one base to another, such that usually the one placed in front in some sense subcategorizes the one that follows (e. g. *audiobook*, *download*, *heavyweight*, *rainforest*, *spacewalker*).

Further Reading

1. Matthews, P. H. (1991). *Morphology*. Cambridge: Cambridge University Press.
2. Adams, V. (2000). *An Introduction to Modern English Word-formation*. London: Longman.
3. Fromkin, V., Rodman, R. and Hyams, N. (2007). *An Introduction to Language*, 8th ed. Boston, MA: Thomson Wadsworth.

● Extended Reading

■ The hierarchical structure of words

We saw earlier that morphemes are added in a fixed order. This order reflects the hierarchical structure of the word. A word is not a simple sequence of morphemes. It has an internal structure. For example, the word *unsystematic* is composed of three morphemes: *un-*, *system* and *-atic*. The root is *system*, a noun, to which we add the suffix *-atic* resulting in an adjective, *systematic*. To this adjective, we add the prefix *un-* forming a new adjective, *unsystematic*.

In order to represent the hierarchical organization of words (and sentences), linguists use tree diagrams. The tree diagram for *unsystematic* is as follows:

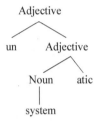

This tree represents the application of two morphological rules:
1. Noun+atic → Adjective
2. Un+Adjective → Adjective

Rule 1 attaches the derivational suffix *-atic* to the root noun, forming an adjective. Rule 2 takes the adjective formed by rule 1 and attaches the derivational prefix *un-*. The diagram shows that the entire word — *unsystematic* — is an adjective that is composed of an adjective — *systematic* — plus *un*. The adjective is itself composed of a noun — *system* — plus the suffix *-atic*.

Like the property of discreteness discussed earlier, hierarchical structure is an essential property of human language. Words (and sentences) have component parts, which relate to each other in specific, rule-governed ways. Although at first glance it may seem that, aside from order, the morphemes *un-* and *-atic* each relate to the root *system* in the same way, this is not the case. The root *system* is "closer" to *-atic* than it is to *un-*, and *un-* is actually connected to the adjective *systematic*, and not directly to *system*. Indeed, **unsystem* is not a word.

Further morphological rules can be applied to the given structure. For example, English has a derivational suffix *-al*, as in *egotistical*, *fantastical* and *astronomical*. In these cases, *-al* is added to an adjective — *egotistic*, *fantastic*, *astronomic* — to form a new adjective. The rule for *-al* is as follows:

3. Adjective+al → Adjective

Another affix is *-ly*, which is added to adjectives — *happy*, *lazy*, *hopeful* — to form adverbs *happily*, *lazily*, *hopefully*. Following is the rule for *-ly*:

4. Adjective+ly → Adverb

Applying these two rules to the derived form *unsystematic*, we get the following tree for *unsystematically*:

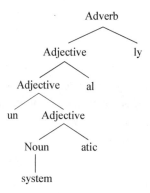

This is a rather complex word. Despite its complexity, it is well-formed because it follows the morphological rules of the language. On the other hand, a very simple word can be ungrammatical. Suppose in the above example we first added *un-* to the root *system*. That would have resulted in the nonword, **unsystem*.

*Unsystem is not a possible word because there is no rule in English that allows *un-* to be added to nouns. The large soft-drink company whose ad campaign promoted the *Uncola* successfully flouted this linguistic rule to capture people's attention. Part of our linguistic competence includes the ability to recognize possible versus impossible words, like **unsystem* and **Uncola*. Possible words are those that conform to the rules; impossible words are those that do not.

Tree diagrams make explicit the way speakers represent the internal structure of the morphologically complex words in their language. In speaking and writing, we appear to string morphemes together sequentially as in *un+system+atic*. However, our mental representation of words is hierarchical as well as linear, and this is shown by tree diagrams.

The hierarchical organization of words is most clearly shown by structurally ambiguous words, words that have more than one meaning by virtue of having more than one structure. Consider the word *unlockable*. Imagine you are inside a room and you want some privacy. You would be unhappy to find the door is *unlockable* — "not able to be locked". Now imagine you are inside a locked room trying to get out. You would be very relieved to find that the door is *unlockable* — "able to be unlocked". These two meanings correspond to two different structures, as follows:

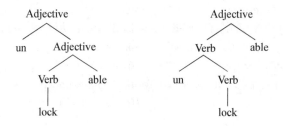

In the first structure the verb *lock* combines with the suffix *-able* to form an adjective *lockable* ("able to be locked"). Then the prefix *un-*, meaning "not", combines with the derived adjective to form a new adjective *unlockable* ("not able to be locked"). In the second case, the prefix *un-* combines with the verb *lock* to form a derived verb *unlock*. Then the derived verb combines with the suffix *-able* to form *unlockable*, "able to be unlocked."

An entire class of words in English follows this pattern: *unbuttonable*, *unzippable* and *unlatchable*, among others. The ambiguity arises because the prefix *un-* can combine with an adjective, as illustrated in rule 2, or it can combine with a verb, as in *undo*, *unstaple*, *unearth* and *unloosen*.

If words were only strings of morphemes without any internal organization, we could not explain the ambiguity of words like *unlockable*. These words also illustrate another important point, which is that structure is important to determining meaning. The same three morphemes occur in both versions of *unlockable*, yet there are two distinct meanings. The different meanings arise because of the two different structures.

— Fromkin, V.

Exercises

I. Fill in the blanks with the proper forms of the words in brackets.

1. It's not that you're so _____ (social), but a man who likes people doesn't wind up in the Arctic.
2. A special show was _____ (range) to give free admission to the family members of the miners.
3. It is said the general _____ (descend) to eat with the soldiers every Sunday.
4. The new law _____ (power) the police to search private houses in an emergency.
5. We've had 200 applicants for the job, but we only plan to _____ (view) about 20 of them.
6. She sued for divorce on the grounds of her husband's alleged _____ (conduct) with his secretary.
7. She doesn't like _____ (door) sports even though she knows that it is good for her health.
8. They come up with some programs to improve _____ (telecommunicate) in developing nations.
9. No terms except _____ (conditional) and immediate surrender can be accepted.
10. A bar with _____ (adjust) weights at each end is lifted for sport or exercise.

II. Use *in-* (*il-*, *im-*, *ir-*), *non-*, *un-* to form new words of the following.

1. correct: _____
2. friendly: _____
3. wrap: _____
4. free: _____
5. rational: _____
6. consistent: _____
7. remarked: _____
8. business: _____
9. green: _____
10. expected: _____

III. Fill in the blanks with the proper forms of the appropriate words in the following box.

| sound | change | sense | dispatch | attribute |
| exemplify | compass | home | mobile | light |

Animals possess sensory powers that humans lack. __1__ pigeons fly with great speed and accuracy when __2__ with messages to faraway places. How do pigeons orient themselves in unfamiliar regions? This remains something of an enigma. The mystery, however, is partly explained by a pigeon's ability to see ultraviolet __3__, which reveals the sun's position even through clouds. In addition, pigeons can hear __4__ waves that have traveled hundreds of miles. These waves enhance a pigeon's __5__ of direction by indicating distant mountains and seas. Pigeons even appear to discern __6__ in the earth's magnetic field.

Bats have impressive __7__ equally worthy of acclaim. As nocturnal animals, they search for food in complete darkness. They do so by screeching in tones higher than any human can hear and then locating prey by the returning echoes.

Scorpions also __8__ the night hunter. Tiny leg hairs enable them to feel vibrations in the sand made by a(n) __9__ insect as far as two feet away.

People with knowledge of the pigeon, bat and scorpion can attest to the fact that such "innovations" as the magnetic __10__, radar and the motion detector are nothing new.

IV. True or False decisions.
1. Compounding is a main type of word-formation adding one base to another, such that usually the one placed in front in some sense subcategorizes the one that follows. (   )
2. Compounding can occur only in the three major word classes, nouns and, to lesser extent, adjectives and, to least extent, verbs. (   )
3. A compound can be formed by placing any lexical item in front of another. (   )
4. The relations consequently involved in compounding are frequently resemblance, function, or some other salient or defining characteristic. (   )
5. Although all compounds are directly "derived" from the clause-structure functions of the items concerned, we shall adopt a mode of presentation which links compounds to sentential or clausal paraphrases. (   )
6. "Bee-sting" is a noun compound, which belongs to the type "subject and verb". (   )
7. All the following items belong to the type "verb and object": turntable, watchdog, push-button, treadmill and drawbridge. (   )
8. "Haircutting, handshaking and letter-writing" are "object+verbal noun in -ing". This type is very productive. (   )
9. In "punchball: verb+object" and "chewing gum: verbal noun in -ing+object", the syntactic paraphrase obscures the "purpose" relationship: "The ball is for punching", "The gum is for X to chew". (   )
10. In American English, compounds are not usually written solid as soon as they have gained some permanent status. (   )

Chapter 6
The Formation of English Words (2)
— Minor Types

> **Points for Thinking**
> 1. What are the ways in which words are formed by means of abbreviation?
> 2. Give examples to illustrate the morphological features of acronymic word-formation.
> 3. Do you think network abbreviations are conducive to our daily communication? Are there any advantages and/or disadvantages of using network abbreviations?
> 4. How many ways are there in which some words may be formed by joining part of one word with part of another?
> 5. Give examples to indicate the overlapping features of reduplications and onomatopoetic words.

The Bible tells a familiar story of people's attempt to build the Tower of Babel high enough to enable them to avoid drowning in the event of a second flood. We can picture the immense amount of talking that went into this project — in the laying of plans, the procuring of materials and the actual building. There must have been the hum of talk from thousands of tongues. Then words changed in form to suit their varying uses. Especially in informal usage, builders tended to shorten polysyllabic words and make up new ones. Later on we learned of two facts from the biblical story about some different ways of word-building: the first of which is that abbreviation started to be involved in English word-formation for convenience's sake; the second fact is that ignorance sometimes could be creative. A new word might come into being in the language because of an incorrect morphological analysis, e. g. *peddle* being derived from *peddler* on the mistaken assumption that the *-er* was the agentive suffix.

6.1 Abbreviation

Abbreviation is lexically regarded as one of the minor means in English word-formation. We can distinguish four highly productive ways in which abbreviation is involved, namely clipping, initialism, acronym and blending.

6.1.1 Clipping

Clipping is one way in which we shorten a relatively long word and thereby create a new one without changing its meaning, e. g. the word *dormitory* being clipped, forming the new word *dorm* which is called a clipped word. We use the longer term if the situation is more formal and the shorter term if the situation is more informal. However, the new term may entirely replace the longer original word.

Clipped words such as *fax* for *facsimile*, *flu* for *influenza* and *prof* for *professor*, are now in very common use. There are also orthographic abbreviations such as *Dr.* (doctor), *Mr.* (mister), *AZ* (Arizona) and *MB* (megabyte), where the spelling of a word has been shortened but its pronunciation is not (necessarily) altered.

There are several types of clipping that are popular in speech and writing, e. g.

Type 1: Clippings take place at the beginning of the words, e. g. aerodrome → *drome*, aeroplane / airplane → *plane*, bicycle → *cycle*, bulldozer → *dozer*, caravan → *van*, earthquake → *quake*, hamburger → *burger*, helicopter → *copter*, microfiche → *fiche*, omnibus → *bus*, parachute → *chute*, periwig → *wig*, raccoon → *coon*, telephone → *phone*, telescope → *scope*, violoncello → *cello*;

Type 2: Clippings take place at the end of the words, e. g. advertisement → *ad*, automobile → *auto*, bicycle → *bike*, coca cola → *coke*, demobilize → *demob*, discotheque → *disco*, doctor → *doc*, demonstration → *demo*, dormitory → *dorm*, examination → *exam*, exposition → *expo*, facsimile → *fax*, gasoline → *gas*, gentleman → *gent*, helicopter → *heli*, hippopotamus → *hippo*, Japanese → *Jap*, kilogram → *kilo*, laboratory → *lab*, lavatory → *lav*, liberation → *lib*, literature → *lit*, mathematics → *math*, memorandum → *memo*, microphone → *mike*, miniskirt → *mini*, mitten → *mitt*, photograph → *photo*, pornography → *porn*, rhinoceros → *rhino*, stereophonic / stereotype → *stereo*, television → *tele*, trigonometry → *trig*, tuxedo → *tux*;

Type 3: Clippings take place both at the beginning and the end of the words, e. g. influenza → *flu*, refrigerator → *fridge*, prescription → *script*, detective → *tec*;

Type 4: Clippings take place in the middle of the words, e. g. assistant → *asst*, fluidonics → *fluidics*, fossilization → *fossilation*, idololatry → *idolatry*, mathematics → *maths*, pacificist → *pacifist*, symbolology → *symbology*, spectacles → *specs*;

Type 5: Clipping of some vowels takes place with major consonants retained in the clipped word, e. g. the Commonwealth → *Cwlth*, department → *dept*, Hong Kong → *HK* (Note: These are called journalist clippings, used mainly in the press circles particularly in the newspapers or on the web.);

Type 6: Phrasal clipping takes place in the phrases, e. g. daily paper → *daily*, weekly paper → *weekly*, final examinations → *finals*; popular music → *pop*, public house → *pub*, zoological garden → *zoo*.

Some spellers choose to write the clipped form of some words. Clipped words are favored because they are easier to spell and to learn by heart. What is important is that clippings usually appear in informal usage and some of them are especially used in certain circles of people. The challenge occurs when students are asked to write the longer form of a clipped word. Some common clipped words are listed below:

mum — chrysanthemum *pen* — penitentiary
champ — champion *con* — convict
pike — turnpike *co-op* — cooperative
ref — referee *cuke* — cucumber
rev — revolution *stats* — statistics
sub — submarine *grad* — graduate
taxi — taxicab *gym* — gymnasium
teen — teenager *tie* — necktie
limo — limousine *typo* — typographical error
vet — veteran; veterinarian

Task

I. Do you know the original forms of the following clipping words?
1. lunch 2. movie 3. pram 4. symbology
5. pacifist 6. Wikipedia 7. Chimerica 8. jeggings

Key:
1. luncheon   2. movie picture   3. perambulator   4. symbolology   5. pacificist
6. wiki-wiki+encyclopedia；Wikipedia 维基百科是一种采用 wiki 协作系统的在线百科。wiki-wiki 一词来源于夏威夷语，原意为"快点快点"。
7. China+America；one of New York Times' buzzwords for 2009；《纽约时报》评选出的 2009 年流行语之一，所谓"中美国"。
8. Jean leggings（牛仔打底裤：牛仔裤与打底裤的结合）。

II. Look at the following pairs of words. Consult a dictionary to find their meanings.
1. cute — acute   2. mend — amend   3. spy — espy   4. peel — appeal
Note: They are pairs of clippings and original words. The words in each pair have different meanings.

6.1.2　Initialism

Initialism is a reduction process in which initialization in words is used. It is generally not a powerful process in English word-building. Still, there are many initialisms in some fields such as bureaucracies and organizations. Hatch, E. and Brown, C. (1995) gave an example, "after the 1994 earthquake, Los Angeles residents who hoped to find housing quickly learned that the acronym HUD was not the name of a movie but the Department of Housing and Urban Development. Those who wanted loans had to deal with SBA and FEMA, the small business and federal emergency agencies." Since China entered the World Trade Organization in 2001, *WTO* has become more popular in the life of the Chinese people. *SARS* (severe acute respiratory syndrome) and *A H1N1* virus (swine flu) have helped a lot of people know *WHO* and *WHA*, which stand for World Health Organization and World Health Assembly.

There are two types of initial-words.

Type 1: The letters represent full words.

AA — Automobile Association (of Great Britain),
AAA — American Automobile Association (triple A),
AAAA — Amateur Athletic Association of America,
ABC — American Broadcasting Company,
AD/A. D. — Anno Domini (in the year of the Lord/since Christ was born),
AP — Associated Press,
BBC — British Broadcasting Corporation,
BC/B. C. — before Christ/Bachelor of Chemistry,
BRT — Bus Rapid Transit,
CNN — Cable News Network,
CNS — China News Service,
DNA — deoxyribonucleic acid,
EQ — emotional quotient/educational quotient,
ESP — English for special purposes / extra-sensory perception,
KL — Kuala Lumpur,
FBI — the Federal Bureau of Investigation,
GPS — global positioning system,
HM — Her/His Majesty,
HIV — human immunodeficiency virus,
ICBC — Industrial and Commercial Bank of China,
IAAF — International Amateur Athletic Federation,
IABA — International Amateur Boxing Association,
IAEA — (UN) International Atomic Energy Agency,
ICE — International Corpus of English,
IOC — International Olympic Committee,
ISBN — International Standard Book Number,
GMT — Greenwich Mean Time,
LA — Los Angeles,
MIT — Massachusetts Institute of Technology,
NET — (US) National Educational Television,
OPEC — Organization of Petroleum Exporting Countries,
SCI — science citation index,
SCO — Shanghai Cooperation Organization,
UFO — unidentified flying object,
UN — the United Nations,
VHF/vhf/v. h. f. — very high frequency,
VHS — video home system,
VIP — very important person,
VOA — Voice of America,
WHO — World Health Organization,
WFB — World Fellowship of Buddhists,
WFP — World Food Program.

Type 2: The letters represent constituents in a compound or just elements of a word.

ABM — antiballistic missile,
BBQ — barbeque/barbecue,
bd. — board/bond,
CAL — computer-assisted learning,
Cdn — Canadian,
CDR/Cdr./cdr. — commander,
GHQ — General Headquarters,
IA — Iowa,
ID — identification (card),
MSN — Microsoft Network,
TB — tuberculosis,
TV — television,
WBE — web-based education,
wgt. — weight,
WH/Wh/wh — watt-hour(s).

Interestingly, some initial-words can be used to represent short clauses or sentences:

DIY — Do it yourself, DK — don't know, DNF — did not finish,
DNP — did not play, IOU — I owe you.

It is important to note that even though such words are originally created as initialisms, speakers quickly forget such origins and the initialisms become new independent words:

ATM — automated teller machine,
BBE — bachelor of business education,
CBD — central business district,
CEO — chief executive officer,
CPPCC — Chinese People's Political Consultative Conference,
CSE — Certificate of Secondary Education,
CSM — corn, soya, milk (a kind of mixed milk powder),
D. J. — disk jockey,
DJ/D-J — Dow-Jones average,
NETFS — National Educational Television Film Service,
FAQ — frequently asked questions,
FM — frequency modulation,
GB — Great Britain,
IAF — International Astronautical Federation,
IAMAP — International Association of Meteorology and Atmospheric Physics,
ICJ — International Court of Justice,
ICN — International Council of Nurses,
ICU — intensive care unit,
ICW — interrupted continuous waves,
MA — Master of Arts,
MP — member of parliament,
NEW — net economic welfare,
NPC — National People's Congress,
PhD — Doctors of Philosophy,
PM — prime minister,
SALT — Strategic Arms Limitation Talks,
SD — Super Dollfie,
TP — traffic policeman,
ZIP — zone improvement plan.

With the rapid development of science and technology worldwide, more and more initialisms from computer science and the Internet have been created and have come into the everyday life of English users:

ADSL — asymmetrical digital subscriber line,
AGP — accelerated graphics port,
AI — artificial intelligence,
ASP — active server page,
ASCII — American Standard Code for Information Interchange,
AV — audio-visual,
BBS — bulletin board system,
CAD — computer-aided design,
CAI — computer-assisted instruction,
CAM — computer-assisted manufacturing,
CD — compact disk,
CDMA — code division multiple access,
CDPD — cellular digital packet data,
CD-R — compact disk recordable,
CD-ROM — compact disc read-only memory,
CD-RW — compact disk rewritable,
CGI — common gateway interface/computer-generated imagery,
CPS — cards per second/characters per second,
CPU — central processing unit,
CRT — cathode-ray tube,
DDE — dynamic data exchange,
DDoS/DDOS — distributed denial of service,
DDS — digital data service,
DMA — direct memory access,
DNC — direct numerical control,
DNS — domain name system/domain name server,
DPI — dots per inch,
EBCDIC — extended binary coded decimal interchange code,
FTP — file transfer protocol,
HTML — hypertext markup language,
HTTP — hypertext transfer protocol,
IBM — International Business Machines,
IC — integrated circuit,
IDE — Integrated Drive Electronics,
IP — Internet Protocol,

ISDN — integrated services digital network,
IT — information technology,
LCD — liquid crystal display,
LP — line printer,
MIDI — musical instrument digital interface,
NSP — network service protocol,
PPM — pages per minute,
SCSI — small computer system interface,
TCP — transmission control protocol,
TDMA — time-division multiple access,
UPS — uninterruptible power system,
USB — universal serial bus,
VCD — video compact disk,
VGA — video graphics array,
VLSI — very large scale integration,
VPN — virtual private network,
VRML — virtual reality modeling language,
WAN — wide area network,
WAP — wireless application protocol,
WWW — World Wide Web.

English is no doubt a very powerful language in the global economy and its initialisms are playing an important role in international business and trade.

B/L — bill of lading,
C/D — customs declaration,
CFR — cost and freight,
CIF — cost, insurance & freight,
CO — certificate of origin,
COD — cash on delivery,
CPI — consumer price index,
D/A — documents against acceptance,
doc — document,
D/P — documents against payment,
EBPP — electronic bill presentment and payment,
EBT — electronic benefits transfer,
EMS — express mail special,
GDP/gdp/g.d.p. — gross domestic product,
GNP — gross national product,
G. W. — gross weight,
GSP — generalized system of preference,
imp. — import/imported/importer,
IMF — the International Monetary Fund,
L/C — letter of credit,
MAX — maximum,
M/m/med. — medium,
MT — metric ton,
MV — merchant vessel,
n. w. — net weight,
PPBS — Planning-Programming-Budgeting-System,
WTO — World Trade Organization.

> **Task**
>
> I. The following initialisms are from Latin. What do they stand for?
> 1. e. g. —   2. id. —   3. i. e. —   4. etc. —   5. viz —   6. v. —
> **Key:** 1. example gratia   2. idem   3. id est   4. et cetera   5. videlicet   6. vide
>
> II. Do you often employ the following initialisms in the practical and daily writings?
> 1. c/o   2. p. s.   3. s/m/w
> **Key:** 1. care of   2. postscript   3. single/married/widow(er)

6. 1. 3 Acronym

Acronym is a kind of shortening. The word comes from Greek, meaning *heads of names*. An acronym is a word composed of the initial letters of the words of a phrase and is pronounced as a word, e. g. *AIDS* /ˈeɪdz/ — acquired immune deficiency syndrome, *ASEAN* /ˈæsiːən/ — Association of Southeast Asian Nations, *NATO* /ˈneɪtəʊ/ — the North Atlantic Treaty Organization; *UNESCO* /juːˈneskəʊ/ — United Nations Educational, Scientific and Cultural Organization. The words *radar* and *laser* are acronyms: each of the letters that spell the word is the first letter (or letters) of some other complete word, that is, *radar* derives from *radio detecting and ranging; laser* derives from *light amplification (by) stimulated emission (of) radiation*. Acronyms of this kind derive from phrasal names specially devised for their acronymic convenience. Other examples are as follows: *APEC* — Asia Pacific Economic Cooperation, *DOS* — disk operating system, *LAN* — local area network, *RAM* — random access memory, *ROM* — read only memory, *SARS* — severe acute respiratory syndrome, *TOEFL* — Test of

English as a Foreign Language, *TESOL* — Teachers of English to Speakers of Other Languages, *WASP* — White Anglo-Saxon Protestant.

> **Task**
> I. What do the following stand for?
> 1. nilk   2. LOTAF   3. GOK
> **Key:** 1. "no income, lots of kids"   2. "lifestyle of touch and fun": It refers to people who are interested in and enjoy using touch screen digital devices, such as iTouch and iPhone.
> 3. "God only knows."
>
> II. How do you say them? What do they refer to?
> 1. sonar   2. hipar   3. colidar   4. maser   5. sofar
> **Key:** 1. /ˈsəʊnə/; sound navigation and ranging 声纳, 声波导航和测距装置
> 2. /ˈhaɪpə/; high power acquisition radar 高功率探测雷达
> 3. /ˈkəʊlɪdə/; coherent light detection and ranging 相干光探测器
> 4. /ˈmeɪzə/; microwave amplification by stimulated emission of radiation 微波激射
> 5. /ˈsəʊfə/; sound fixing and ranging 声发, 声波水下远距离定位的海岸测音设备

6.1.4 Blending

Blending, the process in which some words are formed by joining part of one word with part of another, is a minor, although fashionable, technique for forming new words. These new words such as *biopic* (biography+picture) and *camcorder* (camera+recorder) are called blends or portmanteau words. They may involve the overlapping of sounds (*motel* from *motor* and *hotel*), the overlapping of letters (*smog* from *smoke* and *fog*), or no overlapping of any kind (*breakfast*+*lunch* → *brunch*, *Oxford*+*Cambridge* → *Oxbridge*).

Most blends are formed through blending by one of the following methods:

1) The beginning of one word is added to the end of the other, e.g. automobile+home → *autome*, binary+digit → *bit*, Channel+Tunnel → *Chunnel*, dove+hawk → *dawk*, education+entertainment → *edutainment*, gleam+shimmer → *glimmer*, information+commercial → *infomercial*, simultaneous+broadcast → *simulcast*, smoke+fog → *smog*, spoon+fork → *spork*, stagnation+inflation → *stagflation*, splash+spatter → *splatter*, squirm+wriggle → *squiggle*, video+telephone → *videophone*.

2) The beginnings of two words are combined, e.g. American+Indian → *Amerind / Amerindian*, communication+satellite → *comsat*, cybernetic+organism → *cyborg*, formula+translation → *Fortran*, high+fidelity → *hi-fi*, high+technology → *hi-tech*, interconnection+network → *internet*, motor+pedal → *moped*, psychological+warfare → *psywar*, science+fiction → *sci-fi*, situation+comedy → *sitcom*, teletype+exchange → *telex*.

3) The beginning of one word is added to another word, e.g. documentary+drama → *docudrama*, emotion+icon → *emoticon*, Europe+Asia → *Eurasia*, language+sign → *lansign*, medical+care → *Medicare*, medical+chair → *medichair*, motor+town → *motown*, parachute+troop → *paratroop*, television+diagnosis → *telediagnosis*.

4) The end of one word is added to the end of another word, e.g. internet+etiquette → *netiquette*, internet+citizen → *netizen*, internet+grassroots → *netroots*, internet+espionage → *netspionage*.

5) A word is added to the end of the other, e.g. air+hotel → *airtel*, book+automobile → *bookmobile*, fact+fiction → *faction*, guess+estimate → *guesstimate*, slim+gymnastics →

slimnastics, talk+marathon→*talkathon*, travel+catalogue→*travelogue*.

6) Two words are blended around a common sequence of sounds. It may be called phonetic spelling. For example, the word *Californication*, from a song by the Red Hot Chili Peppers, is a blend of *California* and *fornication*. Other examples are as follows: high+jack → *hijack*, all correct→ *OK* → *okay*, disk jocky → *DJ* → *deejay*, master of ceremony → *MC* → *emcee*, very important person→ *VIP*→*veep*.

Words formed by blending are generally nouns, as seen above, with some exceptions. A few of them are verbs: breath+analyse→*breathalyse*, melt+weld→*meld*; while some others are adjectives: alphabetic+numeric→*alphanumeric*, fantastic+fabulous→*fantabulous*.

Blend words are words that are crunched together to form new words. Knowing the origin of each word can be of help to the spellers. When two words are combined in their entirety, the result is considered a compound word rather than a blend. For example, *bagpipe* is a compound, not a blend of *bag* and *pipe*.

Task

I. Do you happen to know the origins of the following blend words?
1. galumph   2. chortle   3. dawk   4. bit
5. telex   6. Amerind   7. Eurasia   8. moped
Key: 1. gallop+triumph   2. chuckle+snort   3. dove+hawk   4. binary+digit
5. teleprinter+exchange   6. American+Indian   7. Europe+Asia
8. motor-assisted+pedal-cycle

II. See "Extended Reading". — Miscellaneous modes. — Blends

---

6. 1. 5 Network abbreviations

Presently, people tend to encounter more frequently special abbreviations or phonetic spellings such as *b/c* for *because*, *B4* for *before*, *4-ever* for *forever* and *w/o* for *without*, which are known as network abbreviations. Those words have become so commonplace that they are finding their ways into e-mails, cellular communication and other Internet writings. Network communication has a unique style of its own, which is highly colloquial in informal situations. Luckily, network abbreviations are not very difficult to learn, for they are now so prevalent in our daily life and so colorful to attract people's attention. People, particularly netheads and cell phone holders, like to use them so often that they become easy to be remembered.

Linguistically, network abbreviations can represent words, phrases, clauses and sentences:
1) Network abbreviations stand for words:

 ADDR — address, *ASL* — age, soon, location, *B* — bad, *BF* — boyfriend, *BY* — bye-bye, *DL* — download, *EZ* — easy, *FUD* — fear, uncertainty, doubt, *FW* — forward, *GD&R* — grinning, ducking & running, *GF* — girlfriend, *GR8* — great, *ID* — identity, *L8R* — later, *MSG* — message, *PLS* — please, *PPL* — people, *PSW* — password, *R* — are, *SRI* — sorry, *THX/TKS* — thanks, *U* — you, *UR* — your, *WE* — whatever, *Y* — why.

2) Network abbreviations refer to phrases:

 AAMOF — as a matter of fact, *ADN* — any day now, *AFK* — away from keyboard, *AKA* — also known as, *AMBW* — all my best wishes, *ASAP* — as soon as possible, *BAK* — back at keyboard, *AWOL* — absent without leave, *BBL* — be back later,

BBN — bye bye now, *BFD* — big fucking deal, *BFN* — bye for now, *BOT* — back on topic, *BRB* — be right back, *B2B* — business-to-business, *B2C* — business-to-consumer, *BTW* — by the way, *BYAM* — between you and me, *CMF* — count my fingers, *CWOT* — complete waste of time, *EOD* — end of discussion, *EOT* — end of transmission, *F2F* — face to face, *F2T* — free to talk, *FAI* — frequently argued issue, *FOS* — freedom of speech, *FTTT* — from time to time, *FU* — fucked up, *FWIW* — for what it's worth, *FYA* — for your amusement, *FYI* — for your information, *GA* — go ahead, *GLG* — goofy little grin, *GTG* — got to go, *GTH* — go to hell, *HHOJ* — ha ha, only joking, *HHOK* —ha ha, only kidding, *IAC* — in any case, *IAE* — in any event, *IMCO* — in my considered opinion, *IMHO* — in my humble opinion, *IMNSHO* — in my not so humble opinion, *IMO* — in my opinion, *IOW* — in other words, *IRL* — in real life, *JAM* — just a minute, *JIC* — just in case, *JK* — just kidding, *JTLYK* — just to let you know, *KIT* — keep in touch, *KMA* — kiss my ass, *KUTGW* — keep up the good work, *LAT* — lovely and talented, *LLAP* — live long and prosper, *LMA* — last minute addition, *LOL* — laughing out loud / lots of love, *MorF* — male or female, *MOTD* — message of the day, *MOTOS* — member of the opposite sex, *NBFD* — no big fucking deal, *NBIF* — no basis in fact, *NFG* — no fucking good, *NFW* — no fucking way, *NP* — no problem, *NRN* — no reply necessary, *OBTW* — oh, by the way, *OTF* — on the floor, *OTOH* — on the other hand, *PITA* — pains in the ass, *POV* — point of view, *QOS* — quality of service, *R&N* — right and now, *ROTFL / ROFL* — rolling on the floor, laughing, *RSN* — real soon now, *SITD* — still in the dark, *SOHF* —sense of humor failure, *SorG* — straight or gay, *TBC* — to be continued, *TMI* — too much information, *TMK* — to my knowledge, *TMTT* — too much to type, *TTBOMK* — to the best of my knowledge, *TTFN* — ta ta for now, *TTYTT* — to tell you the truth, *VG* — very good, *WAG* — wild ass guess, *WEG* — wicked evil grin, *WRT* — with respect to, *WTF* — what the fuck, *WTH* — what the hell, *YA* — yet another, *YR* — yeah, right.

3) Network abbreviations represent clauses or sentences:

AFAIK — as far as I know, *BSY* — be seeing you, *CU* — see you, *CUL* — see you later, *HAND* (*HND*) — have a nice day, *HTH* — hope this helps / hit the hay, *IC* — I see, *ICQ* — I seek you, *IDK* — I don't know, *IDKY* — I don't know you, *IDTS* — I don't think so, *IHNI* — I have no idea, *ILY* — I love you, *IWBNI* — it would be nice if, *IYSS* — if you say so, *KISS* — keep it simple, stupid, *LTNS* — long time no see, *MHOTY* — my hat's off to you, *MYOB* — mind your own business, *OIC* — oh, I see, *OMG* — oh, my gosh, *PM* — pardon me, *PMFJI* — pardon me for jumping in, *Re me* — Remember me? *Sec . . .* — wait a second, *SYS* — see you soon, *TA* — thanks again, *TAFN* — that's all for now, *TIA* — thanks in advance, *TM* — trust me, *TTUL* (*TTYL*) — talk to you later, *TYVM* — thank you very much, *WB* — welcome back, *WIIWD* — what it is we do, *WYMM* — Will you marry me? *YDKM* — you don't know me, *YGBK* — you got to be kidding, *YHBT* — you have been trolled, *YHL* — you have lost, *YMMV* — your mileage may vary, *YNK* — you never know, *YOYOW* — you own your own words, *YSYD* — yeah, sure you do, *YTTT* — You telling the truth, *YWIA* — you are welcome in advance.

An increasing number of young people in the English-speaking countries love to create buzzwords, or voguish words or phrases. For example, in Britain traditional words with new meanings are prevalent such as *Brighton rock* = sock, *Britney Spears* =

beers, *daisy roots* = boots, *frog and toad* = road, *Jay Kay* = takeaway, *trouble and strife* = wife. In the United States, new words called "instant messaging-speak or IM-speak" are creeping into students' writing assignments. Examples are as follows: *chickenhead* for "an unattractive woman", *exogal* for "an extremely thin contemporary", *muffin top* for "a bulge of flesh over low-cut jeans", *prositot* for "a child dressed as a pop star", *squares* for "cigarettes", *whale tail* for "the appearance of thong underwear above the waistband of a pair of low-slung jeans or a skirt", *DLERES PCNU* for "delicious pumpkin", *I WUNT TUBAROXSTR* for "I want to be a rock star". However, most of teachers call on their students to use proper grammar and spelling when they speak and write in a world outside their social networks.

It is difficult to express emotions using regular words alone when you are on the Internet talking to someone you cannot see. People, particularly young persons, like to use emoticons, that is, combinations of symbols used to express their feelings. In some dictionaries we can find them in the pages of an introduction to "computer words", e. g. ":)" pleased and amused, ";)" wink (showing that you are making a joke), ": (" displeased or sad, ":-))" very happy, ": -0" surprised or shocked.

6.2 Back-formation

We derive such words as *burgle* and *peddle* from *burglar* and *peddler*. This process is known as back-formation and the words derived are called back-formations or back-formation words.

In the historical point of view, a number of newly coined words have entered the English lexicon in this way. Based on back-formation with such pairs as *edit/editor*, *beg/beggar*, new words *preempt* and *televise* were formed from the existing words *preemption* and *television*. Back-formation is a form of shortening in which the omitted material is or is perceived to be a formative, typically an affix. Its omission produces a new form with a meaning related to but distinct from that of the etymon. Back-formation has been a surprisingly productive source of new words.

Verbs are the part of speech most often backformed, and the etymons are often nouns in *-er, -ar, -or*: *audit* ← auditor, *barnstorm* ← barnstormer, *cobble* ← cobbler, *commentate* ← commentator, *dive-bomb* ← dive bomber, *hawk* ← hawker, *housekeep* ← housekeeper, *lase* ← laser, *name-drop* ← name-dropper, *panhandle* ← panhandler, *scavenge* ← scavenger, *stoke* ← stoker, *swindle* ← swindler, *typewrite* ← typewriter.

Other verbs are formed from action nouns, many with suffixes such as *-ion, -(a)tion* and *-ing*, but also a variety of others: *aggress* ← aggression, *appreciate* ← appreciation, *attrit* ← attrition, *automate* ← automation, *demarcate* ← demarcation, *destruct* ← destruction, *diagnose* ← diagnosis, *donate* ← donation, *emote* ← emotion, *enthuse* ← enthusiasm, *escalate* ← escalation, *extradite* ← extradition, *gangle* ← gangling, *jell* ← jelly, *negate* ← negation, *proliferate* ← proliferation, *reminisce* ← reminiscence.

Some verbs are formed from adjectives: *cose* ← cosy, *drowse* ← drowsy, *groom* ← groomy, *henpeck* ← henpecked, *isolate* ← isolated, *laze* ← lazy, *sulk* ← sulky.

Nouns are also backformed from adjectives: *greed* ← greedy, *peeve* ← peevish; and from other nouns such as *lech* ← lecher, *pup* ← puppy. Occasionally, an adjective is formed from a noun: such as *difficult* ← difficulty, and from other adjectives: *ept* ← inept, *flappable* ← unflappable.

A particular productive type of back-formation relates to the noun compounds in *-er* and *-ing, -ship, -(a)tion*: *baby-sit* ← baby-sitter, *backform* ← back-formation, *caretake* ← caretaker, *daydream* ← daydreamer, *eavesdrop* ← eavesdropping, *firebomb* ← firebomber, *free-associate* ← free association, *gatecrash* ← gatecrasher, *housekeep* ← housekeeper, *lip-read* ← lipreading, *proofread* ← proofreading, *spring-clean* ← spring-cleaning, *tape-record* ← tape recording, *window-shop* ← window-shopping, *muckrake* ← muckraking, *one-upman* ← one-upmanship, *mass-produce* ← mass-production, *self-actualize* ← self-actualization.

> **Task**
> I. Do you know the background stories of the following back-formation words?
> 1. to bant   banting   Frederick Banting
> 2. to maffick   Mafeking
> 3. to deep-freeze   "Deep Freezer"
> **Key:**
> 1. *To bant* is back-formed from *banting*, which is named after a Canadian doctor Frederick Banting.
> 2. *To maffick* is derived from *Mafeking*, which is the name of a place in South Africa.
> 3. *To deep-freeze* is a back-formation derived from "Deep Freezer", a famous business brand.
>
> II. See "Extended Reading". — Miscellaneous modes. — Back-formation

6.3　Onomatopoeia

When children start to learn English, they might happen to read the following sentences in *Watching the Storm*: "I see the lightning. *Flash! Flash! Flash!* I hear the thunder. *Crash! Crash! Crash!* I hear the wind swing the gate. *Bash! Bash! Bash!* I see raindrops falling. *Splash! Splash! Splash!* I see people running. *Dash! Dash! Dash!*" Flash, crash, bash, splash and *dash* are called onomatopoeic words associated with relative sounds. Onomatopoeia is one of the minor devices used to form echo / echoic words related to the imitation of sounds made by human beings, animals and some other things. Most of such words are highly informal or familiar.

1. Echo words to imitate sounds of people

babble — make a sound like a baby who cannot talk yet,

boohoo / boo-hoo — show that someone is crying,

chuckle — laugh quietly, especially in a private or secret way,

giggle — laugh in a nervous, excited, or silly way that is difficult to control,

grumble — say something complaining continuously in a quiet way,

ha ha / ha-ha — represent the sound of laughter,

murmur — make a soft sound, especially when speaking in a low voice,

sob — cry while breathing in sudden short bursts,

ta-ta /tæˈtɑː/ — say goodbye in an informal way,

titter — laugh quietly, especially because you are nervous or embarrassed,

whimper — make small sounds of pain, fear, or sadness,

whisper — say something very quietly so that other people cannot hear.

2. Echo words to imitate sounds of animals

apes — *gibber*; bees — *buzz*; beetles — *drone*; birds — *twitter*;

cocks — *crow*; dogs — *bark, howl, growl, whine, yelp*;

ducks — *quack*; frogs — *croak*; hens — *squawk*; kittens — *mew*;

lions — *roar*; mice — *squeak*; pigs — *grunt*; pigeons — *coo*; snakes — *hiss*.

3. Echo words to imitate sounds from nature and some other things

1) from natural phenomena: a long *roll of thunder* from the sky; the *pattering of rain* on the windshield; If thunder *growls*, it makes a low unpleasant noise.

2) from water: When the sauce starts to *bubble*, remove it from the heat. / *ebb, lap, ooze, ripple, splash, trickle*;

3) from doors, windows, etc.: The door *banged* shut. / The postman beat *a tattoo* on the window. / knocking on the door: *rat-a-tat*;

4) from ball games, etc.: *ping-pong*;

5) from clocks, watches, bells, etc.: Christmas bells were *jingling* outside. / *chink, clang, clank, clink, ding, ding-a-ling, dingdong, gangle, jangle, knelling, pealing, ring, tap, tick-tock, tink, tinkle, tinting, tolling*;

6) from guns, cannons, etc.: The heavy guns of the Red Army went off at the foot of the mountain — *Bump! Bump!* / A bullet *whined* angrily past him. / The neighbors say they heard four *shots*. / *pop, pompom, ack-ack*;

7) from objects: The dead branches broke off the tree with a *crack*. / The long rope *snapped* suddenly. / *bang, clash, clink, thump, tinkle*.

Reading Task

Read the following poem "The Cataract of Lodore" by Robert Southey (1774 – 1843), a well-known English poet in the 19th century. Pay special attention to the onomatopoetic words in the poem:

Here it comes sparkling,
And there it lies darkling,
Eddying and whisking,
Spouting and frisking,
And rattling and battling,
And guggling and struggling,
And bubbling and troubling and doubling,

And rushing and flushing and brushing and gushing,
And flapping and rapping and clapping and slapping,
And thumping and pumping and bumping and jumping,
And dashing and flashing and splashing and clashing,
And at once and all o'er with a mighty uproar,
And this way the Water comes down at Lodore.

6.4 Reduplication

Reduplication, in linguistics, is a minor morphological process by which the root or stem of a word, or part of it, is repeated, through which a new compound word is formed either by doubling an entire word (total reduplication), e.g. *tick-tick* (of a clock) or part of a word (partial reduplication), e.g. *ticktack* (of heart beating).

Reduplication is used in inflections to convey a grammatical function, such as plurality, intensification, etc., and in lexical derivation to create new words. It is often used when a speaker adopts a tone more "expressive" or figurative than ordinary speech and is also often, but not exclusively, iconic in meaning. Reduplication is the standard term for this phenomenon in linguistics and literature. English uses some kinds of reduplication, mostly for informal expressive vocabulary. There are three types:

Type 1. Rhyming reduplications: *arty-crafty, arty-farty, bow-wow, claptrap, easy-peasy, fuddy-duddy, gang-bang, hanky-panky, harum-scarum, helter-skelter, heebie-jeebies, higgledy-*

piggledy, hobnob, hocus-pocus, hoity-toity, hot-pot, hotch-potch, hurdy-gurdy, hurly-burly, hurryscurry, itsy-bitsy, itty-bitty, loosey-goosey, lovey-dovey, mumbo-jumbo, namby-pamby, nimbly-bimbly, nitty-gritty, nitwit, nosy-posy, okey-dokey, pall-mall, pee-wee, picnic, piggy-wiggy, razzle-dazzle, roly-poly, rumpy-pumpy, teeny-weeny, tidbit, walkie-talkie, willy-nilly, wingding;

Type 2. Exact reduplications (baby-talk-like): *bonbon, bye-bye, choo-choo, chop-chop, din-din, dum-dum, fifty-fifty, gee-gee, go-go, goody-goody, knock-knock, no-no, pee-pee, poo-poo, pooh-pooh, quick-quik, rah-rah, so-so, tech-tek, tsk-tsk, tuk-tuk, tut-tut, wakey-wakey, wee-wee*;

Type 3. Ablaut reduplications: *bibble-babble, chit-chat, criss-cross, dilly-dally, ding-dong, fiddle-faddle, flim-flam, flip-flop, gibble-gabble, hedge-podge, hippety-hoppety, hocus-pocus, kitcat, knick-knack, mish-mash, niddle-noddle, ping-pong, pitter-patter, prittle-prattle, riff-raff, rickrack, riprap, seesaw, shilly-shally, sing-song, splish-splash, teeny-tiny, teeter-totter, tick-tock, ticky-tacky, tip-top, tittle-tattle, wish-wash, wishy-washy, zig-zag.*

In the ablaut reduplications, the first vowel almost is always accented and the reduplicated ablaut variant of the vowel is unstressed. There is also a tendency for the first vowel to be front and the second vowel to be back.

Task
I. What are the common features of the following groups of reduplications in meaning respectively?
Group 1: knick-knack, itty-bitty, roly-poly, teeny-weeny.
Group 2: nosy-posy, piggy-wiggy, ta-ta, wee-wee.
Group 3: arty-crafty, boohoo, hurly-burly, claptrap, criss-cross, fiddle-faddle, flim-flam, hanky-panky, harum-scarum, helter-skelter, heebie-jeebies, higgledy-piggledy, hocus-pocus, hedge-podge, hoity-toity, hurry-scurry, namby-pamby, willy-nilly, wishy-washy.
Group 4: bibble-babble, dilly-dally, gibble-gabble, niddle-noddle, prittle-prattle, seesaw.
Key:
Group 1: words expressing "small";   Group 2: words for children;
Group 3: words with derogatory sense;   Group 4: words of repetition.

II. See "Extended Reading". — Miscellaneous modes. — Reduplicatives

This chapter introduces some other ways in which words are formed besides the three major ones for word building discussed in Chapter 5. Abbreviation is lexically viewed as one of the minor means in English word-formation. In this chapter, we've discussed four highly productive ways in which abbreviation is involved, i. e. clipping, initialism, acronym and blending. Clipping is one way in which we change words by shortening a word and thereby create a new one, e. g. *dormitory* — *dorm*. Initialisms and acronyms are words formed from the initial letters of words that make up a new word. Initialism is a reduction process in which initialization in words is employed, e. g. *EU* (European Union); *NBA* (National Basketball Association). With the increasing usage of English in various areas of human society over the world, more and more initialisms have been created and have come into the everyday life of English users. An acronym is a word composed of the initial letters of the words of a phrase and is pronounced as a word, e. g. *ASEAN* /ˈæsiːən/ — Association of Southeast Asian Nations. New acronyms are freely produced, especially by scientists, administrators, and particularly for names of organizations. Blends are formations in which a compound is made by *blending* one word with another, e. g. *motor+hotel* — *motel*. The last part of abbreviations is concerned with network abbreviations, including special acronyms, phonetic spellings and some newly coined buzzwords of IM-speak. Back-formation is one of the minor types for word-formation in English. *Peddle* was derived from *peddler* on the mistaken assumption that the *er* was the agentive suffix. Such words are called back-formations. Onomatopoeia is one of the minor devices used to form echo/echoic words related to the imitation of sounds made by human beings, animals and some other things, for example, *bubble, squeal, thump*. These words can also be called onomatopoetic words or imitative words. Reduplication is something like the fact that some compounds have two or more constituents that are either identical or only slightly different, e. g. *walkie-talkie, criss-cross*. Most of the reduplicatives are informal or familiar, many of which are overlapped with onomatopoetic words, e. g. *din-din* (dinner), *bow-wow* (of dog).

Further Reading

1. Spenser, A. and Zwicky, A. M. (eds). (2007). *The Handbook of Morphology*. Oxford: Blackwell Publishers.
2. Fromkin, V., et al. (2007). *An Introduction to Language, 8th edition*. Boston, MA: Thomson Wadsworth.
3. Akmajian, A., et al. (2001). *Lingnistics: An Introduction to Language and Communication, 5th edition*. MA: The MIT Press.
4. Quirk, R., et al. (1985). *A Comprehensive Grammar of the English Language*. London: Longman.

Extended Reading

Miscellaneous modes

Back-formation

Pairs of words like *advise — advisor, burgle — burglar, inspect — inspector, edit — editor*, suggest an identical relationship between the members which in the synchronic viewpoint of the ordinary language user is perfectly correct. But as a matter of historical fact, while *advisor* and *inspector* were indeed formed from *advise* and *inspect* by suffixation, we have derived *burgle* and *edit* from *burglar* and *editor*, analyzing these on the analogy of other agential nouns. This is the process known as "back-formation", and in addition to well-established items, whether from long ago (like *laze* from *lazy*) or more recently (like *televise* from *television*), new formations of this kind continue to be made. The process is particularly fruitful in creating denominal verbs. It should be noted that new formations tend to be used with some hesitation, especially in respect of the full range of verbal inflexions. For example, the textual instance cited in App I. 12 was significantly in the base form, *self-destruct*, but although clearly used as a verb, there is less obvious clash with the well-established verb *destroy* than when (as occasionally) ordinary verb inflections are added: "The organization *self-destructed* in 1985". So also we had the agential *baby-sitter* before the verb *baby-sit*, and the base form ("Will you *baby-sit* for me?") before inflected forms ("He baby-sat for them"). Other back-formations continue to display their lack of established acceptability *(They) sight-saw, *(She) housekept*.

A particularly productive type of back-formation relates to the noun compounds in *-ing* and *-er*, for example, the verbs:

  bottle-feed   brain-wash   chain-smoke   day-dream   dry-clean

fire-watch   house-hunt   house-keep   lip-read   sight-see
sleep-walk   spring-clean   window-shop

Less commonly, we have nouns from adjectives by back-formation: e. g. *polymer* from *polymeric*.

Reduplicatives

Some compounds have two or more constituents which are either identical or only slightly different, e. g. *goody-goody* (chiefly noun, " a self-consciously virtuous person ", informal). The difference between the two constituents may be in the initial consonants, as in *walkie-talkie*, or in the medial vowels, e. g. *criss-cross*. Most of the reduplicatives are highly informal or familiar, and many belong to the sphere of child-parent talk, e. g. *din-din* ("dinner"). The most common uses of reduplicatives (sometimes called "jingles") are:

[i] to imitate sounds, e. g. *rat-a-tat* (knocking on door), *tick-tock* (of clock), *ha ha* (of laughter), *bow-wow* (of dog);

[ii] to suggest alternating movements, e. g. *seesaw, flip-flop, ping-pong*;

[iii] to disparage by suggesting instability, nonsense, insincerity, vacillation, etc. : *higgledy-piggledy, hocus-pocus, wishy-washy, dilly-dally, shilly-shally*;

[iv] to intensify, e. g. *teeny-weeny, tip-top*;

...

Blends

As the term suggests, blends are formations in which a compound is made by "blending" one word with another. Enough of each is normally retained so that the complex whole remains fairly readily analyzable. To this end also, and preserving the normal attributes of the compound such that the end-part is the thematic base to which the new initial part is related, the blend tends to have as a whole the prosodic shape of the untruncated end-part. Thus on the basis of *ho'tel* we preface enough of *motor* both to achieve the new contrast with *hotel* (a hotel specially equipped for the needs of motoring guests), and to achieve the dominance of the base pattern: *mo'tel*.

So too with a special kind of *lunch* which has some of the features of *breakfast*, we have coined *brunch*; if the meal had been primarily conceived as a kind of *breakfast*, we might have had instead *'lunkfast*. Thus, we may conclude that a *spork* (first recorded in 1976) is a fork that looks like a spoon, rather than a spoon that looks like a fork (which might have given us *foon*). Note the distinction between *tigon* (where the sire is a *tiger*) and *liger* (where the sire is a *lion*). In such formations, an attempt seems to be made at matching the pragmatic position with a linguistic form.

Blending is a very productive process, especially in commercial coinages, which suggests that its rather daring playfulness is popular. Where many types of neologism are criticized adversely (e. g. as "unnecessary jargon"), blends seem rather to be enjoyed. Perhaps in consequence, many of them are short-lived or never achieve currency beyond the advertising copy in which they may originate, e. g. *swim'sation* of a *swimsuit* that will cause a *sensation, lubri'tection* of a new *lubricant* that will provide engine *protection*.

Others not merely become well-established but act as a highly productive model for new formations, cf: *'cheeseburger, 'beefburger, 'shrimpburger; washe'teria, candy'teria, luncha 'teria*, etc (and we note again that a matching in prosodic shape is a determining factor in establishing the blended form). Others again achieve a brief surge of productivity, in response to an outstanding event. In the years following the Washington Watergate scandals, the name *'Watergate* became a model for such blends, being the thematic element in items like *'Muldergate,*

'Billiegate, 'cattlegate. All of these denoted specific cases of political crisis resulting from scandalous deception connoted by the underlying *Watergate*, the whole of which (with the associations) had to be understood in each alternative formation.

Some further and more general examples:

'breathalyser	[breath+'analyser]
e'lectrocute	[electro+'execute]
'Eurovision	[European+'television]
'heliport	[helicopter+'airport]
multi'versity	[multiple+uni'versity]
'newscast	[news+'broadcast]
'paratroops	['parachute+troops]
smog	[smoke+fog]
'telecast	[television+'broadcast]
'travelogue	[travel+'catalogue]

There is rather more radical abbreviation in *bi'onic* (*biological+electronic*). Items like *bit* ("binary digit"), *interpol* ("international police"), *moped* ("motor pedal-cycle"), *telex* ("teleprinter exchange"), are outside the general pattern outlined above, both in the way in which the word fractions are made up and in the disregard for the prosody of a thematic starting-point.

— Quirk, R., et al.

Exercises

I. True or False decisions.

1. Blending is the formation of new words by combining parts of two words or a word plus a part of another word. ( )
2. Clipping, a way of making a word, is to shorten a longer word by cutting a part off the original and adding a new part to the original. ( )
3. Words formed through acronymy are called initialisms or acronyms, depending on the spelling of the new words. ( )
4. Back-formation is the method of creating words by removing the supposed suffixes. ( )
5. Motel is formed through clipping. ( )

II. Fill in the blanks with proper words according to the first letters given.

Acronym

An acronym (pronounced AK-ruh-nihm, from Greek acro — in the sense of extreme or tip and onyma or name) is an a___1___ of several words in such a way that the abbreviation itself forms a word. According to Webster's, the word doesn't have to already exist; it can be a new word. Webster's cites "snafu" and "radar", two terms of World War Two vintage, as examples. Implicit is the idea that the new word has to be pronounceable and ideally easy to remember.

Frequently, acronyms are forms that use e___2___ words (and sometimes the acronym is invented first and the phrase name represented is designed to fit the acronym). Here are some examples of acronyms that use existing words: BASIC (Beginner's All-Purpose Symbolic

I __3__ Code), NOW (National Organization for Women), WHO (World Health Organization).

Abbreviations that use the f __4__ letter of each word in a phrase are sometimes referred to as initialisms. Initialisms can be but are not always acronyms. AT&T, BT, CBS, CNN, IBM and NBC are initialisms that are not acronyms. Many acronym lists you'll see are really lists of acronyms and initialisms or just lists of abbreviations. (Note that abbreviations include shortened words like "esp." for "especially" as well as shortened phrases.)

Summing up:

An abbreviation is a s __5__ of a word or a phrase.

An acronym is an abbreviation that forms a word.

An initialism is an abbreviation that uses the first letter of each word in the phrase (thus, some but not all initialisms are acronyms).

Furthermore:

An acronym so familiar that no one remembers what it stands for is called an a __6__. (For example, few people know that COBOL stands for Common Business O __7__ Language.)

An acronym in which one of the letters stands for the actual word abbreviated therein is called a r __8__ acronym. (For example, VISA is said to stand for VISA International Service Association.)

An acronym in which the short form was original and words made up to stand for it afterwards is called a b __9__. (For example, SOS was originally chosen as a distress signal because it lent itself well to Morse code. Long versions, including Save Our Ship and Save Our Souls, came later.)

An acronym whose letters spell a word meaningful in the context of the term it stands for is called an a __10__. (For example, BASIC, which stands for Beginner's All-purpose Symbolic Instruction Code, is a very simple programming language.)

1. _____   2. _____   3. _____   4. _____   5. _____
6. _____   7. _____   8. _____   9. _____   10. _____

III. Read the following passage and fill in the appropriate words with the help of the first letters given.

Back-formation

Sometimes a root word looks to the untrained eye like a combination of a r __1__ and one or more "a __2__" — that is, prefixes or suffixes. For instance, some nouns ending in -ar, -er, or -or seem to be made up of a v __3__ with a suffix on the end: *burglar*, for example, seems to mean "one who burgles," and *scavenger* seems to come from *scavenge*. Historically, though, it's the other way round: the "simple" or "root" forms are actually derived from the longer words. There's also the word p __4__, which seems to be the plural of pea — in fact the original word was *pease* (as in "pease-porridge hot"), a mass noun, and only later did people assume that if you could have peas, you must be able to have a pea. People looked at the word *sleazy* and thought they at the end were turning the noun *sleaze* into an a __5__ — the way *frosty* comes from *frost* or *wealthy* comes from *wealth* — but in fact there was no noun *sleaze* until after there was an adjective *sleazy*.

The resulting words are called back-formations. Here's a list of the more common ones, far from complete: *accrete* (from accretion), *destruct* (from destruction), *diagnose* (from diagnosis), *edit* (from editor), *emote* (from emotion), *enthuse* (from e __6__), *escalate* (from escalator), *flab* (from f 7), *funk* (from funky), *injure* (from injury), *intuit* (from intuition), *kidnap* (from kidnapper), *orate* (from oration), *peddle* (from peddler), *televise* (from television) and *tweeze* (from tweezers).

These back-formations aren't necessarily wrong; most of those above are now part of S 8 English. And of course some can be used for c 9 effect: you might say someone is *gruntled*, for instance, or *ept*, or *chalant*. (Check out Jack Winter's "How I Met My Wife", published in *The New Yorker*, for a whole bunch of back-formations from negatives.)

But when they're new, they'll strike many people as odd. L 10 , for instance — which seems to be the root of the noun *liaison* — is actually derived from it; and in America, at least, it's still struggling for acceptance. Be careful.

IV. **Translate the following sentences from English to Chinese, paying attention to onomatopoeic words.**
1. *Crack*! The stick broke in two.
2. Only the ventilator in the cellar window kept up a ceaseless *rattle*.
3. Round the corner of Crescent Bay, between the pile-up masses of broken rock, a flock of sheep came *pattering*.
4. The cock in the yard *crowed* its first round.
5. He felt as if he must shout and sing, he seemed to hear about him the *rustle* of unceasing and innumerable wings.
6. They *splashed* through the mire to the village.
7. The logs were burning *briskly* in the fire.
8. "Impertinent!" *snorted* Imalds.
9. Then a dog began to *howl* somewhere in a farm house far down the road — a long, agonized wailing, as if from fear.
10. I seldom opened my door in a winter evening without hearing it; *Hoo hoo hoo, hooner hoo*, sounded sonorously, and the first three syllables accented somewhat like *how deardo*; or sometimes *hoo hoo* only.

Chapter 7
The Meanings of English Words (1)
— Aspects of Meaning; Change of Meaning

Points for Thinking
1. Why are meanings of words hard to define?
2. Can you name some non-denotational meanings of words?
3. Are euphemisms really helpful in our communication?
4. Why are metaphor and metonymy the most basic devices in meaning shift?
5. Can meanings change through both radiation and concatenation?

... most (linguistically innocent) people have an intuition that meaning is intimately bound up with individual words; indeed, this is above all what words are for. While such an intuition seriously underestimates other aspects of meaning, it is not in itself wrong, and an adequate introduction to meaning should not shrink from the slipperiness and complexity of word meaning simply because it cannot be neatly corralled into a favored formalization.

— Cruse, D. A.

7.1 Aspects of Meaning

Whenever we are puzzled by the meanings of a word, we turn to the dictionaries for help. A dictionary seems to be the obvious place to find a record of the meanings of a word. Regardless of some special purposes, the very ordering of different definitions or senses of a word in a dictionary may imply that words have a basic or core meaning listed as the first sense, followed by peripheral meanings. But actually the understanding of the intricacies of various aspects of word meanings is not that easy. We would like to examine the most common terms associated with word meanings: denotation, reference, sense, denotational and non-denotational meanings.

7.1.1 Denotation and reference

Lyons (1977) defines the denotation of a word as "the relationship that holds between that lexeme and persons, things, places, properties, processes and activities external to the language system", actually the relation held between an abstract linguistic unit and a whole class of extra-linguistic objects. Reference is often used in a more restricted sense, as a name for the particular "things" that a word refers to in a particular utterance. Lyons points out that reference depends on concrete utterances, not on abstract sentences. Take the word *fruit* in the statement "She held a *fruit* in each hand." for example, the denotation of *fruit* is "sweet and soft edible part of a plant, containing seeds", while the reference of *fruit* is, in this particular utterance, two fruits.

So denotation is the set of potential referents of a word in a particular meaning, whereas reference is the actual subset referred to in an actual utterance.

7.1.2 Sense and reference

Sense is a relationship which is internal to the language system. It is what can be simply called the meaning of "meaning". The sense of a word is "a relationship between the words or expressions of a single language" (Lyons, 1977). Still take the word *fruit* as an example: there are many readings conventionally associated with the word. Apart from the basic meaning, we also have a technical meaning "the part of a plant, bush, or tree that contains the seeds"; in *fruits of nature*, the meaning is more general, as it refers to "everything that grows and that can be eaten by people"; and in *fruits of his work*, the meaning figuratively refers to the "result or outcome of an action". Each of these readings constitutes a separate sense of *fruit*, and each sense may be thought of as a set of things in the outside world.

The difference between sense and reference is that every word that has meaning has sense but not every word has reference. Many words do not refer to anything in the world but do have senses, e.g. *but, and, yes, no, if* and *however*.

7.1.3 Denotational and non-denotational meaning

The denotational meaning of a word is also named as its denotative, referential, descriptive, cognitive or logical meaning. It refers to the relationship between a linguistic sign and its referent. The denotational meaning is the basic concept of the word, comparatively stable. It is usually the meaning we grasp first when we learn a word. In "His *mother* is a doctor", the word *mother* means "a female parent of a child or animal" which is unmistakable to anyone who speaks English.

A word also contains non-denotational types of meaning. They constitute the additional properties of a word. They may be of specific emotive values, stylistic overtones or pragmatic values. They are all the meanings associated with the word. We shall talk about four types of non-denotational meanings of the word: connotative meaning, affective meaning, stylistic meaning and collocative meaning.

1. Connotative meaning

The connotative meaning of a word is the meaning over and above its denotational meaning. Compare the words *home* and *house*: both can be defined conceptually by the feature "place of residence for human beings". But to most people, *home* stands for something more than *house*. It also brings up an association of family, love, affection, security, etc. This is the connotative meaning of the word *home*, and is generally shared by people of the same cultural or social background.

However, with people from different cultures, certain words may give rise to quite different connotations. The word *dragon*, for example, is associated with the connotations of power, prosperity, blessing, good fortune, majesty that an emperor or a king may enjoy in Chinese culture, but it is linked with violence, evilness and fierceness of a monster in English culture.

Connotative meanings also vary widely within the same culture. The same word *mother* may vary greatly from child to child. Their reactions to the word are dependent on their personal experiences with *mother* who may have struck them as kind or indifferent, loving or intimidating, etc. In this sense, connotative meaning is personal.

Information Box

Different Connotative Meanings of the Color Words

	red	yellow	blue	white	black
Chinese	loyal	royal	crafty	treacherous	just
English	fiery	coward	depressed	pure	evil

2. Affective meaning

Affective meaning expresses the speaker's attitude or emotion. Most English words are neutral in affective meaning but some words do explicitly display amelioration or pejoration of the speakers. Words with positive overtones are used to show approval or appreciation such as *famous, firmness, painstaking, slim* while *notorious, obstinacy, pedantic, skinny* are words with negative overtones showing disapproval or contempt.

The affective meaning of a word is perhaps conveyed by all the exclamatory words like *oh* for "expressing a strong emotion or to emphasize what you think about something", *goodness* for "surprise or sometimes angry", *pshaw* for "annoyance, disapproval or disagreement" and *hurrah* for "showing that you are pleased".

The affective meaning may vary from culture to culture and from individual to individual. Sometimes, it relies on the context to decide the ameliorative or pejorative meanings of the word, for example:

The men were drunk, *aggressive* and looking for a fight.

A successful businessman has to be *aggressive*.

It was alleged that they had *plotted* to blow up the White House.

He was already bent over the table, *plotting* a new course.

Aggressive in the first sentence conveys a disapproving sense "behaving in a threatening way as if to fight or attack someone" while in the second sentence, it conveys an approving sense "someone is very determined to succeed or to get what he wants"; similarly, *plot* in the first use means "to make a secret plan to harm a person or organization" which is pejorative whereas in the second use of "to mark, calculate or follow the position of a moving aircraft or ship", it is more neutral.

3. Stylistic meaning

Stylistic meaning refers to varying degrees of formality and status of words in the language. It is closely associated with synonyms and the concept of register, that is, it depends on the type of situation, the addresser or the addressee, the location and the topic to be discussed, etc. Many synonymous words can be divided into different stylistic dimensions marked as "formal", "informal", "slang", "regional dialect" and "social dialect".

In daily English use, most people are not so careful as to make precise distinctions among a group of synonymous words. We simply divide words into "formal" and "informal" or sometimes "formal", "general" and "informal". In the following groups, the formality degree of the words increases from left to right:

sack	*fire*	dismiss
mate	*friend*	companion
chap	*man*	gentleman
daddy	*father*	male parent

Slang is an ever-changing set of colloquial words and phrases generally considered distinct from and socially lower than the standard language. It is used to establish or reinforce social identity especially within a group or with a trend or fashion in society at large. Some very familiar slangs are: *to kick the bucket* (to die), *cool* (very good), *hot* (impressive or sexually exciting), *a bimbo* (an attractive but unintelligent young woman), *crack* (a form of cocaine) and *green* (US dollar). The following conversations contain some of the commonly used slang in contemporary American English.

Ex. 1 — Do you need any help with the assignment?
— No, I'm *all set*.

All set, a colloquial phrase with high frequency of usage means I'm good or I'm ready or No, thanks, I'm fine.

Ex. 2 — *Dude*, I have been trying to reach you for 3 days.

Dude is a term Americans use to address other male individuals.

Ex. 3 — Chris loved to *pig out* at Chipotle during the semester.
— Yeah, he loved chili food.

Pig out, just as its name suggests, is used to describe an over-eating person.

Ex. 4 — That assignment's really horrible.
— Yeah, *no kidding*.

No kidding here means "Correct, I know that."

Regional dialects and social dialects are both related to the users. People in different regions or from different social classes use different words to refer to the same thing. So, people eat *sweets* and use *washroom* in British English, but *candies* and *bathroom* in American English and *lollies* and *toilet* in Australian English. Even in British English, we also have regional dialects as England English and Scottish English, so *a small girl* in England English is *a wee lass* in Scottish English.

Social dialects give people the label of the class they belong to. Upper-class people use the words *mackintosh*, *house*, *rich* and *lavatory paper*, for instance, while the middle classes frequently say *raincoat*, *home*, *wealthy* and *toilet paper*. The following examples show how the upper-class speak differently from the lower-class.

Ex. 1 Darling, please stop being *beastly* to your sister. (horrible)

Ex. 2 You're *jolly* well going to write your thank-you letters whether you like it or not. (very)

Ex. 3 I am feeling rather *tight* now. (drunk)

Ex. 4 There's no need to fly into a *bate* just because I confiscated your horse. (bad mood)

Ex. 5 It's been *yonks* since I wore my tiara. (ages)

Ex. 6 I've been feeling *seedy* all morning. (ill)

Ex. 7 I know it's a *bind*, but you may have to sell one of your castles. (problematic situation)

4. Collocative meaning

Collocative meaning consists of the association a word acquires on account of the meanings of words which tend to occur in its environment. That is, part of the word meaning is closely related to the words it co-occurs with. *Suspicious* as in *a suspicious woman* means the woman is thinking that someone might be guilty of doing something wrong or dishonest, but in *a suspicious character*, it means the character makes you think that something bad or illegal is happening. So the meaning of the word *suspicious* is partly determined by the words it collocates with.

The collocative meaning of a word is frequently overlooked by non-native English users. Take Chinese learners for example. We use the word *large* quite at will. According to a corpus study of Chinese learners, *large* is used to collocate with *amount, sum, number, scale, population, money, costs, progress, areas, school, mistake, part, improvement, country, attention, harm, knowledge, practice, change* and *problem*. But actually *large* does not collocate with *problem, improvement, knowledge, change, mistake, cost, practice* in the native use. The idiomatic expressions are *major problem, marked improvement, extensive knowledge, dramatic change, serious mistake, high cost* and *a lot of practice*.

The study of denotational and non-denotational meanings is important in determining the word meaning in a given context. Of course, as D. Bolinger (1980) said, "... meanings are as elusive as a piece of wet soap in a bathtub", the understanding of word meanings calls for a panoramic view.

Task
How do you say it?
大问题＿＿＿＿＿＿＿　　大变化＿＿＿＿＿＿＿　　大改进＿＿＿＿＿＿＿
大规模＿＿＿＿＿＿＿　　大花费＿＿＿＿＿＿＿　　大错误＿＿＿＿＿＿＿

7.2　Change of Meaning

The meaning of a word is always changing. Every word has a variety of senses and non-denotational meanings which can be added, removed, or altered over time. The meaning change is usually processed in two ways: meaning development and meaning shift. When the new meaning developed does not change the category the original meaning belongs to, it is meaning development. For example, *carriage* originally means "horse-drawn, wheeled vehicle for hauling people", and then with the appearance of the railway, it derived a new meaning as in "railway carriage". Both the new meaning and the original meaning of the word refer to the same category. Meaning shift is different. The new meaning of a word is obtained by rhetorical devices and the meaning shifts from the literal to the figurative. The meaning shift of the word *sweet* from *sweet apple* to *sweet person* is a typical example. The literal meaning of *sweet*, "sugary", changes to the figurative meaning "kind, gentle and friendly".

7.2.1　Causes of meaning change

Basically, there are two categories of causes. The first category is traditionally termed as historical or extra-linguistic; and the second, linguistic.

1. Extra-linguistic causes

Extra-linguistic causes of semantic change can be interpreted as various changes in the life of the speech community, changes in the economic and social structure, changes of ideas, scientific concepts, ways of life, and other spheres of human activities as reflected in word meaning. In other words, extra-linguistic causes of meaning change are those connected with the evolution of the human minds and are influenced by science, politics, technical development, etc. Whenever new objects are created, new concepts and phenomena appear, and new names emerge. The ways we have for providing new names are: coining new words, borrowing foreign ones and applying some old word to a new object or notion.

Scientific advances or social changes bring about the extensions of words to new uses. The word *car* goes back to the Latin *carrus*, which used to denote "a four-wheeled wagon". In Middle English it meant "a vehicle"; in Modern English the word *car* is a general word for any vehicle, without specifying the type. Thus the name of *car* does not change, yet its content has greatly differed. The word *mill* is another case in point. When the first textile mill appeared in England, the old word *mill* was applied to these early industrial enterprises. In this way, *mill*, a Latin borrowing of the first century BC, added a new meaning to its former meaning "a building in which corn is ground into flour". The new meaning was "textile mill".

Words referring to transportation by air have experienced great modification in meaning. The term *plane* was formerly found chiefly in modest scientific contexts, as in the term *plane geometry*. But now it has a greater frequency. Similar items like *pilot* and *jet* have a considerably different meaning from that associated with these words before the age of flight.

Many words, due to the technical evolution of the society, start to denote meanings in physical and chemical terms or even in everyday words. The word *atom*, originally considered undividable, having the meaning of "a body too small to be divided", is but a philosophical term, then it gets its scientific sense as in *atomic energy*, *atomic bomb*, and now we know that it is not undividable. But as it is still "small" in a sense, we use it to mean "a very small amount of something" in daily life as in the sentence *There isn't an atom of truth in the rumor*.

Psychological factors play a basic part in meaning change, which leads to the elevation or degradation of word meanings. A high social position usually wins moral approval, and words related to it get meanings elevated, for example, *free*, *gentle* and *noble*. But at the same time, an inferior position often receives moral disapproval, or even being looked down upon, so words like *churl*, *knave* and *villain*, which are neutral in origin, are biased to mean ignoble, immoral persons. The meaning change of the word *cowboy* well illustrates the point. *Cowboy* was originally used in England with the obvious meaning "a boy who took care of cows". It may not necessarily be a boy, but indicates low status. Then in America, after the Civil War, people who learned the skills of controlling cattle are called *cowboys*. Yet they were usually poorly paid and worked under the harshest conditions. Building on this legend, *cowboy* today is still used to mean someone who is reckless, impulsive and aggressive. It can also be modified to mean someone who merely puts on airs of being tough or sophisticated: a *drugstore cowboy*.

Psychological factors can be found in words related to racism and nationalism. The word *black* used to be an insulting term for the African-Americans before the 1960s, but as blacks mounted a campaign with the slogan "Black is beautiful", the meaning of *black* became more serious, e. g. *Black English*, *Black history*, *Black studies*, *Black capitalism*, *Black nationalism*. The Englishmen always take pride of their own nation and like to show their national priority over other nations, so there are expressions in English like *to take French leave* (to leave your job without permission); *pardon my French* (say sorry for swearing); *to talk like a Dutch uncle* (to tell someone severely that you disapprove of what they have done); *Dutch auction* (a public sale at which the price is gradually reduced until someone will pay it); *Dutch courage* (courage or confidence that you get when you drink alcohol).

Psychological factors in lexical change are also frequently found in taboos. We tend to avoid direct reference to unpleasant or socially stigmatized concepts such as death, old age, illness and sexuality. Euphemism is used in this situation. Neutral or mild words take the place of stigmatized terms, like *to pass away* for "to die", *senior citizen* for "old people", *to terminate with extreme prejudice* for "to murder". Euphemisms continue to develop. Through frequent use, some euphemistic words may be regarded as too explicit, so new euphemistic terms spring up.

There are no groups in the society that can better change and influence the use of words and meanings of words than young people. Their willingness to accept and create new things and their deliberate pursuit for new interpretations give rise to a large number of new words and new meanings. *Bling bling* stands for "flashy or expensive jewellery"; *hella* is used to give emphasis to something as in "Brad Pitt is *hella* good-looking". *Hook up* means "to get romantically involved with someone"; *laters* is a short version of "see you later"; *phat*, pronounced fat, means "cool, good-looking, hot or tempting". So we hear "Catherine Zeta-Jones is really *phat*".

2. Linguistic causes

Meanings also develop due to linguistic causes. That is, certain causes lie in the language system itself. Changes of word meanings may be caused through the influence of other words, or words in the same semantic field.

Borrowing from other languages brings a lot of synonyms into the English language, which elicits the changes of word meanings. The Old English verb *steorfan* (starve) meant "to perish". When the verb *to die* was borrowed from the Scandinavian languages, these two synonyms, which were very close in their meanings, collided, and as a result, *to starve* gradually changed into its present meaning: "to die (or suffer) from hunger". *Pig*, *sheep* and *cattle* have the same experience. In Old English, these three words shared the name of animals and their meat. With the borrowing of the French words *pork*, *mutton* and *beef*, the native English words were kept only for live animals.

Some words change their meanings because of the addition or disappearance of words. The word *tide* originally includes the meaning of "time, season, hour, water current". Then with the invention of the words *time*, *season* and *hour*, *tide* only retains the meaning of "water current".

Shortening contributes another linguistic cause. When a phrase is shortened to one word, the word retains the meaning of the whole phrase. *Uniform* is used for "uniform dress", *duplicate* for "duplicate copy", and *daily* for "daily newspaper". In these instances, a single word assumes the original meaning of the phrase.

> **Task**
> What factors can cause the change of words' meanings?

7.2.2 Types of meaning development

1. Generalization

Generalization, which is also known as the enlarging, widening, extension, expansion, or broadening of meaning, is a process by which a word which originally had a specialized meaning has now become generalized or has extended to cover a broader and often less definite concept. For instance, the verb *to arrive* (French borrowing) began its life in English in the narrow meaning "to come to shore, to land". In Modern English it has greatly widened its meaning and developed to mean "to come", e.g. *to arrive* in a village, town and city, *to arrive* at a hotel, college, or theatre. The word *place* is derived from Latin *platea*, "broad street", but its meaning grew broader than the street, including "a particular city", "a business office" and "an area dedicated to a specific purpose".

There are some ways that meanings can be broadened.

Words denoting specific things applied to indicate more general things:

Word	Old Meaning	Extended Meaning
butcher	one who kills goats	one who kills animals
manuscript	hand-written script	any script
pipe	a musical wind instrument	any hollow oblong body

Words denoting concrete things applied to indicate abstract concepts:

Word	Old Meaning	Extended Meaning
grasp	to hold sth. by hand	to understand
pain	fine / punishment	sufferings
handicap	horse-race	barrier

Technical terms applied to non-specialized use:

Word	Old Meaning	Extended Meaning
alibi	a legal term	excuse
feedback	a computer term	response
montage	a film-making term	an art form

Proper names applied to refer to common things:

Word	Old Meaning	Extended Meaning
Spencer	an Earl of Spencer	a short waist-length jacket
Sandwich	an Earl of Sandwich	a form of light refreshment
Wellington	Duke of Wellington	a boot

2. Specification

Specification, known as the opposite of generalization, is the narrowing or restriction of meaning. For instance, the word *meat* originally referred to "any type of food", but comes to mean "the flesh of animals as opposed to the flesh of fish". *Deer* formerly meant "any beast", but now only refers to "a certain kind of beast". As the opposite of generalization, ways for meaning specification undergo the opposite way of generalization.

Words denoting general things applied to indicate more specific things:

Word	Old Meaning	Narrowed Meaning
stink	smell	terrible smell
starve	die	die of hunger
poison	drink	poisonous drink

Words denoting abstract concepts applied to indicate concrete things:

Word	Old Meaning	Narrowed Meaning
room	space	a part of the inside of a building
affection	emotion	a gentle feeling of love
catch	to get hold of	a hook

Common words applied to special use:

Word	Old Meaning	Narrowed Meaning
capsule	a pill	an aerospace term
acquisition	getting	a finance term
clear	to make emptier	a computer term

Common words applied to refer to proper nouns:

Word	Old Meaning	Narrowed Meaning
the City	any city	business center of London
the Prophet	any wise man	Mohammed

the Cape   any cape   the Cape of Good Hope

One more common way for the specification of word meaning is the shortening of a phrase.

microwave = microwave oven   Danish = Danish pastry
silver = silver coin   iron = an iron machine

3. Amelioration

Amelioration is the process by which a word's meaning improves or becomes elevated, coming to represent something more favorable than it originally referred to. It can also be called elevation or ascent of meaning. The word *nice* is a good example. Its original meaning was "ignorant", was then changed to "foolish" and is now elevated to mean "delightful / pleasant". When we use the words *enthusiasm*, *shrewd* or *nimble*, they are highly agreeable. But these words were all developed from meanings once unfavorable. *Enthusiasm* meant "abuse", *shrewd* was associated with "evil" or "wickedness" and *nimble* was thought to be "good at taking things without permission".

Titles or address terms are the group of words that undergo the most obvious amelioration.

Word	Old Meaning	Elevated Meaning
marshal	manservant attending horses	the highest rank in the army
lord	master of the house	baronet (aristocratic title)
knight	servant	rank below baronet
earl	man	count
governor	pilot	head of a state
minister	servant	head of the government department
chamberlain	servant	high official of royal courts
ambassador	messenger	an official in a foreign country

4. Pejoration

Pejoration is the process by which a word's meaning worsens or degenerates, coming to represent something less favorable than it originally did. It can also be termed as degradation, degeneration, deterioration or catachresis of meaning. How the word *silly* which used to mean "blessed" came to mean "silly" is really an interesting story. It can be deduced like this: since people who are blessed are often innocent, the word gradually came to mean "innocent". Some of those who are innocent might be innocent because they don't have the brains to be anything else, and some of those who are innocent might be innocent because they knowingly reject opportunities for temptation. In either case, as the more worldly-wise would take advantage of their opportunities, the innocent must therefore be foolish, which of course is the current primary meaning of the word *silly*.

The tendency of pejoration is found to have taken place in many words which were once names for the common people or for females.

Word	Old Meaning	Degenerated Meaning
villain	person who worked in a villa	evil or wicked person or scoundrel
boor	peasant	rude / ill-mannered person
churl	peasant	uncultivated or mean person
wench	country girl	prostitute
hussy	housewife	woman of low morals
quean	woman	prostitute

5. New meanings

What we mean by new meanings of a word is that new meanings are added to the existing word. This is a very economical and convenient way to express the new things or ideas accepted. Yet it still needs time to test its endurance and acceptance.

Computer technology brings us a totally new world, and we call it a *virtual* world. In this world we *visit* a *virtual* library and do *virtual* shopping. We *hit* the *icon* to *open* the program and download *data*; we *chat*, *stream* and *email* by the Internet. We *compress* the file to send it in *attachment*. If you are unlucky, the mail might be *bounced* back. Those italicized words get their new meanings due to the development of the computer science.

In the music field, new styles of art forms give names to a lot of common words, e. g. *garage* (a type of popular music played on electronic instruments, with a strong fast beat and singing), *house* (a type of dance music, usually with a fast beat, that is repeated in a very regular pattern. It is made by using special electronic instruments, such as a synthesizer, or by using a special computer program), *jam* (a song or piece of music, especially by a rap or rock group), *jungle* (a type of popular British dance music that has a fast beat and uses samples), *sample* (a small part of a song for a CD or record in a new song).

New meanings of words often start in oral or informal usages. What's *candy*? It's not sweets, but informally, "something that is entertaining or pleasant to look at, but which you do not approve of because you think it is not serious". So we say that most video games are just brain *candy*. If you hear somebody say "The guy Elaine is talking to is just her latest *crush*", you should understand that Elaine has a strong feeling of romantic love for this man.

6. Old meanings

By old meanings, we mean some meanings which either totally disappeared from the word or are no longer active in use. In the long development, most English words would lose one or two meanings. The lost meanings are called the obsolete meanings, and the old-fashioned meanings are archaic meanings. Some examples of obsolete meanings and archaic meanings are:

Word	Obsolete Meaning
merit	reward or punishment due
odds	degree of unlikeness
plate	a silver coin
point	physical condition
Word	**Archaic Meaning**
lie	to reside temporarily
nation	aggregation
offer	to make an attempt
offset	to start
remember	to remind

Archaism refers to an old-fashioned or obsolete use of a word, phrase or usage. The word *thou*, the singular form of *you*, is an archaism. *Thou* is now seen in current English usage only in literature that deliberately seeks to evoke an older style, though there are also some still-read older works that use *thou*, especially religious texts like *The King James Bible*. Archaisms are most frequently encountered in poetry, law, ritual writing and speech.

The following are some well-known phrases from *The King James Bible*. What do you think they mean?

By their fruits *ye* shall know them.

Death, where is *thy* sting?
Fell on stony ground.
How are the mighty fallen.

In terms of poetry, William Shakespeare's "Sonnet 18" is a good example to see how some of the archaic forms of verbs and pronouns were employed in the period of Middle English.

Shall I compare *thee* to a summer's day?
Thou art more lovely and more temperate:
Rough winds do shake the darling buds of May,
And summer's lease *hath* all too short a date.

Task
Find out how the following words experienced meaning change with the help of an etymology dictionary.

villain	manuscript	knight	handicap	starve	boor
ambassador	catch	silver	alibi	sandwich	clear

7. Euphemisms

Some words or expressions are used to substitute what is considered indecent, unpleasant, rude or taboo. These substitutes are called euphemisms. Euphemism is a device dictated by social conventions which are sometimes apt to be over-sensitive or seeking refinement. The word *lavatory* has produced many euphemisms, e. g. *powder room, washroom, restroom, retiring room, public comfort station, ladies', gentlemen's, water-closet, W. C. , public conveniences*.

Euphemisms are widely used in every aspect of life, but they are most frequently found in occupations and social problems, illness and death, sex and marriage life.

Many a time we marvel at the kind of grand jobs persons around us are taking, but if asked further, we discover that they are just euphemistic titles. What do you think *sanitation engineer, landscape architect, domestic engineer, plant superintendent* and *chimney consultant* really are? They are but *garbage collector, gardener, servant, foreman* and *chimney sweep*. The preference for the use of *engineer* and *consultant* is really because they give the image of a decent and prosperous job!

Poverty is an unavoidable social problem, but the euphemistic terms used can make it hard to be traced. The country only has *the low-income group, the have-nots, a man of modest means* or *a negative saver* but not *the poor*. A comic well depicts the phenomenon by saying "I used to think I was poor. Then they told me I wasn't poor, I was needy, I was deprived. Then they told me underprivileged was over used. I was disadvantaged. I still don't have a dime. But I have a great vocabulary."

As for our health, we may experience everyday *blues*, or the things *getting* us *down*. We may *look off color* or *under the weather* but we will not be ill. No one around us will contract cancer or AIDS but *long illness* or *social disease*.

The idea of death and aging sees dozens of expressions: *pass away, lose one's life, breathe one's last, go west, eternal sleep, seasoned, well-preserved, advanced in age, past their prime, senior citizen, an elder statesman, the longer living*, to name just a few.

Pregnancy is another topic calling for delicate references. We can find euphemistic substitutes for it as *in an interesting condition, in a delicate condition, in the family way, with a baby coming, big with child, expecting, eating for two, swallow a watermelon seed, learn all* about *diaper folding*, *rehearsing lullabies* and *wear the apron high*.

Furthermore, sex is a taboo topic all the time no matter in which era, country or culture, so "many euphemisms have developed to describe genitals, sexual acts, sexual body parts, and body products" (Timothy, 1999: 144). There are a series of implicit terms to replace *have sex*, e. g. *making love, sleeping together.* Typical sex-related euphemism could be divided into: menstruation (*the woman's complaint*); masturbation (*self-abuse*); birth control (*rubber*); intercourse (*hanky panky*); orgasm (*come*); body parts (*members*); and body functions (*tinkle*) (Timothy, 1999: 144).

Euphemism, currently, also prevails in politics, economy, military and diplomacy.

Euphemism is a tool which is continually exploited by politicians. A much-quoted example during media coverage of the 2003 war with Iraq was the expression *regime change*. Though alleged by politicians to be a neutral reference to "a change in leadership", it quickly became associated with the idea of overthrowing a government or regime by external military force, and imposing a new government according to the interests and/or ideas promoted by that force.

In the business field, companies are being *reengineered* and even *right-sized*; laid-off workers have to be *unassigned* for being *nonessential*; their jobs are said to be *no longer going forward*. *Downsize* is a recent example that has found broad acceptance in the language and is not particularly thought of as a deceptive attempt to smooth over the pain of large-scale firings.

The purpose of military euphemisms is to minimize defeats, destruction and the violence of war. Thus *adjustment of the front* is a nicer way of saying *retreat; air attack* is but *air support; collateral damage* is damage that is unintended or incidental to the intended outcome. The last term originated in the US military forces. To put it more obvious, *collateral damage* is nothing more than a term for "state-sponsored mass murder".

Diplomacy is a rich source for euphemisms. As diplomats often seek to minimize international tensions, they frequently camouflage both their true motives and their real failures. When we hear *their talk was frank* or *they held a serious and candid discussion*, we should know that they both present their positions, but disagree with each other. In the speech of the diplomats, there are no *poor countries* but *developing countries* or *undeveloped countries*.

7.2.3 Meaning shift

When the meanings of a word shift or transfer from the literal to the figurative, that is, by using figures of speech to express the suggested or symbolic meaning, the words experience meaning shift.

1. Metaphor

If a new meaning appears as a result of associating two objects due to their similarity, it is a metaphor. Take the word *box* for example. The meaning of *box* "a small separate enclosure forming a part of the theatre" has developed on the basis of its former meaning "a rectangular container used for packing or storing things". The two objects become associated in the speaker's minds because boxes in the earliest English theatres indeed resembled packing cases. They are enclosed on all sides and heavily curtained even on the side facing the audience so as to avoid curious or insolent stares.

Association based on similarity can be found in the outward similarity of two concrete things or between the concrete object and the abstract concept. Usually it starts with the human body as it is the most familiar thing we can use to measure many other things.

Similarity between the human body and the object:

the *head*: the *head* of cane, the *head* of an arrow, the *head* of a bed;

the *mouth*: the *mouth* of a river, the *mouth* of a pocket, the *mouth* of a bottle;

the *tooth*: the *teeth* of a saw, the *teeth* of a rake, the *teeth* of a gear;

the *eye*: the *eye* of a potato, hook and *eye*, the *eye* of a needle.

Similarity between animals and plants:

wing chair, *wings* of an airplane, the *wings* of a stage, *gooseneck* lamp, *hare* lips, the *nut* of a screw, the *root* of a hair, the *root* of the tongue, the *stem* of a glass, the *stem* of a word, shoe *tree*, a family *tree*.

The above transferences are between the concrete and the concrete, but there are also those between the concrete and the abstract.

The primary meaning of the noun *branch* is "limb or subdivision of a tree or bush". On the basis of this meaning, several more meanings are developed. One of them is "a special field of science or art", which brings us into the sphere of the abstract. The noun *bar* developing from the original meaning "extra difficulty in the horse race" to the meaning "barrier" as in *social bar, and racial bar* is another instance of the concrete — abstract shift. The concrete meaning of *stage* is a "platform on which to perform" but when it develops to mean "theatre, drama, or acting as a profession", it acquires an abstract meaning.

Meaning extension by metaphor is a natural process almost undergone by every word. Sometimes we are so familiar with the present meanings that we do not even realize that they have developed from certain meanings by means of metaphor. For example, the word *illuminate* originally meant "to light up", but has been broadened to mean "to clarify", "to edify". These meanings seem so natural as to be integral parts of the words, where senses such as "to celebrate" and "to adorn a page with designs" seem like more obvious additions. Some meanings of the words have been taken for granted so that they are simply regarded as part of the regular meanings of the words. The use of *bug* to refer to "an error in computer logic" is a metaphorical extension, but now we just regard it as a meaning ingrained in the word *bug*. The computer industry has a host of words whose meanings have been extended through such metaphors, like *mouse*, *windows* and *virus*. In conclusion, George Lakoff, a linguist and Mark Johnson, a philosopher, state in their renowned work *Metaphors We Live By* that all of us, not just poets, speak in metaphors whether we realize it or not, and metaphors not only make our thoughts more vivid and interesting but that they actually structure our perceptions and understanding.

2. Metonymy

Metonymy in meaning shift refers to the phenomenon that two objects are associated because they often appear in everyday situations, with the image of one easily accompanied by the image of the other. In the sentence *He took to the bottle*, it is *drinking* that he took to rather than the real *bottle*. *Bottle* for *drinking* is natural as it is the substitution of the container for what is contained inside.

There are many types of contiguity: the common function, material and object, container and contained, location and its government or organization.

For the common function: the *arms* of an arm-chair, the *foot* of a bed, the *leg* of a table, a good *eye* for distance, a silver *tongue*, to have a good *nose*;

For the material and the objects: *copper* (coin made of copper or bronze), *silver* (silver coins or silver money), *iron* (a heavy object with a handle on top for making clothing and cloth smooth);

For the container and contained: *bowl* (rice or food in the bowl), *kettle* (water in the kettle), *wardrobe* (the clothes that someone has);

Location and the organization: *White House* (the official home of the President of the United States), *Downing Street* (the government of Great Britain), *Hollywood* (American film industry and its products).

Contiguity sometimes originates from geographical or proper names. *China* in the sense of "dishes made of porcelain" originates from the name of the country which is believed to be the birthplace of porcelain. *Tweed*, a coarse wool cloth, gets its name from the river Tweed and *cheviot*, another kind of wool cloth, is from the Cheviot Hills in England.

Oftentimes, metonymy can serve as a kind of contextual language in daily life.

The ham sandwich wants his coffee now.

This is what can be called "café language", but is perfectly intelligible to all. A customer is momentarily distinguished by the fact that he has ordered a ham sandwich. Similar examples are:

Which's *beef pie*?

The omelet left without paying the bill.

There are frozen metonymies. Some meanings of the words are completely replaced by their metonymic meanings that their original meanings are abandoned. *Paper* comes from *papyrus*, it is the association of material for its products, but no one would remember that paper was once a plant like grass that grows in water to make paper. More examples are *book* for *boc* "material for making book" and *tally* for *talea* "material for counting". Only by the study of etymology can we discover their association.

Apart from metaphor and metonymy, some other figures of speech can also cause meaning shift.

3. Synaesthesia

Synaesthesia denotes a process whereby one sensory stimulus may evoke a stimulus in a different sensory organ. In meaning extension by synaesthesia, there is only one percept not two. That is, a word relating to one sense transfers to another sense, thus its meaning changes. In the example of *a sweet melody*, sense of taste is used to refer to sense of hearing, so the meaning of *sweet* changes to mean "melodious". By studying more examples of *sweet*, we can get different meanings as "pleasing" in *sweet smell*, "lovely" in *sweet sight*, "delicate / skilful" in *sweet touch*.

Synaesthesia is typically at work with adjectives, since adjectives denote properties in things. What is amazing is that one adjective can be used to put through five senses. The word *sharp* is such an all-round word.

sharp pepper: having a slightly bitter taste (sense of taste);

a sharp smell: irritating the nose (sense of smell);

sharp words: severe, angry and criticizing (sense of hearing);

sharp eyes: able to see and notice details very much (sense of sight);

sharp wind: very cold and severe (sense of touch).

4. Synecdoche

Synecdoche involves the substitution of the part for the whole or the whole for the part. It is sometimes regarded as a special kind of metonymy. Examples concerning a part of something for the whole are:

The ship was lost with all *hands* on board.

His parents bought him a new set of *wheels*.

Here *hands* stand for the "sailors" and *wheels* for "car". Similarly, we use *mouths to feed* for "hungry people", *white hair* for "an elderly person" and *the press* for "news media".

Examples concerning the whole of something for a part of it are:

Use your *head* to figure it out.

Michigan just passed a law addressing this problem.

In these two examples, *head* symbolizes "brain" while *Michigan* is for "the government of Michigan".

5. Onomatopoeia

Onomatopoeia is a word that imitates the sound it is describing. Two main sources of onomatopoeia in meaning shift are the sound that suggests its consequences and the sound that suggests animal noises.

Crack is a sudden quick sound like the sound of something breaking; now it denotes "a very narrow space between two things or two parts of things". *Bump* is the sound made by hitting or knocking against something; now it refers to "the area of skin that is raised up because of hitting or knocking". *Splash* is the sound of a liquid hitting something or being moved around quickly; now it also means a mark made by a liquid splashing onto something else.

Animal noises are imitated by people, e. g. *moo* for cow, *mew* for cat, *coo* for pigeon, *bow-wow* for dog, *quack* for duck, *cackle* for hen, *hum* for bee, *squeak* for mouse, *hiss* for snake.

It is interesting to note that different languages may have different animal noises for the same animal. Take the dog for example. In English we have *bow-wow* or *bark*, in Chinese *wōu-wōu*, in German *wau wau*, in Japanese *wan wan*, in Arabic *haw haw*, to name just a few.

Task

The following italicized words all experienced meaning shift from the literal to the figurative. Try to define what figure of speech is used in each case.

| the *mouth* of a river | White House | *sweet* melody | social *bar* | *splash* |
| *bump* | a good *eye* for distance | the *press* | *white* hair | *sharp* words |

7.3 Mechanisms for Meaning Change

Most words in English are polysemic with more than two meanings and the mechanisms for meaning change often consist of the following two ways, radiation and concatenation.

7.3.1 Radiation

Radiation is a process of meaning change in which there is a multiplication in the senses of a word. It can be expressed in the shape of a spider graph. That is, all the new meanings developed are independent of each other.

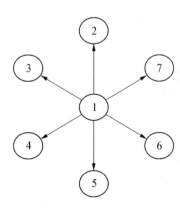

Take the example of the word *pipe*. Its primary meaning is (1) "a tube through which a liquid or gas flows, often under the ground", and from this we have (2) "a thing used for smoking tobacco"; (3) "a simple musical instrument shaped like a tube and played by blowing"; (4) "a hope, idea, plan etc. that is impossible or will probably never happen" *pipe dream*; (5) *spoken* "used to say that someone must accept what you have just said, even though they do not like it" *put that in your pipe and smoke it*; (6) bagpipes. All these meanings can exist or disappear without the influence of the other, and they are related only in one way or another with meaning (1).

7.3.2 Concatenation

Concatenation is a process in which the second meaning of the word develops from the primary meaning, while the third meaning does not start from the primary meaning but from the second meaning, thus the third meaning has little to do with the primary meaning. If it goes on, we can only find the new meaning related to the preceding meaning, but little connection can be found with the primary meaning.

The meanings of the word *candidate* has experienced concatenation. The primary meaning of *candidate* is "a man wearing a white-robe", later it means "an office seeker in white gowns", and then "a person who seeks an office", and finally "a person proposed for a place, award, etc.". The final meaning really makes the primary meaning unrecognizable.

It is true that English has never ceased to change since the day it came into being. It is truer that the change of the word meaning is the most abundant. The meaning change of a word, to some extent, is a result of the way we run our daily lives and it will never be too surprising to see new meanings keep on propping up. So it is interesting to be a sensitive observer of the English language.

Task
Do you know what radiation and concatenation are?

This chapter probes the nature of word meaning and its realization in the language. Terms of denotation, reference, sense, denotational meaning and non-denotational meaning are discussed in pairs. Four types of non-denotational meanings of words, connotative meaning, affective meaning, stylistic meaning and collocative meaning, are given more detailed illustrations. The chapter also discusses the change of meaning with the development of civilization and thoughts and a number of recognized ways in which words change in meanings. Extra-linguistic and linguistic causes both play a part in meaning change. Meanings of a word get developed mainly by generalization, specification, amelioration, pejoration, birth of new meanings and death of old meanings. Many times there are mixed changes of a word meaning, but only the dominant influence is traced and highlighted. Euphemism is categorized as a special phenomenon. Meanings of a word also shift from the literal to the figurative by means of metaphor, metonymy, synaesthesia, synecdoche and onomatopoeia. The mechanisms underpinning the change of meaning are radiation, a spider-graph shaped way, and concatenation, a chain-line development.

Further Reading

1. Schendl, H. (2003). *Historical Linguistics*. Shanghai: Foreign Language Education Press.
2. Antrushina, G. B., Afanasyeva, O. V. and Morozova, N. N. (1999). *English Lexicology*. Moscow: Drofa Publishing House.
3. Trask, R. L. (2000). *Historical Linguistics*. Beijing: Foreign Language Teaching and Research Press.

● Extended Reading

■ Why do word meanings change?

One of these is the need, mentioned at the beginning of this chapter, to adapt language to new communicative requirements. Apart from borrowing or coining new words, speakers frequently use existing words whose meanings are metaphorically or metonymically extended. Thus *torpedo* originally referred to a "flat fish ... which emits electric rays", *tank* to a "large container for holding liquids"; at least with torpedo, the new military meaning has become the primary one. When existing objects change their form but retained their basic function, the old word may, but need not, be retained as well. English *torch* has kept its original meaning, but now also refers to a "small portable electric lamp", while German has formed the new compound *Taschenlampe*, literally "pocket lamp" for the latter, but refers to the former as *Fackel*.

Another, psychological factor in semantic change is basic human tendency to emphasize and exaggerate. Constant use of words may wear off their specific meaning, so that new, more expressive terms are sought. Thus we witness a constant change of English intensifying adverbs meaning "very", from Old English *swipe* to Middle English *full* and modern *very* (Old French *verrai* "true"), *really*, *extremely*, *awfully*.

A central psychological factor in lexical change is taboo, our tendency to avoid direct reference to unpleasant or socially stigmatized concepts such as death, old age, illness and sexuality. In tabooed fields, speakers resort to the strategy of using euphemisms, i. e. neutral words for referring to stigmatized concepts, like *to pass away* for *to die*, or *to sleep with somebody*. But through frequent use the euphemistic word may itself come to be regarded as too explicit, so that new euphemistic terms are used. Tabooed fields themselves may also change. In many modern Western societies, old age, it seems, has become taboo, leading to euphemisms like *senior citizen* and *the elderly*, while we have become increasingly explicit in sexual matters. In some societies the force of taboo is so strong that neither the name of a deceased person nor any word resembling this name may be used any longer. In such speech communities a constant and rapid turnover even of basic vocabulary takes place.

Apart from such extralinguistic factors, linguistic forces behind semantic change have been proposed, though they are less easy to prove.

Among these is the fact that the vocabulary of a language is not simply a list of formally more or less related words, but is also structured into groups of semantically related words, so called semantic (or lexical) field. The meaning relations between words seem to play a major role in semantic change, as the above discussion of the changes of *bird* and *fowl* has illustrated. These two words referring to birds changed their relative status as superordinate (bird in general) and subordinate term (specific kind of bird). At least part of the vocabulary is structured in this way, such as verbs of motion, verbs of saying, etc. A meaning change of any member of a semantic field typically affects the (range of) meanings of the other members as well, and this also applies to changes in the field due to the addition or disappearance of a word.

It has frequently been observed that the borrowing of a word for which a synonymous native word exists either leads to the disappearance of one of the two or to their semantic differentiation (cf. above for *ceapman* vs. *merchant*). Thus the broad meaning of Old English *hefon* heaven and sky narrowed down to heaven as a result of the borrowing of Scandinavian *sky*, which originally meant cloud. There seems to be a tendency for languages (or rather their speakers) to avoid synonymous words for reasons of economy. A related tendency is to reduce the extent to polysemy, i. e. the attachment of too many different meanings to a single word. Finally, when two words with similar or opposite meanings become homonyms, i. e. formally identical, this may lead to communicative difficulties, often referred to as homonymic clash. Thus Old English *lœtan* to let and *lettan* to hinder evidently had almost opposite meanings, but became homonyms under the form *let*. The gradual disappearance of the meaning to hinder (which is still preserved in the phrase *without let or hindrance*) seems to be due to this clash. In general, however, homonyms are sufficiently disambiguated in the context for both forms to continue to exist side by side, cf. *meat — meet*, *waste — waist*.

■ How do word meanings change?

A basic distinction relates to the **extension** and **narrowing of meaning**. In the case of extension a word meaning becomes more general, as when English *bird*, which originally denoted only a young bird, developed to bird (in general); this change can be described as the loss of the meaning component (or semantic feature) [+young]. But meaning extension can also involve the development of an additional new word meaning. The main mechanism in this latter type of extension, and possibly in semantic change in general, is **metaphor**, which involves the transfer of a term because of an imagined similarity. Thus *neck* part of the body was metaphorically extended to refer to anything resembling a neck such as *a bottle neck*; in a similar way most words for body parts have been metaphorically extended (cf. *head of state*, *foot of a mountain*, *heart of the organization*, etc.). **Metonymy**, another mechanism of extension, rests on physical contiguity and typically uses the name of an attribute to denote the whole entity, such as *White House* for the American president, *crown* for the king or queen, or place names for specific products, like *cognac* and *jersey*.

The inverse process of narrowing occurred, for example, in English *fowl*, where the original meaning bird (in general) narrowed down to fowl, i. e. a specific kind of bird (cf. Old English *fugol* and the cognate German *Vogel*, both meaning bird); similarly *meat*, originally food, as still preserved in *mincemeat*. Furthermore, words with multiple meanings, so-called polysemes, may lose a particular meaning in the course of time.

A particular type of semantic change, known as semantic bleaching, is connected with the process of grammaticalization, as when English *will* developed from its original full verb meaning to want into the modern auxiliary *will*, which now only has grammatical meaning.

Meanings have also been classified with regard to speaker evaluation, as neutral, positive or negative, and such evaluations are also subject to change. This typically happens because of the associations words take in different uses or contexts, i. e. in the process of speech, but such associations or connotations may in time become part of the systematic meaning of a word, its denotation. This can be nicely illustrated by some English terms for the status and occupations of people. An **amelioration** or improvement of meaning has occurred in the case of *knight*, originally boy, youth, attendant, which had improved by Middle English to its modern meaning. (The German cognate *Knecht* farm-hand clearly developed in the opposite direction.) A negative evaluation or **pejoration of meaning** has developed in terms such as *knave* (Old English *cnafa* boy, servant, cf. the cognate German Knabe boy), *churl* (Old English ceorl peasant, low-ranking freeman), *villain* (Middle English feudal serf), which were once rather neutral terms for members of lower social ranks. Most of these examples mirror extra-linguistic social changes, i. e. the increasingly low status of certain social groups. In a similar way, many terms referring to women have undergone pejoration, while the corresponding terms for men have remained neutral or have improved, cf. *master* vs. *mistress*, *bachelor* vs. *spinster* — which again mirrors the traditional lower status of women in our society.

— Schendl, H.

 **Exercises**

I. What are the non-denotational meanings of the italicized words in the following sentences?
1. They *chucked* a stone at the *cops*, and then *did a bunk* with the *loot*.
2. Knowledge of inequality has stimulated envy, *ambition* and greed.
3. A *handsome man* is always attracted to a *pretty woman*.
4. My love is a red, red *rose*.

II. Work out the meanings of the word *way* in the following sentences and discuss what kind of trend is happening to the meanings of *way*.
1. We had to pick our *way* along the muddy track.
2. She showed them the *way* to do it.
3. There is quite a *way* still to go.
4. He lives somewhere Lincoln *way*.
5. Can I help you in any *way*?

III. Many technical terms are used in daily life and get their meanings extended. Find out the general meanings of the following words by matching the pairs.
1. scenario   (   )   a. any stimulus in hastening a result
2. charismatic   (   )   b. habitual
3. compulsive   (   )   c. having popular appeal
4. catalyst   (   )   d. practical opinion or body of opinions
5. syndrome   (   )   e. typical example of something
6. philosophy   (   )   f. distinctive or characteristic pattern of behavior
7. complex   (   )   g. obsession of any kind
8. interface   (   )   h. description of a possible course of events
9. bottom line   (   )   i. connection
10. paradigm   (   )   j. conclusion, clincher

IV. Point out the shortening form of the following phrases in their new meanings.
1. crescent moon   新月   _____
2. the main ocean   海洋   _____
3. a lyric poem   抒情诗   _____
4. correspondence of letters 通信   _____
5. port duties   关税   _____
6. a natural born fool   白痴   _____
7. cut-price sale   减价出售   _____
8. expecting a baby   妊娠   _____
9. doleful dumps   郁闷   _____
10. gate money   入场费   _____

11. concert of music   音乐会   _____
12. price of fare   车费   _____
13. cardinal red   深红色   _____
14. stage play   戏剧   _____
15. enormity of the crime 罪大恶极   _____

V. Study the meanings of the italics and discuss the different functions of euphemism in our life. What do you think of the phenomenon of more and more euphemisms?

1. She was *less favored by beauty*.
2. Tom's driving ability *had plenty of room for improvement*.
3. They are now at their *final rest*.
4. May I use the *restroom*?
5. Someone *borrowed money without asking* from my purse.

VI. With the illustration of the word *expire* to describe the possible process of meaning change.

First, before there were such things as tickets and licences with limited periods of validity, this just meant "die". Then it was metaphorically extended to mean "come to the end of a period of validity", which existed as a clear figurative use alongside the literal use. Nowadays, the "die" sense is quite uncommon and used literarily.

Chapter 8
The Meanings of English Words (2)
— Sense Relations

Points for Thinking
1. How would you explain the phenomenon that in a group of synonyms, it is always one word that will frequently occur to our mind and will be picked up most often?
2. Have you ever noticed that a word may have a morphological antonym and a lexical antonym? Can you tell the difference of different antonyms?
3. List all the meanings that you can think of for the lexemes *lemon* (noun). And think over how the word *lemon* gets polysemic?
4. How can you tell the difference of hyponymy relation and taxonymy relation with the group of words *animal, cow, pig, sow*?
5. In hierarchical relations, does the structuring of the vocabulary operate in a systematic way?

Traditionally the study of meaning has been understood as the study of how we "name" objects, properties, events, processes, and actions we encounter in the world around us. It is not surprising, then, that a number of terms coined on the basis of the root-onym "name" are used to cover a variety of semantic relations between words in the language.

— Stockwell, R. & Minkova, D.

Sense relations are the relations held between words within the vocabulary. They are paradigmatic and about the choice between words, the substitution of one word for another in a particular context. The two most obvious sense relations are those of "sameness" and "oppositeness", called synonymy and antonymy respectively. Other sense relations are polysemy, homonymy and hierarchical relations.

8.1 Synonymy

8.1.1 Definition

The term *synonymy* comes from the Greek word *sunonumon* meaning "having the same name". Several definitions made by different linguists are listed below:
- [Synonymy] is the case where two constituents are as similar as possible, where there is no difference in meaning between a sense of one and a sense of the other (Katz, 1972: 48).
- Synonymy is held to be sameness of meaning of different expressions (Harris, 1973: 11).
- Two words are synonyms if they can be used interchangeably in all sentence contexts (Jackson, 1988: 65).
- Words that have the same sense in a given context are synonyms (Kreidler, 1998: 10).

These definitions differ in many ways, but their striking similarity is that they all state that synonymy involves similarity of meaning. So, sets of lexical units (either word to word or word to phrase) that have identical, or nearly identical meanings are referred to as synonyms. In any of the dictionaries of synonyms, we can find a list of synonyms for a word. For example, in *Chambers Dictionary of Synonyms and Antonyms*, *approve* has as many as 37 synonyms, more or less related. Among them are *agree to, assent to, back, consent to, OK, second, support,* and *uphold*.

8.1.2 Sources of synonyms

English is particularly rich in synonyms for the historical reason that its vocabulary comes from two different sources, native words and borrowed words. Anglo-Saxon words are native words on the one side and French, Latin or Greek words are borrowed ones on the other side. Thus we have pairs of words like *rope* and *cable*, *buy* and *purchase*, *world* and *universe* and many others. There are also triples, one native, one from French and one directly from Latin: *ask, question, interrogate*; *time, age, epoch*.

We will notice the fact that the native words are generally shorter than their French or Latin synonyms. They also tend to belong to the ordinary, colloquial language, while French or Latin words apply to a more formal context.

Varieties of English also add a lot of synonyms to the English language, among which American English contributes a large part.

American English	British English
elevator	*lift*
sidewalk	*pavement*
gasoline	*petrol*
tube	*subway*

As people of these two countries accept both uses of the words, they are pairs of synonyms in English.

Synonyms are not evenly spread throughout the vocabulary. Generally speaking, synonyms are much more frequent in verbs and adjectives than in nouns. And synonyms are particularly frequent in areas which are in some way emotionally or socially sensitive for human beings, and where there is a special need to tailor language precisely to context.

8.1.3 Types of synonyms

In talking about equivalence of meaning, we may find some equivalence precise and others relative. *A big house* and *a large house* may convey the same idea of size, but in "That was a big help" and "He was in large part to blame for what had happened", the two words *big* and *large* are not interchangeable. Such cases imply that even between identifiable synonyms there is some, however slight, difference in meaning.

Synonyms can be divided into two types with different degrees of sameness. They are "strict" or "absolute" synonyms and "loose" or "relative" synonyms.

Absolute synonyms can be defined as items which are equally normal in all contexts. That is, a free choice would have no effect on the meaning, style or connotation of what is expressed. For example: *sofa: settee*, and *pullover: sweater*. But perfect synonyms are uneconomical; they will only create unnecessary redundancy in a language. Besides, finding uncontroversial pairs of absolute synonyms is no easy job. This is because in most cases even the closest synonyms will still have some slight differences in usage. Truly absolute synonyms can exist in some narrow fields. For instance, the word *gorse* is a plant defined as any evergreen shrub of the leguminous genus. It is also called *furze* or *whin*. We see this plant has several names, and we doubt that there are any subtle differences between these names. So in this example in the field of botany we come across, presumably, absolute synonyms.

Loose synonyms are synonyms different in shades of meanings. Usually the grouped synonyms have a shared basic meaning. In *Webster's Dictionary of Synonyms*, *choice*, *option*, *alternative*, *preference*, *selection*, *election* are comparable when they mean "the act or opportunity of choosing or the thing chosen". But those synonyms cannot substitute for each other in some contexts. *Choice* usually implies "the right or the privilege to choose freely from a number"; *option* stresses "a specifically given right or power to choose one from among two or more mutually exclusive actions or courses of action"; *alternative* typically stresses "restriction of choice between two mutually exclusive things"; *preference* emphasizes "the guidance of one's choice by one's bias"; *selection* implies "a wide range of choice and the need of discrimination or taste in choosing" and *election* adds to *selection* the implication of "an end or purpose which necessitates the exercises of judgment". So it is proper to use those synonyms in the following ways.

He had no *choice* in room number.

The students have no *option* in the matter of vocations.

The only *alternative* to liberty, in Patrick Henry's estimation, was death.

He said he had no *preference* and would wait until others had declared their *preferences*.

She didn't have time for the careful *selection* of a hat.

The students will make their *election* of courses at the end of the term.

8.1.4 Distinguishing synonyms

It may not be difficult to tell the difference between some synonyms when you know that they are from different varieties of English: British, American or Australian English or regional dialects within a country or an area. *Tap: faucet*, *lift: elevator* and *bonnet: hood* are synonymous pairs in British and American English; *anyway: anyroad*, *child: bairn* and *nothing: nowt* are synonymous pairs from standard British and northern British English.

Difficulty may arise when synonym groups relate to different styles or different degrees of formality of the context. *Gentleman*, *man* and *chap*; *pass away*, *die* and *pop off* are synonym trios differing in degrees of formality. *Destroy: zap*, *prison: clink* and *steal: nick* are synonymous pairs from different styles, one is from standard English and the other from slang English.

The most striking distinction comes from synonym groups with different associative meanings. They may differ either in their evaluative or emotive meanings or collocational restrictions. In the group of *well-known*, *famous*, *notorious* and *celebrated*, *notorious* bears a negative evaluative connotation, while *well-known* and *celebrated* a positive one. *Famous* is rather neutral in emotion. Emotive difference plays a great part between *politician* and *statesman*, *hide* and *conceal*, *liberty* and *freedom*. *Politician* is used with a strong suggestion of derogation or contempt while *statesman* is more positive in meaning. Similarly, *conceal* implies intention or effective hiding; *liberty* carries the implications that the power to choose what one wishes or deliverance or release from restraint or compulsion. These two have more evaluative meanings. Collocational restrictions do not seem to be a matter of meaning differences, but of the company words keep. Thus *rancid* occurs with *bacon* or *butter*, *addled* with *eggs*, *rotten* with *fruit* or *wood*, *sour* with *milk*. It is also common to find *a flock of birds*, *a herd of elephants*, *a swarm of bees*, *a shoal of fish*, *a gang of hooligans* and *a group of people*.

Distinguishing synonyms is the most difficult for language learners in their accumulation of vocabulary. It is most advisable to study both the basic meaning or denotation and the non-denotative meanings of the words. And it deserves keen observation and careful use of the words in English learning.

8.1.5 Context-dependent synonyms

As for synonyms, it is generally agreed that the common features are more salient than their differences. That is why we can make a list of synonyms in the dictionary. But in certain contexts, synonyms may contrast, and this is especially true of loose synonyms.

I *like* you, but I cannot *love* you.

The young man was *strolling* and his child was *trotting* by the side.

Romeo should *smile*, not *grin*.

He was *killed*, but I can assure you he was not *murdered*.

In related contexts, the above pairs of words clearly demonstrate that the substitution of one word for another is impossible. The context firmly binds them in their proper places. On the other hand, if two words, originally different in meaning, both fit in a particular context, they are also defined as context-dependent synonyms (Palmer, 1981). Based on this criterion, the verbs *lead* and *live* are synonyms in the given context of lead/live+a life.

Task

How can you distinguish the following pairs of synonyms?

lift: elevator _____ steal: nick _____

politician: statesman _____ famous: notorious _____

a swarm of: a flock of _____

8.2 Antonymy

8.2.1 Definition

The term *antonymy* is defined as "oppositeness of meaning"; words that are opposite in meaning are antonyms (*The Oxford English-Chinese Dictionary 2nd edition*, 2012). Oppositeness plays an important role in structuring the vocabulary of English. And the omnipresent antonyms are a key feature of everyday life. On your way out, it is impossible to ignore the instructions which tell you whether to *push* or *pull* the door, pay no attention to whether traffic lights are telling you to *stop* or *go*, and visit a public lavatory without checking which is the *gents* and which is the *ladies*. It is often the case that a pair of antonyms occur together.

8.2.2 Types of antonyms

Three types of antonyms are commonly identified: complementary antonyms, gradable antonyms and converses.

Complementary antonyms are those in an either/or relation of oppositeness, e.g. *male: female, dead: alive, true: false, win: lose*. An animate being can be described as either a *male* or a *female, dead* or *alive* but not in the middle state. The assertion of one implies the denial of the other member of the pair.

Gradable antonyms represent a more/less relation. They occur normally with a wide range of degree modifiers. Thus for pairs like *long: short, heavy: light, thick: thin, wide: narrow, expensive: cheap*, modifiers like *very/slightly/rather/quite/a bit/too* can often be found. But the modified gradable antonyms do not represent absolute values. They still need to be interpreted in relation to some reference value. It's absolutely right to discover that *a very very big mouse* is still much smaller than *a very very small elephant*. So gradable antonyms can be viewed as terms at the end-points of a continuum and these terms allow comparison.

Converse antonyms are considered to be a kind of directional opposite. For each pair of antonyms, one expresses the converse meaning of the other, e. g. a*bove: below*, *lend: borrow*, *wife: husband*.

Our office is *above* the hairdresser's.

The hairdresser's is *below* our office.

Prepositions *above* and *below* express the converse view of the directions.

Can you *lend* me $20 till Friday?

Can I *borrow* $20 from you until Friday?

Verbs *lend* and *borrow* express the converse practices.

Jane is Richard's *wife*.

Richard is Jane's *husband*.

Nouns *wife* and *husband* express the relationship in converse ways.

8.2.3 Some features of antonyms

1. Markedness

The notion of *markedness* is often applied to pairs of opposites: one term is designated as the marked term and the other as the unmarked term of the opposition. The unmarked term is usually more neutral, general and positive and can include the concept of the marked term while the marked term is often purpose-centered.

In gradable antonym pairs of adjectives, for example, to ask "How short is the street?" already assumes that the street has been identified as short. The use of *long* does not make an assumption either way. Similarly, even if it is admitted that three feet is rather low, it is still asked and answered like this:

How *high* is it?

It's three feet *high*.

*It's three feet *low*.

The noun forms of the adjective pairs bear the similar feature of markedness. In *height / lowness*, *height* is neutral. In English, it is likely that the "larger" term appears to be unmarked, but this does not appear to be a universal feature.

Task

Underline the unmarked word in the following antonym pairs.

| old: young | tall: short | long: short | heavy: light |
| wide: narrow | deep: shallow | thick: thin | high: low |

---

2. Morphological and semantic opposites of a word

Many antonyms in English words are created by adding negative affixes: *tie, untie*; *interested, disinterested*; *criminalize, decriminalize*; *union, anti-union*; *stop, non-stop*; *moral, amoral*; *normal, abnormal*; *helpful, unhelpful*. These are morphological opposites of the words. Although it is a very effective way in creating opposites, it is not at all clear why we still make up semantic opposites of a word. But it is not rare that a word has two antonyms: one is a morphological opposite and the other semantic opposite, e. g. *happy: unhappy / sad*, *kind: unkind / cruel*, *true: untrue / false*. As to the two antonyms, usually the morphological one is wider in sense than the semantic one. For example, the two antonyms of *happy* are hardly equivalents, *unhappy* describes a wider range of ways of being not happy, which can be sad, angry, disappointed and so on whereas *sad* is rather specific. In this case, *happy: unhappy* is a scale indicating more or less of a property, and *happy: sad* is at two ends of a scale for incompatible properties.

3. A word with more antonyms

The polysemous nature of a word necessarily brings more than one antonym of the word in the context, and very often it depends on the accompanying words to decide the exact meaning of the word. For the same *fresh*, it is really indispensable to decide the antonyms by considering the different collocations:

fresh bread: *stale* bread   *fresh* air: *stuffy* air
fresh flowers: *faded* flowers   *fresh* look: *tired* look

The same is true with the word *dull*:

dull weather: *sunny* weather   *dull* noise: *sharp* noise
dull pain: *acute* pain   *dull* children: *intelligent* children

This reminds us to be cautious of recklessly picking up one word in mind for all the opposites of a word used in contexts.

8. 2. 4 The use of antonyms

Antonymy is not evenly distributed among the categories of parts of speech. Most antonyms are adjectives which is just natural because qualitative characteristics are easily compared and contrasted: *deep, shallow; near, far; clean, dirty*. They can also be found among adverbs: *slowly, quickly; frequently, rarely; closely, distantly*; among verbs: *go, stay; float, sink; lose, find*; among nouns: *joy, sadness; friend, enemy; love, hatred*.

Antonyms are quite useful for stylistic purposes in writing. They are used either as balanced phrases, or as antithesis to achieve contrast and emphasis: *a matter of life and death, pro and con, back and forth*.

Welcome *joy*, and welcome *sorrow*,
Lethe's weed and Hermes' feather,
Come *to-day*, and come *to-morrow*,
I do love you both together!
I love to mark *sad* faces in fair weather;
And hear a *merry* laughter amid the thunder;
Fair and *foul* I love together.

(From *A Song of Opposites* by J. Keats)

Task
Which part of speech forms the most antonym pairs? Can they also be found in other part of speech?

8. 3 Polysemy

8. 3. 1 Definition

Polysemy is a relationship that holds between different senses of the same word. The meanings are related to each other. As a rule, polysemy is a result of one meaning being extended metaphorically over time to bear new shades of meanings. Conventionally each of these senses is numbered and listed under the head word in a dictionary. For instance, the noun *board* is said to be polysemous because it may mean: 1) a flat wide piece of wood, plastic etc. that shows a particular type of information, 2)a flat piece of wood, plastic, card etc. that one uses for a particular purpose such as cutting things on or for playing indoor games, 3)a group of people in an organization who make the rules and important decisions, 4)a long thin flat piece of wood used for making floors, walls, fences etc., 5)the meals that are provided for you when you pay to stay somewhere, 6)[plural] the stage in a theater, 7)[plural] the low wooden wall around the area in which you play ICE HOCKEY, 8)[AmE] examinations that you take in the US when you apply to a college or medical school (*Longman Dictionary of Contemporary English*, 2004).

8.3.2 Literal meaning and transferred meanings

One of the most familiar kinds of relationships between meanings is that of metaphor where a word appears to have both a "literal" meaning and one or more "transferred" meanings. The words for parts of the body provide the best illustration of metaphors. For example, we speak of the *hands* and *face* of a clock, the *foot* of a bed or a mountain, the *leg* of a chair or table, the *tongue* of a shoe, the *eye* of a needle, etc. Intuitively, we assume that words such as *eye*, *face*, *foot*, *hand*, *leg* and *tongue* are first applied to the body, from which they derive their literal senses.

Many adjectives may be used either literally for the quality they refer to or with the transferred meaning of being the source of the quality. For instance, in the literal sense, we may say that "John is *sad*" (He feels sadness.). But in the transferred sense, when we say that a book, a film or a story is *sad*, we do not imply that "it feels sadness", rather, we mean that it causes someone else to feel sad.

8.3.3 Ambiguity

In most cases, only one of the meanings of a polysemous word will fit into a given context, but occasionally ambiguity may also arise. Consider the words *engaged* and *bat* in the following contexts:

Are you *engaged*?

Look at the *bat* under the tree.

Ambiguity results from the fact that *engaged* may mean either "have arranged to do something" or "have agreed to get married", while *bat* may mean either "flying mammal" or "implement used to hit the ball in the cricket".

Despite the difficulties with polysemy, we have to admit that polysemy is an essential condition for the efficiency of the language. If it were not possible to attach several senses to a single word, this would mean a crushing burden on our memory; we would have to grasp a separate term for every conceivable "object" we might wish to talk about, and be absolutely precise in our choice of words. Consequently, polysemy must be considered as an invaluable stipulation of economy and flexibility in language.

Task
Why do we have polysemy instead of inventing more words for every new object?

8.4 Homonymy

8.4.1 Definition

Homonymy refers to a situation where we have two or more words with the same linguistic form. Homonyms are words which are identical in pronunciation and spelling, or, at least, in one of these aspects, but different in meaning. Dictionaries usually treat them as different words and give them respective main entries.

8.4.2 Types of homonyms

All homonyms share one aspect in common, that is, they have unrelated meanings. So according to their differences in spelling and sound, we can identify three types of homonyms.

Homonyms with the same sounds and spellings are termed homonyms proper, e.g. *bear* /bɛə/ "a large strong animal" and *bear* /bɛə/ "to bravely accept or deal with a painful or unpleasant situation";

Homonyms which are the same in sound but different in spelling are homophones, e.g. *sew* /səʊ/ "to use a needle and thread to join pieces of cloth together" and *sow* /səʊ/ "to plant or scatter seeds on a piece of ground";

Homonyms with the same spellings but different sounds are homographs, e.g. *minute* /ˈmɪnɪt/ "one of the 60 parts into which an hour is divided" and *minute* /maɪˈnjuːt/ "extremely small".

Another kind of division of homonyms is shown by their syntactic behavior and spelling:

Lexemes of the same syntactic category, and with the same spellings, e.g. *lap* "circuit of a course" and *lap* "part of body when sitting down";

Of the same category, but with different spellings, e.g. the verbs *ring* and *wring*;

Of different categories, but with the same spelling, e.g. the verb *keep* and the noun *keep*;

Of different categories, and with different spellings, e.g. *not*, *knot*.

8.4.3 Sources of homonyms

One source of homonyms is borrowing. A borrowed word may, in the final stage of its phonetic adaptation, duplicate in form either a native word or another borrowing. *Match*, n. "a game; a contest of skill, strength" is a native word, and *match*, n. "a slender short piece of wood used for producing fire" is a French borrowing. *Bank*, n. "shore" is a native word, and *bank*, n. "a financial institution" is an Italian borrowing.

Phonetic changes which words undergo in the course of their historical development make two or more words which were formerly pronounced differently develop identical sound forms and thus become homonyms. *Night* and *knight*, for instance, are not homonyms in Old English as the initial *k* in the second word is pronounced. The noun *sea* descends from the Old English form "sæ", and the verb *to see* from Old English "sēon".

Word-building also contributes significantly to the growth of homonymy, and the most important type is conversion. Such pairs of words as *helicopter*, n. and *to helicopter*, v.; *record*, n. and *to record*, v. are numerous in the vocabulary.

Shortening is another way by which to increase the number of homonyms, e.g. *fan*, n. in the sense of "an enthusiastic admirer of some kind of sport or of an actor, singer, etc." is a shortening produced from *fanatic*. Its homonym is a Latin borrowing *fan*, n. which denotes "an implement for waving lightly to produce a cool current of air". *Plane*, n. is a shortening for *aeroplane* and it turns out to be a homophone for *plain*, adj.

8.4.4 Polysemy or homonymy

Oftentimes, we find a word with two or more meanings, and we are puzzled as to whether it is one word with different meanings (polysemy) or two different words with the same shape (homonymy). The etymology of the word may help. If it is known that identical forms have different origins, they are treated as homonymous and given separate entries. But if it is known that they have the same origin, even if they have different meanings, they are treated as polysemic and given a single entry in the dictionary. But etymological criterion is far from satisfactory. For instance, *pupil* "in school" and *pupil* "of the eye" are usually listed as different words, so they should be homonyms, but in fact they have the same historical origin, while for the word *ear*, *ear of corn* is in no way related historically to *the ear of the body*. Most people today would regard them as the same word with different meanings, which is polysemy. So it is important to note that there is no clear-cut dividing line between polysemy and homonymy as there is often a conflict between historical criteria and present-day intuition in sorting out cases of polysemy and homonymy.

8.4.5 Application of homonymy

The very characteristic of either the same spelling or the same pronunciation of homonyms makes them one of the most important sources of popular humor.

— "Waiter!"
— "Yes, sir."
— "What's this?"
— "It's *bean* soup, sir."
— "Never mind what it has *been*. I want to know what it is now."

Bean, n. and *been*, p. p. of *to be* are homophones. So the joke is based on a pun which makes use of the same sound.

Officer (to driver in a parked car): Don't you see that sign "*Fine* for parking"?

Driver: Yes, officer, I see and agree with it.

The driver is taking advantage of the homonyms *fine*, v. (to make someone pay money as a punishment) for *fine*, adj. (all right).

Enjoy it!
1. Father (reprovingly): "Do you know what happens to liars when they die?"
   Johnny: "Yes, sir, they lie still."
2. 7 days, without 7-Up, makes one weak.

8.4.6 Elimination of homonym clashes

In the process of communication, it seems that homonyms sometimes lead to confusion and misunderstanding. Yet in practice, there is far less risk of confusion, because most homonyms belong to different word classes. *Knows* (verb) and *nose* (noun), *rights* (noun) and *writes* (verb) fall into two different word classes. Besides, when in context, many homonyms are no longer problematic as it is difficult to have a context in which both members of a given pair might occur interchangeably.

Another easy and simple way to eliminate homonym clashes is to write down the words used. Homonymy in the language as a whole, spoken as well as written, is reduced by writing conventions.

8.5 Hierarchical Relations

Words can be related hierarchically. Some words have a more general meaning, while others have a more specific meaning in referring to the same entity. For example, *bird* and *hawk* may be used to refer to the same object, but *hawk* is a more specific term of the object than *bird*. Indeed, *bird* may be used to refer to objects that are not *hawks*, but which share with them the essential features of "a creature with wings and feathers, lay eggs, can usually fly". Similarly, my *finger* hurts and my *nail* hurts may refer to the same phenomenon, but the second is merely a more specific way of locating the pain.

For hierarchical relations we can divide them into hyponymy, taxonomy and meronymy.

8.5.1 Hyponymy

Hyponymy is a relation of inclusion. *Daffodil* is a hyponym of *flower*. Logically, if something is a *daffodil*, it must be a *flower* because the meaning of *flower* is embedded in *daffodil*. So we say that *daffodil* is a hyponym of *flower*, and conversely, that *flower* is the superordinate of *daffodil*.

Another special hyponymy relation is the ADULT-YOUNG relation, as shown in the examples:

dog	puppy
cat	kitten
cow	calf
pig	piglet

Hyponymy is one of the most important structuring relations in the vocabulary of a language. It is most evident in the classification of natural phenomena, e.g.

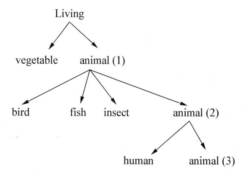

This is by no means a complete hyponymy, but it can illustrate some features of hyponymy relation. First, hyponymy is a transitive relation: *animal (1)* is a hyponym of *living*, but is in turn the superordinate to its hyponyms *bird*, *fish*, *insect*, etc. So, it can be deduced that *insect* is *living*. Second, the same term may appear in several places in the hierarchy as it is polysemic. Thus, *animal (1)* is used in contrast with *vegetable* to include *birds, fishes, insects* as well as *mammals*; *animal (2)* in the sense of "mammal" to contrast with *birds, fishes* and *insects*, to include both *humans* and *beasts*; *animal (3)* in the sense of "beast" to contrast with *human*. Thus it occurs three times in the hierarchical classification of nature.

When we are more interested in the co-hyponyms of the hierarchical relation to make all-rounded inclusion, oddity appears to the superordinate terms. For the members of *round*, *square*, *oval*, and *sweet*, *bitter*, *sour*, *salty*, the superordinate terms we find for them are *shape* and *taste*. But actually they are adjective hyponyms included in noun superordinates. Once more, for *shirt*, *sweater*, *overcoat* with the superordinate term *clothing* and *table*, *wardrobe* and *chair* with the superordinate term *furniture*, they are all countable hyponyms included in uncountable superordinates. These are what we called quasi-hyponymy.

8.5.2 Taxonymy

Taxonymy is often regarded as a sub-type of hyponymy, which can be framed as:

An X is a kind/type of Y.

X is the taxonym and Y is the superordinate. So if X is a taxonym of Y, the result is normal:

A *rose* is a type of *flower*.

A *pear* is a kind of *fruit*.

However, as a sub-type of hyponymy, there are a number of cases that are only normal in the hyponymy description but not in taxonymy:

A stallion is a horse.

*A stallion is a type of horse.

A queen is a woman.

*A queen is a kind of woman.

The question of what distinguishes taxonyms from other hyponyms is not an easy one to answer. It appears that a taxonym must engage with the meaning of its superordinate in a particular way by further specifying what is distinctive about it. *A stallion is a type of horse. Stallion* specifies sex, but this is not a specification of what distinguishes horses from other animals. And the key distinctive characteristic of a woman in the class of human beings is her sex rather than her title, so *queen* does not serve to specify this.

Taxonymy is a transitive relation: if A is a taxonym of B, and B a taxonym of C, then A is necessarily a taxonym of C. So, from the taxonymy tree of plant, we can read:

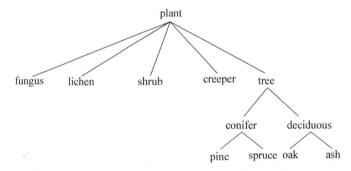

Pine is a kind of *conifer*, which is a kind of *tree*, which is a kind of *plant*.

Co-taxonyms are strict incompatibles, and they are supposed to share an equal rank with the others. Thus *fungus*, *lichen*, *shrub*, *creeper*, *tree* are all co-taxonyms of *plant*; *hammer*, *saw*, *chisel*, *ax* are all co-taxonyms of *tool*. Sometimes, it is really hard to tell which one is a more typical example of a plant or a tool. But in some other cases, we do have some more typical or prototypical taxonyms. *Apple* and *olive* are co-taxonyms of *fruit*, but it is likely that *apple* is closer to our judgment of a standard *fruit*. It occurs far more early in our mind than *olive* when we are asked to name some fruits.

If possible, with a distinctive feature of division, we may have endless numbers of taxonymy layers. But for the lexical taxonymy, we usually include no more than five layers, among which there must be one layer that includes the basic term. For example, to draw the taxonymy tree of *cow*, we can have many layers: *organism*, *animal*, *mammal*, *placental mammal*, *hoofed mammal*, *cloven-hoofed mammal*, *bovine*, *cow*, etc. But when we are asked, "What is a *cow*?", we would intuitively answer "A cow is a kind of *animal*" rather than to say "A cow is a kind of *mammal*" or "A cow is a kind of *hoofed animal*". So *animal* should be a layer listed in the taxonymy tree, no matter how many layers we are going to list. This way of inference is in accord with our thinking habit and cognitive structure.

8.5.3 Meronymy

Meronymy is used to describe a part-whole relationship between lexical items. We can identify this relationship by using sentence frames like:

X is part of Y. / Y has X.

Thus in the case of *finger*, *hand*, we can say *A finger is part of hand*, or *A hand has fingers*. Meronymy relation can be presented by a hierarchy of superordinate and meronym terms, e. g.

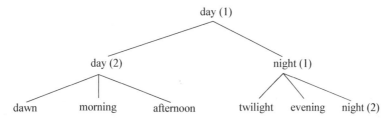

Reading from the bottom of the hierarchy, *twilight*, *evening* and *night (2)* are meronyms of *night (1)*; *night (1)* and *day (2)* are meronyms of *day (1)*. Both *day* and *night* serve as superordinate terms and meronym terms.

According to the necessity and integrality of the part-whole relation, we can divide the parts into the necessary meronym and the optional meronym. For instance, although *beard* is a part of *face*, it is not necessary to *face*. On the other hand, *fingers* are necessary to *hand*. Thus *beard* is only the optional meronym of *face* while *fingers* are necessary meronym to *hand*. More examples of necessary meronyms are *engineer, car; lens, telescope*; optional meronyms are *collar, shirt; cellar, house*.

8.5.4 Features of hierarchical relations

As a hierarchical relation, hyponymy is an unproblematical transitive relation. X is Y, and Y is Z, that X is Z. So, a *spaniel* is necessarily a *dog*, and a *dog* necessarily an *animal*, that a *spaniel* is necessarily an *animal*. Taxonymy is also transitive though there are some exceptions. It's odd to say that *spaniel* is a type of *animal*. Meronymy is somewhat complicated as it may be transitive or may not be. A transitive example is: *nail* is a meronym of *finger*, and *finger* of *hand*. We can see that *nail* is a meronym of *hand*, for we can say "A *hand* has *nails*". A non-transitive example is: *pane* is a meronym of *window* (A *window* has a *pane*), and *window* of *room* (A *room* has a *window*); but *pane* is not a meronym of *room*, for we can't say "A *room* has a *pane*."

Part-whole relations exist among many words in the vocabulary. A *plant* has *root, stem, leaf, flower, bud, shoot*; a *man* is made up of *head, hand, body, foot*. Most human artifacts are made up of parts, which we usually want to label with their own terms. A *knife* consists of a *blade* and a *handle*. A *fountain pen* is made up of *a cap, a barrel, a nib, a reservoir* (for the ink); the *cap* is made up of the *cap* itself and the *clip*. Most obviously, the meronym relation applies to entities that have concrete reference.

When talking about systematic hierarchical relationship in nature, we can distinguish two types of classificatory systems: 1) those commonly known to most people, the folk, who live in the same community and speak the same variety of a language; and 2) those known primarily to specialists such as scientists or experts. For ordinary language users, we do not neatly classify and analyze things in the systematic way that scholars and scientists attempt to do. But what's certain is that hierarchical relationship is a very efficient way for us to get things classified and meanings related.

> **Information Box**
>
> The most inclusive dictionary about the hierarchical relations is *The Oxford-Duden Pictorial Dictionary* which is a direct translation from the German version of *Bildwörterbuch*. It gives 11 catagories, namely, Atom, Universe, Earth; Man and his Social Environment; Nature as Environment, Agriculture and Forestry; Trades, Crafts, and Industry; Printing Industry; Transport, Communications, and Information Technology; Office, Bank, Stock Exchange; Community; Recreation, Games, Sport; Entertainment, Culture, and Art; Animals and Plants.

This chapter seeks to explore the various types of sense relations that exist between words, both within the vocabulary as a whole and in use in sentences. It is mainly about paradigmatic relations that hold between items which can occupy the same position in a grammatical structure. Synonyms are words bearing at least one similarity in sense and the large amount of synonyms in English causes difficulties in distinguishing one from the others. Antonyms are about opposites, and what is interesting about them is their markedness, morphological and semantic opposites. Most English words are polysemic and ambiguity occurs frequently. Homonyms are words identical in sound and spelling, or at least, in one of these aspects, but different in meaning. Homonyms are used to achieve humorous effect. Hierarchical relations include hyponymy, taxonomy and meronymy. It is a very efficient way for us to get things classified and meanings related. Hyponymy is a relation of inclusion; taxonymy is often regarded as a sub-type of hyponymy, which can be framed as a kind/type of; meronymy is used to describe a part-whole relationship.

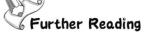

Further Reading

1. Cruse, D. A. (1986). *Lexical Semantics*. Cambridge: Cambridge University Press.
2. Cruse, D. A. (2004). *Meaning in Language: An Introduction to Semantics and Pragmatics*. New York: Oxford University Press.
3. Jackson, H. and Ze Amvela, E. (2000). *Words, Meaning and Vocabulary: An Introduction to Modern English Lexicology*. Trowbridge: The Cromwell Press.

● Extended Reading

■ Types of synonyms

Many linguists do take this position and make a distinction between "strict" or "absolute" (Cruse, 1986) synonymy and "loose" synonymy. In the strict sense, two words that are synonyms would have to be interchangeable in all their possible contexts of use: a free choice would exist for a speaker or writer of either one or the other word in any given context. The choice would have no effect on the meaning, style or connotation of what was being said or written. Linguists argue that such strict synonymy does not exist, or that, if it does, it exists only as semantic change is taking place.

Strict synonymy is uneconomical; it creates unnecessary redundancy in a language. To have a completely free choice between two words for a particular context is a luxury that we can well do without. Indeed, it would appear that where, historically, two words have been in danger of becoming strict synonyms, one of them has either changed its meaning in some way or fallen out of use. For example, when the word *sky* was borrowed from Old Norse into English, it came into competition with the native English word *heaven*, both words denoting both the physical firmament and the spiritual realm of God and the angels. In due course, *sky* came to denote just the physical, and *heaven* just the spiritual; though each is still sometimes used in the context where the other would normally be expected. Similarly, when *spirit* was borrowed from French (ultimately from Latin), it was in competition with the native English *ghost* (compare: *Holy Ghost*, *Holy Spirit*): spirit has taken over as the term with the more general meaning, and *ghost* is more or less restricted to "disembodied spirit" meanings.

When we speak of synonymy, then, we mean varying degrees of "loose" synonymy, where we identify not only a significant overlap in meaning between two words, but also some contexts at least where they cannot substitute for each other. Take the synonyms *find* and *discover*, they are substitutable in the context *Lydia found/discovered the ball behind the garden shed*, but not in the context *Marie Curie discovered radium in 1898* or in the context *Franz found it easy to compose sonatas*. As is evident in this case, synonyms may be substitutable where their meaning overlaps, but where a meaning falls outside of the shared area (*discover* = "be the first one to come across something", *find* = "experience something in some way") one cannot be used instead of the other. Synonyms may overlap in meaning to a greater or lesser degree, though it is not clear how this might be measured, nor whether there is a limit at which the notion of synonymy becomes meaningless.

Types of antonyms

Oppositeness is perhaps not such a pervasive meaning relation in the vocabulary of English as synonymy, but it has an important role in structuring the vocabulary of English. This is especially so in the adjective word class, where a good many words occur in antonymous pairs, e. g. *long — short, wide — narrow, new — old, rough — smooth, light — dark, straight — crooked, deep — shallow, fast — slow*. While antonymy is typically found among adjectives it is not restricted to this word class: *bring — take* (verbs), *death — life* (nouns), *noisily — quietly* (adverbs), *above — below* (prepositions), *after — before* (conjunctions or prepositions).

Besides having morphologically unrelated antonyms, as in the examples above, English can also derive antonyms by means of prefixes and suffixes. Negative prefixes such as *dis-*, *un-* or *in-* may derive an antonym from the positive root, e. g. *dishonest, unsympathetic, infertile*. Compare also: *encourage — discourage* but *entangle — disentangle, increase — decrease, include — exclude*. Similarly, the suffixes *-ful*, *-less* may derive pairs of antonyms, e. g. *useful — useless, thoughtful — thoughtless*, but this is by no means always the case, e. g. *hopeful* and *hopeless* are not antonyms, *grateful* has no counterpart **grateless*, *selfless* has no counterpart **selfful*.

Unlike synonymy, antonymy covers a number of different types of oppositeness of meaning. Three types are commonly identified: gradable antonyms, contradictory or complementary antonyms, and converses. Antonym pairs of these types express oppositeness in rather different ways, though it is not clear that we as speakers are necessarily aware of these differences or that they play a part in how we store antonyms in our mental lexicon.

Gradable antonyms include pairs like the following:

beautiful	ugly
expensive	cheap
fast	slow

These pairs are called gradable antonyms because they do not represent an either/or relation but rather a more / less relation. The words can be viewed as terms at the end-points of a continuum or gradient. The more/less relation is evident in a number of ways: the terms allow comparison, e. g. "My arm is longer/shorter than yours", "I love a good book more than a good meal"; the adjectives can be modified by "intensifying" adverbs, e. g. *very long*, *extremely hot, extraordinarily beautiful*. The terms do not represent absolute values; for the adjectives the value depends on the noun being described; the length of arms is on a different scale from the length of, say, roads. In such pairs of adjectives, one is usually a marked term, the other unmarked. This manifests itself, for example, in questions such as "How long is the street?" To ask "How short is the street?" already assumes that the street has been identified as short. The use of long does not make an assumption either way. Also, in giving dimensions, you would use the "larger" term, e. g. "The street is 400 meters *long*" (not *short*).

The following are examples of contradictory or complementary antonyms:

asleep awake
dead alive
on off

These pairs of antonyms are in an either/or relation of oppositeness. An animate being can be described as either *dead* or *alive*, but not as some grade of these or as being more one than the other. The assertion of one implies the denial of the other member of the pair: if you *permit* some behavior, then it is not *forbidden*; if you *lose* a contest, then you have not *won* it; if a switch is *on*, then it is not *off*.

The following are examples of converse antonyms:

above below
before after
behind in front of

For each pair of antonyms, one expresses the converse meaning of the other. In the case of sentences with *buy* and *sell*, for example, the same transaction is expressed from different (converse) perspectives:

Lydia bought the car from Kirsten.
Kirsten sold the car to Lydia.

Polysemy

Polysemy refers to the situation where the same word has two or more different meanings (from Greek *poly*, "mangy" + *semeion*, "sign"). For instance, the noun *board* is said to be polysemous because it may mean: (1) a long thin flat piece of cut wood, (2) a flat surface with patterns, used for playing a game on, (3) a flat piece of hard material used for putting food on, (4) a flat piece of hard material fastened to the wall in a public place to pin notices on, (5) the cost of means, (6) a committee or association, as of company directors or government officials, set up for a special responsibility (*Longman Dictionary of Contemporary English*, 1978: 105). Similarly, the word *flight* is defined in at least the following ways: (1) the act of flying, (2) the distance covered or course followed by a flying object, (3) a trip by plane, (4) the aircraft making the journey, (5) a group of birds or aircraft flying together, (6) an effort that goes beyond the usual limits, (7) a set of stairs as between floors, (8) swift movement of passage (*LDOCE*, 1978: 421).

In most cases, only one of the meanings of a polysemous word will fit into a given context, but occasionally ambiguity may also arise. For instance, consider the words *bat* and *bank* in the following contexts:

Look at that *bat* under the tree.

Susan may go to the *bank* today.

Ambiguity results from the fact that *bat* may mean either "flying mammal" or "implement used to hit the ball in cricket", while *bank* may mean either "river bank" or "the bank that deals with money".

Since one meaning cannot always be delimited and distinguished from another, it is not easy to say without hesitation whether two meanings are the same or different. Consequently, we cannot determine exactly how many meanings a polysemous word has. Consider the verb *eat*. Most dictionaries distinguish the "literal" sense of "taking in through the mouth and swallowing" and the derived meaning of "use up, damage, or destroy something, especially by chemical action", which tends to suggest that the verb may have at least two different meanings. However, in the literal sense, we can also distinguish between eating nuts and eating soup, the former with fingers and the latter with a spoon. Moreover, we can talk of drinking soup as well as eating it. It may therefore be said that in this sense at least, *eat* corresponds to *drink*, since the latter involves the "swallowing of liquids". We can push the analysis further by asking whether eating an orange (which can involve sucking) is the same thing as eating an apple (which involves only chewing). It goes without saying that if we push this analysis too far, we may end up deciding that the verb *eat* has a different meaning for every type of food that we "eat".

▪ Lexical gap

... while hierarchical semantic relations of hyponymy and meronymy are undoubtedly important in the structuring of vocabulary, they do not operate in an altogether systematic and unambiguous way. There are many lexical gaps that are shown up when we begin to build words into hyponymy and meronymy trees, and co-hyponyms may not always be distinguished on the same basis (size, purpose, mode of power, etc.). When a new word is coined, or a new object created and named, consideration is hardly given to its place in the structure of vocabulary. A word is coined because it is needed in some mode of discourse. How it then fits into the vocabulary as a whole is a matter for the lexicologists.

— Jackson, H. & Ze Amvela, E.

Exercises

I. How can you decide which one of the pair is relatively more normal?
1. *Brave: courageous*
    1) Little Billy was so brave at the dentist's this morning.
    2) Little Billy was so courageous at the dentist's this morning.
2. *Calm: placid*
    1) She was quite calm just a few minutes ago.
    2) She was quite placid just a few minutes ago.
3. *Almost: nearly*
    1) She looks almost Chinese.
    2) She looks nearly Chinese.

II. **Read the following paragraph from** *A Tale of Two Cities* **by Charles Dickens. How many contrasts can be found and what effect have they achieved?**

It was the best of times, it was the worst of times, it was the age of wisdom, it was the age of foolishness, it was the epoch of belief, it was the epoch of incredulity, it was the season of Light, it was the season of Darkness, it was the spring of hope, it was the winter of despair, we had everything before us, we had nothing before us, we were all going direct to Heaven, we were all going direct the other way — in short, the period was so far like the present period, that some of its noisiest authorities insisted on its being received, for good or for evil, in the superlative degree of comparison only.

III. **Choose the right word to fill in each sentence.**
1. He waited with (baited, bated) breath.
2. The brother and sister are both (blonds, blondes).
3. There is a (brake, break) in the clouds.
4. Her (bridal, bridle) gown was trimmed with lace.
5. A (pedal, peddle) of the bicycle fell off.
6. Cromwell (reined, reigned) over England like a king.
7. The wreckers began to (raise, raze) the building.
8. Although we watched carefully, the guard remained (stationary, stationery) for one hour.
9. Edgar cannot sail until he has a full (complement, compliment) of men for his crew, and he is still lacking a deck hand.
10. Eric was a tireless scholar, he would (pour, pore) over his books without a break until everyone else in the dormitory had gone to sleep.

IV. **It is said that native speakers are generally in agreement over a fair range of examples of homonymy and polysemy. Which of the following pairs do you think are homonyms, and which are cases of polysemy?**

barge, n. (boat), v. (intervene); court, n. (entourage), v. (woo); dart, n. (missile), v. (move quickly); fleet, n. (ships), adj. (fast); jam, n. (preserve), v. (block); pad, n. (thick material), v. (walk softly); steep, adj. (of gradient), v. (immerse); stem, n. (of plant), v. (stop); stuff, v. (fill), n. (material); watch, v. (observe), n. (timepiece).

V. **Find in column B the superordinates of the words in column A.**

Column A	Column B
1. cotton _____	a. vehicle
2. borrow _____	b. locomote
3. shrub _____	c. fabric
4. van _____	d. optical instrument
5. cruiser _____	e. plant
6. fountain pen _____	f. water craft
7. drum _____	g. pen
8. telescope _____	h. get
9. sing _____	i. musical instrument
10. walk _____	j. vocalize

Chapter 9
Lexical Chunks (1)
— Collocations

Points for Thinking
1. What is lexical chunking?
2. What is the definition of collocation?
3. How do we define the characteristics of collocation?
4. What are the four classifications of collocation?
5. What is the importance for the learning of lexical collocation?

Fig. 9.1 Chunking content breaks large portions of text into smaller, easier-to-read portions.

Chunking is a method of presenting information which splits concepts into small pieces or "chunks" of information to make reading and understanding faster and easier.

A collocation is the occurrence of two or more words within a short space of each other in a corpus.
— Fromkin, V. et al.

9.1 Lexical Chunking

It is clear that the acquisition of the words and their meanings must be partly related to the acquisition of lexical chunks. Much of the vocabulary is learned in this way. This is especially true because learners are likely to eventually know numerous lexical chunks, seeing how they are easy to learn, efficient to use, and cover a wide variety of lexical content.

A learner of English may realize that some variation is possible in certain chunks. Here is a case to show the way of chunking.
    a. *How are you* today?
    b. *How are you* this evening?
    c. *How are you* this fine morning?

d. *How are you* _____ ?

After a learner of English has heard the phrase *How are you today?* several times, it may be acquired as a chunk within the category of "Greeting". However, he may later notice the phrase *How are you* _____ *?* in the sentences of *How are you this evening?* or *How are you this fine morning?* and, at that point, may realize that the underlying chunk is actually *How are you* _____ *?* where the missing part of the sentence can be filled with most time references.

The example shows the possibility for the learner to perceive that what fits in the slot is a separate lexical unit from the rest of the phrase. This chunking process opens the door to learning that lexical unit. Thus chunks can be further divided into smaller lexical units, frequently individual words. Lexical chunks at this stage are partly fixed and partly creative.

9.1.1 Lexical chunks at different levels

The learning of collocation is seen as one level of "chunking". This chunking occurs at all levels of language, and in both spoken and written forms. The following table has provided the examples from written language.

Table 9.1 Chunking and Chunks

	Level	Type of chunking	Examples
1	Letters	Each letter is processed as a unit not simply as a set of separate strokes.	P is processed as a unit, not simply as a small circle and a descending stroke on its left hand side.
2	Morphemes	Each morpheme is processed as a unit rather than simply a set of letters.	Pray is processed as an integrated unit, not simply as a combination of p, r, a, y.
3	Words	Complex words are processed as an integrated unit rather than simply several morphemes.	Prayer is processed as one integrated unit, not simply as a combination of two morphemes: pray and -er.
4	Collocations	Collocations are processed as an integrated unit, not simply as a group of two or more words.	A prayer in the church is processed as an integrated unit, not simply as a group of five words.

Chunking can develop in the direction of smaller parts being chunked, step by step, to become bigger parts. That is to say, smaller chunks are grouped into larger chunks. Let us look at chunking as a process that starts with knowledge of the first level of letters.

When learning to read another language which uses a different script, for example a Chinese student learning to read English, the smallest unit in Level 1 will be the parts or strokes making up the letters. When the learner can see each letter as a unit rather than having to look carefully at the parts to distinguish the letters, then one level of chunking has occurred. Similarly at the higher levels from 2 to 4, which are the levels involving more or bigger chunks, a learner of English may be able to recognize particular words without having to look carefully at each letter. Common combinations have been chunked at the levels of morphemes, words and collocations.

9.1.2 The advantages and disadvantages of chunking

An alternative to chunking is the rule based mainly on processing of the chunks at different levels. In the use of language, the best example on this issue is the case of word building, that is, the use of complex words.

When we learn or use the words like "unable" or "unambiguousness", do we think of these two words from their parts each time we use them as "unable" (un + able) and "unambiguousness" (un+ambigu+ous+ness) or do we simply take them for granted as already integrated or complete units? Generally speaking, people are likely to accept that high frequency complex units like "unable" are integrated as whole chunks. Low frequency complex items like "unambiguousness" are recreated by rules each time we need them.

The main advantage of chunking is to help learners to save the time, that is to reduce his time for processing chunks at the above levels. Instead of having to give close attention to each part of the chunk, the chunking is seen as an integrated unit which represents a saving in time needed to recognize or produce the word or the collocation. As the collocation *a prayer in the church*, the collocation of *a player with promise* is processed by following the steps below:

1. a letter as an integrated unit: *p* is processed as a unit, not as a small circle and a descending stroke on the left hand side;

2. a morpheme as an integrated unit: *play* is processed as a unit, not as a combination of the four letters: *p, l, a, y*;

3. a word as an integrated unit: *player* is processed as a unit, not as a combination of two units *play* and-*er*;

4. a collocation as an integrated unit: *a player with promise* is processed as a unit.

So, instead of having to refer to a rule or pattern to comprehend or produce the chunk, it is treated as a basic unit of chunking.

The main disadvantage of chunking is to learn by heart the chunks at different levels. There are many more chunks than there are components of chunks, and if the chunks are also learned as the individual words within the vocabulary, then there will be more items or chunks to learn by heart. There may also be difficulty in finding an item of chunking among the collocations of a particular word.

9.2 Definition of Collocation

9.2.1 What is collocation?

A collocation is a pair or a group of words that are often used together. These combinations sound natural to native speakers, but students of English have to make a special effort to learn them because they are often difficult to guess. Some combinations just sound "wrong" to native speakers of English. For example, the adjective *fast* and its synonym *quick* have the similar meaning to some extent, English native speakers use them in different collocations — the word *fast* is to collocate with *a car* or *food*, but the word *quick* with *a glance* or *a meal*.

Table 9.2 The Collocation of *fast* and *quick*

	Native speakers say	Native speakers don't usually say
fast	a *fast* car	* a *quick* car
	fast food	* *quick* food
quick	a *quick* glance	* a *fast* glance
	a *quick* meal	* a *fast* meal

Collocation refers to the tendency for certain words to occur together. The term itself comes from the verb *collocate*, and its original meaning is simply "to go together".

Learning collocations is an important part of learning the vocabulary of a language. Some collocations are fixed, or very strong, for example, *take a photo*, where no word other than *take* collocates with *photo* to give the same meaning. Some collocations are more open, where several different words may be used to give a similar meaning, for example *keep to / stick to* the rules. Here are some more examples of collocations:

1. You must *make an effort* and study for your exams (NOT: *do an effort)
2. Did you *watch TV* last night? (NOT: *look at TV)
3. This car has a very *powerful engine*. It can do 200 km an hour. (NOT: *strong engine)
4. There are some *ancient monuments* nearby. (NOT: *antique monuments)

Sometimes, a pair of words may not be absolutely wrong, and people will understand what is meant, but it may not be a natural, normal collocation. If someone says *I did a few mistakes* it will be understood, but a native speaker of English would probably say *I made a few mistakes*.

A word like *clear* as an adjective or an adverb, for example, can be found with a number of nouns or verbs:

	Collocation	Part of speech	Implied meaning
1	a *clear* day	adj.	fine
2	a *clear* sky	adj.	cloudless
3	a *clear* view	adj.	open, no obstruction
4	a *clear* idea	adj.	doubtless
5	a *clear* mind	adj.	keen
6	a *clear* path	adj.	no blockage
7	a *clear* profit	adj.	net
8	a *clear* winner	adj.	absolute
9	a *clear* conscience	adj.	guiltless
10	a *clear* case of cheating	adj.	unmistakable
11	a *clear* record with the police	adj.	with no record
12	*clear* water	adj.	pure
13	to speak loud and *clear*	adv.	distinctively
14	to stand *clear* of the doors	adv.	away from

In each case the term *clear* has a completely different meaning because of the word it is qualifying. In some instances the difference can be quite marked: *strong* has a completely different meaning in *strong* tea from what it does in *strong* language, where it is usually a euphemism for "swearing".

Collocative differences sometimes separate words which are otherwise synonymous:

1. *Quiver* and *tremble* are synonyms, but *tremble* usually collocates with *fear* and *quiver*

with *excitement*;

2. Human beings are able to *wander* and *stroll,* but any cow or living animals can only *wander*;

3. *Profound* and *deep* can both collocate with the feeling of *sympathy*, but only *deep* collocates with *hole* which has a depth.

9.2.2 Some definitions of collocation

One of well-known definitions says that collocations represent the way words combine in a language to produce natural-sounding speech and writing. The combination of words follows certain rules peculiar to each language.

A native speaker of English will say, for example: *strong wind* but *heavy rain* and not the other way round. The word "collocation" is derived from the verb "collocate" meaning "to set or arrange in a set or position", collocation being "a noticeable arrangement or conjoining of linguistic elements ranging from free combinations — *see a man / a car / a house* — to set or fixed or idiomatic expressions — *not to see the wood for the trees.*"

The meaning of a free combination can be derived from that of its components — *to get away* meaning "to escape" and *to get back* meaning "to return". Set expressions have not only a fixed form, but their meaning is given by the elements arranged in a certain order. Through an intrinsic connection, they can be expressed by a single word, and represent complex parts of speech.

One might ask whether collocation should be dealt with within the context of the semantic range of a word. As the word *blond* can describe little more than another word *hair*, there come the following questions:

1. Should we include reference to *hair* in the definition of the semantic range of the word (+ color, -dark, +hair, etc.) or,

2. Should the denotation of a word and the environment in which it occurs be kept separate?

According to the *Oxford Collocations Dictionary* (2002), collocation is a means of combining words in a language to produce natural-sounding speech and writing. Incorrect combinations such as **heavy wind* or **strong rain* do not sound natural in English.

Geoffrey Leech (1969) refers to collocation as simply an idiosyncratic property of individual words. *White coffee* and *white wine* are only relatively *white*.

In the case of *white lies* and *blue jokes*, the logical link with a color is less apparent still. With *white coffee* we are dealing with a set phrase where the meaning can at least be guessed at on the basis of the two constituent words. Conceivably the *white* in *white lie* suggests purity of intention. In the case of *blue joke* knowing what part of the color spectrum is indicated by the word blue gives us no help in understanding what a blue joke is. When the phrase can only be understood as an entity, it is an idiom.

Collocations are mainly lexical items made up of lexical words from two or more different word classes which co-occur habitually. Collocation is quite different from idioms. Each word in a collocational structure contributes its own meaning to the whole intepretation in a distinguishable way. Thus, collocations are obvious in meaning; that is, the intepretation of the collocation as a whole can be worked out from the individual meaning of each word in it.

For example, a collocational phrase, such as *a heavy drinker*, produces its meaning which is a combination of the adjective modefier *heavy* and the modified noun *drinker*. Thus, *heavy drinker* can be interpreted as "someone who drinks much or even too much alcohol". Both words can combine with others relatively freely in the meanings they express in this combination (*heavy smoker* or *elderly drinker*), but *heavy drinker* is itself relatively fixed and hence becomes a collocation. This is also the case with *white wine*. Such wine looks hardly white in color; it is probably somewhere between relatively clear-to-yellowish and amber. The collocational meaning of *white* is at last partially defined by its occurrence together with the noun *wine*.

9.2.3 Meanings of collocational ranges

The distribution of a word within a language is referred to as its collocational range. The principle is best expressed by the linguist Firth who has memorably summarised its importance by the phrase "[we] shall know a word by the company it keeps" (1957). Therefore, the type of linguistic contexts in which a word occurs can provide clues to what that word might mean.

Collocational ranges are unlike grammatical classes in that they are peculiar to each word, and almost certainly no two words in a language share exactly the same range and frequency of occurrence within a range, whereas grammatical classes may each contain many different words as members.

Collocation is the way in which certain words collocate or co-occur repeatedly according to grammatical rules or idiomatic way of saying things. "How words co-occur" is the way words combine to produce natural-sounding speech and writing. For example, in English we can say:

1. The movie *began* in that newly-built cinema at 7:30 p.m.
2. The movie *started* in that newly-built cinema at 7:30 p.m.
3. Tom quickly got into his car and *started* the engine right away.
4. *Tom quickly got into his car and *began* the engine right away.

Even though in a lot of contexts *start* and *begin* may be interchangeable, it is not proper to say "*begin* the engine", as we have to use "*start* the engine" instead.

If, for example, we use the adjectives *strong* and *powerful*, we can say: a *strong/powerful* argument and *strong* tea but never *powerful* tea, and a *powerful* car but never a *strong* car. In the same way, although a garden can be described as either *large* or *big*, a progress and a boy can only be *big*, rather than *large*.

Special cases of collocational ranges are what are called idioms which are used to refer to habitual collocations of more than one word, that tend to be used together, with a semantic function not readily deducible from the other uses of the component words apart from each other:

e.g. She went for him *hammer and tongs*. They ran off *hell for leather*.

Knowledge of such individual features of a language, acquired by long experience, but unnecessary for ordinary daily communication, usually comes at the end of one's learning of a foreign language; hence a complete or near-complete mastery of one is often said to be "idiomatic". Some idioms preserve in use words that have otherwise become obsolete:

e.g. 1. *to and fro*
    2. *waifs and strays*
    3. *kith and kin*

English idioms will be discussed in detail in the next chapter.

9.3 The Features of Collocation

Collocation is not simply a matter of co-occurrence or an association of words. For example, although it is the fact that milk is white, we are not likely to say *white milk*. But in most cases we may find that an expression of *white paint* is common enough. Collocation is important in a practical and pragmatic point of view for the following plausible reasons.

9.3.1 Non-arbitrariness and predictability

The first and most obvious reason of its importance is the fact that collocational words combine in the way, fundamental to all language use. The collocation of words is not arbitrary. To a large extent, word choice is predictable.

When a speaker thinks of drinking, he may use several common collocations with an English verb, such as *have*. The most likely expectations predict a large number of possibilities:

Group 1

have tea,

have coffee,

have milk,

have mineral water,

have orange juice,

or even alcoholic drinks as:

Group 2

have beer,

have wine,

but there would never be any expectations of

Group 3

* *have engine oil*,

* *have shampoo*,

* *have sulphuric acid*.

Though *engine oil*, *shampoo* and *sulphuric acid* are all the same in the form of liquid, they are completely unacceptable as human drinks. The liquids in Group 3 are linguistically not "probable" in the way that those liquids in both Group 1 and Group 2 are in human life.

Then let's have another example of a less common English verb *enhance*, and its choice of objects is limited to a relatively small number of nouns or noun patterns to be made greater in value, such as:

enhance his reputation, or

enhance the standing of the company.

If the verb is *do*, the choice of its objects is far greater than that of objects with *enhance*, such as:

do his best, and

do the honorable thing.

But it is still limited to some extent, never

* *do a failure*, or

* *do a mistake*.

So, the very definition of collocation is usually the way in which words combine and it was given a status which we cannot deny.

These examples of three English verbs *have*, *enhance* and *do* combine with predictable objects and do not come up with obvious mistakes. They tell the very predictability of the collocation and give the clue as to why collocation is an important practical issue.

There are patterns to collocations which can make them easier to understand and make use of. There are parts of collocations in which words are organized and patterned. So the predictable patterning needs to be paid enough attention to in vocabulary learning and use.

9.3.2 Collocation in common

Collocation is the way in which the words of a particular language are combined to produce natural-sounding speech and writing. Thus, when an English word becomes closely associated with a particular context to the exclusion of other words with a similar meaning such that they form what is almost a set phrase, we have one of English lexical chunks, as what linguists call, collocation in its particular term.

A collocation is a lexical chunk of two or more English words that often go together. Native English speakers use these "right" combinations all the time in their daily life. But a lot of cases show that some odd and unnatural combinations may just be considered as "wrong". For example, here is a short paragraph:

After the fall of night, it was getting dark. The group of five soldiers, against the *strong wind* and *heavy rain*, kept marching on along the muddy road. They had the order to get to the next village within an hour.

People in English say *strong wind* but *heavy rain* in a stormy situation. *Strong* has to be collocated with the word *wind* and *heavy* collocated with the word *rain*. It would be odd and absurd to say *heavy wind* or *strong rain*, as they are definitely not exchangeable in collocation.

From a logical point of view, the combination of the word *a complete moon* seems "acceptable" in an abstract case, but most people would prefer to use the collocation of *a full moon* instead. In another case, we can find *white coffee* not usually white, and *black coffee* not really black.

The Chinese people are used to drinking *green* tea and *red* tea, the latter is conventionally called *black tea* in English. It would seem that *white* and *black* are being used to indicate polarity rather than to give an accurate indication of color in coffee or tea themselves.

In using numerals, we can refer to a *herd* of cows but not a *herd* of sheep. English native speakers say a *flock* of sheep instead, though they use *shepherd* to refer to the one who takes care of this particular *flock* of sheep.

In some cases of idiomatic collocation, the association is so obvious in our daily lives that we may well be able to anticipate it; most of people would, for example, expect *She has blond* ... to be followed by *hair*, and *He was armed to* ... to be followed by *the teeth*.

9.4 Characteristics, Classifications and Categories of Collocations

9.4.1 Characteristics of collocations

The characteristics of collocations are commonly summarized as follows:

1. Collocations are frequent co-occurrences of words between which no new word or words can be added. For example: in *back and forth*, it is really unusual to add a word to this collocation like, *back, middle and forth*. And *knife and fork*, not *knife, spoon and fork*;

2. Collocations consist of components that cannot be replaced by a synonym or word of similar meaning. For example: *take pain* or *painstaking*; but not *take aches* or *achestaking*, and *do his homework*, not *make his homework*.

3. Collocations are binomials that cannot be reversed. The order of the words within a collocation is more or less fixed, for example: *rain cats and dogs*, not *rain dogs and cats*, and

from morning till night, never **from night till morning*.

4. Some collocations are predictable; for example: if a person hears a collocational verb *fill ...* he/she automatically expects that *in* or *out* will follow, and another collocational verb *shrug ...*, then *shoulders* will be expected to follow.

From the above characteristics, the two main factors are indicated for their influence on the collocation range of an item as follows:

1. A certain level of specificity: It shows the fact that the more general a word is, the broader its collocational range becomes; the more specific it means and the more restricted its collocational range is. For example: the verb *bury* is likely to have much broader collocational range than any of its hyponyms, such as *inter* or *entomb*. Only dead human body can be *interred* or *entombed*, but it is not only possible to *bury dead body* of either human or animal, but also probable to *bury a treasure*, *your head or face*, *an insult* and *dispute*.

2. The number of senses a collocation has: This means that most words have several senses and they tend to take up a different array of collocates for each sense. For example: in its sense of *manage*, the verb *run* collocates with words like *company*, *school* and *business*. Meanwhile, along with its sense of *operate* or *provide*, it collocates with words like *service* and *course*.

Generally speaking, collocations usually have specific characteristics. Their frequent co-occurrences are observed and their collocates cannot be changed.

9.4.2 Classifications of collocations

The classifications of collocation are categorized as follows:

1. The weak collocations: These refer to collocations that have a wide variety of collocates. Such collocations consist of a number of word co-occurrences and can be easily guessed. Many things can be *long* or *short*, *cheap* or *expensive*, *good* or *bad*. There are more examples as *a white/red/green/long/small shirt*, etc.

2. The medium-strength collocations: These collocations are of the same meaning as they can sometimes be weak collocations such as to *hold a conversation* and to *make a mistake*. Normally learners already know each individual word such as *to hold* and *a conversation* but they are able to use them as a single item or as a collocation.

3. The strong collocations: These collocations are strong or very strong but not unique. Usually, strong collocations have few other possible collocates. For example, *moved to tears* or *reduced to tears*.

4. The most incomprehensive collocations or unique collocations: These refer to collocations which are fixed and cannot be replaced by any other words, such as *foot the bill* and *foot the invoice*. **Foot the coffee* is obviously wrong.

As what has been discussed before, no two words in a language share exactly the same range and frequency of occurrence within a range. Combinations of a definite word in a language can be ranged in a chain of continuum — from the totally free collocations: *see a man/car/book* — to the totally fixed and idiomatic collocations: *not see the wood for the trees*. The last idiomatic collocation is not only fixed in form, it also has nothing whatever to do with *wood* or *trees*. Between these two extremes, there is a whole range of nouns that take the verb *see* in a way that is neither totally predictable nor totally opaque as to meaning.

The chunking of the word *see* can be collocated as the following,

1. The weak collocations:

a) We are going to *see a film*.

b) I could *see tears in her eyes*.

c) May I *see your ticket*?

d) I can hardly *see without my glasses*.

2. The medium-strength collocations:

e) He has always wanted to *see China*.

f) Mary was ill and went to *see her doctor*.

g) They have been *seeing each other* for the whole year.

h) Tom was so busy that he had no time to *see anybody*.

3. The strong collocations:

i) She has failed to *see danger in his attempt*.

j) I didn't *see any reason for you to give up the plan*.

k) Would you please say it again as I failed to *see your point*?

l) We'll be *seeing Kate home* after the birthday party is over tonight.

4. The most incomprehensive collocations or unique collocations:

m) If you are too busy, I'll *see about* the train ticket.

n) The police have taken the steps to *see into* the traffic accident.

o) Once Tom started a job, he would *see it through* to the end.

p) *See to* the chores, will you?

All the combinations above, including those at the very extremes of the range, can be called collocations. And it is combinations such as these — particularly in the "medium strength" area — that are vital to the correct understanding and the proper use of English words in listening, speaking, reading and writing.

9.4.3 Some frequent categories of collocations

In addition, English collocations are generally divided into two major category sets: one as the categories of **Grammatical Collocations** and **Lexical Collocations**, and the other as the categories of **the Upward Collocations** and **the Downward Collocations.**

Grammatical collocations consist of content words (a noun, an adjective or a verb) plus a preposition or infinitive. Meanwhile, lexical collocations consist of neither prepositions nor infinitives. They comprise only content words:

Table 9.3 Grammatical Collocations

	Patterns:	Examples:
1	noun+preposition	a blockade against, a key to, a reply to
2	preposition+noun	by accident, by the way, under way
3	adjective+preposition	pleased with, eager for, generous of
4	verb+preposition	get to, hold against, stick to

Table 9.4 Lexical Collocations

	Patterns:	Examples:
1	noun+noun	traffic accident, a boy friend, a development plan
2	adjective+noun	a good book, fresh water, heavy rain
3	verb+noun	do homework, kick a ball, reach the destination
4	verb+adverb	get up, set off, walk away

Sometimes collocations are also divided into two sub-categories:

1. The Upward Collocations

This category consists of words which habitually collocate with other words more frequently used in English than they are themselves and most of them are prepositions, adverbs, conjunctions and pronouns. For example, the word *back* normally combines with *at, down, from, into, on,* etc. So the word *back* is used with another word, more than standing alone.

2. The Downward Collocations

This category consists of words which combine with other words less frequently than standing by themselves and give a semantic analysis of a word. For instance, *arrive* and *bring* are less frequently combined with other words than the word *back* mentioned in the upward collocations.

There appears to be a systematic difference between upward and downward collocations. Upward collocations, of course, is the weaker pattern in statistical terms, and the words tend to be elements of grammatical frames, or superordinates. Downward collocations by contrast gives us a semantic analysis of a word (Sinclair , 1999: 116). In terms of grammatical classes, therefore, Sinclair notes the collocates of *back*: upward collocates are, for example, *prepositions, adverbs, conjunctions* and *pronouns*, whilst downward collocates consist of a large number of *nouns* and *verbs*.

In conclusion, there are various ways of categorizing collocations. However, the frequent categories found are firstly lexical and grammatical collocations and secondly, the upward collocations and the downward collocations.

9.5 Basic Types of Collocations

9.5.1 Three types from *OCDSE*

The world famous and authentic dictionary, *Oxford Collocations Dictionary for Students of English* (*OCDSE*, 2003) offers the following types of collocations with the three headwords.

Table 9.5 Type One: the speed of *light* (noun)

	Patterns:	Examples:
1	adjective+**noun**	bright, harsh, intense, strong **light**
2	quantifier+**noun**	a beam, ray of **light**
3	verb+**noun**	cast/ emit/ give/ provide/ shed **light**
4	**noun**+verb	**light** gleams/ glows/ shines
5	**noun**+noun	a **light** source
6	preposition+**noun**	by the **light** of the moon
7	**noun**+preposition	the **light** from the window

Table 9.6 Type Two: *pick* and *choose* (verb)

	Patterns:	Examples:
1	**verb**+adverb	*pick / choose* carefully
2	adjective+**verb**	be free to *pick / choose*
3	**verb**+preposition	*pick / choose* between two things

Table 9.7 Type Three: *safe* and *sound* (adjective)

	Patterns:	Examples:
1	verb+**adjective**	make / keep / declare sth. *safe / sound*
2	adverb+**adjective**	perfectly / not entirely / environmentally *safe / sound*
3	**adjective**+preposition	*safe / sound* from attack

9.5.2 Different kinds of collocation from other sources

If we define collocation as the way in which two or more words occur and co-occur together, it is easy to find that the range of its kinds is very wide, and will cover many different kinds of items. Certainly, all of the following are collocations in the sense that we readily recognize that these groups of words are regularly found together.

1. adjective+noun:
   a decisive action / moment
   a quick / proper reply / answer
   an indisputable / impregnable / invincible / irrefutable idea
   a convincing / forcible / powerful / solid / strong / well-grounded argument
2. verb+noun:
   submit / hand in a report
   keep / maintain / preserve an attitude / opinion
   settle / solve / unlock / unravel / untangle / undo a problem
   attain / earn / enjoy / gain / get / obtain / reach / score / secure / win a success
3. noun+noun:
   a bus stop / station
   an arms reduction plan / project
   a twelve-month installment pay / arrangement
4. verb+adverb:
   check / examine thoroughly
   arrive / come / go early / late
   put / set away / in / off / on / out / up
5. adverb+adjective:
   quite early
   extremely inconvenient / uncomfortable
   very / rather / fairly beautiful / handsome / pretty
6. verb+adjective+noun:
   revise the original plan

establish a new school / institute / organization
achieve / make / win a great / huge / immense progress / success
7. noun+verb:
    The rain set in.
    The fog / mist closed in / lifted up.
    The film / program / performance is over.
8. discourse marker:
    Put it another way.
    Call up the other people / students.
    Buy / Purchase more books / magazines / tickets.
9. multi-word prepositional phrase:
    a few years ago
    in front of the house
    with the help of his teacher
10. phrasal verb:
    turn away / in / off / on / up
    get at / into / off / on / out of / over / through
    hold against / by / ... in one's hand / from / over / to / with
11. adjective+preposition:
    aware / conscious of
    eager about / after / for
    famous among / for / through / at / throughout
12. compound noun:
    sleeping car
    fire brigade / engine / escape
    telephone book / booth / box / directory / call / set
13. binomial:
    to and fro
    back and forth
    backwards and forwards
14. trinomial:
    make up for
    put up with
    hook, line and sinker
15. fixed phrase:
    by and large
    not only ... but / also / as well
    on one hand ... on the other hand
16. incomplete fixed phrase:
    a sort of ...
    at the back of
    to one's disappointment / despair / surprise
17. fixed expression:
    see a doctor
    free of charge

go to church / prison / school / work

18. semi-fixed expression:
    How are you . . . ?
    put off the appointment / meeting / plan
    See you later / tomorrow / on Monday / next week.

19. part of a proverb:
    Too many cooks . . .
    Many hands make . . .
    The birds of a feather . . .

20. part of a quotation:
    on the rocks
    go with the stream
    To be or not to be . . .

9.5.3 Some typical collocations of the words: *do* and *make*

Do and *make* are two of the most frequently used words in English. They have developed plenty of collocations in people's daily life.

It has become a necessity in knowing its real meaning while collocating with particular words. The following two columns provide hints to catch the meaning of each collocation.

1. Some typical collocations of *do*:

    do 20 miles   *do* harm
    do a degree (in medicine)   *do* one's best
    do a favor   *do* sums
    do a movie   *do* the amiable
    do a puzzle   *do* the big
    do a room   *do* the cooking
    do business   *do* the host
    do credit (to)   *do* the polite
    do dishes / the washing-up   *do* the shopping
    do flowers   *do* the sightseeing
    do for food   *do* the washing
    do for oneself   *do* your hair
    do good   *do* your homework
    do Hamlet

2. Some typical collocations of *make*:

    make a boat   *make* a fire
    make a bow   *make* a fool of sb.
    make a decision   *make* a journey

make a mistake
make a name
make a noise
make a poem
make a profit
make a promise
make a road
make a speech
make a trouble
make an answer
make an arrangement
make (an) effort
make an impression

make home
make money
make no difference
make progress
make room
make sense
make sure
make tea
make up one's mind
make use of
make war
make way

9.5.4 Collocations with some particular English quantifiers

When one wants to refer to a quantity of something without being precise, a quantifier is to be used for such an expression.

1. A quantifier is often a word or a phrase, for example, words as *some*, *any*, *much*, or *many*, and phrases as *a lot of*, *lots of* and *plenty of*, which are frequently-used quantifiers, for example:

a) He has bought *some* books in the bookstore.
b) Do you have *any* new idea about the conference?
c) How *much* money have you paid for such a book?
d) *Many* students attended the lecture on Chinese literature.
e) *A lot of* papers were collected from the graduate students.
f) *Lots of* money has been invested in the heavy industry.
g) I have gathered *plenty of* data for the writing of my thesis.

2. Other nouns can also play the role of quantifiers when they collocate with *of* and some particular nouns. They are *bunch*, *flock*, *herd*, *piece*, *pack*, *pile*, etc, for example:

a *bunch* of bananas/cherries/flowers/grapes/keys
a *flock* of birds/geese/goats/sheep/tourists
a *herd* of buffalo/cows/deer/elephants/giraffes
a *pack* of cards/gum/hounds/lies/wolves
a *piece* of advice/furniture/glass/news/paper
a *pile* of books/documents/magazines/newspapers/sand

The following is a list of more collocations with quantifiers:

a *bank* of snow
a *block* of ice
a *burst* of energy
a *cake* of soap
a *chest* of tea
a *circle* of friends
a *cluster* of butterflies
a *contingent* of troops
a *crowd* of people

a *drove* of horses
a *flight* of sparrow
a *group* of boys and girls
a *gust* of wind
a *heap* of rubbish
a *hive* of bees
a *jar* of jam
a *letter* of invitation
a *list* of books

a *pane* of glass
a *pot* of flowers
a *pride* of lions
a *ray* of hope
a *school* of whales
a *set* of rules
a *sheaf* of papers
a *shoal* of fish
a *skulk* of foxes
a *slice* of cake
a *stack* of hay
a *swarm* of locusts
a *throng* of pedestrians
a *troupe* of actors
a *tube* of toothpaste
an *item* of news

3. Some nouns of containers are also used as quantifiers. They are *bag*, *basket*, *barrel*, *bottle*, *bowl*, *box*, *bucket*, *can*, *carton*, *cup*, *glass*, *jar*, *mug*, *package*, *packet*, *plate*, *sack*, *spoon*, *tube*, etc., for example:

a *bag* of bottles / flour / potatoes / rice / toffees
a *bottle* of beer / medicine / soda / water / wine
a *box* of chocolate / blocks / candies / marbles / sweets
a *cup* of tea / coffee / salt / sugar / water

4. Some nouns with the suffix of *-ful* are sometimes used as quantifiers, for example:

an *armful* of flowers
a *basketful* of apples
a *busful* of students
a *handful* of seeds
a *houseful* of guests
a *mouthful* of chocolate
a *roomful* of books
a *spoonful* of sugar

9.6 The Significance of Learning Collocations

Developing an awareness of collocation as an important level of language, although a significant hurdle for the language learner, is necessary because of its efficient meaning-creating function and abundance in language. Vocabulary learning is traditionally limited to the learning of definitions of a single word and the usage. The importance of vocabulary acquisition has always been recognized although, at times, vocabulary is treated separately from grammar and skills. Vocabulary should be at the center of language learning because "a language consists of grammaticalized lexis, not lexicalized grammar!" (Lewis, 1993).

It is accepted that choosing words carefully in certain situations is more important than choosing grammatical structures. We cannot effectively communicate if we do not have a good vocabulary knowledge.

Collocations have been proven to be an important part of vocabulary development. Learning collocations can help us understand and use the collocations properly in the following ways:

1. It gives the most natural way to say something. For example, the sentence *Smoking is strictly forbidden* is more natural than *Smoking is strongly forbidden*.

2. It provides alternative ways of saying something, which may be more colorful / expressive or more precise. Instead of repeating *It was very cold and very dark*, we can say *It was bitterly cold and pitch dark*.

3. It helps to improve the style in writing. Instead of saying *Poverty causes crime*, we can say *Poverty breeds crime*; instead of saying *a big meal* we can say *a substantial meal*.

We may not necessarily use these in informal conversations, but in writing they can give our text more variety and make it read better.

Collocation is the occurrence or co-occurrence of words which are collocated together more often than being expected. Collocations are common combinations of words that the native speakers make instinctively. So it is necessary to turn to the lexical approach that vocabulary should be the most important aspect in learning English.

The fact that certain words tend to co-occur is often explained in linguistic terms, with reference to the fact that some word combinations may be viewed as wholes. A distinction between two mechanisms of language production has been made, one as the open-choice principle and the other as the idiom principle. The role of chunks is explained by the simplified means of language production.

The role of chunks is discussed through the fact that they often have a specialized pragmatic/situational meaning which resides in the chunk as a whole rather than in its component parts. With respect to chunking vs. rule formation, collocations and idioms are the widely-adopted forms among which the former is more frequent in our daily application and use.

Meanings of words are considered as the matters of complexity. It has been already suggested that the meaning of a word involves, at least, its reference to an entity in the world of experience, as well as the sense relations it contracts with other words in the vocabulary, and the collocational relations that may hold between it and other co-occurring words.

The present chapter has focused on the forms, definitions, theories and meanings of English collocations. Then it leads to a discussion on types of collocations which is supplied with plenty of examples.

Further Reading

1. Crowther, J., Dignen, S. and Lea, D. (2003). *Oxford Collocations Dictionary for Students of English.* Foreign Language Teaching and Research Press.
2. Finch, G. (2000). *Linguistic Terms and Concepts.* New York: St. Martin's Press.
3. Lewis, M. (1993). *The Lexical Approach.* Hove, England: Language Teaching Publications.
4. Lewis, M. (ed.). (2000). *Teaching Collocation: Further Developments in the Lexical Approach.* Oxford: Oxford University Press.

● Extended Reading

■ Defining collocation

Collocation refers to the tendency for certain words to occur together. The term itself comes from the verb *collocate*, meaning "to go together". A word like *clear*, for example, can be found with a number of nouns, *clear sky*, *clear conscience*, *clear idea*, and *clear road*. In each case the term *clear* has a completely different meaning because of the word it is qualifying. In some instances the difference can be quite marked: *strong* has a completely different meaning in *strong tea* than it does in *strong language*, where it is usually a euphemism for "swearing". Collocative differences sometimes separate words which are otherwise synonymous: *quiver* and *tremble* are synonyms, but we *tremble* with fear and *quiver* with excitement; similarly humans can *wander* and *stroll* but cows can only *wander*; and *profound* and *deep* can both occur with sympathy but only *deep* with hole. The distribution of a word within a language is referred to as its **collocational range**. The principle is best expressed by the linguist Brian Firth, "We know a word by the company it keeps."

— Finch, G.

Collocation is the way words combine in a language to produce natural-sounding speech and writing. For example, in English you say *strong wind* but *heavy rain*. It would not be normal to say *heavy wind* or *strong rain*. And whilst all four of these words would be recognized by a learner at pre-intermediate or even elementary level, it takes a greater degree of competence with the language to combine them correctly in productive use.

Combinations of words in a language can be ranged on a cline from the totally free — *see a man / car / book* — to the totally fixed and idiomatic — *not see the wood for the tree*. This idiom is not only fixed in form, it also has nothing whatever to do with wood or trees. Between these two extremes, there is a whole range of nouns that take the verb *see* in a way that is neither totally predictable nor totally opaque as to meaning. These run from the fairly "weak" collocation *see a film* (which elementary students learn as a "chunk" without pausing to reflect that this is not quite the literal meaning of *see*) through the "medium strength" *see a doctor* to the "stronger" collocations of *see danger / reason / the point*. All these combinations, apart from those at the very extremes of the cline, can be called collocation. And it is combinations such as these — particularly in the "medium strength" area — that are vital to communicative competence in English.

— Crowther, J. et al.

Collocations, idioms and phrasal verbs

Even during the height of structuralism, we knew that the lexicon was complicated. Apart from individual words, we were keenly aware that multi-word expressions were important. We identified phrasal verbs and idioms as two important areas for students. The rest we labeled "idiomatic usage". It is only recently through the rise of corpus linguistics that the extent of the fixedness of much language has been more widely recognized. We know that fixed expressions range from the totally fixed (An apple a day keeps the doctor away), through the semi-fixed (What I'm saying / suggesting / proposing is . . .), to the fairly loose yet still predictable (go on holiday). In one sense all collocations are idiomatic and all idioms and phrasal verbs are collocations — predictable combinations of different kinds. So, how can we use these terms most usefully? It seems sensible to continue using those terms and categories which language teachers have found useful in the past — idioms and phrasal verbs — while introducing the term collocation to name and categorize that language which has previously been ignored or undervalued. Let us look more closely at each of these three categories.

1. Idioms

An idiom is an expression which is relatively fixed and allows little or no change. It is often metaphorical: he put the cat among the pigeons; don't count your chickens. Not all idioms are as pictorial as these two examples. We could think of *catch the bus* or *fired with enthusiasm* as idioms because of the inherently metaphorical use of *catch* and *fire*. The native speaker has no problem with the idea that both fish and buses can be caught or that non-physical things can be on fire. If the same verbs are not used in the learners' L1, it is probable that they will have a problem with the English idiomatic use. We need to broaden our concept of idiom to include much more metaphorical usage, which is frequently hardly even recognized as idiomatic by native speakers.

2. Phrasal verbs

Phrasal verbs contain a verb plus one or more particles: *make up a story*, *put the light out*. The meaning may or may not be obvious from the individual words. Again, learners may have no trouble with the literal *put the cat out* but cannot relate that to *put the light out*. Some teachers consider *get on* (in get on the bus) as a phrasal verb. Others think of it as verb plus preposition. The distinction is not helpful for the classroom where the emphasis is on the phrase as a whole rather than any analysis of it. Arguments aside, the category of phrasal verb is a useful one for both teachers and learners to identify certain items which they are trying to teach and learn.

3. Collocations

As mentioned above, in a sense, all collocations are idiomatic and all phrasal verbs and idioms are collocations or contain collocations, but rather than spending all our time describing and sorting expressions, the real issue for the methodologist is to try to help teachers to make simple categories which will help their students see some order and organization in the lexicon. ELT has always recognized two types of multi-word item where the patterns have been clear — idioms and phrasal verbs. It is time to introduce our students to one more category of language as it really is — collocation.

A collocation is a predictable combination of words: *get lost*, *make up for lost time*, and *speak your mind*. Some combinations may be very highly predictable from one of the component words — *foot the bill*, *mineral water*, and *spring to mind*. Some "strong" collocations have the status of idioms — *shrug your shoulders* — they are not guessable and are non-generative. Some may be so common that they hardly seem worth remarking upon — *a big Fiat, a nice car*, *have lunch*. (As just mentioned, however, native speakers must be careful, because an item which seems unremarkable to them might be a problem to a learner. Because of their L1, some learners may find *eat lunch* or *take lunch* a more obvious choice than *have lunch*.)

— Lewis, M. (ed.)

Exercises

I. True or False decisions.

1. Collocation is the relationship between two words or groups of words that often go together and form a common expression. (   )
2. Collocation is simply a matter of association of ideas. (   )
3. "Crystal clear", "middle management", "nuclear family" and "cosmetic surgery" are examples of collocated pairs of words. (   )
4. Some words are often found together because they make up a compound noun, for example "riding boots" or "motor cyclist". (   )
5. It is a common expression for someone to be "yellow in the face" or "green in the face". (   )
6. A person can be "locked in mortal combat", meaning involved in a serious fight, or "bright eyed and bushy tailed", meaning fresh and ready to go. (   )
7. English has many of the collocated expressions and some linguists disapprove that our mental lexicon is made up of many collocated words and phrases as well as individual items. Some words have different collocations which reflect their similar meanings; e.g. "bank" collocates with "river" and "investment". (   )
8. Although collocation is very largely determined by meaning, it is sometimes fairly

idiosyncratic and cannot easily be predicted in terms of the meaning of the associated words. (　　)

9. The distribution of a word within a language is referred to as its collocational range. (　　)
10. Collocations are syntactic items consisting of lexical words from two different word classes which co-occur habitually. (　　)
11. Collocations are not transparent in meaning; that is, the meaning of the whole can not be worked out from the meaning of each of the words in it. (　　)
12. If one is sufficiently familiar with a language, the co-text of many words can be accurately predicted or at least what kind of co-text they are unlikely to occur in. (　　)
13. A grammatical collocation is a phrase consisting of a dominant word and a preposition or grammatical structure such as an infinitive or clause. (　　)
14. Fixed combinations consist of elements that are joined in accordance with the general rules of English syntax and allow substitution. (　　)
15. Lexical collocations normally consist of nouns, adjectives, verbs and prepositions. (　　)
16. Whereas syntax deals with general classes of words and their combinations, collocations describe specific lexical items and the frequency with which these items occur with other lexical items. (　　)
17. Collocation in its purest sense recognizes only the lexical co-occurrence of words. (　　)
18. Collocations can be dramatic and interesting because unexpected, or they can be important in the lexical structure of the language because of being frequently repeated. (　　)
19. The principle of idiom is not far more pervasive and elusive than we have allowed. (　　)
20. The "prototype" of collocation refers to all habitual combinations as "heavy drinker", "light drizzle", "highlight of this tour", etc. (　　)

II. Cloze.

Until recently most historians spoke very critically of the Industrial Revolution. They __1__ that in the long run industrialization greatly raised the standard of living for the __2__ man. But they insisted that its __3__ results during the period from 1750 to 1850 were widespread poverty and misery for the __4__ of the English population. __5__ contrast, they saw in the preceding hundred years from 1650 to 1750, when England was still a __6__ agricultural country, a period of great abundance and prosperity. This view, __7__, is generally thought to be wrong. Specialists __8__ history and economics, have __9__ two things: that the period from 1650 to 1750 was __10__ by great poverty, and that industrialization certainly did not worsen and may have actually improved the conditions for the majority of the populace.

1. A. admitted   B. believed   C. claimed   D. predicted
2. A. plain   B. average   C. means   D. normal
3. A. momentary   B. prompt   C. instant   D. immediate
4. A. bulk   B. host   C. gross   D. magnitude
5. A. On   B. With   C. For   D. By
6. A. broadly   B. thoroughly   C. generally   D. completely
7. A. however   B. meanwhile   C. therefore   D. moreover
8. A. at   B. in   C. about   D. for
9. A. manifested   B. approved   C. shown   D. speculated
10. A. noted   B. impressed   C. labeled   D. marked

Chapter 10
Lexical Chunks (2)
— Idioms

Points for Thinking
1. What is an idiom?
2. Illustrate with examples the classification of idioms.
3. What are the characteristics of idioms in terms of the grammatical aspect?
4. What is a proverb? Can you list some features of proverbs?
5. Of the figurative idioms, what are the differences between metaphorical idioms and similized idioms?

Cat Got Your Tongue

I was feeling shy when my uncle came.
"Has the cat got your tongue?" he said.
He must have meant, "Why aren't you talking?"
Because my tongue was still in my head.

— Wilson, A. T.

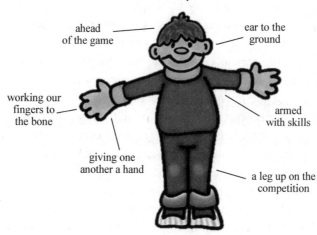

10.1 Definition of Idiom

In the *Cambridge English Dictionary Online* (2020), an idiom is a group of words in a fixed order that have a particular meaning that is different from the meaning of each word on its own. An idiom is generally defined as a phrase whose meaning is difficult or sometimes impossible to guess by looking at the meaning of individual words it contains. In modern linguistics an idiom is defined as a complex lexical item which is longer than a word form but shorter than a sentence and which has a meaning that cannot be derived from the knowledge of its component parts. Meaning is thus the decisive, if not the only criterion for idioms. The word forms of an idiom do not constitute lexical units and do not make an isolable contribution to the meaning of the whole, but show a unitary meaning. As a consequence, some linguists also use a special term for the constituents of idioms, namely formatives (where *word form* would serve the same purpose).

A test for a semantic constituent is that of recurrent semantic contrast (Cruse, 1986: 26-9). In the sentence *you need not jump down my throat* (= "criticize me so fiercely"), take *need* and substitute for it the semantically different but syntactically identical item *may*. This changes the meaning of the sentence, of course, but the point is that the same substitution of forms in a completely different sentence will produce a parallel change of meaning, e. g. *they need / may not sit the exam*. The same test shows that *you* is also a semantic constituent, but that *throat* is not, e. g. semantically unacceptable *you need not jump down my windpipe*. In other sentence frames *throat* and *windpipe* are in recurrent semantic contrast, e. g. *he hit me on the windpipe / throat* and *they operated on my windpipe / throat*. In fact, *jump*, *down* and the possessive *my* are all part of the idiom *to jump down one's throat*. Similarly, if *hit* and *pail* are contrasted with *kick* and *bucket* in the expression *to kick the bucket* it becomes clear that *kick the bucket* is an idiom. The same goes for an adjectival idiom like *red herring*: *red herring* is not to *green herring* as *red book* is to *green book*.

Recurrent semantic contrast does not mean that all idioms are equally difficult to decode. Idioms show different degrees of semantic opacity: *white tops* is less opaque than *white elephant* or *red herring*. Knowledge of the world will play a part in the degree to which speakers feel idioms to be opaque. Many idioms originated in metaphors which some speakers recognize while others remain unaware of their origin. Thus, while *bury the hatchet, give somebody the green light* and *gnash one's teeth* are likely to be intelligible to many, only few will know that *white elephant* ("some expensive but completely useless object") apparently derives from a king of Siam who used to make a present of a white elephant to people he wished to ruin. Dead metaphors often allow constituents to be replaced by synonyms, near synonyms or a semantic paraphrase, e. g. *tomahawk* instead of *hatchet* in *bury the tomahawk*. Some of the literal meaning is still relevant for the interpretation of, for example, *give someone a piece of one's mind*, but another part remains obscure, i. e. the pejorative, scolding meaning.

Few readers will apply the test of recurrent semantic contrast, so the question arises as to what other means there are to recognize that an expression is an idiom. (1) Many expressions have two meanings, a literal and an idiomatic one (e. g. *kick the bucket, go to the country, pull someone's leg*). In such cases only the context will decide which meaning is intended. In other cases, when a literal reading does not make sense in terms of the world as we know it, the likelihood is that we are dealing with an idiom. This applies to *jump down someone's throat, fly off the handle* and *cats and dogs* (in *rain cats and dogs*). (2) Irregular syntax can lead to the same conclusion, e. g. the definite articles in *kick the bucket* and *fly off the handle*, or *one* in *pull a fast one*. The definite article normally has the function of indicating that an item has already been mentioned or is considered unique in the context of the language community, while the pro-form *one* refers to a noun that must precede it. Neither of these conditions is fulfilled in the idioms just cited. (3) Idioms can also be phonologically irregular in that they have an unpredictable stress pattern. In free syntactic groups, the last lexical item usually carries the tonic stress, e. g. *they ran into the 'house*. This is not so in *like a 'house on fire, you can say' that again, learn the 'hard way, and have a' bone to pick with somebody*. Also, in connected spoken discourse, idioms are often signaled by slight pauses or a clear intake of breath. (4) Finally, there is a certain amount of lexical repetition in the environment of idioms, which makes for greater lexical cohesion. Often something is first described in non-idiomatic language, then the sender refers to it with an idiom, before it is picked up again by a non-idiomatic, literal lexical item.

10.2 Classifications of Idioms

Idioms have been classified in applied linguistics according to the image or picture they evoke (e. g. *pull someone's leg* or *that is rather a mouthful* would appear under the heading of body idioms). This can hardly be called semantic of course, for none of the would-be body parts have that meaning in the idiom. Lattey (1986) divides the 500 idioms she has examined into four categories. (1) Those with a focus on the individual (*keep a stiff upper lip, throw in the towel, die a thousand deaths*); (2) those with a focus on the world (*go down the drain, be touch and go,*

that takes the cake (BrE *the biscuit*)); (3) those that refer to the interaction of individuals (*lend someone a helping hand; someone is not fit to hold a candle to someone else*); (4) and those that express the interaction between an individual and the world (*take up arms for something; know something inside out; be all Greek to someone*).

Idioms have been categorized by linguists according to various syntactic criteria. As mentioned above, idioms fall into two groups, depending on whether they are formed in accordance with the rules of present-day English or not. Another classificatory scheme lists idioms according to their parts of speech, e. g. nominal (*black market, red herring*), adjectival (*down-to-earth, happy-go-lucky*) or verbal (*go in for, put up with, cook the books, blow one's top*). More revealing about the structural characteristics of idioms at the sentence level is Fraser's

classification system which looks at what transformations they allow (1970). He set up a so-called "frozenness hierarchy", in which idioms were arranged into six groups, ranging from those which are totally frozen, i. e. admit no transformation at all, to those at the other end of the scale which show almost no restrictions. Fraser considered, for example, insertions, transpositions, gerund use, passive and cleft sentence transformations. The fixed nature of idioms is shown by the fact that there are no idioms which allow all six transformations, while there are some which do not allow any transformation at all, e. g. *bite off one's tongue* and *face the music*. As we see, the more syntactically frozen an idiom is, the greater its semantic opacity is.

Some of the reasons why certain idioms do or do not allow

transformations seem to be idiosyncratic; for others, semantic reasons can be given. Idioms will resist the isolation of one formative for emphasis, for example, in cleft sentence construction (*it was her throat that he jumped down) as well as in adjectival and adverbial modification (*He jumped down her sore throat.) because both operations presuppose that word forms are semantic constituents, which they are not. *Throat* in *he jumped down her throat* has no isolable meaning in the idiom and can therefore not be modified. For the same reason, substitutions are not usually possible in idioms, e.g. *kick the pail, *inter the hatchet, *leap down someone's throat. Insertions are, however, possible in some cases (they are printed in bold here): *that rings a **faint** bell; he is going to come **a hell of** a cropper; the recipes are no great **culinary** shakes.*

10.2.1 Grammatical aspects of English idioms

Some idioms are completely fixed and can be entered into the lexicon as multiple-word entries. They do not allow for syntactic variation or internal modification, as seen in the following examples. The asterisk means that the string of words does not have an idiomatic reading, such as:

(1) A. spick and span / *spick and very span
    B. by and large / *by and much larger
    C. at any rate / *at any special rate
    D. real estate / *real urban estate / urban real estate

The majority of idioms, however, allow for considerably more flexibility, for example the idiom *take into account.* In a normal declarative sentence, there is a direct object between *take* and *into account.* The idiom consists of the verbal head *take* and the "frozen" prepositional object *into account.*

(2) A. John took his teacher's proposal into account.
    B. John took the proposal that his teacher's advisor made yesterday into account.
    C. John took the proposal that Bill claims his teacher's advisor made yesterday into account.

While most idioms involve "frozen" arguments of the verb, some idioms involve "frozen" adjuncts, e.g. *take the bull by the horns.*

Most idioms headed by a verb can undergo passivization, but there are some cases, where the idiomatic meaning is lost in the passive form (e.g. *kick the bucket*).

(3) A. His teacher's proposal was taken into account. (idiomatic)
    B. The police kept tabs on these immigrants. (idiomatic)
    C. Tabs were kept on these immigrants. (idiomatic)
    D. Jack kicked the bucket. (literal and idiomatic)
    E. *The bucket was kicked by Jack. (only literal)

(4) A. Tom took his mother's words into account.
    B. Tom took into account all the nasty things his mother has been telling him when they were living together.

Some idioms can be modified internally, while others cannot.

(5) A. Jack kicked the bucket.
    B. *Jack kicked the tragic bucket.

(6) A. John took the proposal into account.
    B. *John took his teacher's proposal into thorough account.
    C. *John took his teacher's proposal into (several) accounts.

(7) A. The police kept tabs on these immigrants.
   B. The police kept close tabs on these immigrants.

However, it may be argued that (7) is not really idiomatic because *tabs* has the same meaning without the verb *keep*, for example in a newspaper headline *The police kept close tabs on these immigrants*. This is not possible with the phrase *the bucket*, as exemplified by the following impossible headline *Jack kicked the tragic bucket*.

In the idiom *make up one's mind*, the possessive pronoun must agree in gender and person with the subject of *make*. Modification of *mind* and passivization are not possible.

(8) A. John made up his mind.
   B. *John made up her mind.
   C. *John made up his bright mind.
   D. *John's mind was made up by him.

In idioms which are headed by a verb, the verb can of course have different inflectional forms:

(9) A. We take the teacher's proposal into account.
   B. Bill takes the teacher's proposal into account.
   C. Bill took the teacher's proposal into account.
   D. After Bill had taken the teacher's proposal into account, he …
   E. Taking the teacher's proposal into account seemed easy, but …

As the "frozen" complements involved in lexicalized metaphors, the same is not true for the following idioms.

(10) A. He took a walk today. If the weather is fine, he will take one tomorrow.
    B. Standing on the platform, Jack pulled a string or two.
    C. *If Jack doesn't kick the bucket today, he will kick it tomorrow.

The above examples illustrate the syntactic aspects of idiomatic expressions, which must be accounted for in a formal theory of English grammar.

10.2.2 Idioms and simple lexemes

As idioms show unitary meanings in the same way as single word lexemes do, linguists have wondered whether idioms behave more like simple lexemes or more like phrases or clauses. The answer is that they show characteristics of both. If *jump down one's throat* behaved like a single word lexeme the past tense would be *he jump-down-my-throated*, which it is not. Neither *redder herring* nor *red herringer* are found, nor is *roll out the red carpets*, though *red herrings* and *John has bees in his bonnet about many things* are possible. It would seem, then, that nouns, adjectives and verbs in idioms are restricted in their freedom to share in the inflectional processes typical of their part of speech.

10.2.3 Binomials

Binomials, like collocations, consist of two word forms (see Norrick (1988) for a recent discussion). These belong to the same word class and are linked by a grammatical item, frequently *and*. Their constituents can be independently meaningful (as in *bed and breakfast* or *hire and fire*), or they can be idiomatic (*bag and baggage, by and by, head over heels*). There are also three-member combinations (trinomials, e.g. *left, right and centre* or *hook, line and sinker*), but these are much less numerous. The two constituents can be identical, as in *face to face* and *so-and-so*. The basic structure can be expanded, e.g. *from rags to riches, by fair means or foul* and *every Tom, Dick and Harry*. Binomials often preserve words which are rare (e.g. *hale* in *hale and hearty*) or only survive in the binomial expression (e.g. *kith* in *kith and kin*). The collocative potential of binomials varies as with other lexical combinations. *Bed and breakfast*, *high and mighty* and *odds and ends* enter into free combinations, while *high and mighty* forms a collocation with *leave*, and *hook, line and sinker* with *believe (something)* or the synonymous verbs *accept*, *fall for*, *swallow* and *take (something)*.

Syntactically, the two constituents belong to the same word class and can have syntactic functions which neither constituent could have on their own, e. g. the three nouns *hook*, *line* and *sinker* function as an adverbial (*he accepted the story hook, line and sinker*), while the two adverbs *so-and-so* form a noun phrase (e. g. *What do you think of that old so-and-so?*).

The fixed expressions we are dealing with in this section are called irreversible binomials because their word order is, in contrast to collocations, completely unchangeable. This is no doubt connected to the fact that the second (or third in trinomials) constituent is usually phonetically more weighty, i. e. longer, than the first, *bacon and eggs* being one of the few exceptions. Also, none of the items can be exchanged for synonyms. There is no **help and abet* or **aid and help* or **kith and relatives*. Insertions are possible, though infrequent: *they really offered a marvelous bed and an even better breakfast* is a possible expansion of *bed and breakfast*, as is *they do you excellent bacon and not bad eggs*. On the other hand, **this is all an important part and even more important parcel of the whole initiation process* is not acceptable. This example would suggest that the nearer the binomials are to the idiomatic end of the semantic scale, the more fixed they become. The fixed nature of many binomials is heightened by assonance or alliteration. Rhyme is also not uncommon, e. g. *hire and fire*, *make or break*, *town and gown* and *wine and dine*.

Semantically, the two halves of binomials exhibit a whole spectrum of possibilities. They may consist of two near synonyms, which often complement or intensify each other, e. g. *rules and regulations*, *fuss and bother* and *over and done with*. They may also stand in semantic opposition to each other, as in *assets and liabilities*, *give and take* and *war and peace*. More generally, binomials range from completely transparent (*bed and breakfast, bacon and eggs, here, there and everywhere*) to semi-transparent (*kith and kin, left, right and centre, town and gown*) to opaque or completely idiomatic (*high and dry, hook, line and sinker, on the up and up*).

10.2.4 Pragmatic idioms

In this section we will discuss lexical items and expressions whose use is determined by a particular social situation. We will refer to them as pragmatic idioms although there are many other terms such as routines or social formulas or gambits. Pragmatic idioms are not to be confused with pragmatic markers or expressions, often called discourse markers, such as *well*, *you know*, *I mean*, etc.

Among the many situations in which stereotypical, or routinized, language is used are the beginnings (greetings, introductions) and endings (leave takings) of social encounters and letters, eating and drinking, and all sorts of business transactions, as for example at a (railway) ticket counter (*Single or return?*), in a shop (*Can I help you?*, *Next, please*), or in a cafe (*Black or white?*) or wine bar (*White or red?*).

Situations differ in the degree to which the language used in them is predetermined. In many cases there is no choice, as in formal letters where one has to use *Dear* and *Yours* even when one has anything but friendly feelings for the addressee. In other situations, various options are available. When one meets people for the first time and introductions are made, one can use *How do you do?*, *Hello*, *Hi*, *Nice/Pleased to meet you* and *I have been looking forward to meeting you (for some time)*. How do these expressions differ from one another? First, they belong to different levels of personal tenor with *How do you do?* at the formal end, *Hi (there)* at the informal end and *Hello* and the other two somewhere in the middle. *How do you do?* is becoming increasingly rare, not least because of the growing informality of English. When it is used, speakers often try to make it less distant and formal by combining it with *Hello* or *Pleased to meet you*. It is also felt to be typical of a certain social class (upper middle to upper), while *Pleased to meet you* is not so socially restricted. Other expressions are regionally marked, such as *Straight or handle?* (refers to whether one wants a glass with or without a handle in a British pub), or *Time, gentlemen please* (landlord's cry to get his customers to drink up and leave his pub). Another professional restriction can be seen in *Enjoy!*, used by waiters who have just served customers their food — the nearest that English gets to *bon appetite*, *buon appetito*, or *Guten Appetit!*

In contrast to the other types of fixed expression discussed in this chapter, pragmatic idioms often need the context of situation in order to be understood correctly. *Black or white?* in a different context (e.g. *Was the waiter black or white?*) has a completely different meaning. The difficult semantics results in many cases from omission: *Say when* is presumably shortened from *Say when I am to stop pouring* or *Say when you have enough*. Moreover, many situational idioms show a weakened meaning. This is obvious in both *Dear* and *Yours* discussed above and in *How are you?* which is usually no more than a ritual recognition of the hearer's presence, and does not express a deeply felt interest in his or her well-being. *How do you do?* is semantically extreme in that it is difficult to state what meaning it has. Rather than state its meaning, many dictionaries describe its function ("used by people who meet for the first time").

All these aspects — regional and social class dialect and semantics — are still not sufficient when one wants to use them appropriately. It is also important to know the linguistic context. If introductions are made by a third party, and one speaker says *How do you do?*, how does the second person react? In most cases, she or he will reply with the same phrase, and the two people will shake hands. In other words, in order to behave correctly you need to know that *How do you do?* is only the second and third step in a sequence which involves three parties (the person introducing and the two being introduced to each other). Moreover, linguistic behavior is accompanied by non-linguistic behavior (the handshake). However, the increasingly informal social atmosphere in the English speaking world has caused a relaxation of these conventions and it is not uncommon for people to reply with other phatic phrases than *How do you do?* and to refrain from shaking hands.

Hi and *Hello*, as well as being informal, differ from *How do you do?* in that they can be used when one meets the same person or people on a later occasion (often with an added *again*, as in *Hi/Hello (there) again*), while *How do you do?* can only be used once. This also sets it apart from *How are you?* which can be used more than once to the same person(s), though usually not on the same day.

To sum up, a full description of pragmatic idioms has to take into account: their register characteristics (e.g. regional and social distribution, personal tenor etc.); their semantic peculiarities; at what point in a social situation or sequence they come; whether they occur alone or whether reciprocity is usual or indeed necessary (and if so whether the same item or a different one can or must be used); whether there is a change of speaker; and, finally, whether the idiom can be used in an identical situation on a later occasion.

10.2.5 Proverbs

Task
Can you translate the following English proverbs into good Chinese? If not, try to look them up in the dictionary.
- East or west, home is best.
- Two heads are better than one.
- Good company on the road is the shortest cut.
- Constant dropping wears the stone.
- Misfortunes never come alone/single.
- Misfortunes tell us what fortune is.
- Better late than never.
- The tongue is boneless but it breaks bones.
- Entertain an angel unawares.
- World is but a little place, after all.

Commonplaces in the form of truisms, tautologies and sayings (see below) are usually complete sentences, but this is not always the case with proverbs, where shortened versions are quite common. Shortening and other changes (additions, variations, transpositions) do not necessarily affect the intelligibility of proverbs, presumably because they are so well known that even fragments and mutations are easily associated with the full form and, indeed, appreciated for their novelty by senders and addressees alike, e. g. "I will write a long letter to my old mucker in Melbourne, I thought, and kill two birds with one tome. I'll get it all off my chest..." (Frayn M. (1989). *The Trick of It*. London: Viking, p. 17; *tome* instead of *stone*). Mention should also be made of another type of fixed expression, the proverbial saying, which is similarly well established and metaphorical but differs from proverbs in that it is never equivalent to a sentence or utterance. For instance, the following three examples need a subject to form a sentence: *hit the nail on the head* and *carry coals to Newcastle*.

Proverbs as a class are not completely frozen, as is shown by the possibility of various additions and insertions. There are for example expressions that mark proverbs as such, e. g. *(as) they say*, *it is said* or *as the proverb goes*, which can precede, interrupt or follow the respective proverb; e. g. *as the old saw says* in: "the man ... took his mother's life insurance policy and unloaded every nickel of it ... Easy come, easy go, as the old saw says" (Auster P. (1999). *Timbuktu*. London: Faber & Faber, p. 76). Norrick calls these proverbial affixes and contrasts them with proverbial infixes like *proverbial, everlovin'* and *(good) ol'* which "can be inserted before any stressed noun phrase in a proverb" (1985: 45), e. g. *The proverbial pen is mightier than the sword*. Proverb collections often list a number of variant forms, which shows that variability is a characteristic trait of proverbs. Transformations like the cleft sentence construction do not change proverbs out of all recognition (e. g. *it is while the iron is hot that it should be struck*) in contrast to most idioms which would become meaningless if changed in this way or allow only a literal reading.

Proverbs often show irregular syntax (*Like father, like son* "a son will resemble his father", *Handsome is as handsome does* "what counts is not appearance, etc. but one's actions"), while truisms conform to the syntactic rules of contemporary English. The vocabulary used in proverbs tends to be Anglo-Saxon or at least from everyday English and is more varied than that in truisms. Both proverbs and commonplaces are concerned with general rather than specific meanings, which is why the past tense is not normally found with them. Proverbs make a claim to wide, but perhaps not universal, validity while commonplace remarks are expected to apply everywhere and at all times. Proverbs are therefore sometimes syntactically restricted, which comes through in restrictive relative clauses, e. g. *He who pays the piper calls the tune*. Truisms do not have this feature, e. g. *You / we (all) live and learn*, *You only live once*, *Business is business*. Many proverbs are metaphorical and may pose problems for understanding while commonplaces are usually literal and easy to process. Proverbs also show features like hyperbole, metonymy and paradox. Proverbs survive because of their formulaic expression and memorable form (see below). While the proverb pattern is no longer productive, commonplaces flourish in everyday communication. Three patterns are distinguished: tautologies (*enough is enough*, *orders are orders*), truisms (*We only live once*) and sayings based on everyday experience (*Accidents happen*, *You never know*, *It's a small world*). Particularly productive is the pattern of tautologies, many of which can exist without making their way into the dictionaries. Proverbs, on the other hand, are well established and traditional, recorded in many collections and dictionaries.

Proverbs contain "a good dose of common sense, experience, wisdom and above all truth" (Mieder, 1989: 15). One, perhaps surprising, aspect of folk wisdom is that it expresses the complexities of life in sayings which contradict each other: compare *Opposites attract* and *Birds of a feather flock together* or *Fine feathers make fine birds* and *Clothes do not make the man*. Proverbs show structural patterns as well as prosodic features not (typically) found with commonplaces, such as its two part structure, alliteration, assonance, rhyme and lexical repetition: *once bitten, twice shy*; *easy come, easy go*; *a friend in need is a friend indeed*; *all that glitters is not gold*.

Proverbs, in the same way as collocations, binomials and idioms, are folklore items, have no known authors and cannot be traced to specific sources. As far as the users of both proverbs and commonplaces are concerned, they can be said to be associated with the older rather than the younger generation. A recent trend in written documents is to play with the form and meaning of proverbs. While they shy away from straightforward use, the sophisticated still employ them to make a witty point, as in "A Ms is as good as Male" (quoted in Mieder, 1993: 71).

To sum up, commonplaces are: complete sentences; fall into three classes; claim universal validity; and are non-metaphorical. This explains both why they are easy to understand and why there is no need to list them in dictionaries. Proverbs are: traditional; express general ideas; and show non-literal meaning (metaphorical, metonymic); they can be added to, transformed and abbreviated. Proverbs are equivalent to a sentence and are also prototypically characterized by certain metrical, structural and prosodic features. Both types of expressions tend to be used more by older speakers.

10. 2. 6　Fixed expressions in texts

Idioms may be studied from a structural, systematic perspective. In the following section, let's take a brief look at how these expressions function in texts. The first point is that one often finds more than one such expression in the same place, for example,

Ronald: I think the bank could probably see their way to helping you out.
Sidney: Ah well, that's wonderful news ... that means I can put in a definite bid for the adjoining site — which hasn't incidentally come on the market. I mean, as I said, this is all purely through personal contacts.
Ronald: Quite so, yes.

Sidney: I mean, the site value alone — just taking it as a site — you follow me?
Ronald: Oh, yes.
Sidney: But it is a matter of striking while the iron's hot — before it goes off the boil.
Ronald: Mmm...
Sidney: I mean, in this world it's dog eat dog, isn't it? No place for sentiment. Not in business. I mean, all right, so on occasions you can scratch my back. I'll scratch yours...
Ronald: Beg your pardon?
Sidney: Tit for tat. But when the chips are down it's every man for himself and blow you, Jack, I regret to say...
Ronald: Exactly.

(Ayckbourn, A. (1979). *Absurd Person Singular,* in *Three Plays,* Harmondsworth: Penguin, p. 38)

Here both speakers use fixed expressions, which characterizes an informal atmosphere (the scene takes place at a New Year's Eve party), e. g. *see one's way to doing something*, *help someone out*, *put in a bid*, *come on the market*, *strike while the iron* is *hot*, *tit for tat*, etc. The massing of fixed expressions in Sidney's language is, however, unusual and reflects his desperate attempt to get Ronald's approval. What Sidney has in mind does not seem to be entirely above-board, and he uses all his rhetoric to convince Ronald that what he, Sidney, is planning to do is not only necessary but also common business practice, and therefore quite acceptable. He uses fixed expressions in the belief that Ronald will find it difficult not to agree with them because they express widely accepted maxims. Sidney speaks as one businessman to another, in the hope that this appeal to their common situation will win Ronald over to his side. Ronald's rather curt reactions suggest, however, that he does not see himself on the same level as Sidney (he is Sidney's bank manager), and perhaps resents Sidney's attempt at establishing common ground between them. As Ronald does not seem to be convinced by the first proverb (*strike while the iron*...) and idiom (*go off the boil*) Sidney pulls in one more proverb (*dog eat dog* = "no quarter is given") to make his point. He also emphasizes the need for cooperation (proverb: *scratch my back and I'll scratch yours*). Sidney's final volley consists of another proverb (*tit for tat*) and a commonplace (*it's every man for himself*), a barrage which wears Ronald down so that he concedes the point. Proverbs and commonplaces are here used "as silencers... the last word on the subject" (Redfern, 1989: 120).

In this example, Ronald does not openly disagree with Sidney even though he does not seem to like him particularly. The social relationship of small business customer and bank manager puts certain restraints on possible behavior, as does the party situation. In the next example we find serious disagreement between a wife, who wants a divorce, and her husband, who does not want to grant it:

Arnold: I can't bring myself to take you very seriously.
Elizabeth: You see, I don't love you.
Arnold: Well, I'm awfully sorry. But you weren't obliged to marry me. You've made your bed and I'm afraid you must lie on it.
Elizabeth: That's one of the falsest proverbs in the English language. Why should you lie on the bed you've made if you don't want to? There's always the floor.
Arnold: For goodness's sake don't be funny, Elizabeth.
Elizabeth: I've quite made up my mind to leave you, Arnold.

(Maugham, S. (1931). *The Circle*, in *Collected Plays, vol. 2*, London: Heinemann)

Why does Arnold use a form of the proverb *You've made your bed and you must lie on* it? A possible contextual paraphrase of the third sentence in his second speech would run *As you did (marry me), you must accept the consequences.* In comparison with the literal *marry,* a simple lexeme, *You've made your bed* is figurative language and a multi-word expression. Figurative language can be regarded as unusual when compared with literal language; it stands out and attracts attention to itself. Speakers are especially likely to use figurative language in situations where they want to highlight what they have to say. The proverb is also more weighty than *marry* as it consists of at least four word forms. It makes Arnold's refusal more emphatic. Furthermore, the relative position of literal and figurative expressions is important. When the figurative expression comes first, the literal counterpart has a rational function, usually to comment or provide a gloss. When the literal expression precedes, as here, the figurative item gives the message an emotional coloring. The meaning of figurative expressions is always more than the sum of their parts, so that by using the proverb after the literal counterpart Arnold avails himself of this semantic surplus. There is of course another proverb with similar meaning (*In for a penny, in for a pound*), but the "bed" proverb seems much better suited to the marital context and is in fact often used by or with reference to husbands and wives.

Proverbs are said to have a didactic tendency, suggesting a course of action. This is sometimes expressed directly (*When in Rome do as the Romans do*, *People in glass houses should not throw stones*), but more often indirectly (*The early bird catches the worm*). This indirect quality of the proverb suits Arnold's nature well; he does not need to show his anger openly but can be apologetic (*I'm awfully sorry*), although on stage his intonation and gestures may give him away. The proverb relieves him of the burden of thinking up a good argument for his refusal; it is there ready-made, waiting to be used. It also allows him to remain superficially nice to his wife, pretending to side with her against the moral demands of society (*I'm afraid ...*), while at the same time making his point.

What has been said so far does not, however, explain Elizabeth's very emotional reaction. This is only understandable if she has been put under considerable pressure. Proverbs contain the practical wisdom of a culture as it has accumulated through the centuries. They are thus authoritative statements which it is difficult to contradict. Arnold hides behind the proverb, with which he can expect to do a more effective job than he could by flatly refusing his wife's request. But how can Elizabeth hold her own against the overwhelming weight of proverbial wisdom? One possible move is to counter the proverb with another proverb which proves the opposite point (see above for examples of contradictory proverbs). Another possibility is to leave the level of direct interaction and talk about (the use of) the proverb and what it means. Elizabeth here takes this option and makes a meta-communicative statement about the validity of the proverb. But calling the proverb false will not on its own do the job of debunking the proverb. That is why she adds two more sentences. The first is a rhetorical question, quite suited to the emotional atmosphere. The second sentence, on the other hand, is thought highly inappropriate by Arnold. Elizabeth's use of wordplay to contradict him strikes him as frivolous and unacceptable. But it is of a piece with her overall strategy of fighting against conventions: just as she does not accept the truth of the conventional wisdom of the proverb, neither does she feel restricted to the conventional idiomatic meaning of the proverb and puts a literal interpretation on it. Arnold's use of the proverb, aimed at crushing his wife, has been foiled by the ridiculous effect achieved by Elizabeth, who reactivates the literal meaning of the proverb and thus robs it of any weight it might have.

The use of fixed expressions as foils for witty wordplay can be seen as characteristic of certain situations and text types. Punning is common in shop names, newspapers and commercial advertisements. Puns are also found in the titles of plays (e. g. Oscar Wilde's *The Importance of Being Earnest*) or works of fiction (e. g. A. Lurie's novel *Foreign Affairs,* which deals with the love affair of two Americans in England). Fixed expressions and wordplay based upon them are more frequent in social science texts than in the natural science texts, and more frequent in popular works on science than in technical scientific texts.

Fixed expressions can have several functions. They generally make people feel at ease and create an in-group feeling. This nearness between the sender of a message and its addressee can make it difficult for the addressee to disagree with the sender — this is clearly the effect that Sidney wants to exploit with Arnold. Fixed expressions (idioms, binomials and proverbs) provide stylistic variety and lend emphasis to statements. It has also been suggested that speakers use idioms to organize their discourse and to make evaluations. Proverbs and commonplaces deal with social situations, and their uses are manifold: "to strengthen our arguments, express certain generalizations, influence or manipulate other people, rationalize our own shortcomings, question certain behavioral patterns, satirize social ills, poke fun of [sic] ridiculous situations" (Mieder, 1989: 21).

10.3 Figurative Idioms

cost an arm and a leg
-非常昂贵

all ears
-很专注地倾听

have cold feet
-为了重要的事情而紧张

lips are sealed
-保密

cry your heart out
-哭得很伤心

Figurative idioms are usually classified as metaphorical idioms and similized idioms. Metaphorical idioms create images in a reader's mind. If one knows all the words that make up a metaphor, he has a good chance of getting the intended image.

Jack and Susan are *bread and butter together*.

It is a metaphor for Jack and Susan's good relationship. So, if one knows all the words (*bread, butter, together*, etc.) and he comes from a culture where people enjoy eating bread with butter, he can easily understand the meaning of the metaphor.

Similized idioms, on the contrary, produce a concept which is brought up by the figurative meaning of simile. For example:

I *had* my lunch.

This is a common metaphorical idiom which means metaphorically that *I ate my lunch*, rather than the literally *I possessed my lunch* from the word HAVE.

But the next one can be interpreted as a metaphorical idiom or a similized idiom: I *wolfed my lunch.*

On the one hand, it can be a metaphorical idiom which means that *I acted like a wolf with my lunch*; on the other hand, it is a similized idiom which means that *I ate my lunch in the way as / like a hungry wolf would.*

10.3.1 Metaphorical idioms

Metaphorical idioms are universal in languages. To learn and study their metaphorical meaning is a process of cognitive activity. In order to identify categories of metaphorical idioms, their linguistic features, grammatical structures, grammatical functions and semantic categories have to be taken into account.

An important idea in contemporary cognitive science is that metaphor is not just an aspect of language, but constitutes a significant part of human cognition.

Many concepts, especially abstract ones, are partly structured via the metaphorical mapping of information from a familiar source domain onto a less familiar target domain. For instance, people often metaphorically conceptualize love by mapping their knowledge of physical journeys onto their knowledge of love, such as: LOVE IS A JOURNEY.

Our metaphorical conceptualization of *love* partly motivates the creation and use of linguistic expressions found in everyday speech and literature that refer to love and love relationships, for example,

A. Our marriage is *off to a great start*.
B. Their marriage is *at a crossroads*.
C. Her marriage is *on the rocks*.
D. After seven years of marriage, we're *spinning our wheels* for several weeks.
E. We're *back on track* again.

What role does metaphoric thought of *marriage*, such as our metaphorical concepts for *love*, play in how people use and understand it in different contexts?

There are four different hypotheses which are required for addressing the above question. They are:

1. Metaphoric thought plays some role in the historical evolution of what words and expressions mean.
2. Metaphoric thought motivates the linguistic meanings that have currency within linguistic communities, or is presumed to have some role in people's understanding of language.
3. Metaphoric thought motivates an individual speaker's use and understanding of why various words and expressions mean what they do.
4. Metaphoric thought functions in people's immediate on-line use and understanding of linguistic meaning.

These hypotheses are not mutually exclusive of one another but reflect a hierarchy of possibilities about the interaction between metaphoric patterns of thought and different aspects of language use and understanding.

With the help of these hypotheses, MARRIAGE is first mapped onto the domain of LOVE and then onto the concept of TRAVEL: so, the word *marriage*

1. in A as a journey which starts, stops or comes to an end;
2. in B as a traveller who comes to a choice of his ongoing route;
3. in C as a sailor who has his ship stuck on a rock;
4. in D as a driver who has his car stuck in the mud;
5. in E as a traveller who has lost his way and finds it again.

Here are more examples for metaphorical idioms for the word MARRIAGE:

A. Marriage is like *a beleaguered fortress*, those who are *without* want to get in and those *within* want to get out.

B. Her marriage is full of worries and troubles.

C. The marriage will take place in May.

D. The marriage of words and melody in that song was unusually effective.

E. It is a marriage of Chinese traditional medicine and western medical care.

The word *marriage* has different meaning in each sentence. It refers to:

a place for living a married life in A;

one's experience of her married life in B;

an arranged marital ceremony of a married couple in C;

a sound and beautiful integration in D;

a balanced and functional cooperation in E.

Lakoff and Johnson's renowned *Metaphors We Live By* provides us with insightful investigation into the conceptual metaphors pervasive in everyday life, which will in turn be of much help in our understanding of those commonly used metaphorical idioms. The below are some examples.

(a) AN ARGUMENT IS WAR

◆ He attacked *every weak point in my argument*.

◆ His criticism was *right on target*.

◆ I *demolished his argument*.

◆ Your disagree? Okay, *shoot*!

◆ He *shot down all of my arguments*.

(b) IDEAS ARE FOOD

◆ All this paper has in it are *raw facts, half-baked*.

◆ There are too many facts here for me to *digest them all*.

◆ I just can't *swallow that claim*.

◆ Let me *stew over* that for a while.

(c) THE MIND IS A MACHINE

◆ We're still trying to *grind out the solution to this equation*.

◆ My mind just isn't *operating* today.

◆ Boy, the *wheels are turning* now!

◆ I'm a *little rusty* today.

◆ We've been working on this problem all day and now we're *running out of steam*.

(d) ANGER IS HEAT and BODY IS CONTAINER FOR EMOTIONS

◆ You make my blood *boil*.

◆ She *got all steamed up*.

◆ I can't *keep my anger bottled up* anymore.

◆ His eyes *smouldered with rage*.

10.3.2 Similized idioms

Contrary to the form of metaphorical idioms, similized idioms often take animal words for its mapping of concept, for example:

A. The little boy sat in a corner, as quiet as a *lamb*.

B. He lost his temper and looked as fierce as a *tiger*.

C. Our manager worked without any rest, as busy as a *bee*.

D. Blind as a *bat*, the young man probed his way in the cave.

E. The girl in white on the playground is as playful as a *kitten*.

F. The beggar snatched up the cake and ate it as greedily as a *wolf*.

G. Having served in the army for ten years, he is as strong as a *horse*.

There are more examples of similized idioms in the daily use:

as surefooted as a *goat*
as fast as a *deer* (a *hare*)
as like as two *earrings*
as tender as a *chicken*
as bald as a *coot*
as cunning as a *fox*
as weak as a *cat*
as bold as a *lion*
as fleet as a *deer*
as graceful as a *swan*
as hoarse as a *crow*
as mute as a *fish*
as obstinate as a *mule*
as poor as a church *mouse*
as silly as a *goose*
as slippery as an *eel*
as timid as a *hare*
as agile as a *monkey*
as heavy as an *elephant*
as proud as a *peacock*
as slow as a *snail* (a *tortoise*)
as fat as a *pig*
as hairy as a *gorilla*

The English idioms, as the uses and meanings of English collocations discussed in the last chapter, are widely-adopted forms with respect to Lexical Chunks.

An idiom is a term or phrase whose meaning cannot be deduced from the literal definitions and the arrangement of its parts, but refers instead to a figurative meaning that is known only through common use. In linguistics, idioms are generally assumed to be figures of speech based on their time-honored use. It may be better to refer to idioms as words collocated together which happen to become fossilized, becoming fixed over time. This kind of collocation — words commonly used in a group — changes the definition of each of the words that exist. As an expression, the word-group becomes a team. That is, when the collocated words develop a specialized meaning as a whole, an idiom comes into being.

Therefore, it is widely assumed that the meaning of an idiom must be a set expression of two or more words that means something other than the literal meanings of its individual words. To be more precise, an idiom is a group of words which, when used together, have a different meaning from the one suggested by the individual words, e. g. *it was raining cats and dogs*.

Idioms form an important part of the English vocabulary. They have been created, used and studied throughout the past centuries. As time goes on, new idioms and idiomatic expressions are born to enrich the English vocabulary.

Further Reading

1. Cummings, L. (2007). *Pragmatics: A Multidisciplinary Perspective*. Beijing: Peking University

Press.
2. Poole, S. C. (2000). *An Introduction to Linguistics*. Beijing: Foreign Language Teaching and Research Press.
3. Robins, H. R. (2000). *General Linguistics*. Beijing: Foreign Language Teaching and Research Press.

● Extended Reading

■ What are idioms?

Knowing a language includes knowing the morphemes, simple words, compound words and their meanings. In addition, it means knowing fixed phrases, consisting of more than one word, with meanings that cannot be inferred from the meanings of the individual words. The usual semantic rules for combining meanings do not apply. Such expressions are called *idioms*. All languages contain many idiomatic phrases, as in these English examples:

sell down the river
haul over the coals
eat my hat
let their hair down
put his foot in his mouth
throw her weight around
snap out of it
cut it out
hit it off
get it off
bite your tongue
give a piece of your mind

Idioms are similar in structure to ordinary phrases except that they tend to be frozen in form and do not readily enter into other combinations or allow the word order to change. Thus,

(1) *She put her foot in her mouth.*

has the same structure as

(2) *She put her bracelet in her drawer.*

but whereas

The drawer in which she put her bracelet was hers.
Her bracelet was put in her drawer.

are sentences related to sentence 2,

The mouth in which she put her foot was hers.
Her foot was put in her mouth.

and do not have the idiomatic sense of sentence 1.

On the other hand, the words of some idioms can be moved without affecting the idiomatic sense:

The FBI kept tabs on radicals.
Tabs were kept on radicals by the FBI.
Radicals were kept tabs on by the FBI.

Idioms can break the rules on combining semantic properties. The object of *eat* must usually be something with the semantic property "edible", but in

he ate his hat

eat your heart out

this restriction is violated.

Idioms, grammatically as well as semantically, have special characteristics. They must be entered into the lexicon or mental dictionary as single "items", with their meaning specified, and speakers must learn the special restrictions on their use in sentences.

Many idioms may have originated as metaphorical expressions that "took hold" in the language and became frozen in their form and meaning.

— Fromkin, V. et al.

 Exercises

I. Try to find the idioms in the following sentences and explain them.
1. "Oh, let's play the game," he said, when his partner suggested a way to keep from paying some of their debts.
2. Ever since Hughes went into that business he has been coining money.
3. Men's kickers went out of style and are now a drug on the market.
4. The old woman was in the seventh heaven at meeting her long-lost son.
5. He had the knack of always being in hot water with his wife.
6. When her boyfriend calls, Megan will drop everything to go and meet him. She will leave at the drop of a hat.
7. John's friends were going to have a surprise party for him, but Tom spilled the beans.
8. The teacher tore his heart at the boy's stupid answer.
9. The drunk told his troubles to every Tom, Dick and Harry who passed by.
10. Most parents are still uncomfortably Victorian when they approach their children about the birds and the bees.

II. Complete the following binomials with proper words.
1. aches and _____
2. bits and _____
3. cease and _____
4. bag and _____
5. head and _____
6. nook and _____
7. peak and _____
8. puff and _____
9. pull and _____
10. really and _____
11. stuff and _____
12. toil and _____
13. twists and _____
14. ways and _____
15. well and _____

III. Translate the following proverbs of William Shakespeare.
1. Home-keeping youth have ever homely wits.
2. Men are not angels.
3. It is hard to laugh and cry both with a breath.
4. More matter, with less art.
5. Lend your money and lose your friend.
6. Have is have.
7. Take all and pay all.

8. Every why has a wherefore.
9. Every man should take his own.
10. Tell the truth and shame the devil.
11. Care is no cure.
12. Brevity is the soul of wit.
13. The course of true love never did run smooth.
14. A woman is the weaker vessel.
15. All the world's a stage.
16. All cats love fish but fear to wet their paws.
17. There is measure in all things.
18. It is a wise father that knows his own child.
19. Cowards die many times before their deaths; The valiant never taste of death but once.
20. ... so young a body, with so old a head.

Chapter 11
The Use of English Words (1)
— Words in Context

> **Points for Thinking**
> 1. What is the relationship between words and their meanings?
> 2. What is the function of semantic property in semantics?
> 3. How can we explain the distinction of semantics and pragmatics?
> 4. What does lexical pragmatics study?
> 5. What are the uses of lexical narrowing, approximation and metaphorical extension?

Lexical semantics is a subfield of linguistic semantics. It is the study of how and what the words of a language denote.

Words may either be taken to denote things in the world, or concepts, depending on the particular approach to lexical semantics.

Pragmatics studies the ways that context affects meaning. The two primary forms of context important to pragmatics are linguistic context and situational context.

11.1 Words and Their Meanings in Use

In chapters 7 and 8, we have touched a little upon the meanings of words. Now it is time that we look at the words within the fields of lexical semantics and lexical pragmatics. So first, there needs to be a necessary passage on such a topic, "What does MEANING mean?" Let's read the following dialogue from a well-known novel:

(1) "There's *glory* for you!"

"I don't know what you mean by '*glory*'," Alice said.

Humpty Dumpty smiled contemptuously.

"Of course you don't till I tell you. I *meant* 'there's a nice knock-down argument for you!'"

"But '*glory*' doesn't *mean* 'a nice knock-down argument'," Alice objected.

"When I use a word," Humpty Dumpty said, in rather a scornful tone, "it *means* just what I choose it to *mean* — neither more nor less."

"The question is," said Alice, "whether you can make words *mean* so many different things."

— Lewis Carroll's *Alice's Adventures in Wonderland*

The contextual use of words comes to the point. It would be pointless without considering the real use of words in our daily verbal communication. Not all language use is equally meaningful in the same ways. Knowing a language includes knowing the agreed-upon meanings of words with certain strings of sounds and knowing how to combine these meaningful units into larger units that also convey meaning.

All the speakers of a language share conventionally a basic vocabulary — the sounds and meanings of words. Humpty Dumpty, as we read from the quotation, was unwilling to accept this convention. Alice, on the other hand, is right in saying "*glory*" does not *mean* "a nice knock-down argument". Fortunately, there are few Humpty Dumptys around us. Though it seems that anybody is free to change the meanings of any word at his own will, he would be unable to communicate with anyone else, if he did so.

11.2 The Meanings of Words: "Mean" and "Meaning"

Now here are two sentences for us to think about the meanings of the two particular English words "*mean*" and "*meaning*".

(2) Situation A: Teacher (to the pupils in the classroom): Now, who can tell us the *meaning* of "WAR"?

(3) Situation B: A wounded soldier (to a group of politicians): Do you guys really know the *meaning* of "WAR"?

In (2), the word "WAR" requires its literal meanings from a dictionary or an encyclopedia. It is just a direct requirement for the word's definition. But in (3) the word "WAR" goes beyond any of its literal meanings, which arouses the attention to the death and destruction caused by a real warfare. It states out a call for an earnest request of "Ending the War" or a simple exclamation of "No War".

While this word-meaning pairing is generally accepted, there have been a bewildering array of approaches and theories with respect to the nature and organization of word meanings. In a large part, this is due to the word meanings as protean in nature, that is to say, the semantic value of a given word is prone to offer quite significant variations across instances of use. To illustrate it, let us consider the word *fast* in the following utterances:

(4) a. That parked BMW is a *fast* car.
 b. That car is traveling *fast*.
 c. That doddery old man is a *fast* driver.
 d. That's the *fast* lane (of the motorway).

The semantic values associated with the word *fast* appear to be somewhat different. In (4a) *fast* has to do with the potential for rapid locomotion. In (4b) it has to do with observable rapid locomotion. In (4c) it relates to caused motion beyond an established norm: a speed limit. And in (4d) it concerns a venue for rapid locomotion.

Here are more frequently cited examples from C. K. Ogden and A. Richards, two well-known linguists on the topic of "What does a WORD mean?" They managed to distinguish 16 different meanings of the word "mean" (so called as "mean meaning").

(5) a. John *means* to write.
   b. A green light *means* go.
   c. Health *means* everything.
   d. His look was full of *meaning*.
   e. What is the *meaning* of life?
   f. What does "capitalist" *mean* to you?
   g. What does "cornea" *mean* in a dictionary?

(Ogden, C. K. and Richards, I. A., 1923)

The above sentences show us seven meanings of the word "mean" in particular situations:
(6) a. John has his *intention* to write.
   b. It refers to the *indication* of "green light" in the traffic rule.
   c. It explains the *importance* of health for any person.
   d. A special *import* came out from his look.
   e. The speaker directly asks for a *viewpoint* on human life.
   f. The speaker demands for the implicated meaning *conveyed* by "capitalist".
   g. The speaker wants to know what "cornea" *refers to* in reality.

It is the last sentence that comes closest to the focus of literal meaning; the study of the literal meaning is the main focus of lexical semantics. Of greater importance is the study of the way in which words convey different meanings in human speech and writing.

11.3 Lexical Semantics

11.3.1 The semantic study on meaning

Generally speaking, semantics has been largely concerned with discovering what "meaning" is, as a focus in its own right.

Modern semantics regards meanings of words as part of linguistic knowledge and therefore as a part of the human communicative competence. The human mental storehouse of information about words and morphemes is what linguists have been calling the LEXICON (or lexical entry). The study of the lexicon is carried out within the field of Lexical Semantics.

In a similar way, it is argued that to say "words having meaning" means only that they are used in a certain way in a particular sentence. For example, the word "*fish*" has its literal meaning, or definition as:

any cold-blooded creature, living in the water and using its fins and tail to swim, characteristically having gills and a streamlined body.

Let us consider how about the uses of the word "*fish*" in the following four sentences:
(7) a. I like *fish*.
   b. He caught a *fish*.
   c. You are such a poor *fish*.
   d. He looked eager to *fish* for compliments.

It is not difficult to understand the varied meanings of the individual word *fish* in these four sentences: It means "the cooked *fish*" in (7a); "a particular *fish* one caught" in (7b); "a poor or unlucky person" in (7c), and "look for or try hard to seek for" in (7d). If there are more sentences, there will be more meanings of *fish* beyond its literal one in any dictionary.

Dictionaries are filled with words and their definitions (called literal meanings). So is the brain of every human being who speaks a language. Every speaker of a language could be called as a walking dictionary for knowing the meanings of thousands of words. The knowledge of word meanings permits a language user to use them to express the thoughts and to understand when hearing or reading them, even though someone, probably (not always), stops and asks himself, "What does the noun *boy* mean?" or "What does the verb *walk* mean?"

The enquiries on meaning of words have undoubtedly increased our understanding of the nature of the problem, but an accepted definition of "meaning" is as far away today as it was in Plato's time. Why should this be so? For example,

(8) a. The tree is 15 meters *high*.
    b. The street is 500 meters *long*.
    c. The lake is 5 meters *deep*.
    d. The river is 100 meters *wide*.

Any of the above sentences does not mean that there is an abstract property of "*height*", "*length*", "*depth*" or "*width*", that exists independently of the objects *tree, street, lake* and *river*. It is now widely held that "meaning" is not something separable from language use. Meaning is no similar to those measures such as "*height*", "*length*", "*depth*" or "*width*", which have some kind of independent existence. To say that objects "have a certain height" means only that they are so many units high; so are the objects with their "length", "depth" or "width".

11.3.2 Semantic properties

Words have meanings. We need to understand and interpret the meaning of words, even though they may be composed of several morphemes, as noted in previous chapters. Suppose someone says:

(9) John F. Kennedy was *assassinated* in 1961.

If the word *assassin* is in our mental dictionary of English, we know that it was some *person* who murdered an important/political *figure* named John F. Kennedy. The knowledge of the meaning of *assassin* tells us that it could not likely be an animal who had done the murdering act, and that John F. Kennedy could not possibly be a shop assistant who had previously worked in a neighborhood store. Knowledge of *assassin* includes knowing that the word *assassin* is

1) firstly an act by one or more human beings, then
2) playing the role of a murderer or murderers, and more
3) causing the death of one or more important/political figures.

These pieces of information, then, are parts of the semantic properties of the word *assassin* upon which speakers of the language agree. The meaning of all nouns, verbs, adjectives, and adverbs — the content words — and some of the function words, such as *with* and *over* can at least partially be specified by such properties.

In the following discussion, a double quotation mark " " is used to indicate the semantic property of a word or a group of words and *italics* are used for referring to the group of words sharing a common semantic property.

The same semantic property may be part of the meaning of many words. "Female" is a semantic property of English nouns that helps to define the words in the following columns of words:

(10) A   B
    tigress   woman
    hen   maiden
    ewe   lass
    vixen   bride
    doe   girl
    mare   aunt

The words *woman*, *maiden*, *lass*, *bride*, *girl* and *aunt* in Column B are also distinguished by the semantic property "human", which is also found in the following words:

(11) A   B
    doctor   baby
    teacher   child
    parent   kid
    manager   youngster
    bachelor   youth

The meanings of the words in Column B are also specified as a semantic property of "young", while the words in Column A could be "either young or old". That is, part of the meaning of the words *baby*, *child*, *kid*, *youngster* and *youth* is that they are both "human" and "young".

The meanings of words have other properties. The word *father* has the properties of "male" and "adult", as do *uncle* and *bachelor*, but *father* also has the property of "parent", which distinguishes it from *uncle* and *bachelor*.

Hen, in addition to "female" and "animal", must also have a property of "poultry". Words have general semantic properties such as "human" or "parent" as well as specific properties that give the word its particular meanings.

The same semantic property may occur in words of different categories. The word *hand* is in the semantic property of "a part of body", and also the property of the verb "pass something to somebody by using one's hand". The semantic property of "female" is part of the meaning of the noun *mother*, of the verb *breast-feed a baby*, and of the adjective *pregnant*. It is similar in the meaning of English verbs. The word "cause" is a verbal property of *enrich*, *strengthen*, *break*, *kill*, and so on.

(12) A   B
    enrich   cause to become rich
    strengthen   cause to become strong
    break   cause to be broken
    kill   cause to die

Semantic properties of verbs, as nouns, can be classified in different ways. With or without considering the duration of time for an activity is shown in the following lists of verbs.

(13) A   B
    Semantic Property   Verbs Having It
    activity: learn, read, play, work, walk;
    process: move, grow, extend, change, run;
    bodily sensation: feel, ache, itch, hurt, injure;
    transitional event: fall, arrive, die, lose, leave;
    momentary: throw, shake, nod, strike, knock.

Similarly, the verbs *bring*, *fall*, *stride*, *walk* and *run* are grouped to show the semantic property of "motion"; the verbs *hit*, *kiss*, *touch* and *connect* to show of "contact"; the verbs *build*, *imagine*, *make* and *produce* to show of "creation", and the verbs *see*, *hear*, *feel* and *taste* to show of "sensibility".

11.3.3 Semantic features and componential analysis

For the most part, no two words have exactly the same meaning. Additional semantic properties make for increasingly finer distinctions in meaning. The motion verb *walk* is strikingly distinguished from the verb *run* by the property of "being slower than" and *roam* from *walk* by properties like "aimlessly" and "without any plan".

The word is the part of knowledge that speakers have about individual words, including their semantic properties. Words that share a semantic property are said to be in a semantic class, for example, the semantic class of "female" words in (10). Semantic classes may intersect, such as the class of words with the properties "human" and "young". The words *child* and *kid* are members of this class.

Whether a word's meanings can be broken down into parts is one of the main issues in a theory of concepts / meanings. In some cases, the presence of one semantic property can be inferred from the presence or absence of another. For example, speakers of English know the word "*man*" denotes a "*human*" who is "*adult*" and "*male*". So, words referring to family relationship lend themselves to such a binary approach. The words like *daughter*, *son*, *mother* and *father* denote either a male person or a female person, either an early generation or a later generation, and so on.

As intersecting classes share some features, members of the class of words referring to human females are marked "plus" for the features "human" and "female". Due to such intuitions, semanticists have tried to develop theories of meaning that "unpack" words in "simpler" terms or semantic (binary) "features" such as [± HUMAN], [± ADULT], [±MALE].

So this is the way of representing semantic properties by the use of semantic features. Semantic features are a formal or notational device that indicates the presence or absence of semantic properties by pluses and minuses. For example, the words in (14) such as *woman*, *father*, *boy*, *girl*, and *baby* would appear as a semantic class in the following (with other information omitted):

(14)
woman	father	boy	girl	baby
+female	+male	+male	+female	±male/female
+human	+human	+human	+human	±human
−young	+parent	+young	+young	+young

And the words in (15) *mare*, *stallion*, *colt*, *calf* and *heifer* appear as a semantic class in the following (with the distinction between two families of domestic animal).

(15)
mare	stallion	colt	calf	heifer
+female	+male	+male	+male	+female
+equine	+equine	+equine	−equine	−equine
−young	−young	+young	+young	+young

English verbs might be similarly "unpacked" in terms of meaning components, so a proposal for the "decomposition" of "melt" might be something like "cause to become liquid"; whereas "freeze" would be "cause to become solid". Therefore, the lexical semantics attempts to explain language intuitions about how words are related as synonymy, antonymy, hyponymy, meronymy (whole-part relations, e. g. "finger" is part of a "hand") and polysemy by referring to subsets of "features" that words share. Such decompositional theories have been the focus of considerable research as in the field of lexical semantics over the years.

This approach to word meaning attempts to break words down into features by analogy with phonemes. For example, in (16), these differences are encoded as binary features, whereas in the following table, they are taken from a tree in Cruse (1986), cited in Hatch and Brown's *Vocabulary, Semantics, and Language Education* (1995).

(16) Features for table settings

	Silverware	Dishes	Glasses	Linens	Setting	Serving
Knife	+	–	–	–	+	–
Ladle	+	–	–	–	–	+
Plate	–	+	–	–	+	–
Platter	–	+	–	–	–	+
Wineglass	–	–	+	–	+	–
Wine carafe	–	–	+	–	–	+
Napkin	–	–	–	+	+	–
Tablecloth	–	–	–	+	–	+

(17) Features for table settings could also be rearranged in such a diagram:

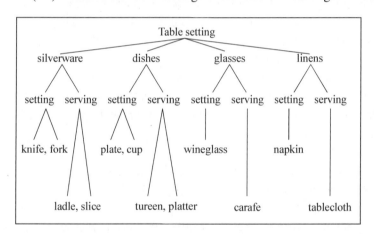 

(from Cruse, 1986: 147; Hatch and Brown, 1995: 37)

Although these are interesting "common-sense" diagrams, the problems with making relationships among words formally precise are considerable. For example, the diagram in (18) suggests an analysis of domesticated birds (as opposed to *pets*, such as *parrots*). They could be split into "water" and "land" birds (webbed-feet might be a distinguishing feature). However, for *duck* vs. *goose*, does [±long neck] play a role as features? If so, how can "swan" be distinguished from "goose"? Which feature(s) will distinguish a *chicken* or a *duck* from a *turkey*? How can we include "pheasant" and "quail" raised for providing *meat*, and laying *eggs*, and so on?

(18) Domestic Birds:

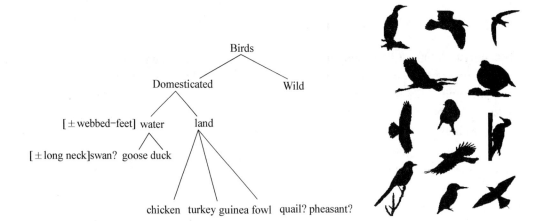

Another difference between nouns may be captured by the use of the feature [±Count]. Consider these data (an asterisk showing the ungrammaticality):

(19) I have two *dogs*.　　　*I have two *rice(s)*.
　　 He has many *dogs*.　　 *He has many *rice(s)*.
　　 *He has much *dogs*.　　 He has much *rice*.

Nouns that can be enumerated — one potato, two potatoes — are called count nouns. They may also be preceded by the quantifier *many* but not by *much*. Nouns such as rice, water, and milk, which cannot be enumerated or preceded by *many*, are called mass nouns. They may be distinguished in the lexicon with one feature:

(20) 　dog　　 potato　　 rice　　　 water　　 milk
　　 +count　　+count　　 −count　　−count　　−count

Our linguistic knowledge about words helps us distinguish their semantic properties, and the relationships. Consider the following knowledge about words that speakers of English have:

(21) If something *swims*, it is in a liquid.
　　 If something is *splashed*, it is a liquid.

Now there is a non-native speaker of English who said these two sentences:

(22) a. *I saw a swan swimming in a *doop*.
　　 b. *Our boat splashed through the *doop*.

Though the word *doop* is not an existing English word, any hearer who understands English would agree that the speaker used this non-English word to refer to the lexical feature of "liquid". Thus, the word *doop* has the semantic feature [+liquid]. Even without knowing what *doop* refers to in the real world, we are able to understand the *doop* in the following situations:

(23) a. pouring *doop*,
　　 b. drinking *doop*, or
　　 c. forming *dooplets* and
　　 d. plugging a hole where *doop* is leaking out.

The words *pour*, *drink*, *leak*, and *droplet* are all used with items relating to the property "liquid". Similarly, we would know that "cutting the *doop* in half", "melting this *doop*", or "bending that *doop*" are semantically ill-formed expressions because considering the words *cut*, *melt* and *bend*, none of these activities apply sensibly to objects that have the semantic feature of [+liquid].

11.4 Lexical Semantics and Lexical Pragmatics

The aim of semantics is to study the linguistic meaning of morphemes, words, phrases, and sentences. Lexical semantics, as a subfield of semantics, is concerned with the meanings of words, and the meaning relationships among words, and phrases, or other language units larger than words or phrases.

The aim of pragmatics is to provide an explicit account of interpretation in particular language contexts. It studies how the context affects meaning, for example, how the sentence "It's cold in here" comes to be interpreted as "close the windows" in certain situations. Lexical pragmatics, as a branch of pragmatic study, tries to give a systematic and explanatory account of pragmatic phenomena that are connected with the semantic meanings of lexical items — words. Cases in point are the pragmatic meanings of words, such as adjectives, systematic polysemy, the distribution of lexical and productive causatives, blocking phenomena, the interpretation of compounds, and many phenomena presently discussed within the framework of Cognitive Semantics.

11.4.1 The distinction between semantics and pragmatics

The sentences in (5) of this chapter show that in everyday English, the word *mean* has a number of different uses which are shown in the brackets respectively:

(24) a. John *means* to write. (intends)
    b. A green light *means* go. (indicates)
    c. Health *means* everything. (has importance)
    d. His look was full of *meaning*. (special import)
    e. What is the *meaning* of life? (point, purpose)
    f. What does "capitalist" *mean* to you? (convey)
    g. What does "cornea" *mean*? (refer to in the world)

There are similar examples as the following, most of which are not relevant to the scope of linguistic meaning:

(25) a. That was no *mean* (insignificant) accomplishment.
    b. This will *mean* (result in) the end of our regime.
    c. I *mean* (intend) to help if I can.
    d. Keep off the Grass! This *means* (refers to) you.
    e. His losing his job *means* (implies) that he will have to look for jobs again.
    f. Lucky Strike *means* (indicates) fine tobacco.
    g. Those clouds *mean* (are a sign of) rain.
    h. She doesn't *mean* (believe) what she said.

These uses of the word *mean* can all be paraphrased by other expressions (indicated in parentheses above). None of them is appropriate for our discussion of word meanings. Rather, we will use the terms *mean* and *meaning* as they are used in the following examples:

(26) a. Postpone *means* "to put things off".
    b. In saying "It's getting late", she *meant* that we should leave.

These two uses of the word *mean* exemplify two important types of meaning: a linguistic meaning (26a) and the meaning of the speaker (26b).

Such a distinction can be illustrated with the following example:

Suppose that a son has been arguing with his father, and the latter exclaims, "The door is right *behind* you!". The son would assume, quite properly in this context, that his father, in uttering this sentence, means that the son is told to leave — although the father's actual words indicate nothing more than the location of the door.

This illustrates how a speaker can mean something quite different from what his or her words literally mean. Pragmatics describes it as the speaker's meaning.

11.4.2 The varieties of meaning

In general, the linguistic meaning of an expression is simply the meaning or meanings of that expression in the language. In contrast, the speaker's meaning can differ from the linguistic meaning, depending on whether the speaker is speaking literally or non-literally. When we speak literally, we mean what our words mean, and in this case there is no important difference between the speaker's meaning and the linguistic meaning. But when we speak non-literally, we mean something different from what our words mean.

Pragmatic uses of language are usually the types of non-literal language use, as, for example, when someone is described as having

(27) a. *raven* hair,
     b. *ruby* lips,
     c. *emerald* eyes, and
     d. teeth of *pearl*.

Taken the words literally, this description would indicate that the person in focus is a monstrosity; however, taken pragmatically or non-literally, it is quite a compliment. A crucial feature in human communication is the ability on the part of the hearer to determine whether a speaker is speaking literally or non-literally. The non-literal use of words is also interpreted as metaphorical uses of language. Metaphor is the main focus of the next chapter.

Returning now to the topic of linguistic meaning, it is helpful to keep in mind the distinction between the linguistic meaning of an expression and a given speaker's literal or non-literal use of the expression. The varieties of meaning we have specified so far are summarized in (28).

(28) Some varieties of meaning

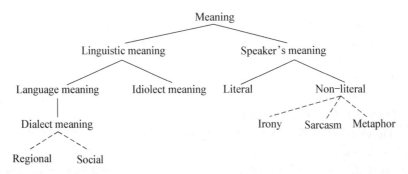

As the figure shows, in talking about the linguistic meaning of an expression, we must note that meanings can vary across dialects and across individual speakers.

(A) The dialect meaning concludes the regional varieties and social varieties, as is shown in the above figure. The word *bonnet*, which has different meaning in British English and American English, is a typical example of the regional varieties of meaning.

(29)

	a type of hat	the hood of a car
Br. English	yes	yes
Am. English	yes	no

Hence, for a word such as *bonnet* we cannot isolate a single meaning valid for all forms of English; rather, our understanding or production of the meaning of this word will be relative to a specific dialect of English.

Another example is the word *tog* in English which refers to clothes one wears in formal dinner, but in New Zealand, it refers to clothes one wears to swim in. The following table is a brief summary of regional dialects between British English and American English.

British English	American English
pavement	sidewalk
boot	trunk
bonnet	hood
petrol	gas
baggage	luggage

Dialect
People from different regions say things differently
People use different words to say the same thing
Let's Say Hello

Howdy!   Yo!   ???

(B) Regional dialects are varieties associated with speakers living in a particular location, while social dialects are varieties associated with speakers belonging to a given demographic group (e.g. women versus men, or different social classes). The most important social dialect in America is African-American Vernacular English (AAVE), also known as Black English or Ebonics. AAVE speakers do use some words which are not found in other varieties, and use some English words in ways that differ from the standard dialects. In some cases, the morphological form is from English but the meaning appears to be derived from West African sources. Take a look at the following examples.

cat: "a friend, a fellow, etc." cf. Wolof *-kat* (a suffix denoting a person)
cool: "calm, controlled" cf. Mandingo *suma* "slow" (literally "cool")
dig: "to understand, appreciate, pay attention" cf. Wolof *deg, dega* "to understand, appreciate"
bad: "really good"

In West African languages and Caribbean creoles a word meaning "bad" is often used to mean "good" or "a lot/intense". For instance, in Guyanese Creole *mi laik am bad, yu noo* means "I like him a lot".

(C) Things might get complicated when we note the meanings of words can vary across individual speakers within the same dialect. The term idiolect, made up of the Greek *idio* (personal, private) + *(dia)lect*, was coined by linguist Bernard Bloch. An *idiolect* is the distinctive speech of an individual. It is clear that the idiolectal meaning of a word can differ from person to another. To illustrate just how individual an idiolect can be, take this dialogue from Tom, played by Aziz Ansari, in NBC comedy *Parks and Recreation*, where he explains his own personal "slanguage":

"*Zerts* are what I call desserts. *Tray-trays* are entrees. I call sandwiches *sammies*, *sandoozles*, or *Adam Sandlers*. Air conditioners are *cool blasterz*, with a *z*. I don't know where that came from. I call cakes *big ol' cookies*. I call noodles *long-a** rice*. Fried chicken is *fri-fri chicky-chick*. Chicken parm is *chicky chicky parm parm*. Chicken cacciatore? *Chicky catch*. I call eggs *pre-birds* or *future birds*. Root beer is *super water*. Tortillas are *bean blankies*. And I call forks ... *food rakes*." (2011)

The meanings of the above-italicized words are unique to the speaker and by no means to other individuals, even those who can be said to speak the same dialect.

The investigation of word meanings in language use has connected semantics with pragmatics in the lexical study. The two fields of linguistics are so far only loosely related.

A particular kind of accounts for the contrast division between lexical semantics and general pragmatics has been developed in this research area. Determining whether various meanings of a word in various contexts are properly represented lexically or pragmatically is not a simple task.

Different researchers adopt different criteria in this respect, which, to some extent, is inevitable, given their different assumptions about the role of the words and the expressive power of the lexical component and pragmatics. But there is no doubt that lexical semantics has to interact with pragmatics to explain various word meanings in utterances. Thus, a new linguistic discipline, namely lexical pragmatics, is emerging.

11.5 Lexical Meaning and the Context

When we use language there is content, but language is not only a way of telling, but also a way of doing. The linguistic subfields of semantics and pragmatics are both concerned with the study of meaning.

Semantics studies the literal meaning — the basic meanings of the words. Semanticists assume that words do have basic meanings, and that a given syntactic structure corresponds with a determinate way of composing the meanings of its words and phrases.

Pragmatics, on the other hand, attempts to explain the non-literal meaning — what someone means by saying on a particular occasion. The literal meaning of a word often differs from what someone means by uttering it on a given occasion.

Whenever language is used, there is a speaker with his intent, and more often than not, the non-literal or implicit intent is hidden behind the literal meaning (i. e. "between the lines") of what is said.

For example, ten minutes after a lesson began, a student hurried into the classroom and took his seat, the teacher stopped and said to the student,

(32) T: My goodness, you're *early* today!

S: Sorry, Madam. I promise I won't be *late* again.

Coming to school early is good for a student. Generally, the word *early* can show the teacher's compliment to the student. Is it so in this particular case? Of course not. It simply reveals the teacher's annoyance for the teaching being interrupted by the late-comer. Then we might have more questions to think about.

How could she use the word *early* to mean *late*?

As the student apologized, what helped him to interpret *early* for *late*?

To any language user, the answer is quite clear and simple, just from consideration of the communicative situation or more properly the context.

This difference arises because of the way that the context of utterance influences interpretation. It is natural that we sometimes complain if someone quotes what we say out of context because this may distort our intended meaning.

But what is a context of utterance, and how does it influence interpretation?

11.5.1 The definition and classification of the context

Context is an expandable notion and is used in various senses. Generally it can be classified as being linguistic (a narrow sense) and non-linguistic (a broad sense). Ellis defines context in the following way:

The "context" of an utterance can mean two different things.

1) It can refer to the situation in which the utterance is produced; this is the "situational context".

2) It can refer to the linguistic environment or the surrounding language; this is the "linguistic context".

Both types of context influence the choice of language forms and therefore have an effect on the output. In a narrow sense, the context has been regarded, from a purely linguistic point of view, as a linguistic unit preceding and following a word, a phrase or a sentence. So the context is just the previous and anticipated words, phrases or sentences in which a particular word takes its place.

(33) a. I *told* him to go.
 b. I *asked* him to go.
 c. I *warned* him to go.
 d. I *allowed* him to go.
 e. I *advised* him to go.
 f. I *ordered* him to go.
 g. I *persuaded* him to go.

A linguistic context can extend its coverage to a linguistic unit larger than a sentence — paragraphs, an entire chapter and even the whole text. Thus some linguists prefer "co-text" to "context" in this sense.

(34) a. He left after I had *told* him to.
 b. He left after I had *requested* him to.
 c. He left after I had given him a *warning*.
 d. He left after I had given him a *permission*.
 e. He went after I had given him a piece of *advice*.
 f. He left after I had given him an *order*.
 g. He left after I had *persuaded* him to.

In a broad sense, the context has been defined as the set of background assumptions that are necessary for an utterance of a word, a phrase, a sentence or even a discourse to be intelligible.

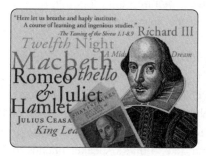

The context here extends to the immediate physical and social environment as well. It covers the people, time, place, and even the whole related backgrounds. Now the term *context* has been extended still further to encompass the so-called "context of culture".

The word *Shakespeare* in the following sentences calls for a necessity of a knowledge on British literature, an essential component of the cultural context.

(35) a. *Shakespeare* is famous for his dramas.
   b. Can I borrow your *Shakespeare*?
   c. We're going to see *Shakespeare* in London.
   d. I hated *Shakespeare* when I was in the middle school.

Shakespeare refers to the British playwright William Shakespeare in (35a), a book with Shakespeare's plays in (35b), a play of Shakespeare in (35c) and the school course of British literature in (35d).

11.5.2 The role of the context

Either of the linguistic context and the nonlinguistic context can play a role in interpreting an utterance of a word, a phrase or a sentence. They are both reflected and affected by our contributions to language use.

The features of the context can first be reflected in the fact that we often "watch our language" by avoiding the misuse of certain words or phrases. More subtly, our language has structural devices, often called stylistic variants, that allow us to organize a language unit to produce our meaning. Consider the following simple conversation.

(36) A: What happened to the *crops*?
   B: The *crops* were destroyed by the flood.
   *B: The flood destroyed the *crops*.
   **B: The farmers lost their *crops* in the flood.

In (36) speaker A's utterance focuses on "the *crops*", but the answers given by speakers *B and **B focus on "the flood" and "the farmer". This disruption in continuity of topic (a failure to observe the relevance rule) makes these contributions inappropriate and difficult to understand.

The features of the context can also be affected by making it appropriate for the same speaker to go on and say one sort of thing rather than another. For instance, When someone asks "Do you have the *time*?", the hearer should not simply say, "Yes, I do." Here is a very common dialogue between two friends.

(37) A: Do you have the *time*?
   B: Yes. What's going on?/Is there anything wrong?
   A: OK. Would you mind helping me to send this to Mr. Smith?

(38) A: Do you have the *time*?
   B: No. I'm sorry. I'm fully occupied.
   A: OK, never mind. I can do it by myself.

Thus, the language structure can both reflect and affect the structure of the discourse by a single speaker. It would be appropriate for both the speaker and the hearer to be cooperative in language communication.

The context has a part to play; we use different words in different situations, with different people. People who are familiar with each other can greet by saying a simple "Hi!" to each other. A defendant in court avoids using this to the judge in charge of his case. The language used in that situation would still have meaning, but not the same meaning.

The context interacts with the semantic content of an utterance in two fundamental ways. It is crucial in determining the proposition (or question, command, etc.) that a speaker intends to express by a particular utterance, and it is in turn updated with the information conveyed by each successive utterance.

Gaps such as these between the **literal** meaning of a word, phrase or a sentence and what it is used to convey — the **pragmatic** meaning — are common in everyday life. In non-literal uses of sentences, the idea conveyed is not the same as the literal meanings of the words. Exaggeration is one very common type, as are metaphor, sarcasm and irony. Politeness is another common reason to avoid speaking too directly or literally.

(39) a. The basketball player is 10 feet *tall*. (extremely tall)
b. The soldier is built like a brick *house*. (extremely solid)
c. My sister is buzzing around like a *honey-bee*. (busy, preoccupied)
d. Even a *pig* wouldn't eat such kind of food. (it is indescribably bad)
e. That movie was really, really a *winner*! (really bad; wins nothing)
f. I'm sorry. Your grades were not too *good*. (really rather poor)

11.6 Meanings of English Words in Lexical Pragmatics

Lexical pragmatics is a rapidly developing branch of linguistics that investigates the processes by which linguistically-specified ("literal") word meanings are modified in use.

The goal of lexical semantics is to investigate the relations between words and the concepts they encode, and to account for the fact that the concept communicated by the use of a word often differs from the concept encoded. Well-studied examples include the following subfields:
1. narrowing (e. g. *drink* used to mean "alcoholic drink"),
2. approximation (e. g. *square* used to mean "squarish") and
3. metaphorical extension (e. g. *dragon* used to mean "frightening person").

In much of the literature of the past, narrowing, approximation and metaphorical extension have been seen as distinct pragmatic processes and studied in isolation from each other.

Later in the 1990s, a simpler model of linguistic semantics was adopted to treat words as encoding mentally-represented concepts, elements of a conceptual representation system or "language of thought", which constitute their linguistic meanings and determine what might be called their linguistically-specified meanings.

In the 21st century, relevance theorists, Sperber, Wilson, and Carston, have been defending the alternative view that narrowing, approximation and metaphorical extension are outcomes of a single pragmatic process which fine-tunes virtually the interpretation of every word.

11.6.1 Narrowing of the meaning

In lexical pragmatics, narrowing is the case where a word is used to convey a more specific sense than its original encoded meaning. Narrowing results in a restriction of the linguistically-specified denotation. It carries out an effect to highlight a proper subpart of the linguistically-specified denotation. Here are some illustrations.

(40) a. Lie on bed for a week and *drink* enough water.
b. I asked her for a *drink* of water.
c. Mrs. Smith does not smoke or *drink*.
d. He had been *drinking* himself into a stupor for six hours.
e. I'm going to have a *drink* with some friends this evening.

f. There are plenty of food and *drink* at the wedding party.

Only in (40a) and (40b) the word *drink* keeps its original meaning as "drink liquid" or "some liquid (usually water)". The other four *drinks* convey more specific meanings, "drink alcohol", or "drink significant amounts of alcohol". In daily life, the word drink should be accompanied by water, tea, coffee, or even to say "soft drink" if the liquid is non-alcoholic.

(41) a. All *birds* lay eggs and some birds can fly.

b. Several *birds* are perching on the electricity line.

c. At Christmas dinner party, the *bird* was delicious.

d. A *bird* flew over the fence and into the backyard.

e. A *bird*, high in the sky, invisible, sang its pure song.

In (41a – e), each use of *bird* would highlight a different subset of birds except the one in (41a) which demotes its encoded meaning as "a creature with feathers, two legs, two wings which lays eggs."

(42) a. There is usually a strong relationship between *mother* and child.

b. *Mother*, you are looking so beautiful in such a dress.

c. Mary and Jane are two working *mothers*.

The word *mother* in (42a) would generally convey the encoded sense "a mother in general; a female parent", while in (42b) it refers to "a mother in particular; one's mother" and in (42c) it indicates not just that Mary and Jane satisfy the definition "female parent who works", but that they are stereotypical working mothers, bringing up young children while earning the living by working outside the home.

(43) a. There would be a sudden drop in *temperature*.

b. The weatherman said tomorrow would be in a very high *temperature*.

c. I have a *temperature*. I need to go to see a doctor.

The word *temperature* in (43a) and (43b) would normally refer to the "weather or climate", preserving its encoded meaning as "the amount of heat something has or there is in a place". On the contrary, the one in (43c) does not convey the truism that the speaker has some *temperature* or other, but that her *temperature* is high enough to be worth seeing a doctor.

11.6.2 Approximation of the meaning

Approximation is a variety of broadening where a word with a relatively strict sense is extended to a kind of state in which something exists to a lesser or an uncertain degree. It is also called a "pragmatic halo" that strictly speaking falls outside its linguistically-specified denotation. Approximation often includes the loose uses of round numbers, geometric terms and negatively-defined terms as in the following examples.

(44) a. There are *about* 800 pupils in this primary school. (not exactly the number)

b. Please stay here and wait for me for *half an hour*. (not exactly 30 minutes)

c. All the children formed a *circle* and sat down on the grass. (seemingly a circle)

d. the textbook will cost *little* money. (cheap; not much money)

e. This experienced surgeon will give you a *painless* operation. (suffering from less or no pain)

As with narrowing (cf. 40 – 43 above), different degrees and types of approximation are appropriate in different circumstances; compare the interpretations of *round* in the following examples.

(45) a. The earth is *round*. (shaped like a ball, but in fact it is not)

b. She admired the church's antiquated *round* arches. (curved in shape like the letter C)

  c. She was happy, her eyes *round* and bright like two diamonds. (wide open because of excitement or surprise)

  d. Mrs. Johnson has a *round* middle-aged face. (shaped like a circle)

  e. That's a nice *round* number. (a number ending with "0")

11.6.3 Category extension of the meaning

Category extension, as approximation, may also be seen as one variety of broadening, in which a word is used to convey a more general sense, with consequent widening of the linguistically-specified denotation.

It is typified by the use of salient brand names *Xerox* and *BMW* to denote a broader category "photocopy machine" and "automobiles", including items from less salient brands. Personal names as *Chomsky*, *Einstein* and common nouns both lend themselves to category extension. Here is one previous example with the word *Shakespeare*:

(35) e. You are a *Shakespeare* of the 21st century.

Some more creative uses are illustrated in the following examples.

(46) a. Federer is the new *Sampras*. (use of Roger Federer, tennis player, at Wimbledon 2003)

  b. Brown is the new *black*.

  c. Mint is the new *basil*.

  d. Is oak the new *pine*?

In (46a), *Federer* and *Sampras* evoke the category of gifted tennis players of a certain type. In (46b) — a typical piece of fashion — *black* evokes the category of staple colors in a fashion wardrobe; echoes are found in cookery and interior design writing. As *basil* in (46c) evokes "herb of the moment"; so does *pine* in (46d) the "trendy furniture wood". These examples of category extension are not analyzable as approximations. The claim in (46a) is not that *Federer* is a borderline case, close enough to being *Sampras* for it to be acceptable to call him *Sampras*, but merely that he belongs to a broader category of which *Sampras* is a salient member.

This chapter offers a brief survey of the English words and their meanings in use, which extends to the discussion of lexical semantics, the distinction of semantics and pragmatics, the roles of context in use, and lexical pragmatics with the pragmatic process of lexical interpretation. The chapter is divided into three parts.

The first part of the chapter goes to the discussion on the relationship of words and their meanings. It leads to the topic of lexical semantics with an analysis on semantic features and properties.

The second part presents a distinctive contrast between semantic study of lexical meaning and that of pragmatic study.

The third part presents an introduction to the meanings of words in contexts, and it turns to a brand-new branch of study on meanings of words — lexical pragmatics, which investigates the processes by which linguistically-specified ("literal") word meanings are modified in use. Narrowings, approximations and metaphorical extensions are outcomes of a single pragmatic process which fine-tunes virtually the interpretation of every word.

Further Reading

1. Cruse, D. A. (1986). *Lexical Semantics*. Cambridge: Cambridge University Press.
2. Cruse, D. A., Hundsnurscher, F., Job, M. and Lutzeier, P. (eds). (2002/2005).

Lexicology: An International Handbook on the Nature and Structure of Words and Vocabularies. Volumes I, II. Berlin: Walter de Gruyter.
3. Sweetser, E. (1990). *From Etymology to Pragmatics: Metaphorical and Cultural Aspects of Semantic Structure.* Cambridge: Cambridge University Press.
4. Sperber, D. and Wilson, D. (1995). *Relevance: Communication and Cognition.* 2nd ed. Oxford: Blackwell.

● Extended Reading

On the linguistics front, in the late 1960s and early 1970s a campaign was launched by some of Noam Chomsky's disaffected pupils in generative semantics (as it was then called), notably Jerry Katz, J. R. Ross and George Lakoff, to challenge their teacher's treatment of language as an abstract, mental device divorced from the uses and functions of language. In their search for the means to undermine Chomsky's position, the generative semanticists, who were attracted to the philosophical work by Austin, Grice, Strawson, and Searle, helped to empty what the philosopher Yehoshua Bar-Hillel called the "pragmatic wastebasket" (see Harris 1993 for a discussion of the linguistics wars they waged). As a result, a great deal of important research was done in the 1970s by linguists such as Laurence Horn, Charles Filhnore, and Gerald Gazdar to "bring some order into the content of [the pragmatic] wastebasket", as wisely advised by Bar-Hillel (1971: 405). The publication of Stephen Levinson's celebrated textbook *Pragmatics* in 1983 systematized the field and marked the coming of the age of pragmatics as a linguistic discipline in its own right.

Since then, the field of inquiry has continued to expand and flourish. In the last two decades we have witnessed new developments such as Laurence Horn's and Stephen Levinson's neo-Gricean pragmatic theories, Dan Sperber's and Deirdre Wilson's relevance theory, and important work by philosophers such as Jay Atlas, Kent Bach, and Francois Recanati. "More recently", as the editors of a newly published *Handbook of Pragmatics* declared, "work in pragmatic theory has extended from the attempt to rescue the syntax and semantics from their own unnecessary complexities to other domains of linguistic inquiry, ranging from historical linguistics to the lexicon, from language acquisition to computational linguistics, from intonational structure to cognitive science" (Horn and Ward 2004: xi). One thing is now certain: the future of pragmatics is bright.

— Huang, Y.

All of this knowledge about meaning extends to an unlimited set of sentences, just like your syntactic knowledge, and is part of the grammar of the language. The job of the linguist is to reveal and make explicit this knowledge about meaning that every speaker has.

The study of the linguistic meaning of morphemes, words, phrases, and sentences is called **semantics**. Subfields of semantics are **lexical semantics**, which is concerned with the meanings of words, and the meaning relationships among words; and **phrasal** or **sentential semantics**, which is concerned with the meaning of syntactic units larger than the word. The study of how context affects meaning — for example, how the sentence "It's cold in here" comes to be interpreted as "close the windows" in certain situations — is called **pragmatics**.

— Fromkin, V. et al.

(1.2) You and you, but not you, stand up!
(1.3) a. The authorities barred the anti-globalization demonstrators because they advocated violence.
   b. The authorities barred the anti-globalization demonstrators because they feared violence.
(1.4) John is too long for his glasses.
   a. glasses = spectacles
   b. glasses = drinking vessels
(1.5) (Cited in Levinson, 2000: 174)
   They are cooking apples.
   a. What are they doing in the kitchen?
      They are cooking apples.
   b. What kind of apples are those?
      They are cooking apples.

The three uses of the pronoun you — called a deictic expression — in (1.2) can be properly interpreted only by a direct, moment by moment monitoring of the physical aspects of the speech event in which the sentence is uttered. In other words, the deictic parameter can be fixed only if the deictic expressions are accompanied by physical behavior of some sort (such as a selecting gesture or an eye contact), which requires an extralinguistic physical context. Next, in (1.3), the assignment of reference for the anaphoric pronoun *they* depends crucially on our background assumption about who would most likely be advocating or fearing violence. This extralinguistic information is responsible for the two opposing interpretations, namely, *they* referring back to the anti-globalization demonstrators, as in (1.3a) or linked to the authorities, as in (1.3b). Finally, (1.4) is a case of lexical ambiguity, and (1.5) a case of syntactic ambiguity. In disambiguating them, contextual or real-world knowledge is needed to select the reading the speaker has intended. All this indicates that certain linguistic phenomena can be handled naturally only by recourse to extralinguistic, pragmatic factors such as context, real-world knowledge, and inference. Put another way, in order to fill the gap created by linguistic underdeterminacy, pragmatics has to be included as a component in an overall theory of linguistic ability.

— Huang, Y.

■ Semantics and pragmatics

There are two main fields within linguistics that study meaning. Semantics focuses on the literal meanings of words, phrases, and sentences; it is concerned with how grammatical processes build complex meanings out of simpler ones. Pragmatics focuses on the use of language in particular situations; it aims to explain how factors outside of language contribute to both literal meanings and nonliteral meanings which speakers communicate using language.

Most linguists who study meaning combine the study of semantics and pragmatics. While a semanticist is technically someone who studies semantics, in fact most semanticists investigate both semantics and pragmatics.

■ Semantics summary

The two main branches of semantics are lexical semantics and compositional semantics.

Lexical semantics seeks to explain how words mean, while compositional semantics focuses on the process of building up more complex meanings from simpler ones. In this section, we have looked at some of the linguistic categories that can be studied from a semantic perspective, including names, modifiers, predicates and arguments, quantifiers, and intentional elements like modals, tense, and aspect. We have also encountered some theoretical ideas used to explain meaning, such as thematic roles, possible worlds, and events. The goal of semantics is to give a precise theory, using ideas like these, which allows us to understand the lexical and compositional semantics of any human language. Languages are complex and diverse, so achieving this goal is a long way off.

Pragmatics summary

Pragmatics is fundamentally about how the use of context contributes to meaning, both semantic meaning and speaker's meaning. The core topics of pragmatics are indexicality, presupposition, implicature and speech acts, but in reality there is no limit to the ways in which context can influence meaning. Situations can even develop which allow words to mean things they never meant before. For example, several families are having dinner together, and two of the teenagers are, unbeknownst to anyone else, dating. They each separately make an excuse to leave the dinner to their parents, expressing a wish to go work on their chemistry assignment, and they have an enjoyable time together. After this, they start to say things like "Don't you need to work on your chemistry homework?" to indicate a desire to sneak off together — a new pragmatic meaning for sentences of that kind.

— Fasold, R. and Connor-Linton, J.

Pragmatics and Semantics

Semantics and pragmatics are the two subdisciplines of linguistics which are concerned with the study of meaning. That much is largely accepted. However, what constitutes the domain of semantics, and what constitutes that of pragmatics? Can semantics and pragmatics be distinguished? Are they autonomous, or do they overlap with each other? To what extent and how do they interact with each other? These are some of the questions that have puzzled, and are still puzzling, linguists and philosophers of language.

— Huang, Y.

Drawing the semantics-pragmatics distinction

The distinction between semantics and pragmatics has been formulated in a variety of different ways. Lyons (1987), for example, attempted to explain it in terms of the following dichotomies: (i) meaning versus use, (ii) conventional versus non-conventional meaning, (iii) truth-conditional versus non-truth-conditional meaning, (iv) context independence versus context dependence, (v) literal versus non-literal meaning, (vi) sentence (or proposition) versus utterance, (vii) rule versus principle, and (viii) competence versus performance. To these, one may add: (i) type versus token, (ii) content versus force, (iii) linguistic meaning versus speaker's meaning, (iv) saying versus implicating, (v) linguistically encoded versus non-linguistically encoded meaning, (vi) compositionality versus non-compositionality, and (vii) intention dependence versus intention independence (see, e. g. Levinson, (1983), Bach, (1999a), Nemo, (1999), Szabo, (2005)). Of these formulations, three, according to Bach

(1999a, 2004), are particularly influential. They are (i) truth-conditional versus non-truth-conditional meaning, (ii) conventional versus non-conventional meaning, and (iii) context independence versus context dependence.

— Huang, Y.

■ Semantic features

In the previous sections we discussed word meaning in relation to objects in the world, and this permitted us to develop a truth-based semantics. We also explored the meaning of words in relation to other words. But it is also possible to look for a more basic set of semantic features or properties that are part of word meanings and that reflect our intuitions about what words mean.

Decomposing the meanings of words into semantic features can clarify how certain words relate to other words. For example, the basic property of antonyms is that they share all but one semantic feature. We know that big and red are not antonyms because they have too few semantic features in common. They are both adjectives, but *big* has a semantic feature "about size", whereas red has a semantic feature "about color". On the other hand, buy / sell are relational opposites because both contain a semantic feature like "change in location or possession" differing only in the direction of the change.

— Fromkin, V. et al.

However, there is a fundamental difference between word meaning — or *lexical semantics* — and sentence meaning. The meaning of most words and all morphemes is conventional; that is, speakers of a language implicitly agree on their meaning, and children acquiring the language must simply learn those meanings outright. On the other hand, the meaning of most sentences must be constructed by the application of semantic rules. In this section we will talk about the meaning relationships that exist between words and morphemes.

Although the agreed-upon meaning of a word may shift over time within a language community, as we shall see in chapter II, we are not free as individuals to change the meanings of words at will; if we did we would be unable to communicate with each other. As we see from the quotation, Humpty Dumpty was unwilling to accept this convention. Fortunately, there are few Humpty Dumptys. All the speakers of a language share a basic vocabulary — the sounds and meanings of morphemes and words. Each of us knows the meanings of thousands of words. This knowledge permits us to use words to express our thoughts and to understand the thoughts of others. The meaning of words is part of linguistic knowledge. Your mental storehouse of information about words and morphemes is what we have been calling the *lexicon*.

— Fromkin, V. et al.

Exercises

I. Among the alternative words and expressions in the brackets, select one with the closest meaning related to the word MEAN in italic type.
  1. What is *meant* by "mental activity"? (referred to a real object / represented)
  2. Twelve o'clock *means* lunch in our household. (shows / is specially important)

3. It's just a waste of time, I *mean*, what is the point? (suggested/that is to say)
4. A: I'm all right.
   B: What do you *mean* — all right? (indicate/refer to in the real world)
5. "Made in China" does still *mean* something, if not very much. (stand for/that is to say)
6. Hearing the news, she knew that it *meant* trouble. (signified/intended)
7. I am willing to complete this work by myself, and you know I really *mean* it. (be specially important/indicate)
8. Jack said to his girlfriend: "I'm terribly sorry. I didn't really *mean* to be rude." (intend/represent)
9. We should not be too hard on him as a little boy. He *means* well. (stands for/is well-intentioned)
10. I've found a road that was not *meant* to be there. (suggested/imagined/thought)

Chapter 12
The Use of English Words (2)
— Metaphor, Metonymy, etc.

> **Points for Thinking**
> 1. What are the functions of figurative devices?
> 2. What is the use and interpretation of metaphor?
> 3. What is the use and interpretation of metonymy?
> 4. What are the differences between metaphor and metonymy?
> 5. What are the other less-frequently applied figures of speech?

A figure of speech is the use of a word that diverges from its normal meaning, or a phrase with a specialized meaning not based on the literal meaning of the words in it, such as metaphor, simile, and personification.

Figures of speech often provide emphasis, freshness of expression, or clarity. However, clarity may also suffer from their use, as any figure of speech introduces an ambiguity between literal and figurative interpretation.

A figure of speech is sometimes called a rhetoric or a locution.

12.1 An Introduction to Figures of Speech: the Figurative Uses of Words

Figures of speech, much like wildflower seeds tossed onto the fertile ground, are sometimes called the "flowers of rhetoric", which have multiplied the uses into a garden of enormous variety over time. It is true in human verbal communication. The linguistic and applied linguistic study illustrates that the number of figures of speech can seem quite imposing. Indeed, the numbers, names, and groupings of figures have been the most variable aspects of rhetorics over the history of language use.

A figure of speech, sometimes termed as a rhetoric, or locution, is a word that departs from its straightforward, literal meaning. Figures of speech are often used and crafted for emphasis, freshness of expression, or clarity. So it is necessary first to recall what we have talked in the previous chapter — the distinction between lexical semantics and lexical pragmatics.

The aim of semantics is to study the linguistic meaning of morphemes, words, phrases, and sentences. Lexical semantics is a subfield of semantics, concerned with the meanings of words, and the meaning relationships among words, and phrases, or other language units larger than the word.

The aim of pragmatics is to provide an explicit account of interpretation from particular language contexts. Lexical pragmatics as a branch of pragmatic study, tries to give a systematic and explanatory account of pragmatic phenomena that are connected with the semantic meanings of lexical items — words.

In the long history of language study, metaphors and metonymies have been regarded as figures of speech, i. e. as more or less the two major rhetorical devices in stylistics. However, metaphorical expressions like the *head of the office* or *the dialogue between Beijing and Washington* indicate that the two phenomena also play an important part in everyday language communication. Moreover, modern philosophers and cognitive linguists have shown that metaphors and metonymies are powerful cognitive instruments for our conceptualization and interpretation of abstract categories through the use of language.

Figurative use of language (or a figure of speech) usually departs from its literal meanings of the used words through comparing very different ideas or objects from different perspectives.

(1) a. Literal: He feels so tired this evening. As he tries to write, he can think of nothing to say.
   b. Figurative: He feels so tired this evening. As he tries to write, his mind is totally in a *blank*.

Imaginatively and carefully used, the figurative use of a word can convey the meaning more precisely and feelingly than its literal use. Now let's get down to metaphors and metonymies.

12. 2   English Words in Metaphor

12. 2. 1   What is metaphor

Metaphor is a figure of speech in which a word or phrase that originally referred to one thing is intentionally used to designate another, thus making an implicit comparison, as in "a *sea* of troubles" or as originally referring to "a lot of troubles".

Metaphors are interpreted when an utterance calls to mind a metaphorical meaning. This meaning has to be (a) restricted to some ways of calling to mind and (b) systematic, shared between speakers and hearers.

It is this "calling to mind" that requires an explanation for how it happens. For example, comparing the similarity of "Mary" and "her sister" involved in (2a) and "Mary" and "fish" in (2b), we can see that a comparison of their resemblance can respectively be literal, as in (2a), or figurative, as in (2b). The fact that there is a similarity between the objects in (2a) does not imply that there has to be such a similarity in (2b).

(2) a. Mary is like her sister.
   b. Mary is like a fish.

Next, metaphors are open-ended: the exact meaning is often left to the hearer, and this feature has to be captured by an adequate understanding. In Shakespeare's play *Romeo and Juliet*, Romeo may have meant various attributes to his dear girl through (3).

Metaphors not only make our thoughts more vivid and interesting but that they actually structure our perceptions and understanding.
— Lokoff and Johnson (1980)

(3) Juliet is the sun.

Similarity would not explain it. So, pragmatic approaches to metaphor are clearly in need of rules of interpretation that rely on the interlocutors' world knowledge and their ability to think logically. The latter is exploited in the cognitive approaches.

Metaphorical uses of words are mostly

types of non-literal language. A crucial feature in human communication is the ability on the part of the hearer to determine whether a speaker is speaking literally or non-literally. The meaning of the word "giant" in (4a) would be probably interpreted as that of the word "big" in (4b).

(4) a. Sam is a giant.
　　b. Sam is big.

Lakoff and Johnson (1980) have claimed that "our ordinary conceptual system, in terms of which we both think and act, is fundamentally metaphorical in nature". So it is believed that an understanding of metaphor is important for language users because figurative use of words is one of the most productive sources of non-literal meanings. Suppose there is such a conversation between A and B.

(5) A: As we know, man is a wolf.
　　B: Oh, no, man is not a wolf but an ostrich.

In context, "man is not a wolf" is as metaphorical as its opposite "man is a wolf", so we can see that the negation of a metaphorical statement can itself be a metaphor and hence possibly true if taken literally.

The broadest division of metaphors is that people are used to distinguishing the seemingly two kinds of metaphors. One is of conventionalized, lexicalized or "dead" metaphors and the other of inventive, expressive, unexpected or "live" metaphors. They are to be discussed in detail in the following sections.

12.2.2　Types of conventionalized, lexicalized or "dead" metaphors

A dead metaphor is an expression like *leg* of a table/chair, which is in very common use and in the case of which we no longer think of the use of *leg* as metaphorical. Indeed, everyday language is full of such metaphorical expressions. People can find that most words denoting body-parts are used in a multitude of metaphorical extensions. Here are some examples of the body-parts of "human body" in our daily life:

(6) a. Recently, he was promoted to be the *head* of English department.
　　b. The *face* of a city can be changed completely in a year.
　　c. Look out, the *eye* of the tornado is coming this way.
　　d. She tries to give a sympathetic *ear* to his complaint.
　　e. His selfishness really gets up my *nose*.
　　f. I never thought he'd have the *cheek* to ask me for money.
　　g. I answered her in her own *tongue*.
　　h. He *elbowed* his way through the crowd to the front of the hall.
　　i. They bought a table with metal *legs* and a yellow top.
　　j. She stayed in a small village at the *foot* of a high mountain.

There are the similar metaphors in our daily use of words. The following is a list of examples of words referring to body-parts in the upper half of the human body collected by Wilkinson (1993).

(7) a. head　　of department, of state, of government, of a page, of a queue, of a flower, of a beer, of stairs, of a bed, of a tape recorder, of a syntactic construction;
　　b. face　　of a mountain, of a building, of a watch;
　　c. eye　　 of a potato, of a needle, of a hurricane,

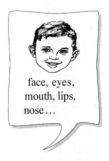

face, eyes, mouth, lips, nose…

of a butterfly, of a flower, hooks and eyes;
d. mouth   of a hole, of a tunnel, of a cave, of a river;
e. lips   of a cup, of a jug, of a crater, of a plate;
f. nose   of an aircraft, of a tool, of a gun;
g. neck   of land, of the woods, of a shirt, of a bottle;
h. shoulder of a hill, of a mountain, of a bottle, of a road, of a jacket;
i. arm   of a chair, of the sea, of a tree, of a coat or jacket, of a record player;
j. hands   of a watch, of an altimeter/speedometer.

What all these examples show is that metaphor is pervasive in everyday language. But the *head-of-department* type is usually not recognized as being metaphorical by language users. This type of metaphor has been called conventionalized, lexicalized or "dead" metaphor. The logic behind these uses is that through its frequent association with a certain linguistic form, the figurative meaning of a word has become so established in the speech community (i.e. conventionalized) that it is entered in the dictionary or vocabulary as one sense of the word in its own right (i.e. lexicalized).

When a unit of a linguistic form and its meaning is conventionalized and lexicalized, the metaphorical force of the word is no longer active, the metaphor is "dead". The most frequent types of conventionalized metaphors are

(8) concretive metaphors
   a. His records throw a new *light* upon certain incidents.
   b. The economy of this country fell into a vicious *circle*.

(9) animistic metaphors
   a. These *angry* clouds on the horizon predicted a coming storm.
   b. The millionaire made a *killing* on the stock market.

(10) humanizing metaphors
   a. A small garden lies along a *charming* river.
   b. She was quite famous for her novels which are usually reader-*friendly*.

(11) synaesthetic metaphors
   a. Some newspapers often give false *color* to the news they report.
   b. It's very *dull* today but I don't think it'll rain.

If we view the uses of words as representing conceptual categories, our knowledge of figurative language can be applied to the relation as follows. Lexicalized metaphors impose a multiple categorization on the entities in the world; one word refers to several categories. The above examples show that metaphor plays a crucial part in forming a complex network of interrelated categories which are all expressed by one word.

12.2.3 Types of inventive, expressive, or "life" metaphors

Examples of metaphors from many fields can easily be provided and some will be given later. These examples show that metaphor is not just a figure of speech in literature but also pervasive in everyday language. This means that metaphors are not just a way of expressing ideas by means of language, but a way of thinking about things. Lakoff and Johnson (1980) argue that we do not just exploit the metaphor "TIME is MONEY" linguistically, but we actually think of, or conceptualize, the so-called "target" category (TIME) via the "source" category (MONEY), i.e. a valuable commodity and limited resource, when we use the following English phrases.

(12) a. If you keep on doing so, you're just *wasting* your time.

b. I need to talk to my teacher, can you *give* me a few minutes.
c. The weekend is coming. How do you *spend* your time?
d. Quicken your steps. We are *running out of* time.
e. May I ask you a question? *Is* that *worth* your while?
f. It *cost* me two hours on this composition.
g. Taking an airplane *saved* us half a day.
h. The time *is not enough for* finishing the project in two months.

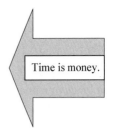
Time is money.

Here the verbs and verbal phrases *waste*, *give*, *spend*, *run out of*, *be worth*, *cost*, *save*, *be enough for* can all be interpreted as the cognition of "money spending". They help to realize the cognition of "TIME is MONEY" metaphorically (figuratively) rather than linguistically. Such a group of words can also be used within the categories of spending and saving energy, efforts, forces, fuel, and so on.

The basic assumption behind the figurative use of words is that although metaphor is a conceptual phenomenon, we have access to the metaphors structuring our way of thinking through the language we use.

One of the consequences of taking the cognitive view is that the notion of "dead" metaphor is rejected. As we have seen, the idea behind the "death" of metaphors is that the conventionalized metaphorical extensions (e. g. *head of department*) get their own entries in the lexicon and are thus considered part of the literal meaning of a word. From a cognitive point of view, this is highly misleading.

12.2.4 The metaphors of language and communication

From a cognitive perspective, the metaphors that have unconsciously been built into the language by long-established conventions are the most important ones.

Now there are more examples of the metaphorical expressions than we use to talk about linguistic expressions describing the language communication process. The metaphorical sentences indicate that we often use the related metaphors to conceptualize how language communication works.

(13) a. Try to pack more *thoughts* into fewer words.
b. They walked back, each in his deep *thoughts*.
c. She wrote down her *idea* on a piece of paper.
d. Insert those *ideas* elsewhere in the paragraph.
e. The sentence was filled with *emotion*.

These five sentences (13a – e) illustrate the conventional metaphorical expressions that when we speak we take up the words *ideas*, *thoughts (usually plural)* and *emotions* which can be put into words and sentences.

(14) a. The doctor put forward his *idea* of treatment to his patient.
b. You may try again to get your *thoughts* across better.
c. Some implied *meaning* is conveyed in his words.
d. None of Mary's *feelings* came through to me.
e. You still haven't given me any *idea* of what you mean.

Examples (14a – e) are linguistic reflections of the metaphor that see language communication as the transfer of thoughts and feelings by means of language.

(15) a. Did you catch the main *idea* of his writing?
b. Let me know if you find any good *ideas* in the essay.

c. I don't get my *feelings* of anger out of his words.

d. Can you extract coherent *ideas* from that prose?

e. The students didn't get hold of their teacher's *thoughts*.

Finally, the last five examples (15a – e) are concerned with how a hearer or a reader unpacks or understands the ideas from the language.

The fifteen types of examples above present us an overall picture of meaning procession as the following:

(16) a. Ideas (or meanings) are objects.

b. Linguistic expressions are containers.

c. Communication is sending.

Thus, ideas, thoughts or emotions as **objects** which are put into **containers** (=words) by a **sender** and sent to a hearer or a reader who takes the **objects** (=ideas, thoughts, emotions) out of their **containers** (=words). Linguistic communication is conceptualized in terms of the **sending** and **receiving** of parcels, which is called as metaphor of CONDUIT (a channel for conveying something).

The importance of this set of examples from a cognitive view of metaphor is that metaphors are not just semantic extensions of one isolated category to another in a different field, but that the connections and relations between categories play an important part. Thus it is not enough to state that IDEAS (OR MEANINGS) ARE OBJECTS and LINGUISTIC EXPRESSIONS ARE CONTAINERS. Instead, the systemic and coherent analogy between the two conceptual domains "sending and receiving of parcels" and "language communication" must be recognized and emphasized. What is more, the wealth of knowledge associated with concepts and conceptual fields must be taken into consideration.

12.2.5 Understanding and interpretation of various metaphors

1. Structural metaphor: ARGUMENT IS A BATTLE

Structural metaphors are often the cases where one concept is metaphorically structured in terms of another, such as:

(17) a. Both sides got their *arguments* ready in the debate.

b. There are strong *arguments* against these projects.

c. I said no and we got into a big *argument* over it.

d. Your *argument* is indefensible.

e. David and Tom had been drawn into a ferocious *argument* about the car.

f. They have withdrawn all their *arguments*.

g. Ok, I just give up my *argument*.

h. My elder brother turned down my *argument*.

i. The proposals are open to *arguments*.

j. The two sides are reconciled after the *argument*.

The cognitive model of BATTLE is not only for the conceptualization of the word "argument" — its structural sequence, but also for the strength and force of a real argument. Similar to a real battle, an argument in human life could also be divided into several stages: initial positions of the opponents (17a – b), followed by the acts of attack and counterattack (17c – e), retreat or withdrawal (17f), and finally the victory of one side over the other (17g – h), or sometimes a suspension or cessation (17i – j).

2. Orientational metaphor: UP and DOWN

Unlike structural metaphors, orientational metaphors are usually the cases where one concept organizes a whole system of concepts with respect to one another. Most of these metaphors have to do with special orientations: up-down; in-out; front-back; on-off; and so on. Here are some examples of the orientational metaphor "up-down":

1) HAPPY IS UP and SAD IS DOWN

(18) a. The boy was in *high* spirits after he won the game.
   b. Cheer up. Let's celebrate the victory.
   c. Thinking about the days at school always gives me a *lift*.
   d. Jack has been *low* these days since he failed in the exam.
   e. The sad news reached him and quickly let him *down*.
   f. The national economy *fell* into a depression.

The physical basis for this metaphor is that an erect posture usually goes along with an active, positive and optimistic state of happiness and a drooping posture typically with a passive, negative and pessimistic state of sadness.

2) MORE IS UP and LESS IS DOWN

(19) a. The sale of English books keeps going *up* now.
   b. He said that the stock index would *rise* next week.
   c. The machinery helps to *increase* the agricultural production.
   d. He made *fewer* misspellings in his last composition.
   e. The family income kept *falling* in the past years.
   f. Their salary has been *cut* by 10% for three months.

The physical basis for this metaphor is that if we add or put more of a substance or physical objects to a pile or into a container, the number increases and the level goes up, and if we take the things away or reduce the number, it results in the decrease of the number or amount.

3) HEALTH/LIFE IS UP and SICKNESS/DEATH IS DOWN

(20) a. Several days later, John got *up* and walked around.
   b. He is said to be at the *peak* of health.
   c. The wounded soldier stood *up* again from his recovery.
   d. The young boy was soaked through and *fell* ill soon after.
   e. Mr. Johnson's health was *declining* in the recent years.
   f. A number of birds were shot dead and *fell* to the ground.

The physical basis for this metaphor is that if a person is in sound health, he will be always *up* except lying down for a rest or a sleep at night. But when the person is suffering from a serious sickness, he is forced to lie down physically for the self-cure or necessary medical treatment. As a matter of fact, a dead body is undoubtedly physically *down*.

3. Ontological metaphor: ARGUMENT IS A BATTLE

Spatial orientations help people to understand concepts in orientational terms. But human experience of physical objects and substance goes beyond orientation. The parts of this experience would be picked up and then be identified as discrete entities or substances of a uniform kind. So we can refer to them, categorize them, group them and quantify them, and reason about them.

(21) The examples of the word "idea" for understanding its ontological concepts:

1) **IDEAS ARE PEOPLE**

   a. Einstein's theory of relativity really gave *birth* to an enormous number of ideas in physics.
   b. Saussure is regarded as the *father* or the founder of the Modern Linguistics by most of linguists and applied linguists.

2) **IDEAS ARE PLANTS**

   a. His maths teacher planted the *seeds* of the great ideas while he was still a school boy.

   b. It will take years for the ideas to come to their full *flourish*.

3) **IDEAS ARE PRODUCTS**

   a. The greatest physician *produced* some new ideas from his experiments.

   b. How could this linguist *generate* this theory?

4) **IDEAS ARE COMMODITIES**

   a. You should *pack* your ideas neatly in the writing.

   b. His ideas don't have any chance in such a *chaotic* condition.

5) **IDEAS ARE RESOURCES**

   a. His mind is totally *blank* and he has no idea of what to do.

   b. Don't *waste* your thoughts on such chores.

6) **IDEAS ARE WEALTH**

   a. He is *rich* in new ideas, and you can ask him for help.

   b. Your idea is *valuable* to our coming task.

7) **IDEAS ARE CUTTING INSTRUMENTS**

   a. His opinion *cuts* directly to the center of the matter.

   b. Their conversation was *interrupted* by the teacher's remark.

8) **IDEAS ARE FASHION**

   a. This kind of idea was *out of date* years ago.

   b. The public is ready to welcome any *new* and helpful thoughts.

12.2.6 The special use of metaphors in literature and in science

1. Metaphors in literary works

Literary metaphors usually require some particular or individual insights from the person who tries to create a figurative expression of metaphor. For example we read such a sentence:

(22) Money is the root of evil.

The words of "money" and "evil" lead us to form a combination of some coherent concepts as:

MONEY HAS POWER, and MONEY IS PLANT;

ROOT IS A PRIMARY SOURCE AND ORIGIN.

Such an interpretation helps us to have a proper understanding of its meaning.

As soon as people form a concept of THE WORLD IS A STAGE, there will be no difficulty in understanding Shakespeare's well-known lines.

(23) All the world's a *stage*,

And all the men and women merely *players*;

They have their *exits* and their *entrances*,

And one man in his time plays many *parts*,

His *acts* being seven ages ...

Consider the following five instances of the word *eye* extracted from Shakespeare's sonnets (The New Penguin, ed. J. Kerrigan, 1986).

(24) a. So long as men can breathe or *eyes* can see,

   So long lives this, and this gives life to thee. (18, 13 – 14)

   b. Is it for fear to wet a widow's *eye*

   That thou consum'st thyself in single life? (9, 1 – 2)

c. Sometimes too hot the *eye* of heaven shines,
     And often is his gold complexion dimmed. (18, 5 - 6)
  d. Lo, in the orient when the gracious light
     Lifts up his burning head, each under *eye*
     Doth homage to his new-appearing sight
     Serving with looks his sacred majesty. (7, 1 - 4)

The category **EYE** is to be identified by lexical semantics as having the following semantic properties.

(25) a. part of the body of people and animals;
  b. located in the head;
  c. organ of sight;
  d. locus for production of tears.

We have no difficulty in interpreting the first two examples (24a and 24b) of the word *eye* as its literal meaning of this category. However, the same can certainly not be said of the next two examples, because they undoubtedly involve figurative uses of the word *eye*.

The word *eye* in the phrase "*eye* of heaven" in (24c) refers to the sun. The word *eye* in (24d) stands for the whole person as the interpretation of the image that *eyes* "do homage" by behaving in a particular way. These two examples are very typical of traditional "metaphor" and "metonymy" respectively.

2. Metaphors in the science domain

With the development of science and technology, metaphors are omnipresent in the field of science. Many of them have primarily been introduced for the aim of explanation. This function can be easily seen from the most metaphorical uses in computer science.

(26) a passage about the computer

While a computer is in *work*, a certain number of user-*friendly* programs provide a surface *screen* which establishes a metaphorical link with the category *office* as a major *software*. The *screen* is a desk-top that can be *tidied up*. There are some permanent *folders* or *files* for *filing* items of *documents*, a *clipboard* where items can be temporarily *stored*, *windows* that can be *opened* and *closed*, and a *trash can* into which superfluous items are *deleted*.

When these simple but rich explanations of programming functions are compared with the kind of non-metaphorical, often abbreviated commands employed in specialist programs (e. g. there are a number of keys on the keyboard: **B** functioning for "bold letter", *I* for "italicized", U for "underline", Ctrl for "control" and Del for "delete"), the literal meaning of the metaphor COMPUTER WORK IS OFFICE WORK becomes really obvious.

In addition to metaphors based on the context of OFFICE WORK, computer programs make use of ANIMAL and ILLNESS metaphors. The particular case is the category COMPUTER MOUSE, in which the metaphor of "*mouse*" amazingly maps the outward appearance and possible movements of a mouse onto the concept of this trackball tool (functioning just as it was originally called). Computer users hold the computer mouse for all the necessary instructions without caring for the abstract principle behind it.

Another use of metaphorical explanation is the malfunctioning of computer programs. Probably the frequently used metaphor in this field is the BUG metaphor, which we use quite naturally when something has gone wrong in the program. But now the WORM metaphor is more likely to be used for the case, such as "millenniums worm" in the year 2000. More complex and also more threatening in computer programs is the VIRUS metaphor. Here what goes wrong with a computer is thought related to the mysterious and invisible spread of viruses which cause an infection in the body of humans or animals. Though ordinary users of language have little idea about the virus as an infectious and dangerous organism, they may have a rich if indirect experience of its unpleasant effects on humans and animals, and this source model is mapped onto the target model of the computer virus.

There are more technical terms, in computer use, taken from the category of office work, as *copy*, *cut*, *paste*, *store*, *retrieve*, *memory*, *upload*, *download*, *databank*, *read*, *write*, *send*, *receive*, *insert*, *format*, and so on. Some of terms are sometimes to be considered as metaphorical extensions, such as *network*, *information highway*, *address*, *E-mail*, *floppy disc*, *cyberspace*, *internet web*, and so on.

12.3 English Words in Metonymy

12.3.1 What is metonymy

At the beginning of the present chapter, we came to know that metaphors and metonymies have been regarded as figures of speech, i.e. as more or less the two major rhetorical devices in stylistics. Consider the following sentences.

(27) a. He is the *head* of the office.
   b. There came the news of a dialogue between *Beijing* and *Washington*.

They indicate that metaphor and metonymy play an important part in everyday language communication. In fact, modern philosophers and cognitive linguists have shown that metaphors and metonymies are powerful cognitive instruments for our conceptualization and interpretation of abstract categories through the use of language. In (27a), the word *head* is used metaphorically and *Beijing* and *Washington* in (27b) are used in metonymy. Here are more examples of metonyms:

General word	Original meaning	Metonymic use
damages	destructive effects	money paid in compensation
word	a unit of language	a promise (to give / keep / break one's word); a conversation (to have a word with)
sweat	perspiration	hard work
tongue	oral muscle	a language or dialect
the press	printing press	the news media

How can metaphor and metonymy, the two major figurative uses of words, be characterized in more general terms and how can they be distinguished from each other? Metaphor has traditionally been based on the notions "similarity" or "comparison" between literal and the figurative meaning of an expression. In contrast, metonymy involves a relation of "contiguity" (i.e. nearness or neighborhood) between what is denoted by the literal meaning of a word and its figurative counterpart.

(28) a. part for whole
   b. whole for part
   c. container for content

    d. material for object
    e. producer for production
    f. place for institution
    g. place for event
    h. the controlled for controller
    i. controller for the controlled
    j. cause for effect

The list above is an incomplete collection of some types of contiguity-relations in metonymy. Examples are given and discussed in the next section.

12.3.2 Metonymy in contiguity-relations

(29) **the PART for the WHOLE**

   a. The captain turned around and spoke to all the *hands* on the deck.
      (hands = sailors)
   b. What they really need is a couple of smart *heads* for the work.
      (heads = people)
   c. The new comer's *face* seemed quite familiar to me.
      (face = a particular person)

(30) **the WHOLE for the PART**

   a. He drove into the gas station, and filled up his *car* by himself.
      (car = petrol tank)
   b. The pupils are busy clearing the *windows* in the room now.
      (window = pane, glass)
   c. Jack sat down on his chair and began to read his *textbook*.
      (textbook = a particular text)

(31) **the CONTAINER for the CONTENT**

   a. He is drunk because he has drunk up three *bottles*.
      (bottles = bottles of alcoholic drinks)
   b. He lost his *schoolbag* and couldn't hand in his homework.
      (schoolbag = schoolbag with all the things inside it)
   c. My *wallet* was stolen just now, so I can't pay it now.
      (wallet = wallet with the money or credit cards inside it)

(32) **the MATERIAL for the OBJECT**

   a. The new married couple bought a small washing machine and an *iron*.
      (iron = a tool for ironing clothes)
   b. I have brought some cooking utensils, some plates and three *glasses*.
      (glasses = drinking vessels made of glass)
   c. The old lady put on her *glasses* and began to read the newspaper.
      (glasses = a pair of lenses used to correct faulty vision)

(33) **the PRODUCER for the PRODUCTION**

   a. Tom recently bought a new *Ford*.
      (Ford = a car produced by Ford company)
   b. The *Xerox* in our office does help us a lot.
      (Xerox = a brand of photocopy machines)
   c. The girl has taken several courses of *Shakespeare* and read a lot.
      (Shakespeare = the literary works by Shakespeare)

(34) **the PLACE for the INSTITUTION**
   a. So far, the *White House* did not say anything about it.
      (the White House = the US presidency or the US government)
   b. The *pentagon* was said to withdraw more soldiers from Iraq.
      (Pentagon = the building in which the United States military establishment works)
   c. *Paris* attracts a great number of foreign tourists every year.
      (Paris = the scenery and historical spots in the city of Paris)

(35) **the PLACE for the EVENT**
   a. The *Watergate* changed the political views of many American people.
      (Watergate = a political scandal in the building of Watergate)
   b. It is said that the present Iraq would be the second *Vietnam*.
      (Vietnam = the Vietnam War in the 1950s and 1960s)
   c. The athletes will never forget the days they spent in *Beijing in 2008*.
      (Beijing in 2008 = the 29th Summer Olympics in Beijing)

(36) **the CONTROLLED for the CONTROLLER**
   a. He looked up and saw a passenger *plane* fly over to the airport.
      (a plane = an aircraft with its crew and passengers on board)
   b. You have to walk to your office. The *buses* are on strike.
      (the buses = the bus drivers, not the real buses)
   c. The *car* stopped in time and avoided a traffic accident.
      (the car = the car driver, not the car itself)

(37) **the CONTROLLER for the CONTROLLED**
   a. *Bush* has caused thousands of deaths in the present Iraq.
      (Bush = the American soldiers sent to Iraq by the Bush government)
   b. *The Chinese Delegation* won 51 gold medals in the 29th Summer Olympic Games.
      (the Chinese Delegation = the athletes of the Chinese Delegation)
   c. The newly-established *orchestra* presented a wonderful concert to the public last night.
      (orchestra = the conductor and the musicians of this orchestra)

(38) **the CAUSE for the EFFECT**
   a. He speaks English with an *accent* because his mother tongue is French.
      (accent = an accent caused by the fact that French is his mother tongue)
   b. The boy fell into *depression* as he had failed again in the exam.
      (depression = depression caused by the failure in the exam)
   c. The secretary was *absent* from the daily meeting for his illness.
      (absent = absence caused by his being ill)

12.4 Other Figurative Uses of English Words

Figures of speech are usually expressions that use language in a non-literal way, such as metaphor or metonymy to achieve a rhetorical effect. In a figure of speech, a word departs from its literal meaning for a non-literal or rhetorical emphasis, freshness of expression, or clarity.

Therefore, a number of other figures of speech need to be mentioned. They are euphemism, synaesthesia, synecdoche, zeugma, and other minor ones.

12.4.1 Euphemism

Euphemism is defined as a substitution of an agreeable or inoffensive expression for the one that may offend or suggest something unpleasant. People normally use this figure of speech to avoid those topics or words that they or their hearers might find distasteful, unpleasant or embarrassing. So they choose euphemistic words to replace unpleasant ones. For instance, there

> When a phrase is used as a euphemism, it often becomes a metaphor whose literal meaning is dropped.

is an attempt to replace the words *handicapped* or *disabled* with the more positive term *differently-abled*, and even more recently, with *physically challenged*. Interestingly, what many people do not know is that the term *disabled* was itself a euphemism for *crippled*, which was abandoned because of its straightforward reference. Let's read the following two paragraphs about the euphemistic effect.

I am an *old cripple*, drawing an *old-age* pension, *working* hard to raise vast quantities of vegetables on an *allotment* and well aware that, one of these days, I shall *die*. All this is fact.

If, however, I listen to the voice of officialdom, it turns out that I am a *disadvantaged senior* citizen, registered as *disabled*, drawing a *retirement* pension, *renting* a *leisure garden* and presumably, *immortal* because I shall never *die* — I shall merely *pass away*.

A match of the words in Column A with the correspondents in Column B presents its reader a sharp contrast.

(39) A (general)   B (officialdom)
  1. old   senior
  2. cripple   disabled / disadvantaged
  3. working   renting
  4. allotment   leisure garden
  5. die   immortal / pass away

The match leads us to the contrast between "I" and "the voice of officialdom". The writer says "All this is fact" to conclude the first paragraph and leaves a blank for the readers to make his own conclusion for the second.

While referring to the unpleasant situations, such as OLD AGE in the western culture, and other unpleasant facts, people seldom say about the topics directly. Instead, they choose euphemistic words to replace them. For example,

(40) A   B
  1. old age   pass one's prime / feeling one's age / second childhood / getting on in years
  2. mad   not all there / soft in the head / simple-minded / of unsound mind
  3. a poor man   in the low-income group / the have-nots / a man of modest means / a negative saver

Nearly in all the world cultures, DEATH is surely regarded as the most unpleasant topic, so English has a lot of expressions to avoid using the words DIE or DEATH:

to age away, to be no more, to be deceased, to be gathered to one's fathers, to be gone, to breathe one's last, to be no longer with us, to get to one's last reckoning, to go hence, to go the way of all flesh, to go west, to join the silent majority, to kick the bucket, to lose one's life, to pass away, to pass on, to run one's race, to yield up the ghost . . .

Euphemisms are sometimes motivated by TABOO rather than the desire not to hurt people's feelings. In daily life some people like to use "man's", "lady's", "washroom", or even "the place to wash my hands" to replace the word "TOILET". Therefore, euphemism is a figure of speech more than just saying something unpleasant in a pleasant way. It has something to do with the human cognitive ability of conceptualization.

12.4.2 Zeugma

Zeugma is a figure of speech by which two or more different words in a sentence are linked to a verb or an adjective which is either strictly appropriate to only one of them, or applying to them in different ways. The latter one would be more common nowadays.

(41) a. Smelling of *musk* and of *insolence*.
    (literal) (figurative)

 b. Delia ran the *family business* and the *marathon*.
    (figurative)   (literal)

 c. She opened the *door* and her *heart* to the homeless boy.
    (literal) (figurative)

 d. Some dam busters blew up *banks* and so did some *bank* robbers.
      (literal)   (figurative)

 e. Heseltine left with a *smile*, a *wave* and his *wife*.
     (literal) (literal) (figurative)

> **Zeugma** is a figure of speech describing the joining of two or more parts of a sentence with a single common verb or noun.

Sentences (41a – e) indicate that this figure of speech can occur with a wide variety of syntactic constructions. Zeugma in all of these cases comes from the use of an ambiguous lexical item: *smell* in (41a), *run* in (41b), *open* in (41c), *bank* in (41d), and *with* in (41e). Therefore, zeugma arises when a single word is applied to modify or govern two or more words in the same sentence.

The use of zeugma is most common in two ways. They are

A. one verb+two (or more) objects

(42) a. Mr. Pickwick *took his hat* and *his leave*.

 b. Those newly made clothes *fit for the man* and *the times*.

In (42a), "*took his hat*" is in a literal sense, and "*took his leave*" is used figuratively for saying good-bye to others. In (42b), "*fit for the man*" is in a literal sense, and "*fit the times*" is used figuratively for being modern and fashionable.

B. Preposition+two (or more) objects

(43) a. Miss Bolo rose from the table considerably agitated, and went straight home, *in a flood of tears* and *a sedan chair*. (Dickens: *The Pickwick Papers*)

 b. The old people gathering in the social hall *for comradeship* and *a hot lunch*.

Here in (43a), "*in a flood of tears*" is figurative and "*in a sedan chair*" is in its literal meaning. In (43b), "*for comradeship*" is figurative and "*for a lunch*" literal.

12.4.3 Several less-frequently applied figures of speech

Sometimes when we speak, we do mean something other than what our words mean. When what we mean to communicate is not compatible with what our expression literally means, then we are speaking non-literally.

There are many other minor figures of speech in language use. This section will introduce **PERSONIFICATION**, **OXYMORON** and **TRANSFERED EPITHET**. They are also ways of making the word's figurative use from its literal meaning. Here are typical examples that are sometimes used non-literally.

1. Personification

As a figure of speech, it gives human form or feeling to animals, or life and personal characters to inanimate objects, or to ideas and abstractions, e. g.

(44) a. This result *argues* against what we believed in the formal theories.
b. It seems that life has *cheated* the young man.
c. The economic depression has *robbed* us of our profits.
d. The January wind has a hundred *voices*. It can *scream*, it can *bellow*, it can *whisper*, and it can *sing a lullaby*. It can *roar* through the leafless oaks and shout down the hillside, and it can murmur in the white pines rooted among the granite ledges where lichen makes strange hieroglyphics. It can *whistle* down a chimney and *set* the hearth-flames *dance* ...

> **Personification** literally means "mask", although it does not usually refer to a literal mask but to the "social masks" all humans supposedly wear.

In (44a – c), the words *argue*, *cheat* and *rob* personify their inanimate subjects. With the use of seven words: *voices*, *scream*, *bellow*, *whisper*, *sing*, *roar* and *whistle* in (44d), its readers seem to hear the invisible *January Wind*. At last, the wind behaves like a little boy as "It can *whistle* down a chimney and *set* the hearth-flames *dance*." It brings the reader not only the hearing of some sounds but also the view of an action of "dance" through the hearth-flames.

Personification is simple to recognize and to understand and is easy for people to use as well.

2. Oxymoron

Oxymoron is usually formed by the conjoining of two contrasting, contradictory or incongruous words or terms, as in

(45) a. The old man told us his *bitter-sweet* memories in the Olympics.
b. This doorman seemed to be in the *proud humility*.
c. We found the bedroom in an *orderly chaos*.

> An **oxymoron** is a figure of speech that combines two normally contradictory terms.

In (45a), *bitter-sweet* describes a mixture of feelings one has in his memory, *proud humility* refers to the quality of being modest, but not servile, and *orderly chaos* gives the fact that there is some order whereas most of things are in disarray.

An oxymoron can be formed in different ways, the most common ones as the followings:

(46) **a. adjective+noun:**
  a living death/ an old child/ a miserable joy/ an enjoyable sorrow
b. adjective+adjective:
  a cold warm welcome/ a poor wealthy man/ a small spacious room
c. adverb+adjective:
  dull bright/ cruelly helpful/ mercifully fatal
d. verb+adverb:
  shine dimly/ glow darkly/ hurry slowly

In daily communication, the appreciation of an oxymoron arises from the attempts to find the hidden truth, the subtle significance in the contrastive images or ideas in such a figure of speech.

3. Transferred epithet

A transferred epithet is a figurative device in which a premodifier is commonly transferred from a person to a thing, as in

(47) a. She threw some cattail roots into a *boiling pot* of water.
   b. He closed his *busy life* as a businessman at the age of seventy.
   c. We spent a very *happy evening* together.
   d. At night the quiet neighbourhood is in the *slumbering darkness* that marks most residential areas.

Logically, the word "boiling" in (47a) actually qualifies "water", but in the sentence it is transferred to the front of "pot". So are the words "busy" in (47b), "happy" in (47c) and "slumbering" in (47d) to be transferred to the front of "life", "evening" and "darkness" instead of qualifying "businessman", "we" and "residents of the areas".

This chapter presents a further discussion on the meanings of words in use, especially the non-literal meanings. It is common that words are often used in figurative senses. Metaphor and metonymy are the two major types of figurative devices for representing the meanings of English words in use. The chapter is divided into two parts.

The first part of the chapter goes to the discussion of the ways in which the two major figures of speech, METAPHOR and METONYMY, are firstly characterized in their respectively general terms and secondly distinguished from each other through their distinctions. A large number of examples accompanied for detailed analyses are taken from some famous linguists among whom Lakoff is one of the most quoted.

The second part leads to a shift to some other less-frequently applied figures of speech. Through the discussion of word meanings in contextual depth and width, the chapter introduces the figurative devices as EUPHEMISM, ZEUGMA, PERSONIFICATION, OXYMORON and some other devices employed in the daily verbal communication.

Further Reading

1. Jaszczolt, K. (2002). *Semantics and Pragmatics*. London: Longman.
2. Lakoff, G. (1987). *Women, Fire and Dangerous Things: What Categories Reveal about the Mind*. Chicago: University of Chicago Press.
3. Lakoff, G. and Johnson, M. (1980). *Metaphor We Live by*. Chicago: University of Chicago Press.

● Extended Reading

■ Reference

If the meaning of a word is not like a dictionary entry, what is it? This question has been debated by philosophers and linguists for centuries. One proposal is that the meaning of a word is its referent, which is the thing or things in the real world that it refers to.

…

Also in support of that "extra something" is our knowledge that, while under certain circumstances the happy swimmer and Jack may have the same reference. The former has some further meaning, for we know that "the happy swimmer is happy" is a tautology — true in every conceivable situation, but "Jack is happy" is not a tautology, for there are circumstances under which that sentence might be false.

■ Sense

If meanings were reference alone, then the meaning of words and expressions would be the objects pointed out in the real world. For example, the meaning of *dog* would be the set of canine objects. This theory of word meaning is attractive because it underscores the idea that meaning is a connection between language on the one hand, and objects and events in the world on the other.

An obvious problem for such a theory, however, is that speakers know many words that have no real-world referents (e.g., *hobbits*, *unicorns*, and *Harry Potter*). Yet speakers do know the meanings of these expressions. Similarly, what real-world entities would function words like *of* and *by*, or modal verbs such as *will* or *may* refer to?

A further problem is that two expressions may refer to the same individual but not have the same meaning. For example, *George W. Bush* and *the President* currently refer to the same individual, but the meaning of *the President* is something like "the head of state", that is, an element of meaning is separate from its *reference* and is more enduring. This element of meaning is often termed **sense**. It is the extra something referred to earlier. *Unicorns*, *hobbits*, and *Harry Potter* have sense but no reference (in the real world). Conversely, proper names typically have only reference. A name like Chris Jones may point out a certain person, its referent, but has little linguistic meaning beyond that. Sometimes two different proper names have the same referent, such as Mark Twain and Samuel Langhome Clemens, or Unabomber and Theodore Kaczinski. It is a hotly debated question in the philosophy of language as to whether two such expressions have the same or different senses.

— Fromkin, V. et al.

Metaphor is for most people a device of the poetic imagination and the rhetorical flourish — a matter of extraordinary rather than ordinary language. Moreover, metaphor is typically viewed as characteristic of language alone, a matter of words rather than thought or action. For this reason, most people think they can get along perfectly well without metaphor. We have found, on the contrary, that metaphor is pervasive in everyday life, not just in language but in thought and action. Our ordinary conceptual system, in terms of which we both think and act, is fundamentally metaphorical in nature.

The concepts that govern our thought are not just matters of the intellect. They also govern our everyday functioning, down to the most mundane details. Our concepts structure what we perceive, how we get around in the world, and how we relate to other people. Our conceptual system thus plays a central role in defining our everyday realities. If we are right in suggesting that our conceptual system is largely metaphorical, then the way we think, what we experience, and what we do every day is very much a matter of metaphor. But our conceptual system is not something we are normally aware of. In most of the little things we do every day, we simply think and act more or less automatically along certain lines. Just what these lines are is by no means obvious. One way to find out is by looking at language. Since communication is based on the same conceptual system that we use in thinking and acting, language is an important source of evidence for what that system is like.

— Lakoff, G. and Johnson, M.

Metaphor

When what appears to be an anomaly is nevertheless understood in terms of a meaningful concept, the expression becomes a metaphor. There is no strict line between anomalous and metaphorical expressions. Technically, metaphors are anomalous, but the nature of the anomaly creates the salient meanings that metaphors usually have. The anomalous *A grief ago* might come to be interpreted by speakers of English as "the unhappy time following a sad event" and therefore become a metaphor.

Metaphors may have a literal meaning as well as their metaphorical meaning, so in some sense they are ambiguous. However, when the semantic rules are applied to "Walls have ears", for example, the literal meaning is so unlikely that listeners use their imagination for another interpretation. The Principle of Compositionality is very "rubbery", and when it fails to produce an acceptable literal meaning, listeners try to accommodate and stretch the meaning. This accommodation is based on semantic properties that are inferred or that provide some kind of resemblance or comparison that can end up as a meaningful concept ...

When a word has multiple meanings that are related conceptually or historically, it is said to be polysemous (**polly-seamus**). For example, the word *diamond* referring to a geometric shape and also to a baseball field that has that shape is polysemous. Open a dictionary of English to any page and you will find words with more than one definition (e.g. *guard*, *finger*, and *overture*). Each of these words is polysemous because each has several related meanings.

...

A metonym is a word that substitutes for an object the name of an attribute or concept associated with that object. The use of crown for king, or for the government ruled by a king, is an example of metonymy. So is the use of brass to refer to military leaders. Metonyms are often employed by the news services. Sportswriters are especially adept, using gridiron to refer to football; *diamond* for baseball; *ice* for hockey; *turf* for horseracing and so on. Metonyms for governments such as *Kremlin*, *White-hall*, *Washington*, and *Baghdad* are commonplace. Metonyms need not be a single word. *Madison Avenue* is a metonym referring to the advertising industry; *Scotland Yard* refers to the Criminal Investigation Department in the United Kingdom. The association is that the Metropolitan Police were once housed in an area of London called Great Scotland Yard.

— Fromkin, V. et al.

Arguments usually follow patterns; that is, there are certain things we typically do and do not do in arguing. The fact that we in part conceptualize arguments in terms of battle systematically influences the shape arguments take and the way we talk about what we do in arguing. Because the metaphorical concept is systematic, the language we use to talk about that aspect of the concept is systematic.

We saw in the "argument is war" metaphor that expressions from the vocabulary of war, e.g. *attack a position*, *indefensible*, *strategy*, *new line of attack*, *win*, *gain ground*, etc., form a systematic way of talking about the battling aspects of arguing. It is no accident that these expressions mean what they mean when we use them to talk about arguments. A portion of the conceptual network of battle partially characterizes the concept of an argument, and the language follows suit. Since metaphorical expressions in our language are tied to metaphorical concepts in a systematic way, we can use metaphorical linguistic expressions to study the nature of metaphorical concepts and to gain an understanding of the metaphorical nature of our activities.

— Lakoff, G. and Johnson, M.

To get an idea of how metaphorical expressions in everyday language can give us insight into the metaphorical nature of the concepts that structure our everyday activities, let us consider the metaphorical concept TIME IS MONEY as it is reflected in contemporary English.

TIME IS MONEY

You are wasting my time.
This gadget will save you hours.
I don't have the time to give you.
How do you spend your time these days?
That flat tire cost me an hour.
I've invested a lot of time in her.
I don't have enough time to spare for that.
You are running out of time.
You need to budget your time.
Put aside some time for ping pong.
Is that worth your while?
Do you have much time left?
He's living on borrowed time.
You don't use your time profitably.
I lost a lot of time when I got sick.
Thank you for your time.

Time in our culture is a valuable commodity. It is a limited resource that we use to accomplish our goals. Because of the way that the concept of work has developed in modern Western culture, where work is typically associated with the time it takes and time is precisely quantified, it has become customary to pay people by the hour, week, or year. In TIME IS MONEY in many ways: telephone message units, hourly wages, hourly hotel rates, yearly budgets, interest on loans, and paying your debt to society by "serving time." These practices are relatively new in the history of the human race, and by no means do they exist in all cultures. They have arisen in modern industrialized societies and structure our basic everyday activities in a very profound way. Corresponding to the fact that we act as if time is a valuable commodity — a limited resource, even money — we conceive of time that way. Thus we understand and experience time as the kind of thing that can be spent, wasted, budgeted, invested wisely or poorly, saved, or squandered.

TIME IS MONEY, TIME IS A LIMITED RESOURCE, and TIME IS A VALUABLE COMMODITY are all metaphorical concepts.

They are metaphorical since we are using our everyday experiences with money, limited resources, and valuable.

— Lakoff, G. and Johnson, M.

When we say "Inflation robbed me of my savings", we are not using the term "inflation" to refer to a person. Cases like this must be distinguished from cases like

The *ham sandwich* is waiting for his check.

where the expression "the ham sandwich" is being used to refer to an actual person, the person who ordered the ham sandwich. Such cases are not instances of personification metaphors, since we do not understand "the ham sandwich" by imputing human qualities to it. Instead, we are using one entity to refer to another that is related to it. This is a case of what we will call metonymy. Here are some further examples:

He likes to read the *Marquis de Sade*. (= the writings of the marquis)

He's in *dance*. (= the dancing profession)

Acrylic has taken over the art world. (= the use of acrylic paint)

The *Times* hasn't arrived at the press conference yet. (= the reporter from the *Times*)

Mrs. Grundy frowns on *blue jeans*. (= the wearing of blue jeans)

New *windshield wipers* will satisfy him. (= the state of having new wipers)

— Lakoff, G. and Johnson, M.

 **Exercises**

I. Complete each phrase of simile with a proper word.

1. as _____ as ink
2. as _____ as brass
3. as _____ as silver
4. as _____ as crystal
5. as _____ as ice
6. as _____ as pitch
7. as _____ as bone
8. as _____ as a pig
9. as _____ as a wolf
10. as _____ as marble
11. as _____ as fire
12. as _____ as two peas
13. as _____ as a hatter
14. as _____ as a ghost
15. as _____ as thought
16. as rich as _____
17. as heavy as _____
18. as easy as _____
19. as blind as _____
20. as yellow as _____
21. as ripe as _____
22. as pleased as _____
23. as green as _____
24. as cunning as _____
25. as thin as _____
26. as poor as _____
27. as gay as _____
28. as busy as _____
29. as soft as _____
30. as large as _____

II. Complete each sentence of metaphorical expression with a word from the box.

broke	broken	do	done	throw	thrown	work	working	hide	write
put	hid	get	ran	give	keep	passed	took	fade	explained

1. Two United Party senators _____ away to form the Federal Party.
2. His father had thought it would be good for his son to _____ away from home and earn some money on his own.
3. I could not decide whether to keep the money he left me or _____ it away.
4. It would be better to _____ away and not attempt to enter the city until she knew what was happening there.
5. I was frightened and I _____ away from my mother and she ran after me and coaxed me to come back.

6. They took my name and address, _____ away all my possessions, and sent me down to the cells.
7. Our medicine has not _____ away with disease.
8. All of this can, of course, be _____ away for other reasons.
9. The sun's warmth began to _____ away.
10. She _____ away within three weeks of her sister and mother.
11. Thirty million tons of refuse are _____ away in the UK.
12. He looked at his drawings of the rocks and _____ them away again.
13. Hamish began to _____ away a vast load of shopping he had brought home.
14. They haven't stopped; they've been _____ away all day.
15. You just _____ away giving your name, address and enclosing three tokens.
16. If you _____ something away, you put it in a place where nobody else can find it.
17. If you _____ away, you continue working hard for a long time.
18. He did not _____ the pamphlet away, but he kept it in his desk.
19. You cannot _____ away with violence by using violence.
20. Australia, after it had _____ away from Antarctica, continued to drift northwards.

Chapter 13
The Dictionaries of English Words (1)
— Types of Dictionaries

> **Points for Thinking**
> 1. What is the fundamental difference between the earliest form of the dictionary and the modern one?
> 2. How is an encyclopedic dictionary different from an encyclopedia?
> 3. What are the characteristics of the learner's dictionaries?
> 4. What information can you find in a dictionary besides the meaning?
> 5. How do the American dictionaries distinguish from the British counterparts?

The worst criminals should neither be executed nor sentenced to forced labor, but should be condemned to compile dictionaries, because all troubles are included in this work.
— Scaliger, J. C. (1540 – 1609)

The word "dictionary" comes from neoclassical Latin "*dictio*", meaning simply "word". It is a list of words of a language, which contains information about their meanings or their equivalents. The dictionary also provides pronunciation, grammatical information, word deviations, etymologies, illustrations, usage guidance and examples in phrases or sentences. According to *Webster's Third New International Dictionary* (*W3*), the definition for "dictionary" runs like this,

> A reference book containing words usually alphabetically arranged along with information about their forms, pronunciations, functions, etymologies, meanings, and syntactical and idiomatic uses.

Dictionaries are human artifacts. The art and craft of compiling dictionaries is called *lexicography*, which is one branch of applied linguistics. It is generally thought to consist of practical lexicography and theoretical lexicography, of which the former is the art or craft of compiling dictionaries while the latter is the scholarly discipline of analyzing and describing the semantic relationships within the lexicon (vocabulary) of a language. This is sometimes referred to as metalexicography.

Dictionaries can be classified by many criteria, many of them obvious to everyone, such as purpose (general or special), size (unabridged, desk or pocket), language (monolingual or bilingual), reader (children or adults), media (printed or electronic) and etc. To most people, dictionaries and encyclopedias are closely linked and are sometimes considered interchangeable but they are essentially different kinds of reference works with different purposes. As a matter of fact, an encyclopedia is not concerned with the language per se but provides encyclopedic information concerning each headword. Encyclopedic dictionaries have the characteristics of both linguistic dictionaries and encyclopedias.

Most dictionaries are found in the form of a book, but more and more dictionaries at present are produced as software running on an electronic PDA or a general-purpose computer. Some dictionaries are arranged in the alphabetical order, but others are arranged by topics, such as science, biography, geography, mathematics, history and philosophy.

> **Information Box**
>
> *Dictionary*: A book dealing with the individual words of a language (or certain specified classes of them), so as to set forth their orthography, pronunciation, signification and use, their synonyms, derivation and history, or at least some of these facts: for convenience of reference, the words are arranged in some stated order, now, in most languages, alphabetical; and in larger dictionaries the information given is illustrated by quotations from literature; a word-book, vocabulary, or lexicon. (OED)

13.1 The Development of Dictionaries

13.1.1 Dictionaries in Britain

The dictionary is probably much older than is generally believed. The history of English dictionaries is roughly divided into four periods: the period before 1604 (the birth of Robert Cawdrey's *Table Alphabetical*), the period between 1604 and 1755 (the publication of Samuel Johnson's *A Dictionary of the English Language*), the period between 1755 and 1928 (the production of the masterpiece *Oxford English Dictionary*) and the period from 1928 up till now.

The earliest word reference books for the English-speaking people were bilingual glossaries that provided English equivalents for Latin or French words. The practice continued through the 16th century in which school masters sometimes collected the glosses and listed them together; the resulting collection, called a *glossarium*, is today called a *glossary*. Schoolmaster Robert Cawdrey's *Table Alphabetical* is generally regarded as the first genuine dictionary in English. It contained roughly 2,500 words, each matched with a synonym or a brief definition. According to its title page, it was intended for "Ladies, gentlewomen, or any other unskillful persons" so that "they may more easily and better understand many hard English words, which they shall hear or read in the Scriptures, Sermons, or else where". The first three entries in Cawdrey's *Table Alphabetical* show the simplicity and directness of his style.

Abandon, cast away, or yield up, to leave or forsake.

Abash, blush.

Abba, father.

. . .

> **Information Box**
>
> **Samuel Johnson** (18 September [7 September] 1709 – 13 December 1784), often referred to as Dr. Johnson, was an English author who made lasting contributions to English literature as a poet, essayist, moralist, novelist, literary critic, biographer, editor and lexicographer. Johnson was a devout Anglican and political conservative, and has been described as "arguably the most distinguished man of letters in English history".

Another early comprehensive inventory of English was the *Universal Etymological English Dictionary* (1721) by Nathan Bailey, reissued in 1730 as the *Dictionarium Britannicum: Or A More Compleat Universal Etymological Dictionary Than Any Extant*. The dictionary used quotations from literary works to confirm and supplement definitions, which greatly served Samuel Johnson, "the father of English dictionary".

When his work *A Dictionary of the English Language* was at last completed in 1755, it was at once recognized as England's greatest contribution to lexicography and remained as the model of English lexicography for more than a century — containing about 40,000 word entries, with a total of around 115,000 supporting quotations. In his splendid preface, Samuel Johnson named Francis Bacon, Richard Hooker, John Milton, and Robert Boyle, representing respectively philosophy, theology, poetry, and science as models of the sources from which he had quoted.

A

DICTIONARY

OF THE

ENGLISH LANGUAGE:

IN WHICH

The WORDS are deduced from their ORIGINALS,

AND

ILLUSTRATED in their DIFFERENT SIGNIFICATIONS

BY

EXAMPLES from the beſt WRITERS.

TO WHICH ARE PREFIXED,

A HISTORY of the LANGUAGE,

AND

AN ENGLISH GRAMMAR.

By SAMUEL JOHNSON, A. M.

IN TWO VOLUMES.

VOL. I.

THE SECOND EDITION.

Cum tabulis animum cenſoris ſumet honeſti:
Audebit quæcunque parum ſplendoris habebunt,
Et ſine pondere erunt, et honore indigna ferentur,
Verba movere loco; quamvis invita recedant,
Et verſentur adhuc intra penetralia Veſtæ:
Obſcurata diu populo bonus eruet, atque
Proferet in lucem ſpecioſa vocabula rerum,
Quæ priſcis memorata Catonibus atque Cethegis,
Nunc ſitus informis premit et deſerta vetuſtas. Hor.

LONDON,

Printed by W. STRAHAN,

For J. and P. KNAPTON; T. and T. LONGMAN; C. HITCH and L. HAWES;
A. MILLAR; and R. and J. DODSLEY.

MDCCLV.

(Title page from the second edition of Samuel Johnson's dictionary)

Occasionally, Samuel Johnson indulged his prejudices and his wit as in the entry *oats* ("a grain, which in England is generally given to horses, but in Scotland supports the people") and *lexicographer* ("a writer of dictionaries; a harmless drudge, that busies himself in tracing the original and determining the significance of words, in keeping with his estimate of a dictionary making as 'drudgery for the blind … requiring neither the light of learning nor the activity of genius'").

Information Box

Dictionary Facts (1st Edition of *OED*)

Size: 10 volumes, 15,490 pages

Time to complete: 70 years (from approval date)

Publication date: 1884–1928 in 128 fascicles. Published in 10 volumes in 1928 and reissued in 12 volumes in 1933, with addition of one-volume *Supplement*

Price of bound volumes (1928): from 50 to 55 guineas for the set, depending on binding

Number of pages edited by James Murray: est. 7,200

Number of entries: 252,200

Number of word forms defined and/or illustrated: 414,800

Price of fascicles: 12 shillings and six pence for large sections

Number of contributors (readers): est. 2,000

Number of quotations submitted by contributors: est. 5 million

Number of quotations used in dictionary: 1,861,200

Number of authors represented in quotations: 2,700

Number of works represented in quotations: 4,500

A peak of lexicographic work in English dictionary history came with *A New English Dictionary on Historical Principles*, popularly known as the *Oxford English Dictionary* (*OED*). Scottish lexicographer Sir James Augustus Henry Murray became the editor of the dictionary in 1879 with the support of the English Philological Society. Ten volumes appeared between 1884 and 1928, and a 12-volume edition with a single-volume supplement in 1933, which means it took 71 years to complete its first edition. A 4-volume supplement came out between 1972 and 1986 and the 20-volume second edition was published in 1989. For the last decade of the 20th century, the *OED* team worked on the third edition, a process sometimes described as the largest humanities project worldwide. This involves not just adding new words but revising every entry in the dictionary. It is the first comprehensive revision and update that the big dictionary has received in its history. The third edition is not available in paper form — it is published online, integrated into the second edition, and is available by subscription at **www.oed.com**. This revision project is expected to be completed in 2037 with projected cost of about £34 million.

Various other dictionaries are related to the *OED* in content or method. The most prominent one, the *Shorter Oxford English Dictionary* (*SOD*), a 2-volume abridgement with some revision in pronunciation, was issued first in 1933, and later revised twice. The *Concise Oxford English Dictionary* (*COD*) joined *OED* family early in the year of 1911, then with a recent edition in 1999. Another member of the family was the *Pocket Oxford English Dictionary* (*POD*), winning its great popularity by everyday words and clear definitions, particularly suitable for beginners. The dictionary witnessed its 10th edition in 2005.

The Oxford dictionaries have made good use of technological advances and exist in several forms. The *Compact Edition of the Oxford English Dictionary*, a 2-volume photographically reduced version of the 13-volume set, became available in 1971. In 1987 the *Oxford English Dictionary* on CD-ROM was published. The second edition of the CD-ROM version was issued in 1992. With the release of the *OED* on the Internet in 2000, subscribers gained access not only to the 1989 version but also to the work of editors revising it, an effort expected to reach the completion of the third edition.

13.1.2 Dictionaries in the United States

In our review of the development of the English dictionary, we are now going to trace the story in America. The American colonies achieved independence from Britain in 1776. At the same time, there were trends to establish an American language, as distinct from the English language. In keeping with this trend, Noah Webster made his great contribution to lexicography in his work *An American Dictionary of the English Language*. This ambitious work, begun in 1807 and published in 1828, included 12,000 more words and 40,000 more definitions than any previous dictionary of the English language. The dictionary is, in essence, characterized by its emphasis on typically American usage, as distinguished from the British usage.

However, Webster's view was not shared by all his fellow Americans. Such a one was Joseph Emerson Worcester (1784 – 1865), who edited a new edition of *Johnson's Dictionary, as improved by Todd and abridged by Chalmers, with Walker's Pronouncing Dictionary combined, to which is added Walker's Key*, which was published in America in 1828. The first "dictionary war" was thus fired between Webster and Worcester and continued for almost 20 years. In 1830, Joseph Worcester published his own dictionary, *A Comprehensive Pronouncing and Explanatory Dictionary of the English Language with Pronouncing Vocabularies*, which paved the way for modern collegiate dictionaries. To compete with Worcester's challenge, a second edition, "corrected and enlarged", of Webster's *American Dictionary* was published in 1841 while Worcester responded with his *A Universal and Critical Dictionary of the English Language* in 1846. By this time, Webster had died (in 1843, at the age of 85), and the rights to reprint and revise his dictionary had been bought from his heirs by George and Charles Merriam, who were printers and booksellers in Springfield, Massachusetts, and who carried on the fight on Webster's behalf. Today, the name "Webster" is a common property and a virtual synonym for the dictionary.

As a result, the name is used even for those which have nothing to do with Webster's dictionary. A good example is *Webster's New World College Dictionary*, published by World Publishing Company in 1952.

With the development of technology, the dictionary compilers became extremely enthusiastic about the word numbers in the dictionary at the end of the 19th century. Thus, came the second "dictionary war" and the competitor against the Webster was Funk and Wagnalls who claimed 450,000 entries in their *New Standard Dictionary* of 1913. However, *Webster's Second New International Dictionary* in 1934 claimed 600,000, though it is no longer clear exactly what is being counted, certainly not just headwords.

The next "dictionary war" set on its way with the publication of *Webster's Third New International Dictionary of the English Language* (*W3*), edited by Philip Babcock Gove in 1961. In this work, the lexicographer attempted to reflect the contemporary usage and to describe language in a "descriptive" rather than "prescriptive" way. *W3*, as it became known, included many slang words and technical terms. Many critics denounced it for they considered the dictionary failed to follow the language standards as in the example of the item "*ain't*" though the dictionary made a detailed explanation "though disapproved by many and more common in less educated speech, used orally in most parts of the US by many cultivated speakers esp. in the phrase ain't I." During the period of the third "dictionary war", a number of well known dictionaries came into existence in the 1960s. The wide success of the *Random House Dictionary of the English Language*, published by Random House Publishing Company in 1966, proved that new opportunities existed in the dictionary market. Another attractive dictionary at that time was *The American Heritage Dictionary of the English Language*, published by the Heritage Company in 1969 with its fourth edition in 2000. All in all, the *W3* is recognized as a great achievement in the dictionary history though there is controversy over its practice of descriptivism.

Over the past decades, the US has seen an increasing interest in college or collegiate dictionaries. Apart from Webster dictionaries, the more popular ones include *The American Heritage Dictionary*, *The Random House College Dictionary*, *Webster's New Collegiate Dictionary*, etc. These dictionaries of similar scope and size have features of their own and represent a new stage of lexicographical development in America.

13.1.3 Dictionaries in other countries

There are many other English-speaking communities where dictionaries are produced or used. In Australia, all the dictionaries were more or less directly inspired by British models at first: the *Australian Pocket Oxford Dictionary* (1976, with a sixth edition in 2007), the *Australian Concise Oxford Dictionary* (1986, with a fourth edition in 2004), or the *Heinemann Australian Dictionary* (1976). The most well-known dictionary in Australia is the *Macquarie Dictionary*, which has been firmly regarded as the voice of Australian English since its first publication in 1981. The *Macquarie* has been constantly evolving over the past three decades. With the second edition (1991), the dictionary became encyclopedic, including entries on people and places of Australia and the rest of the world. The third edition, published in 1997, made use of Macquarie's corpus of Australian English (known as Ozcorp) with a large number of examples of Australian usage. In 2005, the *Macquarie* witnessed its fourth edition, characterized by its number of citations, which includes etymologies for many phrases (e.g. *save someone's bacon*, *on the wallaby*, etc.) and pays particular attention to Australian regionalisms (e.g. *lubra*, *humpy*, *coolamoon*, *currawong*, *Queensland blue*, *Blackbird*, etc.).

> **Information Box**
>
> This fifth edition of the *Macquarie*, measuring a new awareness of environment and fragility, will mark a turning of the tide in our consciousness, in the span of our response, in the way we give voice to place — and place to voice. (Her Excellency Ms Quentin Bryce, Governor-General of the Commonwealth of Australia.)
>
> A selection of new environmental words in the fifth edition includes *baseline-and-credit*, *biochar*, *cap-and-trade*, *climate wars*, *ecotax*, *ecowarrior*, *emissions trading*, *global warming potential*, *guerilla gardener*, *water footprint*, *wave farm*.
>
> New economic related entries include *moral hazard*, *ninja loan*, *toxic debt* and *zombie debt*.
>
> New words related to popular culture include *Boyzilian wax*, *pimp cup*, *scene kid*, *shwopping* (combination of shopping and swapping through the internet), and *treggings*.

Like most regions of the English-speaking world, Canada has produced dictionaries of regionalisms. The most remarkable one is undoubtedly the *Dictionary of Canadianisms on Historical Principles* (1967) after 12 years of preparation, which was later abridged to *A Concise*

Dictionary of Canadianisms (1973). It is the first scholarly historical dictionary of a variety of English other than British or American English with an emphasis on the cultural distinctiveness of Canada and the words that go with them. Recently, after more than 40 years of existence without any updates, the dictionary has been actively seeking its fully-revised and extended edition. In addition, Canada has its own general-purpose dictionaries, among which *Gage Canadian Dictionary* (1983) is the most authoritative. It is featured by its clear and accurate definitions, IPA (International Phonetic Alphabet) pronunciation key, extensive notes on homonyms and synonyms, hundreds of clear and supportive illustrations and photos, appendix of charts and tables with a Canadian focus, and most important of all, written by Canadians for Canadians.

The *Heinemann New Zealand Dictionary* (1979, with a second edition in 1989) was the landmark publication in New Zealand. It is the first work to integrate New Zealandisms with English words to create a general-purpose New Zealand dictionary. In the dictionary, there is a one-page list of the approximate date of term entry found in New Zealand English but not elsewhere, such as "haka" (1827), "Boohai" (1920), and "bach" (1905). Several other dictionaries were published later on: the *New Collins Concise Dictionary of the English Language, New Zealand Edition* (1982), the *Collins New Zealand Compact English Dictionary* (1984), the *New Zealand Pocket Oxford Dictionary* (1986), and the *Dictionary of New Zealand English* (1997) by the Oxford University Press. All these dictionaries are inspired by the British lexicographical tradition.

On the whole, the lexicographical production in Australia, Canada, New Zealand, and other parts of the English-speaking countries is characterized by the presence of two types of dictionaries — dictionaries of regionalisms, and "local" general-purpose dictionaries. The former are much more encyclopedic, laying more emphasis on the culture, particularly the historical aspects of the rural culture; while the latter strive to improve the inadequacies of the imported dictionaries both from Great Britain and the USA. Here are some pioneering dictionaries in other parts of the world — the *Dictionary of Jamaican English* (1967, with a second edition in 1980), distinguished by the use of spoken material; the *Dictionary of Bahamian English* (1982), the whole of the Caribbeans; the *Dictionary of Africanisms: Contributions of Sub-Saharan Africa to the English Language* (1982) and etc. Strangely enough, India, though active in the domain of the lexicography of Indian languages, has no dictionary of its own, not even the regional dictionary on historical principles which so many countries now have.

13.2 The Contents of Dictionaries

Dictionaries vary widely in terms of different purposes. If you want to make full use of the dictionary, you need to have a good idea of what exactly it contains. Despite the differences in scope, length and depth, dictionaries generally cover some or all of the following.

1. Spelling

Due to the wide divergence between the spelling system and the pronunciation, even native-speaking learners have difficulty in spelling. The dictionary, a best friend of poor spellers, gives accepted spelling for all the words, including those alternate ones. In British dictionaries, the first spelling form is naturally British followed by the American (if any), e.g. BrE *cheque* AmE *check* or vice versa in any American dictionaries. Besides, one can also find in a dictionary the different forms of irregular verbs, e.g. *take*, *took*, *taken*, adjectives, e.g. *good*, *better*, *best* and compounds, e.g. *E-mail, e-mail, email*. As a matter of fact, there are many rules of spelling, but almost all have exceptions. Thus the only safe rule is: when in doubt, look up the word in the dictionary and it will tell you the fact.

2. Pronunciation

Just like spelling, British and American dictionaries provide their respective standard pronunciation for the reader's reference. In some, one can find the British followed by the American and in others vice versa. As for the pronunciation standard, British dictionaries, generally speaking, use the Oxford's system or International Phonetic Alphabet (IPA) either broad or narrow, while American ones employ the Webster's. So it is important to study the key to pronunciation in the guide before the main body of the dictionary or at the foot of the page. In most dictionaries for non-native learners, more than one phonetic systems are available, e.g. two different systems — K.K. and IPA are presented in the *Longman Dictionary of Contemporary English* (2001). One more thing, it is possible that the same dictionary adopts different phonetic systems in terms of different editions.

3. Grammatical information

Although modern linguists have suggested several alternative analyses, dictionaries continue to class words in accordance with the eight traditional parts of speech and inflections (the changes in forms of words) to provide one of the most important indications of a word's part of speech.

Apart from the usual coverage of word classes and inflections, dictionaries also include other grammatical information, which is particularly true of the learner's dictionary, e.g. *OALD*, *LDOCE*, *CIDE*, *CCELD* and etc. All these dictionaries supply a good system of verb patterns which are arranged as supplementary material after the main body as in *OALD* or located properly in the main text as in *LDOCE* or in an extra column alongside each sense of the word in the main body as in *CCELD*. Indeed, the grammatical information provided in the dictionary is easy to understand and remember and becomes a handy help to learners in using the English language.

4. Etymology

The etymology of a word is its history. A dictionary should indicate where each word came from — whether it was borrowed, invented or has always been in the language. While some current English words can be traced back directly to Old English, most words, however, are either generated within the language by combining familiar words (like *raincoat* from the nouns *rain* and *coat*) or are loanwords borrowed from other languages (like *kowtow* from Mandarin). Only a few common terms — *Kodak* is a well-known example — are the arbitrary creations of individuals. The main items of the etymological information are: origin of a word, cognate words in Germanic languages and other Indo-European languages, change of meaning and etymological structure of the word.

Most American desk dictionaries and some British ones give etymological information, as a little knowledge of it may help deepen our understanding of the meanings of words. For ordinary learners, however, it is not necessary to explore too deeply into this subject, but it is valuable for researchers and language professionals.

5. Definition

The main body of the dictionary is no doubt the definitions of words — the explanation of the headword meaning. As most words in English are polysemantic, the senses of words are arranged in different ways. Definitions may be listed either chronologically or in order of popularity. That is, the definitions may proceed either from the first meaning that a word had in the language to the most recent, or from the most common meaning to the least common. Under the entry *nice*, for example, a historical dictionary might begin with "foolish" — which is what *nice* meant when it was first used in English in the 13th century — and end with "agreeable"; another dictionary, however, will place "agreeable" first — since that is currently the word's most prevalent sense — and then list the other meanings in descending order of popularity. In practice, most of the desk dictionaries probably follow Thorndike's principle: Other things being equal, literal uses come before figurative, general uses before special, common uses before rare, and easily understandable uses before difficult, and to sum up: that arrangement is best for any word which helps the learners most.

The approaches to definitions also differ from one to another. Generally speaking, words are defined in formal definition, e. g. *bird*: *a creature that is covered with feathers and has two wings and two legs*; definition by synonym, e. g. *handsome*: *attractive, good-looking, beautiful*; definition by antonym, e. g. *fail*: *to not be successful in achieving sth.* ; definition by context, e. g. *laugh*: *When you laugh, you make a sound with your throat while smiling and show that you are happy or amused. People also sometimes laugh when they feel nervous or are being unfriendly*; operational definition, e. g. *seesaw*: *a game played when children sit on opposite ends of the plank and go up and down alternately*; definition by example, e. g. *blue*: *having the color of a clear sky or the sea/ocean on a clear day*; and lastly, definition by illustration.

Dictionaries used to define words in the form of words or phrases. In recent years, however, especially in some learner's dictionaries, full sentences are widely adopted for the purpose of setting meaning contexts, for example, in *CCELD*, *canal* is defined as, "A *canal* is a long narrow stretch of water that has been made for boats to travel along or to bring water to a particular area." Besides, most of the learner's dictionaries use a controlled vocabulary to make definitions, e. g. 2,000 defining words have been used to write all the definitions in *LDOCE* to ensure that the definitions are clear and easy to understand, and that the words used in explanations are easier than the words being defined.

6. Usage labeling

Although many people are opposed to the practice of marking words with usage labels, teachers and students generally find them essentially helpful. In most medium-sized dictionaries, one may find some or all of the following: 1) temporal labels: archaic, old-fashioned, rare, obsolescent, obsolete; 2) regional labels: British, Canadian, Scottish; 3) style labels: formal, informal, colloquial, slang, biblical; 4) field labels: linguistics, philosophy, psychology; 5) linguistic labels: poetic, literary; 6) level labels: standard, sub-standard, nonstandard, illiterate; 7) attitudinal labels: approving, derogatory, humorous, offensive, vulgar, euphemistic, sexist; 8) sentence structure labels: [vn] ~ sb (with sth)|~ sth (for sb), etc.

These labels will provide guidance for learners of English in their production if they get familiarized with them.

7. Related forms

Along with the grammatical information, some dictionaries include related forms of the word in each entry, among which derivatives, compounds, synonyms, antonyms are the ones most likely to appear. As a matter of fact, dictionaries published in the US show more interests in collecting the information of related forms than the British ones, headed by the collegiate dictionaries.

8. Frequency

Since computers entered the field of lexicography, and with the creation of large English corpora, lexicographers now know a great deal about word frequency. As this information is very valuable to teachers and students of English, more and more efforts have been devoted by lexicographers and linguists.

In theory, with 3,000 most commonly used words, one can talk about or read a lot of things on everyday topics. And if one has learned 7,000 words, then he/she can more or less easily read natural English articles or newspapers with the help of dictionaries. Therefore, the marking of frequency is of vital importance to language beginners and three learner's dictionaries provide frequency information about headwords. Take *Longman Dictionary of Contemporary English* (2003) as an example, it marks the first 3,000 most common English words, used in speech and writing in the form of:

S1 means the first 1,000 most common English words used in speech;

S2 means the second 1,000 most common English words used in speech;

S3 means the third 1,000 most common English words used in speech;

W1 means the first 1,000 most common words used in written English;

W2 means the second 1,000 most common words used in written English;

W3 means the third 1,000 most common words used in written English.

In the dictionary, *capital* is marked as follows: **capital^1** S3 W1, which shows that the word *capital* is both the third 1,000 most common English words used in speech and the first 1,000 most common words used in written English.

And in *McMillan English Dictionary*, a different code of three-frequency band is presented. Very high frequency words have three stars, high frequency words have two stars, and frequent words have one star. The dictionary covers about 7,300 words. Likewise, *COBUILD Dictionary* distinguishes with five frequency bands, totaling 14,600 words. Throughout the dictionary, entries are given markers to indicate how frequently words occur in the language. For example, in the entry of *say*, one can see the marker ◆◆◆◆◆ in the extra column. This means that the word *say* is one of the most frequent words in the English language (Note that the entry for *say* covers the forms *says*, *saying*, and *said* as well, and that the ◆◆◆◆◆ is an indication of frequency for all these forms taken together). The markers are on a scale from 1 to 5, (◆◆◆◆◆ for the most frequent words, ◆◇◇◇◇ for less frequent words.) About half the entries in the dictionary have no frequency markers.

9. Illustrations

Many dictionaries have illustrations, especially those language-oriented dictionaries. Their main purpose is to provide visual support for the description of the meaning content of linguistic units. Illustrations have different functions and different degrees of importance for different users. Adults often use the dictionary to determine more exactly the meaning of words which they have only a vague idea of. On the other hand, a child may have difficulty in understanding what the definition means. A picture, therefore, may activate a memory of something earlier, or at least enable him/her to know the name of something when he does see one. It is also very important for language learners in case where the definition has to be complicated or else inexact.

Illustrations can be classified into various types according to what is depicted. They may have the following categories: 1) single object; 2) several objects of the same class; 3) an object in its surroundings; 4) object in operation; 5) parts of subjects; 6) environment with typical objects; 7) basic objects and concepts in a subject field and 8) encyclopedic redundancy. Moreover, the presentation is of decisive importance as regards the function of the picture. As a matter of fact, a specially made drawing has a different effect from that of a photograph, and a colored picture gives more information than a black-and-white one.

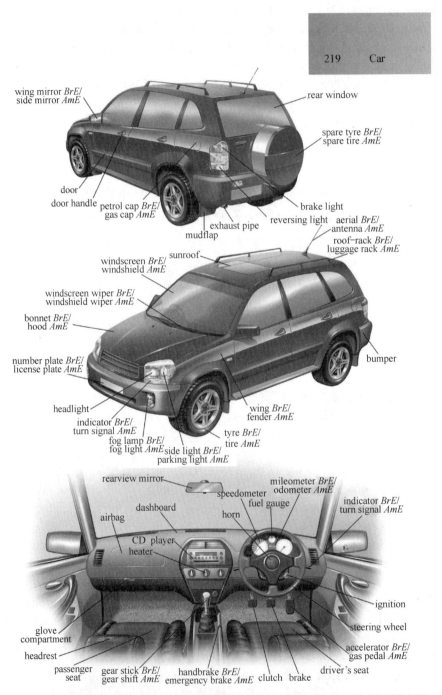

Fig. 13.1 An Illustration from the *Longman Dictionary of Contemporary English* (*LDOCE*)

10. Supplementary matters

Apart from its main body, a dictionary has many supplementary matters, among which irregular verbs, common first names, geographical names, numbers, punctuation and so on are the most common ones. Comparatively speaking, American dictionaries tend to be more practical and reader-oriented than their British counterparts. For example, *Webster's New World College Dictionary* (4th edition) has the following reference supplements: Nations of the World, World City Populations, US Cities by Population, US Metropolitan Core Areas by Population, Cities of Canada by Population, Geographical Data, Monetary Units, Books of the Bible, Geologic Time Chart, Astronomical Data, Presidents of the United States, The Declaration of Independence, Constitution of the United States, Amendments to the Constitution of the United States, etc.

13.3 The Types of Dictionaries

Dictionary is a powerful word. Authors and publishers have found that if they call a reference book a dictionary it tends to sell better than it would if called by another name because the word suggests authority, scholarship, and precision.

13.3.1 Types of dictionaries

"The function of a dictionary is to serve the person who consults it." (Philip, G.) Owing to the complexity of demands on dictionaries, there have been numerous types of dictionaries in terms of different criteria.

1. Prescriptive and descriptive dictionaries

A dictionary can either describe actual linguistic usage or prescribe a certain usage. An example of a mainly descriptive dictionary is *Webster's Third New International Dictionary of the English Language* (*W3*), whereas the *Oxford Dictionary for Writers and Editors* is prescriptive for the spelling and inflexion of English words.

2. Diachronic and synchronic dictionaries

With regard to the time axis, dictionaries are grouped into two kinds: diachronic dictionaries and synchronic dictionaries. Diachronic dictionaries mainly focus on the vocabulary development by showing how the words have developed throughout the history of the language while synchronic dictionaries describe the vocabulary of a certain period. Examples of diachronic dictionaries are the *Oxford English Dictionary* (*OED*) and *Shorter Oxford Dictionary* (*SOD*) while *Webster's New Collegiate Dictionary* (*WNCD*), *Collins COBUILD English Language Dictionary* (*CCELD*) and *Longman Dictionary of Contemporary English* (*LDOCE*) are most famous synchronic dictionaries.

3. General and specialized dictionaries

General dictionaries are intended to provide a comprehensive description of the whole language, with special attention to the vocabulary. The "general-purpose" nature fulfills a number of different functions (information on meaning, spelling, idiomatic use, etc.) and thus satisfies various reference needs of the language user. It is typically monolingual, although it shares many features with the bilingual dictionary, where translation equivalents replace definitions. Here are some of the typical general dictionaries: *Concise Oxford Dictionary* (*COD*), *Webster's New Collegiate Dictionary* (*WNCD*), *Random House College Dictionary* (*RHCD*), etc.

In contrast, specialized dictionaries concentrate either on more restricted information, such as names, idioms, abbreviations, clichés, colloquialisms, dialect words, ESP, euphemisms, hard words, new words, phrasal verbs, phrases and quotations, proverbs and slangs, or on the language of a particular subject field, such as the jargon of the drug scene or the technical terms of mechanical engineering. Dictionaries fall into this kind are: *The Oxford Dictionary of English*

Etymology, *Longman Dictionary of English Idioms*, *Cambridge International Dictionary of Phrasal Verbs*, *The Oxford Dictionary of Euphemisms*, *The BBI Dictionary of English Word Combinations*, *Roget's Thesaurus of English Words and Phrases*, *Longman Lexicon of Contemporary English*, etc.

4. Monolingual and bilingual dictionaries

The major difference between these two types of dictionary is that an English monolingual dictionary will give its information (definitions, etc.) in English, while a bilingual one uses an English entry for which foreign language translations are offered by way of definition (and of course vice versa: foreign entry + English translation equivalents). In some monolingual dictionaries for learners of English, the definitions are written within a controlled vocabulary of around two thousand words. Other learner's dictionaries have a policy of making the definitions simple but not being limited by a fixed defining vocabulary. Learners seem to prefer dictionaries written in a controlled vocabulary.

Bilingual dictionaries are often less helpful than they might be because they do not offer enough context to tell one meaning of a word from another. In addition, finding suitable lexical equivalents is a notoriously difficult task, especially in pairs of languages with different cultures. Nevertheless, in the lexicographic tradition of many languages, the production of bilingual dictionaries started early, e. g. for English and Latin before 1450, English and Welsh in 1547, English and French in 1570, even before the publication of the first monolingual English dictionary in 1604. To some extent, bilingual dictionaries are popular among some language learners simply because they provide meanings in a very accessible way and in most cases they can be bi-directional.

Over the past decades, a new type of dictionary made its appearance, which is called bilingualized dictionary. It is a native language dictionary with foreign language translation. The first bilingualized dictionary published in China is *Oxford Advanced Learner's Dictionary*, published in the early 1970s. Nowadays, not only more and more English dictionaries are being or have been bilingualized, Chinese dictionaries are being bilingualized as well (*The Dictionary of Chinese Language*, Xinhua Zidian). Designed for native Chinese speakers, these dictionaries are useful when you are translating English to Chinese or vice versa, but essentially they are not learner's dictionaries.

5. Printed and electronic dictionaries

With the rapid development of the computer technology, dictionaries are no longer published in paper alone. They may be available on the Internet or in the form of CD-ROMs. Some of the Internet resources are free, but quite a few demand a fee.

An important distinction between printed and electronic dictionaries is that the latter save space on your book shelves and tend to be quicker to use. What is crucial to realize is that there are different types of CD-ROM dictionaries. One type, often available for free, offers the text of a printed dictionary in electronic form and can only be used to access main entry words. Another type tends to make full use of the electronic medium by including visual and video materials and allows users to search for words in the complete text of the dictionary (this is called full-text search), which often finds more words than are listed as head words. We are to discuss in more details in Chapter 14.

6. Unabridged, medium-sized and pocket dictionaries

Dictionaries can be of widely varying sizes, from a hundred or so pages to many thousands. Thus, three types of dictionaries (unabridged, medium-sized and pocket) can be distinguished in terms of the size. There comes, however, a problem that all that one can count is "entries" or "headwords" which is a vague term, because a headword in one dictionary may be subordinated — listed below the main entry — in another. Therefore, size alone, measured by the number of entries, does not make a dictionary better. In fact, entry-counts are good mostly for publicity purposes.

An unabridged dictionary may not be a shortened version of some other dictionary, listing more than 400,000 entries. It is compiled from scratch, which is to say, largely from its own files of citations, with all definitions and arrangements of meanings and examples determined by its own editors. A remarkable example of the unabridged dictionary is the *Webster's Third New International Dictionary of the English Language* (*W3*).

A medium-sized or desk dictionary usually contains about 50,000 to 150,000 entries and it usually saves space at the expense of the obsolete and dialected lexical units. It is therefore appropriate for an intermediate or advanced learner's consultation. Among scores of medium-sized dictionaries, *COD* and *WNCD* might be regarded as the standard in Britain and the United States respectively.

Dictionaries called "pocket" often are bilingual and meant primarily for "travelers". The information they contain is very brief and much simplified. Their pages are small and the number of pages rarely exceeds between 5,000 to 15,000 entries. In addition, they usually have no illustrative examples. If the entries of a pocket dictionary are properly selected, it is a useful reference for the language beginners.

7. Adults and children dictionaries

The fact that dictionaries intended for children have to differ considerably from those for adults is self-evident. Children are less able to make use of the complicated format and it is more difficult for them to determine whether the information given is relevant to their needs of the moment. A dictionary for children must therefore be not just an abbreviated dictionary for adults. Usually, children dictionaries have a shorter word-list consisting of the most "important" words of the language, excluding regionalisms, slang words, etc. They also use different techniques for the explanation of meaning, including, for instance, the use of illustrative examples without definitions.

13.3.2 Learner's dictionaries

The learner's dictionary (also called the pedagogical dictionary), which aims to help non-English learners in some certain way, lies in the endeavors of three teachers of English, coinciding with the growth of the English-as-a-foreign-language industry. Two of them (Harold E. Palmer and A. S. Hornby) worked in Japan and the other in India (Michael West). As a matter of fact, the research projects they made upon English teaching have greatly contributed to the genesis of the learner's dictionary. Michael West played a leading role in promoting the "vocabulary movement", while Harold Palmer worked on the grammatical patterning of words, especially verbs, as later did A. S. Hornby. Palmer and Hornby also investigated collocations and idioms, which inevitably resulted in the first general-purpose learner's dictionary — *Idiomatic and Syntactic English Dictionary* in 1942, marking the birth of the first learner's dictionary. The second generation of the learner's dictionary did not make its appearance until the publication of the second (1963) and third (1974) editions of

> What are the differences between the learner's dictionaries and collegiate dictionaries?

OALD and more significantly, the first edition of the *Longman Dictionary of Contemporary English* (*LDOCE*) in 1978, which greatly challenged the authoritative position of the *OALD* over the past 30 years. With the arrival of the 1980s, the learner's dictionary has developed greatly into a stage characterized by its "user-drivenness" with the assistance of the computer and corpora. There comes the third generation of the learner's dictionary, marked by the fourth edition of *OALD* (1989), the second edition of *LDOCE* (1987) and the first edition of *Collins COBUILD English Language Dictionary* (*CCELD*, 1987).

With increasing attention being paid to the needs of learners, the market witnessed the "year of the learner's dictionaries" in 1995, in which *OALD* published its fifth edition, *LDOCE* its third and *CCELD* its second. Also in that year, there came a new learner's dictionary, *Cambridge International Dictionary of English* (*CIDE*), edited by Paul Proctor, who had been responsible for the first edition of *LDOCE*. In *CIDE*, each major sense has a separate entry, followed where appropriate by a "guiding word" to the meaning. Besides, every grammatical pattern is illustrated by an example, and examples also show typical collocations. Indeed the dictionary focuses on the phraseological potential of words, and it includes an extensive "Phrase Index", in which phrases are entered under all of their constituents, each of which has a reference to the page, column and line number. The "International" in the title is justified on the one hand by its treatment of American and Australian, as well as British English, and on the other by its tables of "false friends" for some sixteen languages, including Japanese, Korean and Thai — Chinese, for some unknown reasons, is ignored. Like other learner's dictionaries, *CIDE* derives from an analysis of the corpus — Cambridge Language Survey Corpus, which is supposed to have 100 million words.

1. Oxford Advanced Learner's Dictionary (OALD)

The first English monolingual learner's dictionary was the *Idiomatic and Syntactic Dictionary of English* by A. S. Hornby published in 1942. It was republished as *A Learner's Dictionary of Current English* by Oxford University Press in 1948 and changed in 1952 to *The Advanced Learner's Dictionary of Current English*. The second edition of the dictionary came in 1963 and the third in 1974 with the replacement of *Oxford* to *The* in the title. The dictionary was a huge financial success and had the advanced learner's dictionary market to itself. This unparalleled success was, of course, the result of the boom in the English language teaching industry worldwide. It is now in its seventh edition as the *Oxford Advanced Learner's Dictionary*. It was edited by Sally Wehmeier and runs up to 1,880 pages both in paper and CD-ROM forms.

Two outstanding features of the *OALD* attract language learners' attention. First, the invention of "Short Cut" gives the reader an easy and quick way to locate the meaning they are seeking for in a polysemous context. For example, the entry "sensitive" has the following six "Short Cut": **sensitive (adj.):** 1 TO PEOPLE'S FEELINGS; 2 TO ART / MUSIC / LITERATURE; 3 EASILY UPSET; 4 INFORMATION / SUBJECT; 5 TO COLD / LIGHT / FOOD, etc. ; 6 TO SMALL CHANGES. Besides, 3,000 defining words are used to ensure the comprehension of the definitions for the learners, some of the definitions being explained in full sentences. The second feature of the dictionary is of its delicate system of grammatical and pragmatic, or else cultural information. To achieve the goal of helping the learners in using the language, the dictionary provides with many specific columns, e. g. Which Words? British / American, More About, Synonyms and Vocabulary Building.

2. Longman Dictionary of Contemporary English (LDOCE)

The *Longman Dictionary of Contemporary English*, which becomes to be the first rival to the *OALD*, was published in 1978 and its latest one was the fourth edition in 2003. The editors, led by Paul Proctor, introduced several innovations. The most striking one is the use of a restricted "defining vocabulary" of 2,000 common words in English, which has now become a standard feature of learners' dictionaries. Another distinctive feature of the *LDOCE* lies in the "word frequency", which presents itself in two forms. The first one attempts to describe words in the dictionary with different codes (e. g. S1 , W3) of the 3,000 most common English words, which has been discussed in detail in 13. 2. The second is to compare the language usage in terms of the frequency in bar, illustrated as follows.

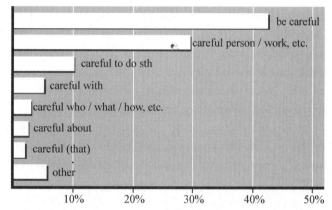

Fig.13.2 This graph shows how common different grammar patterns of the adjective *careful* are.

Fig. 13. 2 This graph shows how common different grammar pattens of the adjective *careful* are.

In addition, the dictionary also tries to convey the linguistic information for each entry in the following ways: 1) "Guide Word", functioning as the "Short Cut" in *OALD*, e. g. **charge (vt.): 1** MONEY; **2** RUSH/ATTACK; **3** WITH A CRIME; **4** BLAME; **5** ELECTRICITY; **6** ORDER; **7** GUN and **8** GLASS. 2) "Word Focus", which deliberately links the words to their related ones, very much like the one in *OALD* — Word Building.

WORD FOCUS: CAR
big cars: limousine, people carrier *BrE*, gas-guzzler
AmE informal, estate car *BrE*
small cars: compact *AmE*, hatchback *BrE*
other types of car: pickup, van, saloon *BrE*/ sedan
AmE, sports car, convertible, SUV *AmE*, off-roader, four-wheel drive/4×4
where you park your car: garage, car park *BrE*/ parking lot *AmE*, multi-storey car park *BrE*, parking space, carport
someone who drives a car: driver, motorist, learner driver
someone who drives a rich or important person's car for them: chauffeur, driver

3. Collins COBUILD English Language Dictionary (CCELD)

COBUILD, an acronym for Collins Birmingham University International Language Database, is a British research group set up at the University of Birmingham in 1980 and funded by Collins Publishers. The group was led by Professor John Sinclair. The most important

achievement of the COBUILD project has been the creation and analysis of a corpus of contemporary text (the Bank of English), and the production of the monolingual learner's dictionary *Collins COBUILD English Language Dictionary* (*CCELD*, 1987), based on the study of the COBUILD corpus. It has its second, third, fourth and fifth editions in 1995, 2001, 2003 and 2006 respectively.

The dictionary thrilled the market with many significant innovations. First, all the definitions are complete sentences; they are intended to sound like the teacher explaining the meaning in the classroom, and they give some idea of typical contexts. Second, all the examples are from the corpus — "real English" — sometimes with minor adaptation, which will be fully discussed in the next chapter. Third, the grammatical information is not included in the main entry, but provided in an "extra column", to the right of the main column. Fourth, there is only one entry per spelling, and senses are listed in frequency order; all inflections are given, whether regular or irregular. Each sense begins a new paragraph, and nearly all senses have at least one example.

All in all, the learner's dictionary focuses on current meaning, omitting outdated uses. Etymology is also omitted in such dictionaries and all headwords are explained in uncomplicated language, typically using a core defining vocabulary of some 3,000 words, thus making the definitions more digestible to learners. There are many example phrases and sentences, but no quotations. Appendices and interspersed notes serve the target readership, providing additional guidance and help to language learners, e. g. with the usage of "false friends" in *CIDE*. Besides, all the four monolingual learner's dictionaries discussed above are available in CD-ROM format.

13.3.3 Collegiate dictionaries

The college, or "collegiate", dictionary is a desk-size dictionary, aimed at native language learners as well as the learners of English as a second language. By comparison with their British counterparts in terms of the content, American collegiate dictionaries have tended to be more "encyclopedic" in their scope. They have routinely included biographical and geographical entries, as well as more extensive scientific and technical information. Diagrams and line drawings also intersperse the text. The collegiate dictionary is much more of an all-purpose reference work. On the other hand, they tend to contain limited information on etymology, and they pay little attention to the other varieties of English than the American.

Although Merriam-Webster's "collegiate" dictionaries were first published in 1898, and were widely used, it is not until from the 1940s that we saw remarkable development of college dictionaries. *The American College Dictionary* (*ACD*), edited by Clarence L. Barnhart, drew upon a distinguished group of linguistic advisers. What distinguishes the *ACD* most from its predecessors is that it applied linguistic studies of that time to its dictionary. In 1953, *Webster's New World Dictionary of the American Language* appeared. Edited by David B. Guralnik and Joseph H. Friend, it simplified its technical definitions to make them more understandable to the layman and gave full etymologies. In 1963, *Webster's Seventh New Collegiate Dictionary*, edited by Philip Babcock Gove and based on *Webster's Third Unabridged International Dictionary* (*NID3*), appeared, and that same year Funk and Wagnalls' new dictionary, the *Standard College Dictionary*, was issued. In 1968, Random House, publisher of the *ACD*, issued the *Random House Dictionary*, *College Edition* (later called the *Random House College Dictionary*, *RHCD*), with 155,000 entries, more than any of the other college dictionaries up to that time. In 1973, the eighth edition of *Webster's New Collegiate Dictionary*, much expanded in vocabulary from the seventh edition, was published, and ten years later *Webster's Ninth New Collegiate Dictionary*, enlarged still more, with nearly 160,000 entries, appeared.

Being a typical American product, the collegiate dictionary distinguishes itself with unique Americanism. Spelling and pronunciation are almost uniformly American. Essays on dictionary-making or language history, written by some linguistic authorities are added in the front of the dictionary. Thus, some of the practices of American lexicography, including numbered definitions, biographical and geographical entries, have been imitated by some British dictionaries.

Owing to the fierce competition in the dictionary market, several college dictionaries have made revisions and innovations at such a rapid pace that they can not be excelled by the British ones, and nearly all the main publishers have a dictionary of this type, including the American Big Five:

- *American Heritage Dictionary of the English Language*, *New College Edition*
- *Merriam Webster's Collegiate Dictionary*
- *Random House Webster's College Dictionary*
- *Webster's New World College Dictionary*
- *Funk and Wagnalls Standard Desk Dictionary*

Being a virtual symbol for the dictionary, Merriam-Webster began to introduce its collegiate dictionary in 1898 and the series is now in its eleventh edition. As a matter of fact, the dictionary has a paper file of 15,700,000 citations from which their lexicographers chose 10,000 new words, for a total of 165,000 entries and 225,000 definitions. In addition, there are 100,000 "changes" from the tenth edition and 40,000 examples and a "significant" increase in idioms to meet the user's demand. The thing that really sets this dictionary apart is the CD-ROM. We can search for words using up to 15 different operations, including "rhymes with", "is a cryptogram of", "homophones are", "etymology includes", etc. Moreover, the online version has a number of search options, including a reverse dictionary (if you can think of the correct words), the etymology of words, and those that are the same part of speech.

This chapter on the introductory knowledge about the dictionary includes three sections — the development of dictionaries, contents of dictionaries and types of dictionaries. The earliest word reference books for the English-speaking people were bilingual glossaries which provided English equivalents for Latin or French words. The dictionary history in Britain and the US, as well as other countries, is discussed in the first section. In the second section, the contents of dictionaries are studied in detail. Dictionaries generally cover some or all of the following: spelling, pronunciation, grammatical information, etymology, definition, usage labeling, related forms, frequency, illustrations and supplementary matters. In the third section, different types of dictionaries are carefully categorized in terms of complexity of demands. Among them, the learner's dictionary and the collegiate dictionary are the most helpful for language learners. Examples and illustrations are presented in this section.

Further Reading

1. Béjoint, H. (2000). *Modern Lexicography: An Introduction*. London: Oxford University Press.
2. Cowie, A. P. (1999). *English Dictionary for Foreign Learners: A History*. New York: Oxford University Press.
3. Hartmann, R. R. K. (1983). *Lexicography: Principles and Practice*. London: Academic Press Inc.

● Extended Reading

▪ What is in a dictionary?

From the perspective of its "macro-structure", there are potentially three parts to a dictionary: the front matter, the body, and the appendices. Some dictionaries do without appendices, but most have front matter, however brief. The front matter usually includes an introduction or preface, explaining the innovations and characteristics of the edition concerned, together with a guide to using the dictionary, which may consist of a single-page diagram or some lengthier account. Other front matter might be an explanation of the transcription system used for indicating pronunciation, a list of abbreviations used in the dictionary, and an essay on some relevant topic, such as the history of the language or varieties of English around the world. Appendices may be various and even non-lexical; here is a selection: abbreviations, foreign words and phrases, ranks in the armed forces, counties of the U. K. and states of the US, weights and measures, musical notation, Greek and Cyrillic alphabets, punctuation, works of Shakespeare.

The body of a dictionary contains an alphabetical list of "headwords". Each headword is accompanied by a number of pieces of information, which together with the headword constitute the "entry". The headword is usually printed in bold type and hangs one or two spaces to the left of the other lines. Entries are presented in two columns on each page, though there may be three columns in some, usually larger dictionaries (e. g. *NODE*, *W3*, but also *ECED*).

The headwords represent the particular selection of vocabulary and other items that the editors have decided merit inclusion, given the size and purpose of the dictionary. General-purpose dictionaries will all tend to share a headword list that encompasses the core vocabulary; the differences will be in the amount of technical and specialist, as well as colloquial, slang and dialect vocabulary they include. Editors will be concerned to be up-to-date, especially in socially and culturally significant areas such as computing, medicine, the environment, fashion, and so on. The inclusion of the latest vocabulary in such areas is often used as a selling point for a new edition.

If you examine the headwords in a general-purpose dictionary, you will find that it includes more than just lexemes. In terms of lexemes, it will include: "simple" lexemes; compounds, possibly all, but at least those written solid (without a hyphen); and derivatives whose meanings are considered to need a separate definition from their roots. Other derivatives are contained within the entry for the root, as "run-ons", usually in bold type but without a definition. The headword list will usually include inflected forms where these are "irregularly" formed and are alphabetically some distance from the citation form (e. g. *bought* in relation to *buy*): the entry will contain just a cross-reference to the citation form. The list may also include items that are not lexemes, especially derivational affixes and combining forms, and abbreviations. In some dictionaries (e. g. *CED*, *NODE*) the headword list includes names of places and people, introducing geographical and biographical entries, e. g.

Birmingham / ˈbʊhmɪŋ(h)em / 2nd largest British city, in the W Midlands of England; a major industrial, service, and transport centre with growing high-tech and light industries; home of two universities, a symphony orchestra, and the National Exhibition Centre; est. pop. 998, 200(1987)

(*LDEL*2)

Angelou / ˈandʒəluː /, Maya (b. 1928), American novelist and poet, acclaimed for the first volume of her autobiography, *I Know Why the Caged Bird Sings* (1970), which recounts her harrowing experiences as a black child in the American South.

(*NODE*)

Some headwords will be entered more than once. This applies to homonyms (1.2), e. g. *spell*, with four entries in *COD*9, and to homographs, e. g. *bow*, with one entry pronounced / bəʊ / and two entries pronounced / baʊ /. In some dictionaries (e. g. *LDEL*) each word class that a headword belongs to will occasion a separate entry: for example, *rear* has four entries in *LDEL*2, one each for the verb, noun, adjective and adverb uses of the headword.

The "micro-structure" of a dictionary refers to the arrangement of the information within the entries. The range and type of information within an entry will vary according to the kind of headword, but will typically include some or all of the following:

- *Spelling*: the headword indicates the normal spelling, but any variations will follow.
- *Pronunciation*: within rounded () or slash // brackets, together with any variations.
- *Inflections*: if these are formed irregularly or occasion some spelling adjustment such as doubling of consonants, dropping of "e" or changing "y" to "i".
- *Word class*: usually indicated by conventional abbreviations, "n" for noun, "adj" for adjective, etc.; verbs are also marked for "transitive" (vt) or "intransitive" (vi).
- *Senses*: where a lexeme has more than one meaning, each sense is usually numbered; where a sense, or group of senses belong to a different word class or subclass, this is indicated before the sense(s) concerned.
- *Definition*: each sense is given a definition, which is an explanation of its meaning.
- *Examples*: where the elucidation of a sense benefits from an illustrative phrase or sentence, usually given in italic type.
- *Usage*: where a sense is restricted in its contexts of use, an appropriate label precedes the sense concerned; if the restriction applies to all the senses of a lexeme, the label precedes any of the senses.
- *Run-ons*: undefined derivatives (with a word class label), idioms, phrasal verbs (if they are not included as headwords), usually in bold type.
- *Etymology*: conventionally in square brackets as the final item in the entry.

Some dictionaries include additional information, for example on collocation or the syntactic operation of words. Learner's dictionaries, especially, contain detailed information on these topics, as well as other additional material. By way of illustration, here is the entry for *drink* from *COD*9:

Drink / drɪŋk / v. & n. v. (past **drank** / dræŋk / ; past part. **drunk** / drʌŋk /) **1 a** *tr.* swallow (a liquid). **b** *tr.* swallow the liquid contents of (a container). **c** *intr.* swallow liquid, take draughts (*drank from* *the stream*). **2** *intr.* take alcohol, esp. to excess (*I have heard that he drinks*). **3** *tr.* (of a plant, porous material, etc.) absorb (moisture). **4** *refl.* bring (oneself etc.) to a specified condition by drinking (*drank himself into a stupor*). **5** *tr.* (usu. foil. by *away*) spend (wages etc.) on drink (*drank away the money*). **6** *tr.* wish (a person's good health, luck, etc.) by drinking (*drank his health*). *n.* **1 a** a liquid for drinking (*milk is a sustaining drink*). **b** a draught or specified amount of this (*had a drink of milk*). **2 a** alcoholic liquor (*got the drink in for Christmas*). **b** a portion, glass, etc. of this (*have a drink*). **c** excessive indulgence in alcohol (*drink is his vice*). **3** (as **the drink**) *colloq.* the sea. **drink deep** take a large draught or draughts. **drink in** listen to closely or eagerly (*drank in his every word*). **drink off** drink the whole (contents) of at once. **drink to** toast; wish success to. **drink a person under the table** remain sober longer than one's drinking companion. **drink up** drink the whole of; empty. **in drink** drunk. **drinkable** *adj.* [Old English *drincan* (*v.*), *drinc* (*a*) (*n.*), from Germanic]

— Jackson, H.

Exercises

I. True or False decisions.

1. The English dictionary originated from the glossary, an interpretation of hard words in English and easy Latin. (   )
2. The dictionary entitled with "Webster's" belongs to the Webster series published by G. & C. Merriam Company. (   )
3. For pronunciation, British dictionaries as well as American ones generally use International Phonetic Alphabet (IPA). (   )
4. Bilingual dictionaries are of the two types. One is that the entries are defined and explained in the same language with translations. The other is that the entries are defined in one language and given in their foreign equivalents. (   )
5. The definitions in *CCELD* are written using a list of defining vocabulary no more than 2,000. (   )

II. Choose the best choice to answer the following questions.

1. Which of the following statements is not true about the *OED*?
    A. The second edition of the *OED* is currently available as a 20-volume print edition.
    B. The *OED* offers the best in etymological analysis and in listing of variant spellings, and it shows pronunciation using the International Phonetic Alphabet.
    C. The first CD-ROM version of the *OED* is published in 1993.
    D. The Philological Society of London calls for a new English Dictionary (later known as the *OED*) in 1857.
2. According to the purpose of dictionaries we have _____ dictionaries.
    A. monolingual, bilingual and multilingual
    B. synchronic and diachronic
    C. pocket, medium-sized and unabridged
    D. general and specialized
3. Pocket dictionaries provide only _____.
    A. the spelling and pronunciation of each word with a few most common meanings
    B. spelling and meaning

C. spelling, meaning and usage
D. pronunciation and spelling
4. Among the following dictionaries, which one provides the definitions of words in full sentences?
   A. *LDOCE.* B. *CCELD.* C. *OED.* D. *OALD.*
5. Which of the following is not a specialized dictionary?
   A. *The Oxford Dictionary of English Etymology.* B. *Practical English Usage.*
   C. *Longman Dictionary of Phrasal Verbs.* D. *LDOCE.*
6. Which of the following statements is not true as far as the *OALD* is concerned?
   A. There are many example phrases and sentences, including quotations and etymologies.
   B. The dictionary was first published in 1948 with A. S. Hornby as editor; the current edition (as of 2005) is the seventh (editor: Sally Wehmeier).
   C. The dictionary previously entitled the *Oxford Advanced Learner's Dictionary of Current English*, is a popular dictionary published by the Oxford University Press.
   D. As its name implies, the dictionary is intended not for linguistic scholars but for non-native speakers who want information about the meaning of current English words and phrases.

Chapter 14
The Dictionaries of English Words (2)
— How to Use Dictionaries

Points for Thinking
1. What factors should be taken into consideration in choosing a dictionary?
2. Is it necessary to read the introduction and guide to the dictionary before you use it?
3. How does lexicography benefit from the development of the corpus?
4. Is it possible that the electronic dictionary will replace the printed one in the near future?
5. What are the advantages of online dictionaries?

A craftsman who wishes to practice his craft well must first sharpen his tools.
— Confucius (551BC – 479BC)

14.1 How to Use Dictionaries

In English, dictionaries are referred to as "reference books". If we want to study a language well, we should first of all learn how to use a dictionary. As a matter of fact, dictionaries can be used for a wide range of purposes. Some are complied chiefly for comprehension (e. g. reading), others are mainly for production (e. g. speaking and writing). The following list covers most of the purposes for dictionary use.

Comprehension (decoding)
- look up unknown words met while listening, reading or translating;
- confirm the meanings of partly known words;
- confirm guesses from context.

Production (encoding)
- look up unknown words needed to speak, write or translate;
- look up the spelling, pronunciation, meaning, grammar, constraints on use, collocations, inflections and derived forms of partly known words needed to speak, write or translate;
- confirm the spelling, pronunciation, meaning, etc. of known words;
- check that a word exists;
- correct an error.

(I. S. P. Nation, *Learning Vocabulary in Another Language*)

As well as being sources of information, dictionaries can be aids to learning. First, dictionaries play an authoritative role in language learning, especially in the case of the word pronunciation. Secondly, dictionaries provide a great deal of information on the usage of each entry with the presentation of definitions and examples. In some learner's dictionaries, the usage, as well as related information (e. g. synonyms and antonyms) of the word is sufficiently given to language learners. Thirdly, modern dictionaries focus greatly on its interactive function. Learners are encouraged to communicate with the dictionary in an easy way (e. g. CD-ROM and online dictionary).

14.1.1 How to choose a dictionary

The success of a learner depends to a large extent on his or her study skills, and the use of dictionaries is one of the most important study skills. The selection of a dictionary constitutes the first step of the dictionary using. Then, what is a good dictionary for dictionary users? Perhaps this is a question with quite different answers. However, the most important thing we have to do is to identify the general information in the dictionary before we choose it. The following factors may greatly influence our decision.

What is the appropriate English dictionary for the students of English majors?

● User's need: Dictionaries are compiled for a certain purpose. Some are compiled mainly for comprehension, and others are chiefly for production. Some dictionaries are explicitly designed for the learner of a certain level, such as collegiate dictionaries, and other dictionaries are for a certain age group, such as dictionaries for children. In brief, the dictionary should be chosen that best suits the learner's specific needs and level. For example, you are suggested to have a desk dictionary if you use it at home and at work while a pocket one will be just sufficient if you only use it for traveling and reference. In another case, if you want to do some translation tasks, the selection of a bilingual dictionary is most important and a monolingual one will turn to be useless.

● Copyright date: With thousands of new words or new meanings being added into the vocabulary, it is not exaggerating to say that "a dictionary begins to go out-of-date the moment it is published". It is felt inadequate though the publishers have spared their efforts to improve the out-of-dateness of the dictionary via constant revisions and in-time supplement. Under this circumstance, what a dictionary user can do is to choose a dictionary with the latest copyright date and watch for the supplement or new edition of the dictionary being used.

● Authoritative publisher: Dictionaries play the role of being the authority for the language learners. Thus, it is of great importance to find an authoritative dictionary, as it is most likely to be the product of competent editors supported by competitive publishers. Oxford, Longman in England and Webster (the G. & C. Merriam Company), Funk and Wagnalls, Random House in the US are some well-established publishers in western countries. Dictionaries published by them are thought to be reliable as they, with a long history, are staffed by learned and experienced editors and consultants and are often equipped with copious materials, some are even corpus-based. This is not an absolute criteria, but it is true that excellent publishers usually produce good dictionaries.

14.1.2 How to use dictionaries

A dictionary is nothing but a tool, so it is very important for the learners to make full use of the dictionary after choosing it.

Task
True or False decision
Contained in the introduction are such matters as the purpose of the dictionary, the coverage, the general layout and the way of compilation, and in most cases, the special merits of the dictionary.

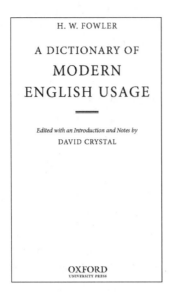
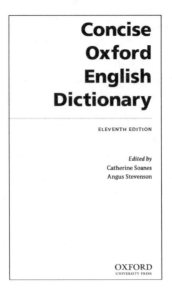

1. Read the introduction and guide of the dictionary

A dictionary user is supposed to read in advance the introduction and guide to the use of the dictionary. The purpose of doing this is to find out what the editors and publishers intend to offer in their works and get to know how the information is presented. Usually, the purpose of the dictionary, the coverage, the general layout and the way of compilation etc. are included in the introduction. In most cases, the special merits of the dictionary and the improvements made in later edition are also mentioned in the introductory part of the dictionary. In brief, the introduction presents the user with a general idea of the dictionary.

As for the guide to the use of the dictionary, it informs the user the presentation of the word information. Different dictionaries may run differently, but usually they contain: 1) arrangements of entries, 2) structure of entries, 3) meaning, 4) spelling, 5) pronunciation, 6) labels, 7) inflections, etc.

2. Make full use of the word entry

To know a word does not mean to know its meaning only. To make full use of the word entry, it is necessary for a dictionary user to pay special attention to its spelling, pronunciation, syllable division, grammatical and pragmatic information, in addition to the meaning itself. Take the word "sensible" for example. Apart from the usual coverage of the word class and definition, the entry also provides the user with plenty of information of grammar, usage labeling and related forms. As a matter of fact, the word entry indeed tells the user a detailed story of the word. Let's take the word *sensible* in the *Oxford Advanced Learner's Dictionary* for example.

sens · ible / ˈsensəbl/ adj.

1 (of people and their behaviour) able to make good judgements based on reason and experience rather than emotion; practical: *She's a sensible sort of person.* ◇ *I think that's a very sensible idea.* ◇ *Say something sensible.* ◇ *I think the sensible thing would be to take a taxi home.*

2 (of clothes, etc.) useful rather than fashionable: *sensible shoes*

3 (*formal* or *literary*) aware of sth: *I am sensible of the fact that mathematics is not a popular subject.* OPP for sense 3 INSENSIBLE HELP Use **silly** (sense 1) or **impractical** (senses 1 and 2) as the opposite for the other senses.

▶ **sens · ibly** /ˈsensəbli/ adv. : *to behave sensibly* ◇ *He decided, very sensibly, not to drive when he was so tired.* ◇ *She's always very sensibly dressed.*

Guide to the use of the dictionary

Verb inflections

dab¹ ■ v. (**dabs, dabbing, dabbed**) press against (something) lightly several times with a piece of absorbent material. ➤ apply (a substance) with light quick strokes. ■ n. **1** a small amount: *a dab of perfume*. ➤ a brief application of a piece of absorbent material to a surface. **2** (**dabs**) Brit. informal fingerprints.
– ORIGIN ME: symbolic of a light striking movement; cf. DABBLE and DIB.

Typical form (in bold)

Example of use (taken from real evidence)

Homonym number (indicates different word with same spelling)

dab² ■ n. a small, commercially important flatfish found chiefly in the North Atlantic. [*Limanda limanda* and other species.]
– ORIGIN ME: of unknown origin.

■ introduces each new part of speech

➤ introduces each subsense

dabble ■ v. **1** move (one's hands or feet) around gently in water. ➤ (of a duck or other waterbird) move the bill around in shallow water while feeding. **2** (often **dabble in**) take part in an activity in a casual or superficial way.

Part of speech

Core sense

Typical pattern (in bold)

WHICH WORD?

sensible · sensitive

Sensible and sensitive are connected with two different meanings of sense.

■ **Sensible** refers to your ability to make good judgements: *She gave me some very sensible advice.* ◇ *It wasn't very sensible to go out on your own so late at night.*

■ **Sensitive** refers to how easily you react to things and how much you are aware of things or other people: *a soap for sensitive skin* ◇ *This movie may upset a sensitive child.*

3. Choose the right meaning

It seems to be quite difficult for the dictionary user to choose the right meaning when polysemy or homonymy arises. Take the word "wheel" (Six people had been injured because a mad man, too drunk to walk, had gotten behind the *wheel*.) for example. The following steps may be taken if the user wants to define the word accurately in *LDOCE*. First, from the context, we can ascertain that *wheel* is a noun, so we may locate the definition to *wheel*¹ noun. Next, three guide words (1. on a vehicle; 2. for controlling a vehicle; 3. in a machine) are to be studied carefully for the purpose of defining the word logically. Finally, read the definition and example sentences in each entry and decide the right meaning of the word *wheel* in the context (2. for controlling a vehicle: [usually singular] the round piece of equipment that you turn to make a car, ship etc. move in a particular direction). Taking the above steps is only one way of choosing the right meaning. Sometimes the situation is more complicated. The meaning we find in the dictionary does not fit the context nicely. This point involves adapting the meaning found in the dictionary to the context of the word in the text. In many cases this will not be a big change. In a few cases, some narrowing or stretching of the meaning may be necessary. An extension or amplification of the meaning in the dictionary is, therefore, needed. For example, in the sentence "The picture *flattered* her", we can not possibly find matching meaning for the word "*flattered*" in the dictionary. All we can do is just to extend the dictionary meaning a bit, which actually means "She looks more beautiful in the picture than herself". Thus, always bear in mind that in some cases, it is not likely to find a fixed dictionary meaning for every word. The latter aspect of using the dictionary is called productive use, that is, turning ideas into languages. It involves finding word forms to express messages. In essence, the user of the dictionary may exercise his own judgment on the basis of his linguistic knowledge and intuition of the language.

Apart from the above mentioned features, three kinds of possible skills are highlighted in the use of a dictionary:

• Check the spelling or pronunciation of the word before using it. In most learner's dictionaries, the working out of the pronunciation requires reading phonetic script, which needs considerable practice.

• Interpret the dictionary's style labels and codes. These labels include: indications of whether the word is in current use or archaic; whether it is formal or colloquial; whether it is only used in the US or U.K.; whether it is impolite, etc.

• Work out the grammar and collocations of the word. Most of the information can come from grammatical information and example sentences in the dictionary. Learners are more likely to make use of the example sentences than they are to try to interpret grammatical coding schemes. As a matter of fact, this grammatical information can be of great use in written and spoken production.

14.2 Corpus and Lexicography

14.2.1 The history of corpus development

The rapid development of the computer science exerts influential impact on modern language research, among which the corpus ranks at the top, especially in lexicography. Derived from Latin, "corpus" has the following definitions.

corpus (13c: from Latin *corpus* body. The plural is usually *corpora*) (1) A collection of texts, especially if complete and self-contained: *the corpus of Anglo-Saxon verse*. (2) Plural also *corpuses*. In linguistics and lexicography, a body of texts, utterances or other specimens considered more or less representative of a language, and usually stored as an electronic database. Currently, computer corpora may store many millions of running words, whose features can be analysed by means of *tagging* (the addition of identifying and classifying tags to words and other formations) and the use of concordancing programs. (cf. McArthur, Tom "Corpus", in: McArthur, Tom (ed.) 1992. *The Oxford Companion to the English Language*. Oxford, 265 – 266).

In David Crystal's opinion, a corpus is a collection of linguistic data, either compiled as written texts or as a transcription of recorded speech. The main purpose of a corpus is to verify a hypothesis about language — for example, to determine how the usage of a particular sound, word, or syntactic construction varies. As a matter of fact, the booming of the corpus gives rise to the corpus linguistics — merging in the 1960s with the combination of corpus and linguistics, which inevitably deals with the principles and practice of using corpora in language study.

In the English-speaking world, the first large-scale project to collect language data for empirical research was Randolph Quirk's *Survey of English Usage* which later led to what became the standard English grammar for many decades: *A Comprehensive Grammar of the English Language* (Quirk et al. 2010). Quirk's Survey was a mixture of spoken and written data: there were about 500,000 words of spoken English within a total of one million words. The spoken component was actually the first to be put in a computer by Jan Svartvik, and became, in the late 1970s, the London Lund Corpus. It was transcribed in an elaborate way with much phonological and even phonetic information. It became the first spoken corpus widely available for use. In fact, the Survey was mostly interested in grammar, not in meaning. Nevertheless, it was one of the very few projects working on empirical data. Due to the pervasiveness of the Chomskyan paradigm, it became increasingly difficult in the 1960s to find acceptance of this kind of data-oriented language research and was indeed the exception in Britain at that time.

The second data-oriented project in the 1960s was the Brown Corpus, named after Brown University in Providence, Rhode Island, where it was compiled by Nelson Francis and Henry Kučera. The corpus consists of one million words, taken in samples of 2,000 words from 500 American texts belonging to 15 text categories as defined by the Library of Congress. The Brown Corpus was a carefully organized corpus, very easy to use, and proofread until it was almost free of mistakes. So is the similarly composed corpus of British English, the LOB (Lancaster-Oslo-Bergen)-Corpus from the 1970s, consisting of about one million words. Both the Brown Corpus and the LOB Corpus are generally defined to be the representatives of the sample corpus with static and closed features.

Table 14.1 Composition of the Brown Corpus and LOB Corpus

Label	Text category	Brown Corpus	LOB Corpus
A	Press: reportage	44	44
B	Press: editorial	27	27
C	Press: reviews	17	17
D	Religion	17	17
E	Skills, trades and hobbies	36	38
F	Popular lore	48	44
G	Belles lettres, biography, essays	75	77
H	Miscellaneous (documents, reports, etc.)	30	30
J	Learned and scientific writings	80	80
K	General fiction	29	29
L	Mystery and detective fiction	24	24

Continued

Label	Text category	Brown Corpus	LOB Corpus
M	Science fiction	6	6
N	Adventure and western fiction	29	29
P	Romance and love story	29	29
R	Humour	9	9
	Total	500	500

The third, and certainly the most important, corpus project was English Lexical Studies, begun in Edinburgh in 1963 and completed in Birmingham. The principal investigator was John Sinclair. It was he who first used a corpus specifically for lexical investigation, and it was he who took up the concept of the collocation. Professor of Modern English Language at Birmingham University, John Sinclair is a first-generation modern corpus linguist and the founder of the COBUILD project. The most important achievement of the COBUILD project has been the creation and analysis of a corpus of contemporary text (the Bank of English), and the production of the monolingual learner's dictionary *Collins COBUILD English Language Dictionary*, based on the study of the COBUILD corpus. As a matter of fact, the Bank of English, successor of the COBUILD, is a collection of English texts which are mainly British, but American and Australian data are also included. Apart from it, the British National Corpus (BNC) is also very influential, covering British English of the late twentieth century. It is a 100-million-word text corpus of samples of written and spoken English from wide range of sources. The written part of the BNC (90%) includes, for example, extracts from regional and national newspapers, specialist periodicals and journals for all ages and interests, academic books and popular fictions, published and unpublished letters and memoranda, school and university essays. The spoken part (10%) consists of orthographic transcriptions of unscripted informal conversations (recorded by volunteers selected from different age, region and social classes in a demographically balanced way) and spoken language collected in different contexts, ranging from formal business or government meetings to radio shows and phone-ins.

Table 14.2 Composition of the BNC World Edition

Text type	Texts	Kbytes	W-units	S-units	percent
Spoken demographic	153	4206058	4.30	610563	10.08
Spoken context-governed	757	6135671	6.28	428558	7.07
All Spoken	910	10341729	10.58	1039121	17.78
Written books and periodicals	2688	78580018	80.49	4403803	72.75
Written-to-be-spoken	35	1324480	1.35	120153	1.98
Written miscellaneous	421	7373707	7.55	490016	8.09
All Written	3144	87278205	89.39	5013972	82.82

14.2.2 Corpus-based lexicography

As mentioned above, the development of computer science gave rise to corpus linguistics, which later on gave birth to a new interdisciplinary branch — corpus lexicography, when integrated with the traditional lexicography. A new innovation of the lexicography has thus started. Many lexicographers, as well as linguists, have placed computer corpus at the center of dictionary-making. Compared with traditional lexicography, corpus-based lexicography has following advantages:

1. Quick data-gathering

When a corpus is being built up from scratch, data-gathering can be enormously speeded up by the use of a high-speed optical character reading machine (OCR), which scans written material, converts it to the digital form and stores it on the tape or on the disc. Moreover, if it is confronted with good-quality paper and print, it can be trained to recognize and input not only a wide variety of typesizes and fonts but also some exotic scripts.

2. Easy access and operation

Computer corpora are essentially bodies of textual material stored in machine-readable form. Being composed and stored electronically, they can be accessed by a computer user, who may easily search, copy, or transfer the material. Corpora are created by inputting texts into a computer through a number of channels, of which the most familiar one to the ordinary computer user is the keyboard of a microcomputer, though scanning is thought to be more efficient.

3. Further analysis and processing

It is assumed that the lexicographer can further analyze and process the original linguistic data for the purpose of reflecting the up-to-date language change, for example,

- new lexical entries are found;
- existing lexical entries are enriched by additional information extracted via corpus analysis (e.g. most common forms, connotation, etc.);
- important aspects of word meaning and grammar which were simply never noticed by linguists who had no data to work with are highlighted;
- word frequency analysis is used for annotating lexical entries;
- collocational information is collected, organized, and presented (e.g. idiom identification).

By systematically analyzing the corpus data we can make discoveries which are then used to update and improve dictionary entries, in order to produce the most accurate description of the language possible. New words are the most obvious manifestation of language change. We monitor new words as they emerge: they may be coming into the language via different routes. But we are also looking for more subtle changes in language — new meanings of existing words, for example, or changes in spelling and hyphenation over a longer period of time, or even grammatical changes. Here is an example showing how the Oxford English Corpus has been used to identify new uses and meanings in the language, and to change dictionary entries as a result. Until recently *edgy* was a word with a single meaning; a typical definition, here taken from the tenth edition of the *Concise Oxford English Dictionary* (1999), would look like this:

edgy *adj.* tense, nervous, or irritable.

But almost any sample of lines from the Oxford English Corpus gives ample evidence of a second meaning as well.

```
       chronological Love Actually. The only thing  edgy   about Actually was the language and the
         After making a name for himself with cool,  edgy   films like My Life as a Dog and What's
       wide-legged baggy-crotch jeans commercial-all edgy   and alternative. And if you can't get
          Drunk Love-the previous reigning champ of  edgy   romance starring comedy giants) and dizzying
             casting of her may have seemed daring and edgy, it's all wrong. Think about it-the
                  's just not as relentlessly concise and edgy as Lola. The pace is more akin to Tykwer
                     much worse than a film that thinks it's edgy and quirky but just plain isn't. Rage
                      one) tries to turn Thief into a fresh,  edgy, cliché-free story, Donald is working
       debacles. And Simple went from one hell of an  edgy   film to an important chunk of independent
                    say? Would it mention his great work in  edgy   films like Pulp Fiction and Twelve Monkeys
                       will be disappointed. Nevertheless, its edgy   stuff, and I came out compelled to see
                     n't constant so it gives you a slightly  edgy,  kind of moving look to it and it does
             not surprised because onscreen you're far   edgier than that. But I want to do it. I'm
              Death, which was very contemporary and   edgy.  Yeah, but I only had a small part in
                       framework, to go in saying, "I'm staying edgy   and I'm not going to compromise". There
                   darker, or high quality comedy side, or the edgy   stuff. What advice would you give to someone
                           To Hollywood, drunkards are figures of edgy   fun right up to the moment when they say
                       Emin Toprak are quite brilliant in these edgy   battles for the remote control, the late-night
              with the demands of live broadcasting. The   edgy   comic style had been familiar since Lenny
                           2003) Erik Gandini and Johan Soderberg's edgy   documentary, subtitled Terrorized Into
```

The new meaning appears to be quite widespread in both British and American English, though it is more commonly found in American English. It represents a clear case of a new sense of an existing word, and the dictionary entry needs to be updated to reflect this change (from the eleventh edition of the *Concise Oxford English Dictionary*, 2004),

   edgy adj. 1 tense, nervous, or irritable. 2 informal avant-garde and unconventional.

Highly competitive to the traditional lexicography, corpus-based lexicography still needs challenging efforts as it needs professional skills and the process of making a dictionary is a quite complicated one. It would greatly benefit the field of corpus linguistics if descriptive corpus linguists and more computationally-oriented linguists and engineers worked together to create the corpora. Generally speaking, a complete process of a corpus entry involves the following phases:

   Planning a corpus. To create a balanced and representative corpus, we, first of all, have to determine what kind of corpus we are going to have, as corpora vary greatly in terms of purposes. For instance, vocabulary studies necessitate larger corpora while grammatical studies smaller corpora.

   Collecting and computerizing written texts. As there are so many written texts available in computerized formats in easily accessible media, such as the World Wide Web, the collection and computerization of written texts have become much easier than in the past. It is no longer necessary for every written text to be typed in by hand or scanned with an optical scanner. If texts are gathered from the World Wide Web, it is still necessary to strip them of HTML formatting codes. But this process can be automated with the software. Indeed, creating a corpus of written texts is now an easy and straightforward enterprise.

   Collecting and computerizing spoken texts. While it is easier to prepare written texts for the entry to a corpus, there is little hope for making the collection and transcription of spoken texts easier. For the foreseeable future, it will remain a painstaking task to find people who are willing to be recorded, to make recordings, and to have the recordings transcribed. There are advantages to digitizing spoken samples and using specialized softwares to transcribe them, but still the transcriber has to listen to segments of speech over and over again to achieve an accurate transcription, which is surely a time-consuming and tiresome task.

Annotating texts with structural markup. The development of SGML-based (Standard Generalized Makeup Language-based) annotation systems has been one of the great advances in corpus linguistics, standardizing the annotation of many features of corpora so that they can be unambiguously transferred from computer to computer. The Text Encoding System (TES) has provided a system of corpus annotation that is both detailed and flexible, and the introduction of XML (the successor to HTML) to the field of corpus linguistics will eventually result in corpora that can be made available on the World Wide Web. There exist tools to help in the insertion of SGML-conformant markup to corpora. Nevertheless, much of this annotation has to be inserted manually, requiring hours of work on the part of the corpus creator.

Tagging and parsing. Tagging is now a standard part of corpus creation, and taggers are becoming increasingly accurate and easy to use. There will always be constructions that will be difficult to tag automatically and will require human intervention to correct. Parsing is improving too, but has a much lower accuracy than tagging. Therefore, much human intervention is required to correct a parsed text.

Text analysis. The most common text analysis program for corpora, the concordancer, has become an established fixture for the analysis of corpora. There are many such programs available for the use on PCs, Macintoshes, and even the World Wide Web. Such programs are best for retrieving sequences of strings (such as words), but many can now search for particular tags in a corpus, and if a corpus contains file header information, some concordancing programs can sort files so that the analyst can specify what he or she wishes to analyze in a given corpus: journalistic texts, for instance, but not other kinds of texts.

One more thing about the corpus is copyright restrictions as obtaining the rights to use copyrighted material has been a perennial problem in corpus linguistics. The first release of the British National Corpus could not be obtained by anyone outside the European Union because of restrictions placed by copyright holders on the distribution of certain written texts. As a result, access to the corpus is restricted to those who participated in the actual creation of the corpus — a method of distribution that does not violate copyright law. It is unlikely that this situation will ease in the near future. While texts are more widely available in the electronic form, particularly on the World Wide Web, getting permission to use these texts involves the same process as getting permission for printed texts, and current trends in the electronic world suggest that the access to texts will be more restrictive in the future, not less. Therefore, the problem of copyright restrictions will continue to trouble corpus linguists in the future.

Task

Explore The Corpus of Contemporary American English (COCA), the only large, genre-balanced corpus of American English. COCA is probably the most widely-used corpus of English, and it is related to many other corpora of English that we have created, which offer unparalleled insight into variation in English. The corpus can be accessed via:

https://www.english-corpora.org/coca/

14.3 Electronic Dictionaries

Dictionaries are generally divided into two kinds in terms of their carrier function — paper dictionaries and electronic dictionaries. With the rapid development of computer technology, there has emerged the electronic dictionary ever since the late 1970s, which marked the entry to the digital era of dictionary compilation. The electronic dictionary, challenging the paper dictionary to a great extent, is nevertheless not a proper substitute for the traditional one in many aspects. It differs from the paper dictionary in the fact that it achieves its goal on the basis of computer and web technology.

An electronic dictionary is, in fact, a small handheld computer with integrated reference materials. In some languages, the usage of the term is slightly broader, including CD-ROM dictionaries and dictionaries used by desktop word-processing programs. The term may be used in a broader sense in English as well, to refer to a machine-readable dictionary or spell checker.

14.3.1 The e-dictionary

The e-dictionary, monolingual or bilingual, takes the form of a calculator but works like a computer. Nowadays popular brands in China are "Youdao", "Casio", "Hanvor", "Besta", "Wenqüxing", "Instant-Dict", "IFLY-TEK", etc. Such dictionaries resemble miniature laptop computers, complete with full keyboards and LCD screens. As they are intended to be fully portable, the dictionaries are battery-powered and made with durable casing material. In these

dictionaries, each headword is followed by its pronunciation, part of speech, a few common meanings of the target language. It is much more convenient to use than a traditional paper dictionary. If one needs to find a word, he or she just types in the word and presses the button, immediately the meanings appear on the screen accompanied with pronunciation recording. Therefore, many learners depend on them so much that they never bother to use a traditional one. This is a mistake. Convenient as it is, they are expected to be helpful in situations like traveling, reading for fun or just checking spelling or pronunciation. If one wants to learn the language,

he/she is strongly recommended to use more of a paper dictionary than an electronic one. Meanwhile, two aspects should be taken into consideration if an electronic one is to be bought. First, make sure that the e-dictionary we buy has complete contents, or at least as much as its original one. Second, the publisher of the dictionary should be authoritative, like one of those well-known paper publishers, such as Oxford University Press, Cambridge University Press and Merriam-Webster Inc.

14.3.2 The CD-ROM dictionary

A number of dictionary publishers have made their dictionaries available in the electronic medium. Before the advent of CD-ROM technology, the third edition of *Collins English Dictionary* was produced on 3.5″ floppy disks, but quite a number of dictionaries are now available in CD-ROM format, including

- *Oxford English Dictionary*, 2nd edition
- *Concise Oxford English Dictionary*, 11th edition
- *Longman Dictionary of the English Language*, packaged with "Infopedia UK", published by SoftKey
- *Encarta World English Dictionary*
- *Oxford Advanced Learner's Dictionary*
- *Longman Interactive English Dictionary*, a version of *LDOCE*
- *Collins COBUILD English Dictionary*
- *Cambridge International Dictionary of English.*

The electronic medium provides a number of possibilities for dictionaries that are not presented by the print versions, as well as the basic functions. At its simplest level, a CD-ROM dictionary allows you to look up a word, just as in a print dictionary. Instead of turning pages to find the word, all you have to do is to enter it in a box and press the "Enter" key or click on a "Search" or "Find" icon to initiate the electronic search. The entry for the word is then displayed in a larger frame, while the headword list with the selected word highlighted is displayed in a smaller frame.

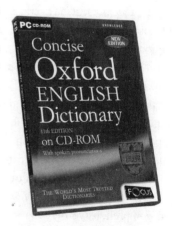

The electronic medium allows considerably more sophisticated exploitation of a dictionary text. The *COD10* on CD-ROM, for example, gives an initial choice between a "Quick" search and a "Full" search. The Quick search relates to the headword list, and the Full search to the complete text of the dictionary. The screen is divided into a headword list on the left and the dictionary entry on the right. The Quick search allows

- a straightforward lookup, by typing the headword in the search box, whose place will be found in the headword list and its entry displayed in the larger righthand window; you can scroll through the dictionary in either direction by moving the cursor from item to item in the headword list.
- a lookup using "wildcards", where, as is now the convention, "?" stands for a single letter, and " * " stands for any number of letters; a search for "?a?e" will find all four-letter words having "a" as their second letter and "e" as their fourth; " * ist" will find all the words ending in "ist"; the results of the search are displayed in the lefthand box, together with the total number of items found (180 for "?a?e", 291 for " * ist").

As a matter of fact, publishers have done more than simply transfer the print dictionary to the electronic medium and some of the CD-ROM versions of learner's dictionaries have begun to take more imaginative possibilities.

14.3.3　The dictionary apps for mobile device

The advent of mobile phones, tablets and their associated app stores has given rise to a large range of free and paid dictionary apps for mobile devices. As sales from the print dictionary industry decline, publishers are trying hard to make up for the loss in revenue using the income from dictionary app sales, particularly over the last 3 years. Software developers are also scrambling to license premium dictionaries from well-known publishers so that they can profit from the smartphone app boom.

A dictionary app can be a handy tool. Many have features such as a word of the day to help expand your vocabulary. Here are some of the best dictionary apps for Android: Advanced English Dictionary, Dict. cc, Dict Box Offline Dictionary, Dictionary by The Free Dictionary, Dictionary.com, English Dictionary, Google Search, Merriam-Webster Dictionary, Pocket Thesaurus, WordWeb, etc.

14.3.4　The online dictionary

Perhaps, the most promising development of dictionary is the online dictionary. Quite different from the traditional and electronic dictionaries, the online dictionary takes the Hypertext Markup Language (HTML) as its working medium and uploads the content onto the webpage with the assistance of the computer language. If we classify the electronic dictionary in terms of net-orientedness, there come two major generations. The first one, prevailed during the period of the 1980s, is in essence the extension of the traditional dictionary while the second (online dictionary), originated from the 1990s and featured itself in net-based framework, is often thought to be an innovation in the lexicographical field.

In online editing, the editor can highlight the identified file in order to see it, change it, transfer it to another part of the file, or delete it on the screen. The great advantage of online editing is the immediate availability of the latest file data.

In the present-day era of information and technology, online access to the dictionary database is certain to become an accepted practice in dictionary making in the near future. Dictionary editors may choose to continue to compose their definitions with pencil and paper, but they (or trained computer keyboard operators) will then transfer the information directly from the editorial office into the file. Longman has already employed such a system in preparing some of its dictionaries, which will undoubtedly be adopted and improved upon by other dictionary houses in the years ahead. Four online dictionary websites concerning language and three extra websites concerning encyclopedia are to be recommended in the following part of the chapter in order to help the language learners.

1. http://dictionary.oed.com/

The *Oxford English Dictionary Online* is widely acknowledged to be the most authoritative and comprehensive dictionary of English in the world. In addition to offering unparalleled access to the wealth of material contained in the 20-volume *Oxford English Dictionary* and 3-volume *Additions Series*, the *Online* enables the "treasure-house" of the English language to move with the times as never before.

For the first time since it was completed in 1928, the *Oxford English Dictionary* is being completely revised; every word and every sense is being fully reviewed, and new words added, to take account of the latest changes in language and scholarship. The revision program, which began in 1993, is released quarterly, offering online subscribers a unique opportunity to follow the progress of the revision project. Some major features and benefits of *OED Online* are as follows:

- Unprecedented access to the 20-volume *Second Edition* and the three *Additions Series* volumes, plus between one and two thousand new and revised entries every quarter;
- Everything from simple word look-ups to sophisticated Boolean searching, using any of the fields in the *Dictionary*, can be done with speed and ease;
- Find a term when you know the meaning but have forgotten the word;
- Use wildcards if you are unsure of a spelling, or if you want to search for words with common characteristics;
- Search for quotations from a specified year, or from a particular author and/or work;
- Search for words which have come into English via a particular language;
- Search pronunciations as well as accented and other special characters;
- Search for first cited date, authors, and works;
- Search for words with a particular part of speech.

The *OED Online* is more than a dictionary and it is an enormous history of the language. However, the *OED Online* is consulted daily by many scholars, but less frequently by general users, owing to its rather high admission charge, approximately $550 per year for a single subscription and a base price of $795 for multiple users.

2. http://www.m-w.com

Merriam-Webster is America's foremost publisher of language-related reference works. The company publishes a diverse array of print and electronic products, including *Merriam-Webster's Collegiate Dictionary* (11th edition), — America's best-selling desk dictionary — and *Webster's Third New International Dictionary*, unabridged.

The *Merriam-Webster Online Dictionary* is based on the print version of *Merriam-Webster's Collegiate Dictionary* (11th edition). The online dictionary includes the main A – Z listing of the *Collegiate Dictionary*, as well as the Abbreviations, Foreign Words and Phrases, Biographical Names, and Geographical Names sections of that book. It also includes 1,000 illustrations and 25 tables. Selected sections of the print *Collegiate Dictionary*, notably the Signs and Symbols

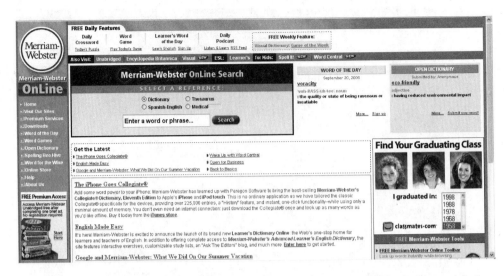

section, are omitted from the online *Collegiate Dictionary* because they include special characters and symbols that cannot readily be reproduced in HTML.

3. http://www.ldoceonline.com/

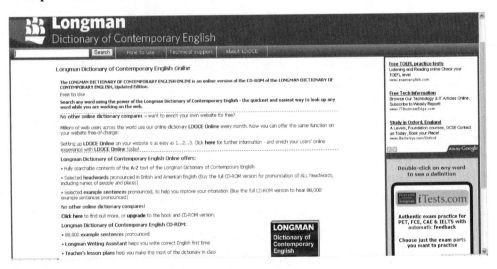

The *Longman Dictionary of Contemporary English Online* is an online version of the CD-ROM of the *Longman Dictionary of Contemporary English*, updated edition. It offers the following matters freely:

● Fully searchable contents of the A – Z text of the *Longman Dictionary of Contemporary English*;

● 88,000 example sentences pronounced;

● Longman Writing Assistant helps you write correct English first time;

● Teacher's lesson plans help you make the most of the dictionary in class;

● Over 1,000 listening exercises as well as extensive exam practice for FCE, CAE, CPE, IELTS and TOEIC.

4. http://dictionary.cambridge.org/

Cambridge Dictionaries Online is simply an electronic version of its paper dictionaries. It aims primarily at learners of English and its principle is to concentrate on describing and

reflecting as accurately as possible common contemporary English usage. Hence, it does not include particularly uncommon words or words whose use is restricted to a particular field of activity. Inclusion policy of the *Cambridge Dictionaries Online* is based largely, but not exclusively, on a word's frequency in the Cambridge International Corpus, 600-million-word database of contemporary English text.

5. http://www.onelook.com

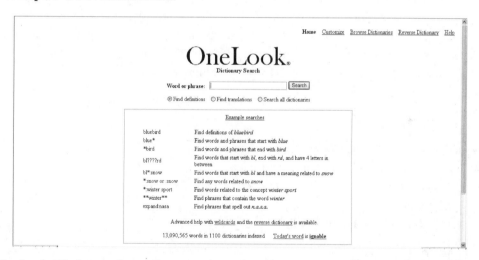

OneLook Dictionary Search is a search engine for words and phrases. If you have a word for which you'd like a definition or translation, you are supposed to turn to this web-based dictionary that defines or translates that word. If you don't know the right word to use, it will help you find it. No word is too obscure: More than 13 million words in more than 1,100 online dictionaries are indexed by the OneLook search engine. Luckily enough, it will spare you very little time to learn how to use this search engine.

Define words: Type a word into the search box on the front page to retrieve a list of dictionary web sites that define that word. Be sure "Find definitions" is selected.

Find words: Type a pattern consisting of letters and the wildcards "*" and "?" to retrieve a list of words matching your pattern. The asterisk "*" matches any number of letters or symbols. The question mark "?" matches exactly one letter or symbol.

Translate words: Type a word into the search box and select "Find translations" to retrieve a list of dictionary web sites that have translations of that word into other languages.

6. http://www.yourdictionary.com

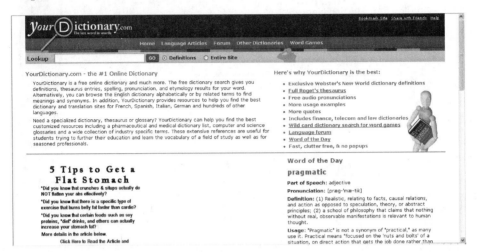

YourDictionary is a free and No.1 online dictionary. The dictionary search gives you definitions, thesaurus entries, spelling, pronunciation, and etymology results for your word. Alternatively, you can browse the English dictionary alphabetically or by related terms to find meanings and synonyms. In addition, YourDictionary provides resources to help you find the best dictionary and translation sites for French, Spanish, Italian, German and hundreds of other languages. Some major features and merits of YourDictionary are as follows:

- Exclusive *Webster's New World Dictionary* definitions;
- Full Roget's thesaurus;
- Free audio pronunciations;
- More quotes;
- Includes finance, telecom and law dictionaries;
- Wild card dictionary search for word games;
- Language forum;
- Word of the Day.

7. http://en.wikipedia.org/wiki/Main_Page

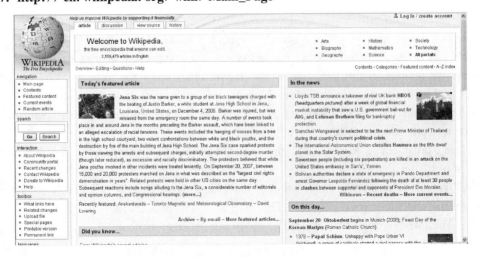

Wikipedia is a multilingual, web-based, free content online encyclopedia. The name Wikipedia is a blend of the words wiki (a type of collaborative web site) and encyclopedia. Wikipedia is written collaboratively by volunteers all over the world. Since its creation in 2001, it has grown rapidly into one of the largest reference web sites, attracting at least 684 million visitors yearly by 2008. There are more than 75,000 active contributors working on more than 10,000,000 articles in more than 250 languages. Up till May 2020, there are 6,073,863 articles in English; every day hundreds of thousands of visitors all over the world make tens of thousands of edits and create thousands of new articles to enhance the knowledge held by the Wikipedia encyclopedia.

Visitors do not need specialized qualifications to contribute, since their primary role is to write articles that cover existing knowledge; this means that people of all ages and cultural and social backgrounds can write Wikipedia articles. Most of the articles can be edited by anyone with access to the Internet. Anyone is welcome to add information, cross-references or citations, as long as they do so within Wikipedia's editing policies and to an appropriate standard.

Because Wikipedia is an ongoing work to which, in principle, anybody can contribute, it differs from a paper-based reference source in important ways. In particular, older articles tend to be more comprehensive and balanced, while newer articles more frequently contain significant misinformation, unencyclopedic content. Users need to be aware of this to obtain valid information and avoid misinformation that has been recently added and not yet removed. However, unlike a paper reference source, Wikipedia is continually updated, with the creation or updating of articles on topical events within seconds, minutes or hours, rather than months or years for printed encyclopedias.

This chapter, a further exploration of its practical use, focuses on three aspects of the dictionary — how to use dictionaries, corpus and lexicography and electronic dictionaries. The first section of the chapter deals with the necessity of learning how to use a dictionary. The most important thing is to know how to choose a dictionary. Three factors, user's need, copyright date and authoritative publisher should be taken into consideration. Some skills on using the dictionary are also mentioned in this section. With the assistance of the computer science, corpus has developed rapidly over the past four decades, thus resulting in the innovation of lexicography. In the second section, the history, as well as some famous corpora, is carefully discussed. Apart from that, this section also studies the function and application of the corpus in modern lexicography. The last section is concerned with the electronic dictionaries, which challenge or will even substitute the printed ones in the future. Three types of electronic dictionaries are categorized — e-dictionary, dictionary apps for mobile device or CD-ROM dictionary and on-line dictionary. Among them, the on-line dictionary has mushroomed during the past decades and exerted an influential impact upon modern lexicography. To make it clear, seven representative on-line dictionaries are recommended for the learners' reference.

Further Reading

1. Béjoint, H. (2000). *Modern Lexicography: An Introduction*. London: Oxford University Press.
2. Jackson, H. (2002). *Lexicography: An Introduction*. London and New York: Routledge.
3. Landau, S. I. (1989). *Dictionaries: The Art and Craft of Lexicography*. Cambridge: Cambridge University Press.

● Extended Reading

■ Computer corpora and lexicography

The progressive computerization of dictionary editing in the 1980s (and 1990s) has gone more or less hand in hand with the transformation of an activity that had long been the essential prelude to large-scale dictionary-making along traditional lines. This was the gathering of large bodies of authentic examples, often from literary sources and, in the case of the *OED*, by amateur readers (Landau 1984; Cowie 1990). Computerized data-gathering has speeded up this process enormously and, in so doing, corrected the bias in traditional gathering techniques towards the unusual or idiosyncratic and encouraged due respect for those more humdrum items that carry the chief burden of communication (Meijs 1992: 146). It has also placed the computer corpus at the centre of EFL dictionary-making.

Computer corpora are essentially bodies of textual material stored in machine-readable form. Being composed and stored electronically, they can be accessed by a computer user, who may automatically search, copy, or transfer the material they contain (Leech and Fligelstone 1992). Corpora are created by inputting text into a computer through a number of channels, of which the most familiar to the ordinary computer user is the keyboard of a microcomputer. The corpus compiler may develop at least part of a corpus in this way, but more often his or her task is one of capturing machine-readable text which already exists as a result of word-processing by others.

Material captured in this way may consist of computerized files originally created for uses quite unconnected with lexicography. These have ranged from mass-circulation newspapers to transcriptions of NASA investigations and the (bilingual) proceedings of the Canadian parliament. Such material, however, does permit searches for specific lexical items with the help of special retrieval systems (Bailey 1986) and had been used by Oxford lexicographers before the setting-up of the *New Oxford English Dictionary* project (in 1982 – 3) to search for items of special interest (Weiner 1987). A large and constantly expanding source of data is of course the daily and weekly press, and since major British and American newspapers are now printed with the aid of computer-driven composition systems, such material can be supplied to the lexicographer in machine-readable form (Cowie 1990).

When a corpus is being built up from scratch, data-gathering can be enormously speeded up by the use of a high-speed optical character reading machine (OCR), which scans written material, converts it to digital form and stores it on tape or disc. A further refinement is the Kurzweil Data Entry Machine (KDEM) which, provided it is confronted with good-quality paper and print, can be trained to recognize and input not only a wide variety of typesizes and fonts but also some exotic scripts (Knowles 1984; Renouf 1987; Butler 1990). Its overriding advantage, however, is its speed of operation: a KDEM can read whole books into the computer far faster than they could be typed via a keyboard (Leech and Fligelstone 1992; cf. Burnard 1992).

— Cowie, A. P.

■ The future of on-line dictionary editing

In the long run, perhaps the most promising development of computer use is on-line editing of dictionaries, as of other kinds of data. *On-line* means "having direct access to the computer file", usually by means of a video screen with an attached keyboard. Although on-line editing has been and is being employed in some dictionary projects, it is still not widely used, which is why discussion of it has been delayed until now.

In on-line editing, the editor can summon to the display unit any identified element of the current file in order to see it, change it, transfer it to another part of the file, or delete it. The great advantage of on-line editing is the immediate availability of the very latest file data. In ordinary editing, no one editor can know what other editors have done to other parts of the file without some delay — often a long one — and without laborious checking of card files or manuscript. Without knowing what is in the file, the editor may make mistakes or duplicate work already done. On-line editing makes style checking easier and has many other advantages.

Up until very recently, however, attempts to prepare dictionaries on-line have been plagued with difficulties and have seldom materialized on a large scale. *The Dictionary of American Regional English*, for example, which as we have seen uses computers extensively, was originally planned to have been written and edited on-line, but it was found to be easier to write it conventionally, while using information produced by computer on video screens. In the United States, the *Random House Dictionary* was one of the first major commercial dictionaries to utilize computers to store and categorize word lists, but the dictionary was not written or edited on-line. Neither was the *American Heritage Dictionary*, which used computers even more extensively to help produce its citation files. A scholarly historical work, the *Dictionary of Old English*, is, however, being edited on-line at the University of Toronto.

However slow it has been to become incorporated in the editorial process, on-line access to the dictionary database is certain to become an accepted practice in dictionary making in the near future. Dictionary editors may choose to continue to compose their definitions with pencil and paper, but they (or trained computer keyboard operators) will then transfer the information directly from the editorial office into the file. Longman has already employed such a system in preparing some of its dictionaries, which will undoubtedly be adopted and improved upon by other dictionary houses in the years ahead.

In the future we can look forward to the increasing use of speech synthesis for proofing pronunciations. The computer will be programmed to interpret phonetic symbols and record them in audible speech. Possibly, some day, one may be able to bypass the written form entirely and utter a word, wait a second or two, and hear in response the word's definition in one's own language, or its equivalent in another. An aural dictionary for the blind recently developed by the Library of Congress consists of audio cassettes and a voice index that the user must play at accelerated speed to find the word he wants, but we may look forward to the day when the sound of a human voice will by itself elicit an aural response of dictionary information about the word spoken.

— Landau, S. I.

Exercises

I. Choose the best choice to answer the following questions.

1. As far as the choice of a dictionary is concerned, which of the following is not worth consideration?
   A. Suitability.   B. Up-to-dateness.
   C. Authority.   D. Comprehensiveness.
2. The first step to make good use of a general dictionary is to _____.

A. read the introduction and guide of the dictionary
B. choose the right meaning
C. know the inadequacies of the dictionary
D. make full use of the entry words

3. Which of the following is not included in the guide of English dictionaries?
   A. Arrangement and structure of entries.   B. Articles from some authoritative experts.
   C. Grammatical labels.   D. Usage labels.

4. To make full use of the corpora, the collected linguistic materials should be carefully studied by the computer, the natural order of which is _____.
   A. concordancing — lemmatizing — parsing — tagging
   B. tagging — parsing — lemmatizing — concordancing
   C. parsing — tagging — concordancing — lemmatizing
   D. lemmatizing — concordancing — tagging — parsing

5. Which habit of using the dictionary is correct?
   A. To use one dictionary all through one's learning career.
   B. The more entries the dictionary has, the better.
   C. The dictionary is an awesome authority. We should not challenge it.
   D. To choose the dictionary which is the most suitable to the user.

6. Which of the following is the largest in the world in terms of the vocabulary?
   A. The Bank of English.   B. British National Corpus.
   C. Longman Corpus Network.   D. The Brown Corpus.

II. True or False decisions.

1. A dictionary begins to go out-of-date the moment it is published. Under this circumstance, what a dictionary user can do is to choose a dictionary with the latest edition. (   )
2. Any dictionary is helpful to a certain degree, but no one is perfect. In other words, every dictionary has its inadequacies. (   )
3. In short, a dictionary should be chosen as big as possible and has more entries than other dictionaries. (   )
4. The Brown Corpus consists of one million words, taken in samples from 500 American texts while the LOB Corpus collects its words from English texts. (   )
5. On-line dictionaries, originated from the 1990s and featured itself in net-based framework, is often thought to be an innovation to its counterpart, printed dictionaries. (   )

III. In buying the dictionary, are you taking the following questions into consideration?

1. Is the paper of good, hard-wearing quality?
2. Will the binding allow it to be opened flat?
3. Are (especially long) entries clearly laid out?
4. Does it have the words you most want to look up? (Keep a note of some words which have caused you problems, and use them as a quick check.)
5. Does it have good international coverage?
6. Does it contain encyclopedic information?
7. Does it have illustrations of difficult concepts?
8. Are the definitions clearly distinguished, and organized on a sensible principle?
9. Are the definitions easy to understand, and helpful (e.g. avoiding vicious circularity, as

when X is defined as Y, and Y is then defined as X)?
10. Does it give citations (examples of usage), and are they real or artificial?
11. Does it give guidance about usage?
12. Does it use a good set of stylistic labels (e. g. formal, slang, medical, archaic)?
13. Does it give etymological information?
14. Does it give guidance about capitalization, spelling variation, and where syllable boundaries go (i. e. where to hyphenate)?
15. Does it give pronunciation variants, and is the phonetic transcription easy to follow?
16. Does it contain idioms, phrases, proverbs, etc. ?
17. Does it contain lists of synonyms and antonyms?
18. Does it give useful cross-references to other words of related meaning?
19. Does it give information about word class, inflectional endings, and other relevant features of grammar?
20. Are there useful appendices (e. g. abbreviations, measures)?

Chapter 15
The Learning of English Words (1)
— The Mental Lexicon

> **Points for Thinking**
> 1. How are the three types of memory related to each other? Illustrate with the figure on the mechanisms of memory.
> 2. How are you to effectively review the English vocabulary according to Ebbinghaus Forgetting Curve?
> 3. What is the mental lexicon? How does it differ from the dictionary?
> 4. In what way does the mental lexicon organize? Illustrate with the model discussed in the chapter.
> 5. What are the variables that influence lexical access?

If any one faculty of our nature may be called more wonderful than the rest, I do think it is memory. There seems something more speakingly incomprehensible in the powers, the failures, the inequalities of memory, than in any other of our intelligences. The memory is sometimes so retentive, so serviceable, so obedient; at others, so bewildered and so weak; and at others again, so tyrannic, so beyond control! We are, to be sure, a miracle every way; but our powers of recollecting and of forgetting do seem peculiarly past finding out.

— Austen, J. (1775 – 1817)

Memory is the ability of the nervous system to receive and keep information, which is critical to humans and all other living organisms. Practically, all our daily activities — talking, understanding, reading, socializing — depend on our having learned and stored information about our environments. Memory enables us to learn new skills and to form habits. Without the ability to access past experiences or information, we would not be able to understand a language, recognize our friends, find our way home, or even have a dinner.

Maybe the interaction between memory and learning does not seem very obvious at first sight, but these two terms often describe roughly the same process. The term *learning* is often used to refer to the process involved in the initial acquisition or encoding of information, whereas the term *memory* more often refers to the later storage and retrieval of information. However, this distinction is quite vague. After all, information is learned only when it can be retrieved later, and retrieval cannot occur unless information has been learned. Thus, psychologists often refer to the learning/memory process as a means of incorporating all facets of encoding, storage and retrieval.

15.1 Memory in the Language-Processing System

15.1.1 Types of memory

A basic and generally accepted classification of memory is based on the duration of memory retention, which identifies three distinct types of memory: sensory memory, short-term memory

(STM) and long-term memory (LTM).

Sensory memory holds information for milliseconds and is separated into two components. The iconic memory is responsible for visual information, whereas auditory information is processed in the echoic memory. The ability to look at an item, and remember what it looked like with just a second of observation, or memorization, is an example of sensory memory. American psychologist George Sperling demonstrated the existence of sensory memory in an experiment in 1960. Sperling asked subjects in the experiment to look at a blank screen. Then he flashed an array of 12 letters on the screen for one-twentieth of a second, arranged in the following pattern:

G	Z	E	P
R	K	O	D
B	T	X	F

Subjects were then asked to recall as many letters from the image as they could. Most could only recall four or five letters accurately. Subjects knew they had seen more letters, but they were unable to name them. Sperling hypothesized that the entire letter-array image registered briefly in sensory memory, but the image faded too quickly for subjects to "see" all the letters. To test this idea, he conducted another experiment in which he sounded a tone immediately after flashing the image on the screen. A high tone directed subjects to report the letters in the top row, a medium tone cued subjects to report the middle row, and a low tone directed subjects to report letters in the bottom row. Based on these partial report experiments, Sperling was able to show that the capacity of sensory memory was approximately 12 items. Because this form of memory degrades so quickly (within a few hundred milliseconds), participants would see the display, but be unable to report all of the items before they decayed.

Sensory memory systems typically function outside the awareness and cannot be prolonged via rehearsal. Iconic memory seems to last less than a second. Echoic memory probably lasts a bit longer, estimating up to three or four seconds. The information in sensory memory vanishes unless it captures subject's attention and enters working memory.

Short-term memory (working memory) is the link between sensory memory and long-term memory and allows one to recall something from several seconds to as long as a minute. We can keep information circulating in working memory by rehearsing it. For example, suppose you look up a telephone number in a directory. You can hold the number in memory almost indefinitely by saying it over and over to yourself. But if something distracts you for a moment, you may quickly lose it and have to look it up again. This is an example of a piece of information which can be remembered for a short period of time. According to George Miller, the capacity of the STM is five to nine pieces of information (the magical number seven, plus or minus two). The term "pieces of information" or, as it is also called, "chunk" might enable one to memorize in a more efficient way. All of the following are considered as chunks: single digits or letters, whole words or even sentences and the like. It has been shown by experiments also done by Miller that chunking (the process of bundling information) is a useful method to memorize more than just single items in the common sense. A very intuitive example of chunking information is the following:

FBIPHDTWAIBM

One is supposed to be able to remember only a few items. However, if the same information is presented in the following way:

FBI PHD TWA IBM

One can remember a great deal more letters. This is because they are able to chunk the information into meaning groups of letters. STM is believed to rely mostly on an acoustic code for storing information, and to a lesser extent a visual code.

Long-term memory, which can store information over decades, consists of the conscious explicit and the unconscious implicit memory. Explicit memory, also known as declarative, can be subdivided into episodic memory and semantic memory. Episodic memory represents our memory of events and experiences in a serial form and is always connected with a specific time and place. For example, you would rely on episodic memory to describe a past family vacation, the circumstances of a childhood accident or the way you felt when you won an award. It is from this memory that we can reconstruct the actual events that took place at a given point in our lives. Semantic memory, on the other end, is a structured record of facts, concepts and skills that we have acquired. It is not tied to the particular time and place of learning. For example, in order to remember that George Bush was president, people do not have to recall the time and place that they first learnt this fact. Procedural memory refers to the skills that human possess. Riding a bicycle, swimming, and hitting a baseball are examples of procedural memory. In brief, LTM can be structured as follows:

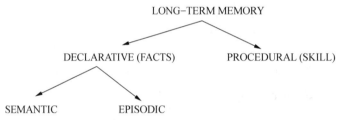

There seems to be no finite capacity to long-term memory. People can learn and retain new facts and skills throughout their lives. Although older adults may show a decline in certain capacities (e. g. recalling recent events), they can still profit from experience even in old age.

On the whole, the mechanisms of memory are not completely understood, but we can postulate that the above three memories (sensory memory, short-term memory and long-term memory) are closely interrelated, as shown in the following figure:

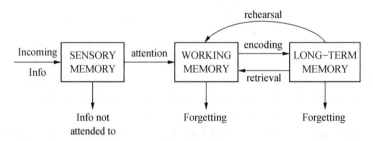

15.1.2 Memory retrieval

Our prior knowledge of pictures and faces allows us to see a "face" in the word "liar".

Once information has been encoded and stored in memory, it must be retrieved in order to be used. Memory retrieval is important in every aspect of daily life, from remembering where you parked your car to learning new skills. Then, what exactly is memory retrieval and what are things that can influence this process?

It is well-known to all of us that retrieval is a process of accessing stored memories. When you are taking an exam, you need to be able to retrieve learned information from your memory in order to answer the test questions. There are four basic ways in which information can be pulled from long-term memory.

1. **Recall:** This type of memory retrieval involves being able to access the information without being cued with any part of the memory. For example, answering a question on a fill-in-the-blank test is a good example of recall.

2. **Recollection:** This type of memory retrieval involves reconstructing memory, often utilizing logical structures, partial memories, narratives or clues. For example, writing an answer on an essay exam often involves remembering bits on information, and then restructuring the remaining information based on these partial memories.

3. **Recognition:** This type of memory retrieval involves identifying information after experiencing it again. For example, taking a multiple choice quiz requires you to recognize the correct answer out of a group of available answers.

4. **Relearning:** This type of memory retrieval involves relearning information that has been previously learned. This often makes it easier to remember and retrieve information in the future and can improve the strength of memories.

However, the retrieval process does not always work perfectly. Psychologists have explored several puzzling phenomena of retrieval that nearly everyone has experienced. These include déjà vu, jamais vu, flashbulb memories, and the tip-of-the-tongue state.

The sense of déjà vu (French for "seen before") is the strange sensation of having been somewhere before, or having experienced your current situation before, even though you know you have not. One possible explanation of déjà vu is that aspects of the current situation act as retrieval cues that unconsciously evoke an earlier experience, resulting in a strange sense of familiarity. Another puzzling phenomenon is the sense of jamais vu (French for "never seen"). This feeling arises when people feel they are experiencing something for the first time, even though they know they must have experienced it before. This phenomenon could be partly explained by the fact that the cues of the current situation do not match encoded features of the earlier situation despite their overt similarity.

A flashbulb memory is an unusually vivid memory of an especially emotional or dramatic past event. For example, the death of Princess Diana in 1997 created a flashbulb memory for many people. People remember where they were, when they heard the news, whom they heard it from, and other seemingly fine details of the event and how they learned of it. Flashbulb memories may seem particularly vivid for a variety of reasons. First, the events are usually quite distinctive and hence memorable. In addition, many studies show that events causing strong emotion (either positive or negative) are usually well remembered. Finally, people often think about and discuss striking events with others, and this periodic rehearsal may help to increase retention of the memory. However, researches have also shown that flashbulb memories are not always faultless, as is often supposed.

Have you ever felt like you knew the answer to a question, but could not quite remember the information? This phenomenon is known as a "tip of the tongue" experience. While you may feel certain that this information is stored somewhere in your memory, you are unable to access and retrieve it. While it may be irritating or even troubling, researches have shown that these experiences are extremely common for both younger individuals and elderly adults though the latter are more prone to the experience. Often when a person cannot retrieve the correct bit of information, some other wrong item intrudes into one's thoughts. For example, in trying to remember the name of a short, slobbering breed of dog with long ears and a sad face, a person might repeatedly retrieve *beagle* but know that it is not the right answer. Eventually the person might recover the sought-after name, *basset hound*. One theory of the tip-of-the-tongue state is that the intruding item essentially blocks the retrieval mechanism and prevents retrieval of the correct item. That is, the person cannot think of *basset hound* because *beagle* gets in the way and blocks the retrieval of the correct name. Another idea is that the phenomenon occurs when a person has only partial information that is simply insufficient to retrieve the correct item, so the failure is one of activation of the target item (*basset·hound* in this example). Both the partial activation theory and the blocking theory could be partly correct in explaining the tip-of-the-tongue phenomenon.

15.1.3 Why people forget

Forgetting, defined as the loss of information over time, is a spontaneous or gradual process in which old memories are unable to be recalled from memory storage. In most cases, we see forgetting as a bother. However, forgetting can also be useful because we need to continually update our memories, e.g. we are likely to forget our old telephone number if we get a new one; otherwise, things will get into a mess. Thus, forgetting can have an adaptive function.

Psychologist Hermann Ebbinghaus was one of the first to scientifically study forgetting. In experiments, Ebbinghaus tested his memory by using three-letter nonsense syllables for periods of time ranging from 20 minutes to 31 days. He then published his findings in 1885 in *Memory: A Contribution to Experimental Psychology*. His results, known as the Ebbinghaus Forgetting Curve, revealed a relationship between forgetting and time. Initially, information is lost very quickly after it is learned. Factors such as how the information was learned and how frequently it was rehearsed play a role in how quickly these memories are lost. The forgetting curve also showed that forgetting does not continue to decline until all of the information is lost. At a certain point, the amount of forgetting levels off.

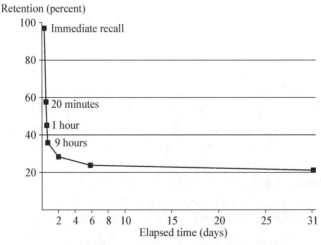

Fig. 15.1　Ebbinghaus Forgetting Curve. (From *Memory: A Contribution to Experimental Psychology* by Hermann Ebbinghaus, 1885/1913)

There are five possible reasons for forgetting: ineffective encoding, decay, interference, retrieval failure and motivated forgetting, which are to be discussed as follows:

1. **Ineffective encoding:** The way information is encoded affects the ability to remember it. Processing information at a deeper level makes it harder to forget. If a student thinks about the meaning of the concepts in his textbook rather than just reading them, he'll remember them better when the final exam comes around. If the information is not encoded properly — such as if the student simply skims over the textbook while paying more attention to the TV — it is more likely to be forgotten.

2. **Decay:** According to the decay theory, memory fades with time. It explains the loss of memories from sensory and short-term memory. However, loss of long-term memories does not seem to depend on how much time has gone by since the information was learned. People might easily remember their first day in junior high school but completely forget what they learned in class last Monday.

3. **Interference:** Interference theory has a better account of why people lose long-term memories. According to this theory, people forget information because of interference from other learned information.

4. **Retrieval failure:** Forgetting may also result from failure to retrieve information in memory, such as if the wrong sort of retrieval cue is used. For example, one may not be able to remember the name of his first-grade teacher. However, the teacher's name might suddenly pop into his head if he visits his old grade school and sees his first-grade classroom. The classroom would then be acting as a context cue for retrieving the memory of his teacher's name.

5. **Motivated forgetting:** Psychologist Sigmund Freud proposed that people forget because they push unpleasant or intolerable thoughts and feelings deep into their unconscious. He called this phenomenon repression. The idea that people forget things they don't want to remember is also called motivated forgetting.

In spite of all these reasons for forgetting, people can still remember a vast amount of information. In addition, memory can be enhanced in a variety of ways, including rehearsal, overlearning, distributed practice, minimizing interference, deep processing, organizing information, mnemonic devices, and visual imagery.

1. **Rehearsal:** Practicing material helps people remember it. The more people rehearse the information, the more likely they are to remember the information.

2. **Overlearning:** Continuing to practice material even after it is learned also increases retention.

3. **Distributed practice:** Learning material in short sessions over a long period is called distributed practice or the "spacing effect." This process is the opposite of cramming, which is also called massed practice. Distributed practice is more effective than cramming for retaining information.

4. **Minimizing interference:** People remember material better if they don't learn other similar material right before or soon after their effort. One way to minimize interference is to sleep after studying material, since people can't learn new material while sleeping.

5. **Deep processing:** People also remember material better if they pay attention while learning it and think about its meaning rather than memorize the information by rote. One way to process information deeply is to use a method called elaboration. Elaboration involves associating the material being learned with other material. For example, people could associate the new material with previously learned material, with an anecdote from their own lives, with a striking

example, or with a movie they recently saw.

6. **Organizing material:** Organizing material hierarchically or in categories and subcategories can be particularly helpful. The way an outline is organized, for example, usually helps people to remember the material in it. Chunking material into segments is also helpful. People often remember long strings of numbers, such as telephone numbers, by chunking them into two-, three-, or four-digit segments.

7. **Mnemonics:** Mnemonics are strategies for improving memory. The different kinds of mnemonics include acronyms, acrostics, narrative methods, and rhymes.

1) Acronyms

Acronyms are words made out of the first letters of several words. For example, to remember the colors of the spectrum, people often use the name ROY G. BIV, which gives the first letters of the colors red, orange, yellow, green, blue, indigo, and violet in the right order.

2) Acrostics

Acrostics are sentences or phrases in which each word begins with a letter that acts as a memory cue. For example, the rather strange phrase *Roses on yachts grow better in vinegar* also helps to remember the colors of the spectrum.

3) Narrative methods

Narrative methods involve making up a story to remember a list of words. For example, people could remember the colors of the rainbow in the right order by making up a short story such as this: Red Smith stood next to an orange construction cone and flagged down a yellow cab. He told the cabbie he was feeling very green and asked to be taken to a hospital. The cabbie took him to a hospital, where a nurse in a blue coat guided him to a room with indigo walls. He smelled a violet in a vase and passed out.

4) Rhymes

Rhymes are also good mnemonics. For example, the familiar rhyme that begins, "Thirty days has September ..." is a mnemonic for remembering the number of days in each month.

8. **Visual imagery:** Some well-known memory improvement methods involve using visual imagery to memorize or recall lists.

1) Method of loci

When using the method of loci, people might picture themselves walking through a familiar place. They imagine each item on their list in a particular place as they walk along. Later, when they need to remember their list, they mentally do the walk again, noting the items they imagined along the path.

2) The link method

To use the link method, people associate items on a list with each other. For example, if a man wants to remember to buy bread, juice, and carrots at the store, he might try visualizing the peculiar image of himself eating a juice-and-bread mush using carrots as chopsticks.

3) Peg word method

When using the peg word method, people first remember a rhyme that associates numbers with words: one is a bun, two is a shoe, three is a tree, four is a door, five is a hive, six is sticks, seven is heaven, eight is a gate, nine is swine, ten is a hen. They then visualize each item on their list being associated with a bun, a shoe, a tree, and so on. When they need to remember the list, they first think of a bun, then see what image it is associated with. Then they think of a shoe, and so forth.

> **Task**
>
> Are You Experiencing Brain Drain?
>
> Instructions: For each of the following statements, answer "T" if the statement is true or "F" if it is false. If you have more than 5 of them "T", perhaps your memory is aging, please take care of it.
>
> 1. My memory is not as good as it used to be.
> 2. It is harder to do mental calculations than it used to be.
> 3. It is more difficult to concentrate than it used to be.
> 4. I often feel fuzzy headed.
> 5. I can't handle stress as well as I used to.
> 6. I get depressed more often than I used to.
> 7. At the end of the day I feel more exhausted than I used to.
> 8. I often have a ringing sound in my ear.
> 9. I often feel jittery and irritable.
> 10. It is more difficult to learn new things than it used to be.
> 11. I sometimes get lost while driving familiar routes.
> 12. I often tell the same stories over and over to the same people.
> 13. I sometimes get confused over what time it is or where I am.
> 14. I often forget important appointments.
> 15. Lately, I have had difficulty naming familiar objects.

15.2 The Mental Lexicon and Its Organization

15.2.1 What is the mental lexicon?

The *mental lexicon* is a concept in linguistics that refers to a language user's knowledge of words. Psycholinguists refer to the representation of words in permanent memory as our "internal lexicon". When a given word in our lexicon has been found, the properties we associate with the word become available for use. These properties include the meaning of the word, its spelling and pronunciation, its relationship to other words, and related information. Much of this is the stuff of which dictionaries are made, but our internal lexicon also contains information that is not strictly linguistic. A part of our knowledge of *elephants*, for example, is that they are said to never forget things, but this is not part of the meaning of the word per se.

One part of our word knowledge is the phonological structure or pronunciation of the word. For example, we know when two words are homophones, which are words that are spelled differently but sound alike (such as *know* and *no*). Similarly, we experience the tip-of-the-tongue (TOT) phenomenon when we are not quite successful at retrieving a particular word but can remember something about how it sounds.

Another part of our knowledge of the word is the syntactic category, or part of speech, to which they belong. Two words belong to the same syntactic category when they can substitute for one another in a sentence. Consider the following sentence: *The lonely bachelor raised the neighbor's pity*. We can replace *lonely* with any number of words, such as *beautiful*, *ugly*, *fat*, *solemn*, and so on. Although the substitutions may change the meaning of a sentence, the sentence remains grammatical. One advantage of using syntactic categories is that we can generate grammatical rules in terms of categories rather than lexical items. Thus, we have no rule that states *lonely* may appear before *bachelor* in a sentence. The rule is that adjectives may modify nouns. To use such a rule, we need to include syntactic categories in the lexical entries in our mental lexicon (Miller, 1991).

Morphological knowledge is also included in our mental lexicon. It would seem, superficially, to be a fairly simple question, but it turns out that there is no easy answer. Any effort to identify vocabulary size will eventually have to confront the morphology of the language. If a person knows the word *go*, he is very likely to know the related words such as *going*, *gone*, *goes*, and so on. Do these count as separate words in his lexicon? How, then, do we estimate the size of a person's mental lexicon? For simple cases, such as the plural morphemes, it could be assumed that when a person knows *book*, the person will also recognize *books* as a word. So, *book* and *books* should count as just one word. Other morphemes, such as *-er*, cause more problems. In some cases, the morpheme produces a predictable shift in meaning, as in *run* and *runner*. But in other cases, the meaning is opaque, as in *sell* and *seller*. In fact, our ability to form various alternative forms of root words effectively means that there is no limit to the number of words in our mental lexicon.

Apart from the above mentioned, semantic knowledge should never be ignored. Then, how is that meaning represented mentally? Linguists, philosophers, and psychologists have identified several important aspects of word meaning, such as *sense* and *reference*, *denotation* and *connotation*, which have been fully discussed in Chapter 7.

To use words effectively in our daily lives, we must utilize our stored knowledge of words, which includes phonological, syntactic, morphological, and semantic aspects. These aspects enable us to pronounce words, create new forms of words, and understand the meanings of words.

The mental lexicon differs radically from a dictionary. There are so many words and they are found so fast. Native speakers can recognize a word of their language in 200 milliseconds or less and can reject a non-word sound sequence in about half a second. This speed is astonishing concerning how many words one would have to search through if he systematically examined the contents of his mental lexicon in order to reject such non-words. Just how many words are we talking about? Adults usually grossly underestimate the size of their vocabulary, guessing that it is between 1 and 10 percent of the real level. In a 1940 study Seashore and Erickson estimated that an educated adult knows more than 150,000 words and is able to use 90% of these. According to another recent study, the reading vocabulary of the average American high school graduate has been assessed at 40,000 words. If proper names of people and places, and idiomatic expressions are included the total will rise to 60,000.

15.2.2 Organization of the mental lexicon

We have discussed some of the information that is related to the mental lexicon. We now turn to two interdependent issues: how the mental lexicon is organized (this section) and how we access lexical information (15.3).

Researches show that words in the mind are "linked together in a gigantic multi-dimensional cobweb, in which every item is attached to scores of others" (Aitchison, 1994). The question here is how these lexical networks are organized. Aitchison points out that there are two types of links which seem to be particularly strong among native speakers of English: connections between co-ordinates (e.g. *salt — pepper*, *butterfly — moth*) and collocational links (e.g. *salt — water*, *butterfly — net*). Aitchison also mentions two more links which are important, although these occur less often; they are superordination (e.g. *butterfly — insect*) and synonymy (e.g. *starved — hungry*).

While Aitchison's research is based on native speakers' data, there is also some evidence of differences in word association between EFL learners and native speakers. Sokmen (1993) analyzes word associations of non-native speakers, and reports that affective associations are more often observed than coordinates and collocations. According to Sokmen, there is an "affective" category that shows a visual image, an opinion, an emotional response, or a personal past experience, such as *table — study* or *dark — scared*, and in her research, most words solicited "affective" associations. This suggests that students develop word associations based on feelings, attitudes, or strong memories and impressions.

In fact, there lies a big difference in word association among individuals. Further, not only does the mental lexicon vary from person to person, but also it is always changing. McCarthy (1990) demonstrates this as follows:

> The mental lexicon is never static; it is constantly receiving new input which has to be integrated into the existing store. Not only do new words come in but information about existing words is added too. This is a more obvious phenomenon for the learner and the L2 lexicon, but it is also true of L1. The webs of meanings and associations constantly shift and re-adjust; new connections are woven, and old ones strengthened.

Currently the main idea regarding the organization of the lexicon is that it is set up as a network of interconnected elements. The elements are concepts or nodes, which are connected to one another by virtue of having various relations with one another. In addition, the network is hierarchical if some of these elements stand above or below other members of the network. The Hierarchical Network Model proposed by Collins and Quillian (1969) (see Fig. 15.2) stands as the prototype of this approach, which mainly illustrates three points to the organization of the mental lexicon.

1. Information is stored in categories;

2. Categories are logically related to each other in a hierarchy: Broad categories of information, like "animal", are subdivided into narrower categories, like "bird" and "fish", which in turn are subdivided into still narrower categories;

3. "Cognitive Economy": Information stored at one level of the hierarchy is not repeated at other levels. A fact is stored at the highest level to which it applies. For example, the fact that birds breathe is stored in the ANIMAL category, not the BIRD category.

However, this model is by far beyond perfect as problems soon emerged. Perhaps the most serious difficulty was that the model assumed that all items on a given level of the hierarchy were more or less equal. *Canary* and *ostrich*, for example, were both subordinates of *bird* and one link away from *bird*, so they should take equal time to verify. In fact, they do not. It seems that this is generally true as some instances of categories are usually verified faster than others.

To modify the hierarchical assumption while retaining the idea of a network, there came another class of models, referred to as Spreading Activation Models. As one example, Collins and Loftus (1975) assume that words are represented in the mental lexicon in a network, but the organization is not strictly hierarchical. In contrast, the organization is closer to a web of interconnecting nodes, with the distance between the nodes determined by both structural characteristics such as taxonomic relations and considerations such as typicality and degree of association between related concepts. Collins and Loftus argue that retrieval occurs by a process of spreading activation: activation begins at a single node and then spreads in parallel throughout the network. This activation attenuates over distance, thus ensuring that closely related concepts are more likely to be activated than distant concepts (see Fig. 15.3).

◎ 英语词汇学（第二版）

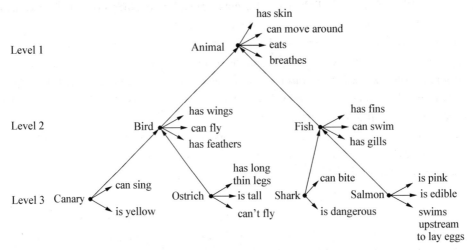

Fig. 15.2 Hypothetical memory structure for a three-level hierarchy. (Adapted from Collins and Quillian, 1969. Reprinted by permission of Academic Press.)

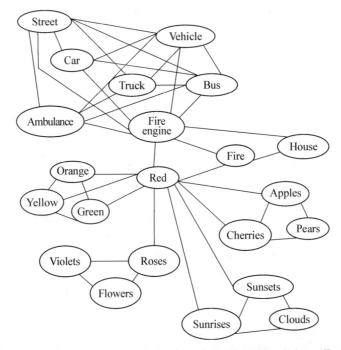

Fig. 15.3 A spreading activation model of semantic knowledge. (From "A Spreading-Activation Theory of Semantic Processing" by A. M. Collins and E. F. Loftus, 1975, *Psychological Review*, 82 (6) p. 412. Copyright © 1975 American Psychological Association. Reprinted by permission.)

Compared with Collins and Quillian's Hierarchical Network Model, additional features of Collins and Loftus's Spreading Activation Model are as follows:

　　1. Concepts and properties are treated equally in the sense that each can be accessed directly. In Collins and Quillian's Model, properties are contained within concept categories: To think of a property, like "can fly", you first have to think of a category, like "bird".

2. Not only are properties linked to concepts, but also to other properties. For example, "can fly" could be linked directly to "can sing".

3. Links between units of information vary in length. The longer the line between two units, the weaker is the degree of association between them.

The Collins and Loftus' Model is a step forward from the overly rigid hierarchical network model, but it too has some limitations. Very little attention is paid to phonological, syntactic, and morphological aspects of words. In a sense, then, it is a model of concepts rather than words. Besides, the disadvantage of the model is that you cannot predict reaction time in a verification task until you have mapped out the individual's network of associations. The theory explains a lot but predicts very little.

15.3 Variables Influencing Lexical Access

The process by which we activate meanings is called "lexical access". A word in our mental lexicon may be activated in several ways. One way is as a result of the perception of the word. If we see *dog* on a printed page, we identify it as a recognizable, familiar word and bring our knowledge of the word to bear on the task of comprehension.

15.3.1 The familiarity effect

Although an enormous vocabulary is available to any speaker of a language, not all of these words have equal status. One of the most firmly established statistical facts about words is that some of them are used far more frequently than others. For example, Hartvig Dahl has counted the frequency of different words in a transcript of 1,058,888 running words of spoken conversations. He found that the most frequently spoken word was the first person singular. The top twenty words are listed below and together they make up 37% of the total sample.

Table 15.1 The Twenty English Words Occurring Most Frequently in Personal Discourse

Rank	Word	Percentage	Rank	Word	Percentage
1	I	6.2	11	was	29.0
2	and	9.7	12	uh	30.4
3	the	12.6	13	in	31.6
4	to	15.4	14	but	32.5
5	that	18.0	15	is	33.3
6	you	20.5	16	this	34.2
7	it	22.4	17	me	35.0
8	of	24.3	18	about	35.8
9	a	26.2	19	just	36.6
10	know	27.6	20	don't	37.3

The familiarity effect illustrates a clear difference between the mental lexicon and a dictionary. In a dictionary it takes no longer to look up a less commonly used word; in the mental lexicon familiar words are more rapidly accessed. This is measured by using a lexical decision task (LDT). People are asked to indicate as rapidly as possible whether or not a string of letters spells an English word. The reaction time is the time between the instant that the word appears and the instant that people answer "yes" or "no". The lexical decision task consistently shows faster response time for high-frequency, high-familiarity words. One speculation about the reason for this effect is that frequently used words are easy to find because they are stored in many different places in the brain.

15.3.2 Variables that influence lexical access

The process of accessing or retrieving lexical information from memory is influenced by a number of factors. Among such factors are the word frequency, lexical ambiguity, morphological complexity, lexicality and semantic priming.

1. Word frequency

Word frequency refers to the fact that people respond much faster to the high-frequency word than the low-frequency one. Researchers selected 30 words from the Brown Corpus with the frequency of the first half averaging 199/1,000,000 and the second half 1/1,000,000. From the following experiments, they found that the subjects spent 71 milliseconds more on those low-frequency words than high-frequency ones, concerning the lexical access.

Rayner and Duffy (1986) have also found that the word frequency plays a role in normal reading. They measured eye fixations to words during reading and found that low-frequency words were fixated for about 80 milliseconds longer than high-frequency words.

2. Lexical ambiguity

Lexical ambiguity arises when the context is insufficient to determine the sense of a single word that has more than one meaning. For example, the word "*bank*" has several distinct definitions, including "financial institution" and "edge of a river", but if someone says "I deposited $100 in the bank", most people would not think you used a shovel to dig in the mud. In most cases, the lexical access of different senses occurs at the same time, but it is the context that helps us to decide which one to retain.

3. Morphological complexity

Some investigators argue that morphological information and base word information are organized separately in the mental lexicon. In this view, a word such as *decision* would be stored as the base word *decide* with a separate representation for *-ion*. In retrieving *decision*, the base word and the morpheme are united. One argument for this kind of arrangement is that it achieves some storage economy since we would not have to store all of the various forms of a word but only the base and the set of morphemes used throughout the language. However, this arrangement complicates the processing of these words: instead of accessing a single word, we would have to access both the base word and the morpheme and then combine them. It is not obvious which of the two proposals, independent storage or combined storage, would be preferable. However, much evidence has shown that high-frequency words tend to be stored independently while low-frequency words are likely to be stored in a combined way.

4. Lexicality

The role of lexicality has been demonstrated in the word identity task. A series of studies have proved that those non-words (e.g. *sajf*) are rejected less rapidly than fully illegal items such as **sjmf*, which is termed as lexicality effect. The pronunciation impossibilities of those illegal items may account for the effect.

5. Semantic priming

According to Carroll (1999), semantic priming occurs when a word presented earlier activates another semantically related word. The priming task consists of two phases. In the first phase, a priming stimulus is presented. Often no response to the prime is required or recorded; in any event, the response to the prime itself is of little interest. In the second phase, a second stimulus (the target) is presented, the participant makes some response to it, and the time taken to make this response is recorded. The response could take many forms, but two of the most commonly used tasks are to ask people to name the word or to decide whether the string is a word. An example is provided in a study by Meyer and Schaneveldt (1971). They used a lexical decision task and found that the time needed to classify the target *butter* as a word varied with the priming stimulus. The time was shorter when the prime was *bread* than when it was *nurse*.

   The learning of the vocabulary is closely linked with one's memory. This chapter mainly explores the learning of English words in two aspects — memory and the mental lexicon. Three sections are included in the chapter. In the first section, "Memory in the Language-Processing System", types of memory, memory retrieval and forgetting curves are introduced in detail. In the second section, "The Mental Lexicon and Its Organization", the definition and organization of the mental lexicon are carefully studied on the experimental basis of some linguists and psychologists. And in the last section of the chapter, "Variables Influencing Lexical Access", word frequency, lexical ambiguity, morphological complexity, lexicality and semantic priming are categorized to show that the learning of vocabulary is a complicated mental process.

Further Reading

1. Carroll, D. W. (1999). *Psychology of Language*. Brooks/Cole Publishing Company.
2. Steinberg, D. D. and Sciarini, N. V. (2006). *An Introduction to Psycholinguistics*. Harlow: Pearson Longman.
3. Nation, I. S. P. (1990). *Teaching and Learning Vocabulary*. New York: Newbury House Publishers.

● Extended Reading

▇ Role of memory in vocabulary acquisition

   Memory has a key interface with language learning. In fact, Ellis (1996) suggests that short-term memory capacity is one of the best predictors of both eventual vocabulary and grammar achievement. I have already brought up the memory-language relationship in the discussion of MWUs and language processing, but there are other, more general, memory issues worth touching on in a discussion of vocabulary acquisition.

   It must be recognized that words are not necessarily learned in a linear manner, with only incremental advancement and no backsliding. All teachers recognize that learners forget material as well. This forgetting is a natural fact of learning. We should view partial vocabulary knowledge as being in a state of flux, with both learning and forgetting occurring until the word is mastered and "fixed" in memory. I found that advanced L2 university subjects (Schmitt, 1998a) improved their knowledge of the meaning senses of target words about 2.5 times more than that of the words forgotten (over the course of one year), but this means that there was some backsliding as well. Interestingly, most of the forgetting occurred with words that were only known receptively; productive words were much less prone to be forgotten.

Of course, forgetting can also occur even if a word is relatively well known, as when one does not use a second language for a long time or stops a course of language study. In this case, it is called attrition. Studies into attrition have produced mixed results, largely because of the use of different methods of measuring vocabulary knowledge. In general, though, lexical knowledge seems to be more prone to attrition than other linguistic aspects, such as phonology or grammar. This is logical because in one sense vocabulary is made up of individual units rather than a series of rules, although we have seen that lexis is much more patterned than previously thought. It appears that receptive knowledge does not attrite dramatically, and when it does, it is usually peripheral words, such as low-frequency noncognates that are affected (Weltens & Grendel, 1993). On the other hand, productive knowledge is more likely to be forgotten (Cohen, 1989; Olshtain, 1989). The rate of attrition appears to be independent of proficiency levels; that is, learners who know more will lose about the same amount of knowledge as those who learn less. This means that more proficient learners will lose relatively less of their language knowledge than beginning learners. Overall, Weltens, Van Els, and Schils (1989) found that most of the attrition for the subjects in their study occurred within the first two years and then leveled off.

This long-term attrition mirrors the results of research on shorter-term forgetting, i.e. when learning new information, most forgetting occurs soon after the end of the learning session. After that major loss, the rate of forgetting decreases. This is illustrated in Fig. 15.4. By understanding the nature of forgetting, we can better organize a recycling program which will be more efficient. The forgetting curve in Fig. 15.4 indicates that it is critical to have a review session soon after the learning session, but less essential as time goes on. The principle of expanding rehearsal was derived from this insight, which suggests that learners review new material soon after the initial meeting and then at gradually increasing intervals (Pimsleur, 1967; Baddeley, 1990, pp. 156–158). One explicit memory schedule proposes reviews 5–10 minutes after the end of the study period, 24 hours later, 1 week later, 1 month later, and finally 6 months later (Russell, 1979, p. 149). In this way, the forgetting is minimized (See Fig. 15.5). Students can use the principle of expanding rehearsal to individualize their learning. They should test themselves on new words they have studied. If they can remember them, they should increase the interval before the next review, but if they cannot, they should shorten the interval.

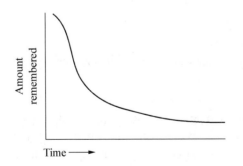 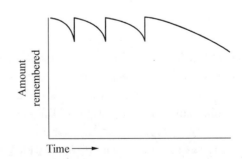

Fig. 15.4 *Typical pattern of forgetting.*   **Fig. 15.5** *Pattern of forgetting with expanded rehearsal.*

Landauer and Bjork (1978) combined the principle of expanding practice with research results demonstrating that the greater the interval between presentations of a target item, the greater the chances it would be subsequently recalled. From this, they suggest that the ideal practice interval is the longest period that a learner can go without forgetting a word. Research by Schouten-van Parreren (1991, pp. 10 – 11) shows that some easier words may be overlearned (in the sense that more time is devoted to them than necessary), whereas more difficult abstract words are often underlearned. A practice schedule based on the expanding rehearsal principle may help in avoiding this problem.

Memory comes in two basic types: short-term memory (also known as working memory) and long-term memory. Long-term memory retains information for use in anything but the immediate future. Short-term memory is used to store or hold information while it is being processed. It normally can hold information for only a matter of seconds. However, this can be extended by rehearsal, for example, by constantly repeating a phone number so that it is not forgotten. Short-term memory is fast and adaptive but has a small storage capacity. Long-term memory has an almost unlimited storage capacity but is relatively slow. The object of vocabulary learning is to transfer the lexical information from the short-term memory, where it resides during the process of manipulating language, to the more permanent long-term memory.

The main way of doing this is by finding some preexisting information in the long-term memory to "attach" the new information to. In the case of vocabulary, it means finding some element already in the mental lexicon to relate the new lexical information to. This can be done in various ways. One is through imaging techniques such as the Keyword Approach. Another is through grouping the new word with already-known words that are similar in some respect. The new word can be placed with words with a similar meaning (*prank* → *trick, joke, jest*), a similar sound structure (*prank* → *tank, sank, rank*), the same beginning letters (*prank* → *pray, pretty, prod*), the same word class (*prank* → *cow, greed, distance*), or other grouping parameter, although by far the most common must be meaning similarity. Because the "old" words are already fixed in the mind, relating the new words to them provides a "hook" to remember them by which they will not be forgotten. New words that do not have this connection are much more prone to be forgotten.

— Schmitt, N.

Exercises

I. Fill in the blanks with proper words according to the first letters given.

1. M_____ is the mental process used to encode, store, and retrieve information.
2. Holding information in memory over time is called s_____.
3. The process of putting information into memory is called e_____. It takes many forms: visual, auditory, semantic, taste, and smell.
4. Pulling information out of memory and into consciousness after it has been stored is called r_____. It includes recognition, recall, and reconstruction.
5. S_____ memory: a temporary place for storing information during which it receives limited processing (e.g. verbal rehearsal).
6. L_____ memory: a relatively permanent store, which has unlimited capacity and duration.
7. Any memory of a specific event that happened while you were present is an e_____ memory.
8. S_____ memory contains generalized knowledge of the world that does not involve

memory of a specific event.

9. D_____, the gradual erosion of memory, is the most common culprit for short-term memory loss.

10. I_____ causes forgetting by interrupting the encoding or retrieving process through the presence of other information.

II. Choose the best choice to answer the following questions.

1. The mental lexicon differs radically from a dictionary in the following aspects except _____.
   A. retrieving speed
   B. size of the vocabulary
   C. tip-of-tongue phenomenon
   D. systematic organization

2. Mental lexicon can be organized by sound and meaning. Besides, the organization can also be influenced by the following except _____.
   A. the age at which the word is acquired
   B. the frequency of use
   C. the formality of the word
   D. orthographical lexical access (as opposed to by-sound)

3. Which of the following is not the variable affecting the lexical access?
   A. The length of the word.
   B. Priming effect.
   C. Lexical ambiguity.
   D. Frequency.

4. "Mental lexicon" is the term first put forward by _____.
   A. Jean Aitchison
   B. A. M. Treisman
   C. Ferdinand de Saussure
   D. A. M. Collins

5. "Spreading Activation Model" for mental lexicon is put forward by _____.
   A. Bock and Levelt
   B. Meyer and Schvaneveldt
   C. Collins and Quillian
   D. Collins and Loftus

III. Test your memory!

A SIMPLE QUIZ TO CHECK YOUR MEMORY AND COGNITIVE SKILLS

This simple test evaluates some aspects of your memory & cognition. The quiz has two components, a performance and a historical section. This is a modified version of a quiz of Dr. Devi's used by *TIME* in a cover article in July, 2000, which may be accessed by getting onto *TIME* online.

PART I OF QUIZ

1a. What year is it?
1b. What season is it?
1c. What month is it?
1d. What day of the week is it?
1e. What is today's date?
2. Remember these words: apple, table, penny.
3. Without looking at your watch, write down what time it is?
   Now look at your watch and write down the actual time.
4. Give the names of the current and previous four US presidents:
5. Give the names of the following items:

Chapter 15 The Learning of English Words (1)

5a: _____

5b: _____

5c: _____

5d: _____

5e: _____

5f: _____

5g: _____

5h: _____

PART II OF QUIZ:
6. Do you remember the address of the last place you lived?
7. Do you find that you repeat yourself more often?
8. Do people get annoyed with you due to your memory?
9. Do you have more trouble remembering lists, such as shopping lists?
10. Do you have trouble remembering events that happened this morning or last week?
11. Do you now have more trouble following directions?
12. Have you been getting lost more often than usual?
13. Do you have trouble finding words?
14. Do you find that you lose or misplace things more often?
15. Do your memory difficulties impair your work / social life?
16. Without going back to the top of the page, write down the three words you were told to remember at the beginning of the quiz:
    GREAT! You are done with the quiz. Now submit for your memory score. The interpretation of your scores is given below.

INTERPRETATION:
PART I OF QUIZ (SUBSECTION SCORE 18):
1) Give yourself 1 point for remembering the exact date (date, day of week, month, season and year). (1 point)
2) Did you remember the three words (apple, table, penny) asked in question 16? Give yourself 1 point for each correct answer. (3 points)
3) If the difference between your guessed time and the correct time is less than 30 minutes, give

yourself 1 point.

4) Give yourself 1 point for each president named correctly. (5 points): Biden, Trump, Obama, Bush, Clinton. The order in which you remembered them is not important.

5) Give yourself a point for each correct answer. (total 8 points)

    5a) Abacus (1 point)

    5b) Acorn (1 point)

    5c) Escalator (1 point)

    5d) Igloo (1 point)

    5e) Pencil (1 point)

    5f) Protractor (1 point)

    5g) Pyramid (1 point)

    5h) Watch (1 point)

PART II OF QUIZ (SUBSECTION SCORE 10):

Question 6: 1 point for remembering your last address.

Questions (7 – 15): Give yourself 1 point each for every question answered "No".

Note that poor scores may be due to factors such as anxiety and inattention and not just from memory difficulties. Doing well on this simple quiz also does not ensure that you have no memory or cognitive difficulties. The best indicator of your memory is your own assessment of your abilities. A perceived consistent change in your mental capacity is a far more sensitive indicator of cognitive difficulties than most tests, including this one. You should seek further help if this is the case.

If you score a 27 or 28, congratulations!

If you score between 22 and 26, you may have some memory difficulties that, if persistent and interfering with function, may need to be evaluated.

If you score 21 or below, and you have noticed that you have difficulty with your memory or thinking abilities of sufficient severity to interfere with functioning, you probably would benefit from a good evaluation.

Chapter 16
The Learning of English Words (2)
— Learning Strategies and Tactics

Points for Thinking
1. How much vocabulary does a second language learner need to know?
2. What does it mean to "know a word"?
3. What are the factors which make the second language vocabulary learning difficult?
4. What is the strategy? Please specify Oxford's taxonomy of language learning strategy.
5. What are the vocabulary learning strategies you are likely to adopt in your vocabulary learning?

Learning strategies determine the approach for achieving the learning objectives and are included in the pre-instructional activities, information presentation, learner activities, testing, and follow-through. The strategies are usually tied to the needs and interests of students to enhance learning and are based on many types of learning styles.

16.1 The Vocabulary Size

A person's vocabulary is the set of words they are familiar with in a language. It is evident that vocabulary is indispensable for successful communication in any language. Besides, the mastery of vocabulary has been seen as central to learning a second language. However, the key role vocabulary plays in language learning has not always been reflected in the amount of attention that has been given to it in the past few decades. The main focus in classroom activities was on the acquisition of grammatical competence and the development of functional communication skills. Vocabulary development was seen as some kind of secondary and auxiliary activity.

As far as the vocabulary size is concerned, there involve three different questions: (1) how many words are there in English? (2) how many words do native speakers know? and (3) how much vocabulary does a second language learner need?

The most straightforward way to answer the first question is to look at the number of words in the largest dictionary, but it is not an easy task for dictionary compilers, as they often see the vocabulary of the language as a continually changing entity with new words being added and old words falling into disuse. In addition, counting words (however defined) is wearisome, complex and difficult, and the experience of dictionary-makers suggests that no matter how well organized the count, there can never be enough data to ensure completeness. A complete list of present-day English words would be impossible to make, but if we had an approximation, it would surely be many times larger than those in the second edition of the *Oxford English Dictionary*, which claimed to have 616,500 forms of the vocabulary. When we look at the vocabulary of *Webster's Third International Dictionary* (1961), the largest non-historical dictionary of the English, we will find that the dictionary only has a vocabulary of around 54,000 word families after excluding entries such as proper names, alternative spellings and dialect forms.

The most notable feature of estimates of the vocabulary size of English native speakers is that there is enormous variation in the estimates: from 400,000 to 600,000 (Claiborne, 1983) or from a half million to over 2 million (Crystal, 1988). Recent research suggests that a university graduate will have a vocabulary of around 20,000 word families. This suggests that native speakers add between 1,000 and 2,000 words per year to their vocabulary, or 3 to 7 words per day.

We are now ready to answer the question "how much vocabulary does a second language learner need?". According to Nation (1990), vocabulary can be divided into three groups: high-frequency words, low-frequency words and specialized vocabulary. Clearly, the learner needs to know the 3,000 or so high frequency words of the language and it is the teacher's focus to help the learners develop strategies to comprehend and learn the low frequency words of the language. Because of the poor coverage that low frequency words give, it is more efficient to spend class time on the strategies of guessing from the context instead of teaching these words. However, we need a vocabulary of about 3,000 words which provides coverage of at least 95% of a text before we can efficiently learn from context. In other words, if one does not know enough of the words on a page and have comprehension of what is being read, one can not easily learn from context.

Just as Meara (1996) has stated, "All other things being equal, learners with big vocabularies are more proficient in a wide range of language skills than learners with smaller vocabularies, and there is some evidence to support the view that vocabulary skills make a significant contribution to almost all aspects of L2 proficiency, vocabulary plays a central role in the language development." It is also assumed that vocabulary size is a good predictor of reading comprehension. Francis and Kucera studied texts totaling one million words and found that if one knows the words with the highest frequency, they will quickly know most of the words in a text:

Vocabulary Size (words)	Written Text Coverage (%)	Vocabulary Size (words)	Written Text Coverage (%)
0	0	4000	86.8
1000	72.0	5000	88.7
2000	79.7	6000	89.9
3000	84.0	15,851	97.8

By knowing the 2,000 words with the highest frequency, one would know 80% of the words in those texts. The numbers look even better than this if we want to cover the words we come across in an informally spoken context. However, we cannot usually guess meanings from context when many words are missing. In order to reach text comprehension, we need to be familiar with 95% of the words in a text and it has been claimed for various languages that the 5,000 most frequent words yield a coverage of 90% to 95% of the word tokens in an average text.

In order to help learners with limited vocabulary either improve language proficiency or achieve effective communication, several word lists have been developed. In 1930, Charles Kay Ogden created Basic English with the book: *Basic English: A General Introduction with Rules and Grammar* (850 words). Other lists include Simplified English (1,000 words) and Special English (1,500 words). The most influential one is the General Service List (GSL), published by Michael West in 1953 with roughly 2,000 words. The words were selected to represent the most frequent words of English and were taken from a 5,000,000 word corpus. It has been used to create a number of adapted reading texts for English language learners. Knowing 2,000 English words, one could understand quite a lot of English, and even read a lot of simple material without problems.

16.2 Vocabulary Acquisition

16.2.1 Vocabulary growth

The learning of vocabulary is the most noticeable feature of the early months of language acquisition and serves as a useful and fundamental tool for communication and acquiring knowledge.

From the point when a child's "first word" is identified, there is a steady lexical growth in both comprehension and production. At the very beginning, in the infancy phase, vocabulary growth requires no effort. Infants hear words and mimic them, eventually associating them with objects and actions. This is the listening vocabulary. Then the speaking vocabulary follows, as a child's thoughts become more reliant on its ability to express itself without gestures and mere sounds. Once the reading and writing vocabularies are acquired — through questions and education — the irregularities of language can be discovered. An indication of the scope and speed of progress can be obtained from a study of American 1-year-olds: the average time it took children to get from 10 to 50 words in production was 4.8 months — about 10 words a month. In comprehension, the children understand an average of 22 new words each month. By 18 months, it is thought that most children can speak about 50 words and understand about five times as many. In fact, young children talk about what is going on around them — the "here and now" — and rapidly build a vocabulary in several semantic fields. The content of early vocabulary is listed as follows:

- People: mainly relatives and house visitors — *daddy*, *baba*, *grandma*, *man*, *postman*;
- Actions: the way things move (*give*, *jump*, *kiss*, *go*), and routine activities in the child's day (*bye-bye*, *hello*);
- Food: occasions as well as products — *din-din*, *milk*, *juice*, *drink*, *apple*;
- Body parts: usually facial words first (*mouth*, *nose*), then other areas (*toes*, *handie(s)*) and body functions (*wee-wee*);
- Clothing of all kinds — *nappy diaper*, *shoes*, *coat*;
- Animal whether real, in pictures, or on TV — *doggie*, *cat*, *horse*, *lion*;
- Vehicles: objects and their noises — *car*, *choo-choo*, *brrm*;
- Toys and games: many possibilities — *ball*, *bricks*, *book*, *dolly*, *peep-bo*;
- Household objects: all to do with daily routine — *cup*, *spoon*, *brush*, *clock*, *light*;
- Locations: several general words — *there*, *look*, *in*, *up*;
- Social words: response noises — *m*, *yes*, *no*, *ta*;
- Describing words: early adjectives — *hot*, *pretty*, *big*;
- Situational words: several "pointing" words — *that*, *mine*, *them*.

Crystal, D.

However, things become much more complicated when they get to school. According to studies, an advantaged student (i.e. a literate student) knows about twice as many words as a disadvantaged student in their first grade. Generally, this gap does not tighten. This translates into a wide range of vocabulary size in the fifth and sixth grades, when students know about 2,500 — 5,000 words. After leaving school, vocabulary growth reaches a plateau. People may then expand their vocabularies by reading, playing word games, participating in vocabulary programs, etc.

16.2.2 Vocabulary knowledge

Next, we are to focus our attention on the vocabulary knowledge. A great deal has been written on the topic of what it means to "know" a word. Most of us will only deal with a very basic form of word knowledge: recognizing a word in the target language and being able to describe one of its possible meanings in the learners' mother tongue. However, applied linguists don't see it this way. Nation (1990) suggests that words are not isolated units of language but are interlocked to form part of more complex systems and levels. He stresses that learning individual items and learning systems of knowledge differ greatly. The first one requires the recognition of a word by memorizing it. The second one requires more complex processes such as determining spelling rules and systemic phonemics of the language. Richards (1976) provided a list of aspects that should be considered when knowing a word. In Richards' view, "knowing" a word means,

a) knowing the degree of probability of encountering the word in speech or print;

b) knowing the limitations imposed on the use of the word according to function and situation;

c) knowing the syntactic behavior associated with the word;

d) knowing the underlying form of a word and the derivations that can be made of it;

e) knowing the associations between the word and other words in the language;

f) knowing the semantic value of the word, and

g) knowing many of the different meanings associated with the word.

Indeed, the learning of a word is thought to progress from receptive to productive knowledge. Put it clearly, a word that can be correctly used, is assumed to be understood by the user, when heard or seen. The opposite however, is not necessarily true. Passive vocabulary size is thus considered to be larger than the active size even though it is not clear how much larger it is.

- Receptive/productive vocabulary

Receptive/productive vocabulary has been defined in relation to the language skills of reading and listening, and speaking and writing. The way the meaning of a word is retrieved and understood by the learner when he/she is exposed to written or oral input describes the process that receptive vocabulary follows and the process of retrieving and producing the appropriate written or spoken language form to get meaning across, defines the productive vocabulary.

- Active/passive vocabulary

Even if we learn a word, it takes a lot of practice and context connections for us to learn it well. A rough grouping of words we understand when we hear them encompasses our "passive" vocabulary, whereas our "active" vocabulary is made up of words that come to our mind immediately when we have to use them in a sentence, as we speak.

- Incidental and explicit learning of vocabulary

Explicit and incidental learning are the two approaches to vocabulary acquisition. Explicit learning focuses attention directly on the information to be learned, which gives the greatest chance for its acquisition. But it is also time-consuming, and for all but the most diligent student, it would be too laborious to learn an adequately sized lexicon. Incidental learning can occur when one is using language for communicative purposes, and so gives a double benefit for time expended. But it is slower and more gradual, lacking the focused attention of explicit learning. One may have to read a great deal of texts or converse for quite some time to come across any particular word, especially if it is relatively infrequent.

For L1 learners, incidental learning is the dominant way of acquiring vocabulary. However, for L2 learners at least, both explicit and incidental learning are necessary, and should be seen as complementary.

16.2.3 Why is second language vocabulary learning difficult?

According to Nation (1990), the learning burden of the second language vocabulary lies in three factors: (1) the learner's previous experience of English and their mother tongue, (2) the way in which the word is learned or taught, and (3) the intrinsic difficulty of the word.

1. Learner's previous experience

There is a lot of evidence to show that the second language vocabulary learning is influenced by the learner's first language vocabulary, as first and second language vocabulary are stored together in an integrated whole rather than as two separate, independently functioning units, which would inevitably encourage borrowing and interference. A Japanese-speaking child was found to use English loanwords in Japanese to learn the related English words quickly. For second language learners, the semantic development in a second language is a process of moving from native to second language meanings and meaning structures. In other words, the second language learner first classifies second language meanings according to the mother tongue. As the learner discovers more about the second language culture, these meanings change. The effect of first language vocabulary on second language vocabulary learning may result in some meanings becoming "fossilized", that is, learners always keep a first language meaning for the second language word. However, many learners finally acquire a second language meaning for the second language word.

A very indicative fact shows that learners with a low level of language proficiency store their vocabulary according to the sounds of words. That is, when such learners remember English words, they tend to connect similar-sounding words like *horse* and *house*. However, learners at higher levels of proficiency store words according to their meanings. They tend to connect *horse* to *cow* while they are remembering it. Generally speaking, as learners become better at a language, whether they are native speakers or second language learners, the way that they organize and store vocabulary in their memory changes. Storage according to form is replaced by storage according to meaning. This means that words similar in sound or spelling to each other should not be introduced early in second language instructions. If they are introduced early, they are likely to be stored together and will interfere with each other.

Indeed, a word will be easy to learn if many features of the word are predictable. For example, if a learner already knows the word *communicate* and the word ending *-tion*, the word *communication* has a very low learning burden. The following table presents the factors of previous experience which affect learning burden. The general principle is: the more predictable and regular the features of the word, the lighter the learning burden.

Table 16.1 Learning Burden

Form		
	Spoken	Does the word contain only familiar sounds or clusters of sounds? Is the stress predictable?
	Written	Is the script like the mother-tongue script? Is the written form predictable from the spoken form? Does the written form follow regular spelling patterns?
Position		
	Grammar	Does the word occur in the same patterns as the corresponding mother-tongue word? Does the word occur in a common pattern or common set of patterns?
	Collocation	Does the word commonly occur with predictable words or types of words?
Function		
	Frequency	Does the mother-tongue word have the same frequency?
	Appropriateness	Does the degrees of politeness, formality, etc. of the word match the corresponding mother-tongue word, or the other English words learned so far?
Meaning		
	Concept	Does the English concept correspond to a mother-tongue concept? Are the various meanings of the word obviously related to a central concept? Is the meaning predictable from the form of the word?
	Associations	Does the mother-tongue word give rise to associated words similar to the English word?

(Nation, I. S. P., *Teaching and Learning Vocabulary*)

2. Organization of the vocabulary learning

The second factor affecting the vocabulary learning is the way in which a word is learned or taught. Some psychologists believe that repetition is not important in vocabulary learning. They simply believe that it is the type of attention that is given to an item which decides whether it will be remembered or not. If the teacher does not use challenging ways to draw the learners' attention to a word, then the learning will be poor. If the learning is poor, the word will need to be repeated for learning. It is evident that there is a relationship between learning and repetition. Several studies indicate that words occurring seven or more times in the coursebook are supposed to be known by most of the learners while over half of the words occurring only once or twice in the books are not known by most of the learners. Therefore, it is important for teachers to add the number of repetitions if the coursebook does not provide enough repetition. Otherwise, efforts spent in dealing with the vocabulary will be wasted. It is strongly recommended by some scholars that the first repetition should occur quite soon after the introduction of a new word. The next repetition can be a day or more away, and the next a week or more, and so on.

Another important thing about the vocabulary learning is that the old material in any lesson is more important than the new one. The reason for this is that the old material has almost been mastered by the learners. If it is not repeated, then it will be forgotten and all the previous work will be wasted. The new material, on the other hand, has not had a lot of time and effort spent on it even if it is forgotten. It is therefore very important for a teacher to keep a rough check on the vocabulary so that enough repetitions and attention will be given.

3. Intrinsic difficulty of the word

The learning burden of a word can also be affected by features of the word itself. It is found that the part of speech of a word affects its learning. Nouns are the easiest to learn, and adjectives are next. Verbs and adverbs are the most difficult to learn. This finding partly agrees with experience in guessing words from context. Nouns and verbs are usually easier to guess than adjectives and adverbs. Moreover, whether words are learned to be recognized (receptively) or to be produced (productively) affects their difficulty. It is easier to learn to recognize a word form and recall its meaning than it is to learn to produce the word on appropriate occasions. A study shows that learning a word productively is 50 to 100 percent more difficult than learning it receptively. Unluckily, a teacher cannot do a great deal about intrinsic difficulty caused by the part of speech and the need for receptive or productive learning.

Task
Cross Word Puzzle

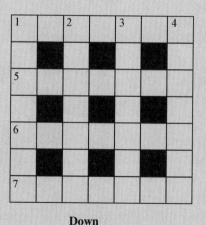

Across
1. Angry
5. Segment
6. Occurring at the beginning
7. No longer in existence

Down
1. Merry
2. Mark or stamp as paid
3. Belief or sentiment
4. Vest

Key:
Across: 1. furious   5. section   6. initial   7. extinct
Down: 1. festive   2. receipt   3. opinion   4. singlet

16.3 Vocabulary Learning Strategies

A strategy is a plan of action designed to achieve a particular goal. The word derives from the Greek word *stratēgos* rooted from two words: *stratos* (army) and *ago* (ancient Greek for "leading"). *Stratēgos* referred to a "military commander" during the age of Athenian Democracy.

Strategy is relevant to many areas of life, from getting the right date for the school disco to running a business. For example, the goal of a company may be to increase profits: the strategy chosen might be to undertake an advertising campaign; invest in a new computer system; or adjust pricing.

16.3.1 Language learning strategies

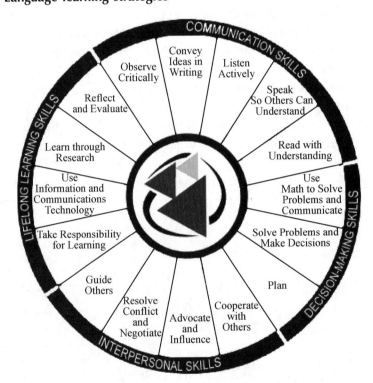

All language learning strategies (LLS) are related to the features of control, goal-directedness, autonomy and self-efficacy. The goal of strategy use is to "affect the learner's motivational or affective state, or the way in which the learner selects, acquires, organizes, or integrates new knowledge" (Weinstein and Mayer, 1986). This broad description of learning strategies may include any of the following: focusing on selected aspects of new information, analyzing and monitoring information during acquisition, organizing or elaborating on new information during the encoding process, evaluating the learning when it is completed, or assuring oneself that the learning will be successful as a way to reduce anxiety. Learning strategies help learners become more autonomous. Autonomy requires conscious control of one's own learning processes. Learning strategies also enhance self-efficacy, individuals' perception that they can successfully complete a task or series of tasks.

There are literally hundreds of different, yet often interrelated language learning strategies. As Oxford has developed a fairly detailed list of LLS in her taxonomy, it is useful to summarize it briefly here. First, Oxford distinguishes between direct LLS, "which directly involve the subject matter", and indirect LLS, which "do not directly involve the subject matter itself, but are essential to language learning nonetheless". Second, each of these broad kinds of LLS is further divided into LLS groups. Oxford outlines three main types of direct LLS: memory strategies "aid in entering information into long-term memory and retrieving information when needed for communication", cognitive strategies "used for forming and revising internal mental models and receiving and producing messages in the target language" and compensation strategies "needed to overcome any gaps in knowledge of the language". She also describes three types of indirect LLS: metacognitive strategies "help learners exercise 'executive control' through planning, arranging, focusing, and evaluating their own learning", affective strategies "enable learners to control feelings, motivations, and attitudes related to language learning" and finally, social strategies "facilitate interaction with others, often in a discourse situation". Theoretical distinctions can be made among these six types; however, the boundaries are fuzzy, particularly since learners sometimes employ more than one strategy at a given time.

1. Memory strategies

Memory strategies help learners link a new item with something known. These devices are useful for memorizing information in an orderly string (e. g. acronyms) in various ways; examples are: by sounds (e. g. rhyming), by body movement (e. g. total physical response, in which the teacher gives a command in English and learners physically follow this) or by location on a page or blackboard (the locus technique). In contrast to cognitive strategies, memory strategies do not typically develop deep associations but instead relate one thing to another in a simplistic, stimulus response manner. Even with their limitations, memory strategies are often the first step in learning vocabulary items.

2. Cognitive strategies

Cognitive strategies help learners make and strengthen associations between new and already-known information and facilitate the mental restructuring of information. Examples of cognitive strategies are: guessing from context, analyzing, reasoning inductively and deductively, taking systematic notes and reorganizing information. Cognitive strategies usually involve hypothesis testing, such as searching for clues in surrounding material and one's own background knowledge, hypothesizing the meaning of the unknown item, determining if this meaning makes sense and, if not, repeating at least part of the process.

3. Compensation strategies

Compensation strategies help learners make up for missing knowledge when using English in oral or written communication, just as the strategy of guessing from the context while listening and reading compensates for a knowledge gap. Compensation strategies (or communication strategies) for speaking include using synonyms, circumlocution and gesturing to suggest the meaning. Compensation strategies for writing encompass some of the same actions, such as synonym use or circumlocution.

4. Metacognitive strategies

Metacognitive strategies help learners manage (1) themselves as learners, (2) the general learning process, and (3) specific learning tasks. Several varieties exist. One group of metacognitive strategies helps individuals know themselves better as language learners. Another set of metacognitive strategies relates to managing the learning process in general and includes identifying available resources, deciding which resources are valuable for a given task, setting a study schedule, finding or creating a good place to study, etc. This set also includes establishing general goals for language learning. Other metacognitive strategies help learners deal effectively with a given language task, not just with the overall process of language learning. This set of metacognitive strategies includes, among other techniques, deciding on task-related (as opposed to general) goals for language learning, paying attention to the task at hand, planning for steps within the language task, reviewing relevant vocabulary and grammar, finding task-relevant materials and resources, deciding which other strategies might be useful and applying them, choosing alternative strategies if those do not work and monitoring language mistakes during the task.

5. Affective strategies

Affective strategies include identifying one's feelings (e. g. anxiety, anger and contentment) and becoming aware of the learning circumstances or tasks that evoke them. Language learning anxiety — which has received an abundance of attention in the last decade — is usually related to the fear of communicating in English (or, indeed, the native language) when a judgment of performance is anticipated. In some cases, the anxiety can sorely ruin the language learning process.

Negative attitudes and beliefs can reduce learners' motivation and harm language learning, while positive attitudes and beliefs can do the reverse. Using the affective strategy to examine beliefs and attitudes is therefore useful for (e. g. learning any language) the native speaker, the teacher and the language classroom. Using a language learning diary to record feelings about language learning can be very helpful.

6. Social strategies

Social strategies facilitate learning with others and help learners understand the culture of the language they are learning. Examples of social strategies are asking questions for clarification or confirmation, asking for help, learning about social or cultural norms and values and studying together outside the class.

16.3.2 Vocabulary learning strategies

Compared with the language learning strategies, vocabulary learning strategies (VLS) is still in an embryonic state. It seems that many learners do use strategies for learning vocabulary, especially when compared to language tasks that integrate several linguistic skills. This might be due to the relatively discrete nature of vocabulary learning compared to more integrated language activities, making it easier to apply strategies effectively. It may also be due to the fact that classrooms tend to emphasize discrete activities over integrative ones and vocabulary learning is most preferable among learners.

Several classification systems for VLS have been proposed by scholars. Of the more established systems, the one developed by Schmitt and McCarthy (1997) seemed best able to capture and organize the wide variety of VLS identified. Their strategy system consists of two major classes: (1) strategies that are useful for the initial discovery of a word's meaning, and (2) those useful for remembering that word once it has been introduced. This reflects the different processes necessary for working out a new word's meaning and usage, and for consolidating it in memory for future use. Then, the strategies are further classified into five groups: determination (DET), social (SOC), memory (MEM), cognitive (COG) and metacognitive (MET). The following table presents the resulting taxonomy of vocabulary strategies. It is organized according to both the Oxford (*op. cit.*) system (see 16.3.1) and the Discovery/Consolidation distinctions.

Table 16.2 A Taxonomy of Vocabulary Learning Strategies

Strategy group	Strategy
Strategies for the discovery of a new word's meaning	
DET	Analyze part of speech
DET	Analyze affixes and roots
DET	Check for L1 cognate
DET	Analyze any available pictures or gestures
DET	Guess meaning from textual context
DET	Use a dictionary (bilingual or monolingual)
SOC	Ask teachers for a synonym, paraphrase, or L1 translation of a new word
SOC	Ask classmates for meaning
Strategies for consolidating a word once it has been encountered	
SOC	Study and practice meaning in a group
SOC	Interact with native speakers
MEM	Connect the word to a previous personal experience
MEM	Associate the word with its coordinates
MEM	Connect the word to its synonyms and antonyms
MEM	Use semantic maps
MEM	Image word form
MEM	Image word's meaning
MEM	Use Keyword Method
MEM	Group words together to study them
MEM	Study the spelling of a word
MEM	Say the new word aloud when studying
MEM	Use physical action when learning a word
COG	Verbal repetition
COG	Written repetition
COG	Word lists
COG	Put English labels on physical objects
COG	Keep a vocabulary notebook
MET	Use English-language media (songs, movies, newscasts, etc.)
MET	Use spaced word practice (expanding rehearsal)
MET	Test oneself with word tests
MET	Skip or pass a new word
MET	Continue to study the word over time

(*Source*: Schmitt and McCarthy, 1997)

1. Discovery strategies

● Determination strategies

If learners do not know a word, they must discover its meaning by guessing from their structural knowledge of the language, guessing from a first language (L1) cognate, guessing from context, using reference materials, or asking someone else. Determination strategies facilitate gaining knowledge of a new word. Learners may be able to discern the new word's part of speech, which can help in the guessing process. They can also obtain hints about meaning from its root or affixes, although not always reliable.

Cognates are words in different languages which have descended from a common parent word, such as *mutter* in German and *mother* in English. Languages also borrow words from other languages, and these loanwords often retain similarities in form and meaning. If the target second language (L2) is closely related to the learner's L1, cognates can be an excellent resource for both guessing the meaning of and remembering new words.

Guessing an unknown word's meaning from the context has been widely promoted in the last two decades. The learner is supposed to have adequate background knowledge of the subject and the strategic knowledge of how to effectively go through the inferencing process. In addition, the context itself must be rich enough with clues to enable guessing.

A third way of initially finding a word's meaning is through reference materials, primarily dictionaries. Even though they are prone to certain shortcomings, bilingual dictionaries seem to be used much more extensively than monolingual dictionaries by L2 learners. Word lists and flash cards, though they have fallen out of favor in the communicative era, as many teachers believe that words should only be presented in the context, are proved to be very useful for initial exposures to a new word.

- Social strategies

A second way to discover a new meaning employs social strategies of using interaction with other people. Teachers often play this role, and they can be asked to give help in a variety of ways: giving the L1 translation if they know it, giving a synonym, giving a definition by paraphrase, using the new word in a sentence, or any combination of these. L1 translations have the advantage of being fast, easily understood by students, and make possible the transfer of all the knowledge a student has of the L1 word (collocations, associations, etc.) onto the L2 equivalent. The disadvantages are that the teacher must know the learners' mother tongue, and that most translation pairs are not exact equivalents, so that some erroneous knowledge may be transferred. Likewise, though synonyms have similar meanings, students need to know collocational, stylistic and syntactic differences in order to use them effectively in a productive mode. Paraphrasing well involves similar kinds of complexities. Of course classmates or friends can be asked for meaning in all of the above ways. In addition, learners can be introduced to new words and discover their meanings through group work.

2. Consolidation strategies

- Social strategies

Besides the initial discovery of a word, group work can be used to learn or practice vocabulary. Here are some of the benefits to cooperative group learning: it promotes active processing of information and cross modeling/imitation; the social context enhances motivation of the participants; cooperative learning can prepare the participants for "team activities" outside the classroom; and because there is less instructor intervention, students have more time to actually use and manipulate language in class. If input is a key element in language acquisition, then it would seem that interacting with native speakers would be an excellent way to gain vocabulary.

- Memory strategies

Memory strategies (traditionally known as mnemonics) involve relating the word to be retained with some previously learned knowledge, using some form of imagery, or grouping. A new word can be integrated into many kinds of existing knowledge (e.g. previous experiences or known words). Grouping is an important way to aid recall, and people seem to organize words into groups naturally without prompting. If words are organized in some way before memorization, recall is improved. Another kind of mnemonic strategy involves focusing on the target word's orthographic or phonological form to facilitate recall.

It is worth noting that memory strategies generally involve the kind of elaborative mental processing that facilitates long-term retention. This takes time, but the time expended will be well spent if used on important words that really need to be learned, such as high-frequency vocabulary and technical words essential in a particular learner's field of study. A learner may not have time to "deeply process" every word encountered, but it is certainly worth attempting for key lexical items.

1) Pictures/imagery

New words can be learned by studying them with pictures of their meaning instead of definitions. Pairing L2 words with pictures has been shown to be better than pairing them with their L1 equivalents. Alternatively, learners can create their own mental images of a word's meaning. Imagery has been shown to be more effective than mere repetition for reading passages, suggesting it could well be more effective for vocabulary too. New words can also be associated with a particularly vivid personal experience of the underlying concept. For example, a learner mentally connects the word *snow* to a memory of playing in the snow during his childhood.

2) Related words

Likewise, new words can be linked to L2 words which the student already knows. Usually this involves some type of sense relationship, such as coordination (*apple* — other kinds of fruit like *pears*, *cherries*, or *peaches*), synonymy (*irritated* — *annoyed*), or antonymy (*dead* — *alive*). These and other sense relationships (hyponymy and meronymy) can be illustrated with semantic maps, which are often used to help consolidate vocabulary.

Some words, particularly gradable adjectives, have meanings relative to other words in their set. For example, in any given situation, *big* is larger than *medium-sized*, but smaller than *huge*. A helpful way to remember these words is to set them in a scale (*huge / big / medium-sized / small / tiny*).

3) Unrelated words

The learner can also link words together that have no sense relationships. One way of doing this is with "peg" or "hook" words. One first memorizes a rhyme like "one is a bun, two is a shoe, three is a tree, etc.". Then an image is created of the word to be remembered and the peg word. If the first word to be remembered is *chair*, then an image is made of a bun (peg word) resting on a chair. Recitation of the rhyme draws up these images, which in turn prompt the target words.

Similarly, a spatial mnemonic strategy can be used to memorize unrelated words. In the Loci Method, one recalls a familiar place, such as a street, and mentally places the first item to be recalled in the first location, the second item in the second location, and so on. To recall the items, one mentally proceeds along the landmarks and retrieves the items which have been associated with each location.

4) Grouping

Grouping is an important way to aid recall, and people seem to organize words into groups naturally without prompting. In free-recall studies, L1 subjects were given lists of words to study and then recall in any order. Typically, words belonging to each meaning category are recalled together, for example, all animals first, before moving on to another category like names. If the words are organized in some way before memorization, recall is improved. The above L1 studies show grouping works for native-speakers, and there is no reason to believe it does not do the same for L2 learners. It may work better for more proficient learners, however, as they have been shown to favor grouping strategies more than beginners did.

5) Word's orthographical or phonological form

Another kind of mnemonic strategy involves focusing on the target word's orthographical or phonological form to facilitate recall. One can explicitly study the spelling or pronunciation of a word. Other options are to visualize the orthographical form of a word in an attempt to remember it, or to make a mental representation of the sound of a word, perhaps making use of rhyming words. The initial letter of a word has been shown to be the most prominent feature in word recognition, with word shape being less important. The learner can make these two features more salient by underlining the first letter or by outlining the word with lines (configuration).

The Keyword Method, which combines the phonological forms and meanings of L1 and L2, is perhaps the most researched mnemonic strategy of all. It entails a learner finding an L1 word which sounds like the target L2 word. Consider, for example, *sentimental*, the English word that Chinese learners must acquire and retain, means *duo chou shan gan de* representing the learner's prior knowledge, or the semantic concept he/she associates with /sentɪˈmentəl/, the keyword *sheng de man tou* creating an imagery of the left-over steamed bread and representing the mediator linking the learner's prior knowledge with incoming information. Moreover, /men/ in English and Chinese /man/ as well as /təl/ and /tou/, the length of the vowels is quite the same. Given these phonetic similarities, the assumption is that when the learner hears or reads the word "sentimental", he/she will be reminded of the word "sheng de man tou" and it is associated with an excessively mental imagery of the left-over steamed bread, and vice versa. A number of studies have found that the Keyword Method is highly effective in enhancing the recall of words.

6) Other memory strategies

Just as a structural analysis of words can be useful for determining their meaning, studying a word's affixes, root, and word class is potentially useful as a way of consolidating its meaning. A knowledge of Latin affixes and roots has two values for an advanced learner of English. It can be used to help the learning of unfamiliar words by relating these words to known words or to known prefixes and suffixes, and it can be used as a way of checking whether an unfamiliar word has been successfully guessed from context.

Some Latin prefixes occur in many different words. For example, the prefix *ad-* in its various forms occurs in 433 of the 20,000 most frequent words in *The Teacher's Word Book* by Thorndike and Lorge. *Circum-* occurs in only 8 words. The root *dur-* (as in *endure*) occurs in fewer words than the root *duc-* (as in *reduce*). Almost one-quarter of the 20,000 words in the list had prefixes. It has also been found in the book that 15 prefixes accounted for 82 percent of the total number of occurrences of prefixes used in words in the list. To make use of prefixes and roots, learners need three skills. They need to be able to break new words into parts so that the affixes and roots are revealed, they need to know the meanings of the parts, and they need to be able to see a connection between the meaning of the parts and the dictionary meaning of the new word.

- Cognitive strategies

Cognitive strategies in this taxonomy are similar to memory strategies, but are not focused so specifically on manipulative mental processing. They include repetition and using mechanical means to study vocabulary. Written and verbal repetition, repeatedly writing or saying a word over and over again, are common strategies in many parts of the world. They are so entrenched that students often resist giving them up to try other ones. Word lists and flash cards can be used for the initial exposure to a word and the main advantage of them is that they can be taken almost anywhere and studied when one has a free moment.

Another kind of cognitive strategy is using study aids. Taking notes in class enables learners to create their own personal structure for newly learned words, and also affords the chance for additional exposure during the review. Students can also make use of any special vocabulary sections in their textbooks to help them study target words.

- Metacognitive strategies

Metacognitive strategies are used by students to control and evaluate their own learning, by having an overview of the learning process in general. As such, they are generally broad strategies, concerned with more efficient learning. To efficiently acquire an L2, it is important to maximize exposure to it. If the L2 is English, the pervasiveness of English-medium books, magazines, newspapers and movies in most parts of the world offers an almost endless resource (if cost is not a problem). The strategy of interacting with native speakers whenever possible also increases input, and could be considered a metacognitive strategy if it is used as a controlling principle of language learning.

Commonly, mechanical strategies (e. g. simple memorization, repetition, and taking notes on vocabulary) are often favored over more complex ones requiring significant active manipulation of information (imagery, inferencing, Keyword Method). If we follow the depth of processing perspective, it would seem that learners often favor relatively "shallow" strategies, even though they may be less effective than "deeper" ones. For example, forming associations and using the Keyword Method have been proved to enhance retention better than rote memorization. However, even rote repetition can be effective if students are accustomed to using it.

Rather than being used individually, multiple VLS are often used concurrently. Good learners do things such as use a variety of strategies, structure their vocabulary learning, review and practice target words, and they are aware of the semantic relationships between new and previously learned L2 words; that is, they are conscious of their learning and take steps to regulate it. Poor learners generally lack this awareness and control.

The Ten Best Vocabulary Learning Tips

Tip One: Read, read, read! Most vocabulary words are learned from context. The more words you're exposed to, the better vocabulary you will have. While you read, pay close attention to words you don't know.

Tip Two: Improve your context skills. To improve your context skills pay close attention to how words are used.

Tip Three: Practice, practice, practice! Learning a word won't help very much if you promptly forget it. Research shows that it takes from 10 to 20 repetitions to really make a word part of your vocabulary.

Tip Four: Make up as many associations and connections as possible. Say the word aloud to activate your auditory memory. Relate the word to words you already know.

Tip Five: Use mnemonics (memory tricks).

Tip Six: Get in the habit of looking up words you don't know. If you have a dictionary program on your computer, keep it open and handy.

Tip Seven: Play with words. Play Scrabble, Boggle, and do crossword puzzles. These and other word games are available for the computer, so you are not dependent on a partner to play.
Tip Eight: Use vocabulary lists.
Tip Nine: Take vocabulary tests.
Tip Ten: Get excited about words! Come to appreciate the sometimes-subtle differences between them. Do you know the difference between something that denotes something else and something that connotes something else? If not, go look it up. Learn to say what you really mean and discover the joys of being able to express yourself in writing.

  This chapter explores another aspect of English vocabulary learning — learning strategies and tactics. The chapter is divided into three sections — the vocabulary size, vocabulary acquisition and vocabulary learning strategies. It has been agreed that vocabulary plays a central role in the language learning process. Then how many words should be learned for both native speakers and second language learners? This is the core issue fully discussed in the first section. The second section mainly deals with the word knowledge — what it means to know a word. Besides, three factors (the learner's previous experience of English and their mother tongue, the way in which the word is learned or taught, and the intrinsic difficulty of the word) influencing the second language vocabulary learning are also studied in this section. In the last section of the chapter, strategy, language learning strategies and vocabulary learning strategies are the three focuses discussed in detail, as well as their effective explanations.

Further Reading

1. Nation, I. S. P. (2001). *Learning Vocabulary in Another Language*. Cambridge: Cambridge University Press.
2. O'Malley, J. M. and Chamot, A. U. (1990). *Learning Strategies in Second Language Acquisition*. Cambridge: Cambridge University Press.
3. Schmitt, N. (2000). *Vocabulary in Language Teaching*. Cambridge: Cambridge University Press.

● Extended Reading

■ Stages of vocabulary acquisition

  Clarke and Nation's (1980) strategy is basically very simple. It begins by getting the learner to look closely at the unknown word, next to look at its immediate context, and then to take a much broader view of how the clause containing tile word relates to other clauses, sentences, or paragraphs. After guessing, there is a simple system of checks to make sure that the guess is the best possible. Once learners have mastered the steps of the strategy and have practiced guessing words by systematically going through the steps, it is no longer necessary to apply all the steps. That is, the strategy is just a means of acquiring the unconscious skill that an efficient reader already has.

  Let us look at the steps involved in the strategy and then apply them.

Step 1. Look at the unknown word and decide its part of speech. Is it a noun, a verb, an adjective, or an adverb?

Step 2. Look at the clause or sentence containing the unknown word. If the unknown word is a noun, what adjectives describe it? What verb is it near? That is, what does this noun do, and what is done to it?

If the unknown word is a verb, what nouns does it go with?

Is it modified by an adverb?

If it is an adjective, what noun does it go with?

If it is an adverb, what verb is it modifying?

Step 3. Look at the relationship between the clause or sentence containing the unknown word and other sentences or paragraphs. Sometimes this relationship will be signaled by a conjunction like *but*, *because*, *if*, *when*, or by an adverb like *however*, *as a result*. Often there will be no signal. The possible types of relationship include cause and effect, contrast, inclusion, time, exemplification, and summary. Punctuation may also serve as a clue. Colons often signal a list of inclusion relationships; dashes may signal restatement. Reference words like *this*, *that*, and *such* also provide useful information.

Step 4. Use the knowledge you have gained from Steps 1 – 3 to guess the meaning of the word.

Step 5. Check that your guess is correct.

    a. See that the part of speech, of your guess is the same as the part of speech of the unknown word. If it is not the same, then something is wrong with your guess.

    b. Replace the unknown word with your guess. If the sentence makes sense, your guess is probably correct.

    c. Break the unknown word into its prefix, root, and suffix, if possible. If the meanings of the prefix and root correspond to your guess, good. If not, look at your guess again, but do not change anything if you feel reasonably certain about your guess using the context.

Experience has shown that using affixes and roots alone as a means of guessing meanings is not very reliable. Also, once a word has been analyzed according to its parts, this guess at its meaning is more likely to result in twisting the interpretation of the context than allowing interpretation of the context to modify the guess of the meaning. So, by leaving the use of affixes and root until the last step in the strategy, the learner is more likely to approach interpretation of the context with an open mind.

Let us apply the strategy to guess the meanings of two infrequent words. The following paragraph is taken from Mackin and Carver (1968: 45 – 50).

[Chinese spectacles] were regarded as objects of *reverence* because the rims of tortoise-shell came from a sacred and symbolic animal, and the lenses were made from sacred stones. People wore them at first not so much to aid eyesight, or for curing eye-ailments, as for good luck, or for the dignity which they *bestowed* on the wearer. Sometimes even empty frames were worn as a mark of distinction.

reverence (line 1)

Step 1. *Reverence* is a noun.

Step 2. Spectacles are objects of reverence. If, because of the *-ence* suffix, we guess that *revere* might be a verb, we could say

People revere spectacles.

Step 3. *Because* indicates a cause-effect relationship. The causes are *The rims of tortoise-shell came from a sacred and symbolic animal* and *the lenses were made from sacred stones*. The effect is *Chinese spectacles were regarded as objects of reverence*.

Step 4. *Reverence* seems related to *sacred* and *symbolic* so it probably means something like *religion* or *holiness*.

Step 5. a. Like *reverence*, *religion* and *holiness* are nouns.

b. Spectacles were regarded as objects of holiness. Spectacles were regarded as objects of religion. The first substitution seems the best.

c. *Re--ver--ence*, *-ence* indicates that the word is a noun. The prefix and root do not help at all.

The dictionary says that *reverence* means *feelings of deep respect*. *Holiness* is close enough to this: 95 percent correct.

bestowed (line 4)

Step 1. *Bestowed* is a verb.

Step 2. Spectacles bestow dignity on the wearer.

Step 3. *Or* indicates that there are alternatives. The other alternatives are *good luck*, and *curing eye-ailments* which are desirable things, so we can conclude that *bestowing dignity* is also a desirable thing.

Step 4. *Bestowed* probably means *gave* or *put*.

Step 5. a. *Gave* and *put* are verbs.

b. Spectacles put dignity on the wearer. Spectacles gave dignity on the wearer. Except for the awkwardness of *on*, both words seem suitable.

c. *Be--stow--ed*. No help here.

The dictionary gives *put*, *place*: 100 percent correct.

  The errors that learners make when guessing words from context give interesting insights into their grasp of the strategy and also into difficulties they encounter while reading. One of the commonest errors in using the strategy was to guess a meaning that was a different part of speech from the word in the passage. Faulty analysis of word parts also led to errors (*laterally* = coming after or later). Failure to understand the context produced some errors. Most learners did not infer *sparse* correctly in the sentence *Desert areas owe their aridity to sparse rainfall*. After talking to some learners it was found that they did not interpret *owe* correctly. When it was explained to them that the sentence means *The aridity of desert areas is caused by sparse rainfall*, most were able to find the meaning correctly.

  Our experience coincides with that of Bright and McGregor (1970, p. 31): "Perhaps the most important thing of all is to remember that the ability to infer in this way is a skill that can only be acquired by practice. Every time we tell a pupil what a word means we are robbing him of a chance to practice this skill."

  The various steps needed in the strategy — namely part of speech, immediate context, wider context, word parts — can be practiced separately before being combined into a strategy (Long & Nation, 1980). So learners can practice recognizing the part of speech of various words in context. They can do the *What does what?* exercise with various nouns, verbs, adjectives, or adverbs in a text. In this exercise the teacher gives the learners a word and the line number of that word in the text. The learners must ask themselves questions like "What does what? Who does what?" if the word is a noun or verb, or "What is what?" if it is an adjective, or "What does what how?" if it is an adverb. They answer these questions by reference to the text. The learners can also practice using the wider context as a separate exercise by analyzing sentences to find the conjunction relationships.

  The guessing strategy can be used in cooperative class exercises or for individual work such as homework. When the strategy is being introduced, the teacher can demonstrate the steps to the learners using a word from the passage. The steps are put up on the board. Then one word is chosen from the passage for the whole class to guess. The teacher then calls on different learners to do each step. So one learner has the task of saying what part of speech the word is, and then another looks at the immediate grammar of the word, and so on. After doing a few words like this the learners can work in pairs and then on their own.

When the learners work in pairs, they work on the steps together and then describe the steps to the rest of the class. The teacher gives them a percentage grade for correctness, as in the examples above.

The research of van Parreren and Schouten-van Parreren (1981) supports the value of an organized system for guessing, with the grammar level being one of the lowest and then meaning and word analysis being higher levels — "a subject can act correctly on a certain level only if there is no problem on one of the lower levels" (p. 238). They found that making a good guess did not involve going through all the levels but involved "estimating how many difficulties guessing a certain word would present and then entering on the apparently most appropriate level. Sometimes however this estimation proved to be wrong and in that case the skilled guesser went down or moved up to the appropriate level" (p. 240).

Guessing words in context obviously leads on to dictionary work. Unless the learners already have a reasonable idea of what a word means, they will be unable to choose the most suitable meaning from those given in the dictionary. Using the dictionary could be the fourth way of checking in Step 5.

Honeyfield (1977a) suggests three types of exercise for practicing guessing words from context. The first is a cloze exercise where gaps are made which must be filled by context words. Such an exercise involves many of the requirements of guessing from context. The major disadvantage is the lack of a form which must be largely ignored while guessing but is useful when checking. The second type of exercise provides multiple-choice answers either for the meaning of the unknown word or for the clues which give the meaning. Finally, he describes a context-enrichment exercise where gradually increasing information is revealed.

All the guessing procedures described so far focus on linguistic information that is present within a text. There are other important sources of information (Drum and Konopak, 1987). These include knowledge that learners already have about particular words through having met them before, knowledge of the subject that they are reading about (this may be knowledge gained through the learner's first language), and knowledge of the conceptual structure of the topic.

To help readers make the most effective use of these other clues to guess words, it may be necessary to show them ways of stimulating this knowledge before or as they begin reading a text.

— Nation, I. S. P.

Exercises

I. **How many words do you know?**
Basic Words Tests

This tests the size of your vocabulary by seeing how many words you know, going from the most frequent down to the least frequent. The words are chosen from the British National Corpus frequency list; definitions have been checked against the *Oxford English Dictionary*. The items get more and more difficult as the test goes on; give up when it becomes just guessing. Complete the definitions; all the spaces are the same size so they do not give clues to the number of letters. Then check your answers and fill in the profile below. The Basic Words Test tests you up to the 20,000 most frequent words. If you get through this, try the Advanced Words Test, which goes beyond the 150,000 level.

Section A   The top 1,000 words
1. a group of people meeting to decide something is a c_____
2. a person who can move heavy objects about is s_____
3. something which many people like is p_____
4. a person who has done well in life is a s_____
5. the group responsible for ruling a country is its g_____
6. a building in which people live is a h_____
7. the part of the body which has eyes and is joined by the neck is the h_____
8. something which is consistent with the facts is t_____
9. a room in which paperwork takes place is an o_____
10. to allow something to happen is also to l_____ it happen

Section B   Words in the top 1,000 – 3,000 band
11. a round object often used as a toy is a b_____
12. something you carry and put things in is a b_____
13. to think about past events is to r_____
14. to divide things among people is to s_____
15. a royal man who rules a country is a k_____
16. to work out the meaning of written words is to r_____ it
17. a part of the body leading to the foot is a l_____
18. to accept something given to you is to r_____ it
19. putting forward a new idea is making a s_____
20. a temporary outdoor place for cooking and sleeping is a c_____

Section C   Words in the 3,000 – 5,000 band
21. to go from one place to another is to t_____
22. natural, unadulterated food is o_____
23. an elected member of local government is a c_____
24. to look quickly at something is to g_____
25. the opposite of male is f_____
26. to find a new idea or a new place is to d_____ it
27. the person who is the best at a competition is the c_____
28. a person who works for someone else is an e_____
29. the written information that tells you how to do or use something is an i_____
30. to try to judge the value, size, speed, cost, etc. of something, without calculating it exactly is to e_____

Chapter 16 The Learning of English Words (2)

Section D   Words in the 5,000 – 10,000 band
31. the house or flat where someone lives is their r_____
32. the place where the race ends is the f_____
33. a long object for climbing walls etc. is a l_____
34. When countries or people refuse to deal with other people because they object to their behavior, they are b_____ them.
35. a pipe or channel through which things flow is a c_____
36. to give way to someone is to y_____
37. a space without any air is a v_____
38. something that can be carried from place to place is p_____
39. getting minerals from the earth is called m_____
40. a man who serves food in a restaurant is a w_____

Section E   Words in the 10,000 – 20,000 band
41. the movement to liberate women is known as f_____
42. a disabled person is sometimes described as h_____
43. a type of tree with silver bark is an a_____ tree
44. one type of British lawyer is called a b_____
45. a person who works without being paid is a v_____
46. a preparation for preventing infectious disease is a v_____
47. something that is not difficult can be called e_____
48. to make something for sale on a large scale is to m_____
49. a kitchen device that cooks by direct heat is a g_____
50. a place known for its healthy waters is a s_____

References

Adams, V. (2000). *An Introduction to Modern English Word-formation*. London: Longman.
Aitchison, J. (1987 / 1994). *Words in the Mind: An Introduction to the Mental Lexicon*. Oxford: Basil Blackwell.
Aitchison, J. (2003). *Words in the Mind*. Malden: Blackwell.
Akmajian, A. et al. (2001). *Linguistics: An Introduction to Language and Communication*, 5th edition. MA: The MIT Press.
Allsopp, R. (1996). *Dictionary of Caribbean Usage*. New York: Oxford University Press.
Amvela, E. Z. (2009). Lexicography and Lexicology. In M. Byrant (ed.), *Routledge Encyclopedia of Language Teaching and Learning* (1st edition). London: Routledge.
Antrushina, G. B., Afanasyeva, O. V. and Morozova, N. N. (1999). *English Lexicology*. Moscow: Drofa Publishing House.
Aronoff, M. and Rees-Miller, J. (eds.) (2001). *The Handbook of Linguistics*. Oxford: Blackwell Publishers Ltd.
Austin, J. L. (1962). *How to Do Things with Words*. Oxford: Oxford University Press.
Bailey, R. and Gorlach, M. (1986). *English as a World Language*. MI: The University of Michigan Press.
Baker, M. (1992). *In Other Words*. London: Routledge.
Barber, C. (2000). *The English Language: A Historical Introduction*. Cambridge: Cambridge University Press.
Barber, K. (2004). *Canadian Oxford Dictionary*. Don Mills, Ontario: Oxford University Press.
Baugh, A. C. and Cable, T. (1993 / 2002). *A History of the English Language*. London: Routledge.
Beaton, A. et al. (2005). Facilitation of Receptive and Productive Foreign Vocabulary Learning Using the Keyword Method: The Role of Image Quality. *Memory*, *13*, 458 – 471.
Benson, M. (1985). Collocations and Idioms. In Ilson, R. (ed.) *Dictionaries, Lexicography and Language Learning*. Oxford: Pergamon Press.
Benson, M., Benson, E. and Ilson, R. (1986). *Lexicographic Description of English*. Amsterdam: Benjamins.
Bialystok, E. (2001). *Bilingualism in Development: Language, Literacy & Cognition*. Cambridge: Cambridge University Press.
Béjoint, H. (2000). *Modern Lexicography: An Introduction*. London: Oxford University Press.
Black, M. (1962). *Models and Metaphors*. Ithaca, NY: Cornell University Press.
Blake, N. F. (1996). *A History of the English Language*. London: Macmillan Press Ltd.
Bloomfield, L. (1933). *Language*. New York: Holt, Rinehart and Winston.
Blutner, R. (1998). Lexical Pragmatics. *Journal of Semantics*. *15*(2): 115 – 162.
Bolinger, D. (1980). *Language: The Loaded Weapon*. London: Longman.
Boonyasaquan, S. (2005). An Analysis of Collocational Violations in Translation. *Journal of*

Humanities, 27, 79 – 91. Bangkok: Srinakharinwirot University.

Brown, C. H. (2002). Paradigmatic Relations of Inclusion and Identity I: Hyponymy. In Cruse, D. A., Hundsnurscher, F., Job, M. and Lutzeier, P. R. (eds.) *An International Handbook on the Nature and Structure of Words and Vocabularies*. Berlin: Walter De Gruyter.

Brown, G. et al. (eds.) (1994). *Language and Understanding*. Oxford: Oxford University Press.

Brown, K. (1995). Syntactic Clues to Understanding. In Brown, G. et al. (eds.) *Language and Understanding*. Oxford: Oxford University Press.

Burns, A. and Coffin, C. (2001). *Analysing English in a Global Context*. London: Routledge.

Cameron, L. and Graham, L. (2001). *Researching and Applying Metaphor*. Cambridge: Cambridge University Press.

Campbell, L. (1999). *Historical Linguistics*. Cambridge: The MIT Press.

Carroll, D. W. (1999). *Psychology of Language*. Brooks/Cole Publishing Company.

Carston, R. and Uchida, S. (1998). *Relevance Theory: Applications and Implications*. Amsterdam: John Benjamins.

Cheshire, J. (1991). *English around the World*. Cambridge: Cambridge University Press.

Claiborne, R. (1983). Our Marvelous Native Tongue. *The Life and Times of the English Language*. New York: Times Books.

Coady, J. and Huckin, T. (1997). *Second Language Vocabulary Acquisition*. New York: Cambridge University Press.

Cohen, A. D. (2000). *Strategies in Learning and Using Second Language*. Beijing: Foreign Language Teaching and Research Press.

Collins, A. M. and Loftus, E. F. (1975). A Spreading-activation Theory of Semantic Processing. *Psychological Review*, 82, 407 – 428.

Collins, A. M. and Quillian, M. R. (1969). Retrieval Time from Semantic Memory. *Journal of Verbal Learning and Verbal Behavior*, 8, 240 – 247.

Collins COBUILD English Language Dictionary. (1989). London & Glasgow: Collins Publishers.

Cowie, A. P. (1999). *English Dictionaries for Foreign Learners: A History*. London: Oxford University Press.

Croft, W. (1993). The Role of Domains in the Interpretation of Metaphors and Metonymies. *Cognitive Linguistics*, 4(4), 335 – 370.

Crowther, J., Dignen, S. and Lea, D. (2003). *Oxford Collocations Dictionary for Students of English*. Beijing: Foreign Language Teaching and Research Press.

Cruse, D. A. (1986). *Lexical Semantics*. Cambridge: Cambridge Universtiy Press.

Cruse, D. A. (1990). Language, Meaning and Sense: Semantics. In Collinge, N. (ed.) *An Encyclopedia of Language*. London: Routledge.

Cruse, D. A. (2001). The Lexicon. In Aronoff, M. and Rees-Miller, J. (eds.) *The Handbook of Linguistics*. Malden: Blackwell Publishers Ltd.

Cruse, D. A. (2004). *Meaning in Language: An Introduction to Semantics and Pragmatics*. New York: Oxford University Press.

Cruse, D. A., Hundsnurscher, F., Job, M. and Lutzeier, P. R. (eds.) (2002 / 2005). *An International Handbook on the Nature and Structure of Words and Vocabularies*. Berlin:

Walter De Gruyter.

Crystal, D. (1995). *The Cambridge Encyclopedia of the English Language.* Cambridge: Cambridge University Press.

Crystal, D. (1997). *The Cambridge Encyclopedia of Language* (2nd edition). Cambridge: Cambridge University Press.

Crystal, D. (1999). The Future of Englishes. *English Today,* 15(2), 10–20.

Crystal, D. (2003). *English as a Global Language.* Cambridge: Cambridge University Press.

Crystal, D. (2006). *Words Words Words.* New York: Oxford University Press.

Cummings, L. (2007). *Pragmatics: A Multidisciplinary Perspective.* Beijing: Peking University Press.

Denning, K., Kessler, B. and Leben, W. R. (2007). *English Vocabulary Elements.* New York: Oxford University Press.

Dirven, R. (1993). Metonymy and Metaphor: Different Mental Strategies of Conceptualization. *Leuvense Rijdragen,* 21(1), 1–28.

Dirven, R. (2002). Structuring of Word Meaning III. In Cruse, D. A., Hundsnurscher, F., Job, M. and Lutzeier, P. R. (eds.) *An International Handbook on the Nature and Structure of Words and Vocabularies.* Berlin: Walter De Gruyter.

Ebbinghaus, H. (1962). *Memory: A Contribution to Experimental Psychology.* New York: Dover. (Original work published in 1850.)

Farghal, M. and Obiedat, H. (1995). Collocations: A Neglected Variable in EFL Writing. *IRAL: International Review of Applied Linguistics in Language Teaching,* 33, 315–331. Retrieved September 2003 from ProQuest Direct (No. 0019042X).

Fennell, B. A. (2001). *A History of English: A Sociolinguistic Approach.* Malden: Blackwell Publishers Inc.

Finch, G. (2000). *Linguistic Terms and Concepts.* New York: St. Martin's Press.

Fox, G. (1998). Using Corpus Data in the Classroom. *Materials Development in Language Teaching.* Cambridge: Cambridge University Press.

Frazer, B. (1970). Idioms within a Transformational Grammar. *Foundations of Language,* 6, 22–42.

Freeborn, D. (2006). *From Old English to Standard English.* Basingstock: Palgrave Macmillan.

Fromkin, V. et al. (2007). *An Introduction to Language,* 8th edition. Boston: Thomson Wadsworth.

Gass, S. M. and Schachter, J. (1989). *Linguistic Perspectives on Second Language Acquisition.* Cambridge: Cambridge University Press.

Goodluck, H. (1991). *Language Acquisition: A Linguistic Introduction.* Malden: Blackwell Publisher Ltd.

Goossens, L. (1990). Metaphtonymy: The Interaction of Metaphor and Metonymy in Linguistic Action. *Cognitive Linguistics,* 1(4), 323–340.

Gozzi, R. (1990). *New Words and a Changing American Culture.* Columbia: University of South Carolina Press.

Gramley, S. (2001). *The Vocabulary of World English.* London: Arnold.

Gramley, S. and Patzold, K. (2004). *A Survey of Modern English.* London: Routledge.

Green, G. (1989/1996). *Pragmatics and Natural Language Understanding.* Hillsdale, NJ: LEA Publisher.

Grice, H. P. (1957). Meaning. *Philosophical Review*, 66(3), 377-388.
Gu, P. (2003). Fine Brush and Freehand: The Vocabulary-leaning Art of Two Successful Chinese EFL Learners. *TESOL Quarterly*, 37, 73-104.
Halliday, M. A. K. (1976). Lexical Relations. *System and Function in Language*. Oxford: Oxford University Press.
Halliday, M. A. K. and Yallop, C. (2007). *Lexicology: A Short Introduction*. London: YHT Ltd.
Hanks, P. (2008). *Lexicology: Critical Concepts in Linguistics*. London and New York: Routledge.
Harris, R. (1973). *Synonymy and Linguistic Analysis*. Oxford: Blackwell.
Hatch, E. and Brown, C. (1995). *Vocabulary, Semantics, and Language Education*. Cambridge: Cambridge University Press.
Hill, J. (2000). Revising Priorities: From Grammatical Failure to Collocational Success. In M. Lewis (ed.), *Teaching Collocation: Further Development in the Lexical Approach* (pp. 47-69). Oxford: Oxford University Press.
Hobbs, J. B. (1999). *Homophones and Homographs: An American Dictionary*. Jefferson: McFarland & Company, Inc. Publisher.
Hornby, A. S. (2000). *Oxford Advanced Learner's Dictionary of Current English* (6th edition), ed. Sally Wehmeier. Oxford: Oxford University Press.
Horst, M. (2005). Learning L2 Vocabulary through Extensive Reading: A Measurement Study. *The Canadian Modern Language Review*, 61, 355-382.
Howard, J. (2002). *Lexicography: An Introduction*. Oxford: Routledge.
Hu, Z. (2001). *An Introduction to Linguistics*. Beijing: Peking University Press.
Huang Y. (2007). *Pragmatics*. Oxford: Oxford University Press.
Huckin, T. et al, (eds.) (1993). *Second Language Reading and Vocabulary Learning*. Norwood, New Jersey: Ablex Publishing Corporation.
Hudson, W. (1989). Semantic Theory and L2 Lexical Development. In Gass, S. M. and Schachter, J. (eds.) *Linguistic Perspectives on Second Language Acquisition*. Cambridge: Cambridge University Press.
Hughes, J. (ed.) (1992). *The Concise Australian National Dictionary*. Melbourne: Oxford University Press.
Jackson, H. (1988). *Words and Their Meanings*. London: Longman.
Jackson, H. and Amvela, E. Z. (2000). *Words, Meaning and Vocabulary: An Introduction to Modern English Lexicology*. London and New York: Cassell.
Jakel, O. (1997). *"Der handgreifliche Intellekt", oder: Mental Activity as Manipulation*. Frankfurt: Lang.
Jakobson, R. (1971). *Selected Writings II: Word and Language*. The Hague: Mouton.
James, C. (1998). *Errors in Language Learning and Use*. London: Longman.
Jaszczolt, K. (2002). *Semantics and Pragmatics*. London: Longman.
Jay, T. (1999). *Why We Curse*. Philadelphia: John Benjamins Publishing Company.
Jeffries, L. (1998). *Meaning in English: An Introduction to Language Study*. Hampshire: Palgrave Macmillan.
Jef, V. (1999). *Understanding Pragmatics*. London: Arnold, Great Britain, Hodder Headline group.
Jenkins, J. (2003). *World Englishes*. London and New York: Routledge.

Johnson, S. (1755). *A Dictionary of the English Language.* Classic Books.
Jones, S. (2002). *Antonymy.* London: Routledge.
Kachru, B. (1988). The Sacred Cows of English. *English Today,* 16, 3–8.
Katamba, F. (2005). *English Words: Structure, History, Usage.* London; NY: Routledge.
Kempson, R. (2001). Pragmatics: Language and Communication. In Arnoff, M. and Ress-Miller, J. (eds.) *The Handbook of Linguistic.* Malden: Blackwell Publishers Ltd.
Kjellmer, G. (1994). *A Dictionary of English Collocations.* Oxford: Clarendon Press.
Knowles, G. (2004). *A Cultural History of the English Language.* Beijing: Peking University Press.
Kovecsex, Z. (1986). *Metaphors of Anger, Pride, and Love: A Lexical Approach to the Structure of Concepts.* Amsterdam/Philadelphia: Benjamins.
Kreidler, C. W. (1998). *Introducing English Semanitcs.* London: Routledge.
Lakoff, G. (1987). *Women, Fire and Dangerous Things.* Chicago: The University of Chicago Press.
Lakoff, G. (1988). Cognitive Semantics. *Meaning and Mental Representation.* Bloomington: Indiana University Press.
Lakoff, G. (1989): The Invariance Hypothesis: Is Abstract Reason Based on Image-schemas? *Cognitive Linguistics,* 1(1), 39–74.
Lakoff, G. and Johnson, M. (1980). *Metaphors We Live by.* Chicago: The University of Chicago Press.
Lakoff, G. and Turner, M. (1989). More than Cool Reason. *A Field Guide to Poetic Metaphors.* Chicago: University of Chicago Press.
Langacker, R. W. (1987). *Foundations of Cognitive Grammar, Vol. I.* Stanford: Stanford University Press.
Lattey, E. (1986). Pragmatic Classification of Idioms as an Aid for the Language Learner. *International Review of Applied Linguistics,* 24(3), 217–233.
Laufer, B. (2005). Focus on Form in Second Language Vocabulary Learning. *EUROSLA Yearbook,* 5, 223–250.
Laufer, B. and Paribakht, T. S. (1998). The Relationship between Passive and Active Vocabularies: Effects of Language Learning Context. *Language Learning,* 48, 365–391.
Leech, G. (1969). *A Linguistic Guide to English Poetry.* London: Longman.
Lehmann, W. P. (2002). *Historical Linguistics: An Introduction.* Beijing: Foreign Language Teaching and Research Press.
Lehrer, A. J. and Arizona, T. (2002). Paradigmatic Relations of Exclusion and Opposition I: Gradable Antonymy and Complementarity. In Cruse, D. A., Hundsnurscher, F., Job, M. and Lutzeier, P. R. (eds.) *An International Handbook on the Nature and Structure of Words and Vocabularies.* Berlin: Walter De Gruyter.
Levi-Strauss, C. (1966). *The Savage Mind.* London: Weidenfeld and Nicholson.
Lewis, M. (1993). *The Lexical Approach.* Hove, England: Language Teaching Publications.
Lewis, M. (ed.) (2000). *Teaching Collocation: Further Developments in the Lexical Approach.* Oxford: Oxford University Press.
Littlemore, J. (2001). Metaphorical Intelligence and Foreign Language Learning. *Humanising Language Teaching,* 3.
Longman Dictionary of Contemporary English, fourth edition. (2003). London: Longman.
Lyons, J. (1977). *Semantics.* Cambridge: Cambridge University Press.

Lyons, J. (1995). *Linguistic Semantics: An Introduction.* Cambridge: Cambridge University Press.
Macmillan English Dictionary: For Advanced Learners of American English. (2004). New York: Palgrave Macmillan.
Malmkjaer, K. (1991). *The Linguistics Encyclopedia.* London: Routledge.
Manser, M. H. (1989). *Chambers Dictionary of Synonyms and Antonyms.* Great Britain: W & R Chambers Ltd. and Cambridge University Press.
Matthews, P. H. (1991). *Morphology.* Cambridge: Cambridge University Press.
May, J. (1993). *Pragmatics: An Introduction.* Oxford: Blackwell.
McArthur, T. (1992). *The Oxford Companion to the English Language.* USA: Oxford University Press.
McArthur, T. (1998). Guides to Tomorrow's English. *English Today, 14*(3), 21 – 26.
McArthur, T. (2001). *Oxford Concise Companion to the English Language.* Shanghai Shanghai Foreign Language Education Press.
McCarthy, J. (1990). *Formalizing Common Sense.* New Jersey: Ablex, Norwood.
McFedries, P. (2004). *Word Spy: The Word Lover's Guide to Modern Culture.* New York: Broadway Books.
Meara, P. (1996). The Dimensions of Lexical Competence. In G. Brown, K. Malmkjaer and J. Williams (eds.) *Performance and Competence in Second Language Acquisition* (pp. 35 – 53). Cambridge: Cambridge University Press.
Merriam-Webster's Collegiate Dictionary, 11th edition. (2003). Springfield, MA: Merriam-Webster Inc.
Meyer, D. E. and Schvaneveldt, R. W. (1971). Facilitation in Recognizing Pairs of Words: Evidence of a Dependence between Retrieval Operations. *Journal of Experimental Psychology, 90,* 227 – 234.
Mieder, W. (1989). *American Proverbs: A Study of Texts and Contexts.* Bern: Peter Lang.
Murphy, M. L. (2003). *Semantic Relations and the Lexicon.* Cambridge: Cambridge University Press.
Nassaji, H. (2003). L2 Vocabulary Learning From Context: Strategies, Knowledge Sources, and Their Relationship with Success in L2 Lexical Inferencing. *TESOL Quarterly, 37,* 645 – 670.
Nation, I. S. P. (1990). *Teaching and Learning Vocabulary.* New York: Newbury House.
Nation, I. S. P. (2001). *Learning Vocabulary in Another Language.* Cambridge: Cambridge University Press.
Nattinger, J. R. and DeCarrico, J. S. (2000). *Lexical Phrases and Language Teaching.* Shanghai: Shanghai Foreign Language Education Press.
Nesselhauf, N. (2003). The Use of Collocations by Advanced Learners of English and Some Implications for Teaching. *Applied Linguistics,* 223. Retrieved February 14, 2007 from ProQuest Direct (ISSN No. 1426001). New York: A Barnes & Noble Paperback.
Norrick, N. R. (1988). Binomial Meaning in Texts. *Journal of English Linguistics, 21,* 72 – 87.
O'Malley, J. M. and Chamot, A. U. (1990). *Learning Strategies in Second Language Acquisition.* New York: Cambridge University Press.
Orsman, H. W. (1998). *The Dictionary of New Zealand English.* Auckland: Oxford University Press.

Ortony, R. (1979). *Metaphor and Thought.* Cambridge: Cambridge University Press.

Oxford Advanced Learner's Dictionary, 7th edition. (2005). Oxford: Oxford University Press.

Oxford Collocations Dictionary for Students of English. (2003). Oxford: Oxford University Press.

Oxford, L. R. (1990). *Language Learning Strategies.* New York: Newbury House Publishers.

Palmer, F. R. (1981). *Semantics,* 2nd *edition.* Cambridge: Cambridge University Press.

Panther, K. and Raddeeo, G. (1999). *Metonymy in Language and Thought.* Amsterdam / Philadelphia: Benjamins.

Poole, S. C. (2000). *An Introduction to Linguistics.* Beijing: Foreign Language Teaching and Research Press.

Procter P. (eds.) (1995). *Cambridge International Dictionary of English.* Cambridge: Cambridge University Press.

Quirk, R. (1995). *Grammatical and Lexical Variance in English.* London: Longman.

Quirk, R. et al. (1985). *A Comprehensive Grammar of the English Language.* London: Longman.

Quirk, R., Greenbaum, S., Leech G. and Svartvik, J. (2010). *A Comprehensive Grammar of the English Language.* London: Longman.

Quirk, R., Greenbaun, S., Leech G. and Svartvik, J. (1972). *A Grammar of Contemporary English.* London: Longman.

Ramson, W. S. (ed.) (1988). *The Australian National Dictionary.* Melbourne: Oxford University Press.

Ravin, Y. and Leacock, C. (2000). *Polysemy: Theoretical and Computational Approaches.* Oxford: Oxford University Press.

Rayner, K. and Duffy, S. A. (1986). Lexical Complexity and Fixation Times in Reading: Effects of Word Frenquency, Verb Complexity, and Lexical Ambiguity. *Memory & Cognition,* 14, 191 – 201.

Redfern, W. (1989). *Clichés and Coinages.* Cambridge: Basil Blackwell.

Redford, Andrew et al. (2000). *Linguistics: An Introduction.* Beijing: Foreign Language Teaching and Research Press/ Cambridge University Press.

Richards, J. C. (1976). The Role of Vocabulary Teaching. *TESOL Quarterly,* 10 (1), 77 – 89.

Robins, H. R. (2000). *General Linguistics.* Beijing: Foreign Language Teaching and Research Press.

Romaine, S. (1995). *Bilingualism,* 2nd *edition.* Oxford: Blackwell.

Romaine, S. (ed.) (1997). *The Cambridge History of the English Language* (Vol. 4). Cambridge: Cambridge University Press.

Schendl, H. (2003). *Historical Linguistics.* Shanghai: Shanghai Foreign Language Education Press.

Schmitt, N. (2000). *Vocabulary in Language Teaching.* Cambridge: Cambridge University Press.

Schmitt, N. and McCarthy, M. (1997). *Vocabulary: Description, Acquisition and Pedagogy.* Cambridge: Cambridge University Press.

Schmitt, N. et al. (eds.) (2002). *Vocabulary: Description, Acquisition and Pedagogy.* Shanghai: Shanghai Foreign Language Education Press.

Schneider, E. W. (1997). *Englishes around the World* (Vol. 1). Amsterdam: John Benjamins

Publishing Co.

Searle, J. (1969). *Speech Acts: An Essay in the Philosophy of Language.* Cambridge: Cambridge University Press.

Searle, J. (ed.) (1971). *The Philosophy of Language.* Oxford: Oxford University Press.

Serjeantson, M. S. (1935). *A History of Foreign Words in English.* New York: Routledge & Kegan Paul PLC.

Sidney I. Landau. (2001). *Dictionaries: The Art and Craft of Lexicography.* Cambridge: Cambridge University Press.

Silva, P. (ed.)(1996). *A Dictionary of South African English on Historical Principles.* Oxford: Oxford University Press.

Sinclair, J. (1999). *Corpus Concordance Collocation.* Shanghai: Shanghai Foreign Language Education Press.

Singleton, D. (2000). *Language and the Lexicon.* London: Arnold.

Skeat, W. W. (2005). *An Etymological Dictionary of the English Language.* Mineola, NY: Dover Publications.

Smith, R. (2005). *Global English: Gift or Curse?*: English Today, *21*(2), 56 – 62.

Soanes, C. and Stevenson, A. (eds.)(2009). *Concise Oxford English Dictionary.* Oxford: Oxford University Press.

Sokmen, A. (1993). Word Association Results: A Window to the Lexicons of ESL Students. *JALT Journal*, *15*(2), 135 – 150.

Sonntag, S. K. (2003). *The Local Politics of Global English.* Lanham: Lexington Books.

Spenser, A. and Zwicky, A. M. (eds.)(2007). *The Handbook of Morphology.* Oxford: Blackwell Publishers.

Sperber, D. and Wilson, D. (1995). *Relevance: Communication and Cognition.* Oxford: Blackwell.

Sperling, G. (1960). The Information Available in Brief Visual Presentations. *Psychological Monographs: General and Applied*, *74*(11), 1 – 30.

Sperling, G. (1967). Successive Approximations to a Model of Short Term Memory. *Acta Psychologica*, *27*, 285 – 292.

Steinberg, D. D. and Sciarini, N. V. (2006). *An Introduction to Psycholinguistics*, 2nd edition. Harlow: Pearson Longman.

Stockwell, R. and Minkova, D. (2001). *English Words: History and Structure.* Cambridge: Cambridge University Press.

Sweetser, E. (1990). From Etymology to Pragmatics. *Metaphorical and Cultural Aspects of Semantic Structure.* Cambridge: Cambridge University Press.

The New Oxford Dictionary of English. (1998). Oxford: Oxford University Press.

The Oxford-Duden Pictorial English-Chinese Dictionary. (1999). Hong Kong: Oxford Universty Press.

The Oxford English Dictionary, 2nd edition. (1989). Oxford: Oxford University Press.

Thomas, J. (1995). *Meaning in Interaction: An Introduction to Pragmatics.* London: Longman.

Tottie, G. (2002). *An Introduction to American English.* Oxford: Blackwell.

Trask, R. L. (2000). *Historical Linguistics.* Beijing: Foreign Language Teaching and Research Press.

Traugott, E. C. and Casher, R. B. (2005). *Regularity in Semantic Change.* Cambridge: Cambridge University Press.

Trudgill, P. and Hannah, J. (1994). *International English*. London: Edward Arnold.

Ullmann, S. (1979). *Semantics: An Introduction to the Science of Meaning*. New York: A Barnes & Noble Paperback.

Ungerer, F. and Schmid, H. J. (2001). *An Introduction to Cognitive Linguistics*. (pp. 45–46) Beijng: Foreign Language Teaching and Research Press.

Ur, P. (2000). *A Course in Language Teaching: Practice and Theory*. Beijing: Foreign Language Teaching and Research Press.

Verschueren, J. (1999). *Understanding Pragmatics*. London: Arnold.

Wardhaugh, R. (1996). *An Introduction to Sociolinguistics*. Blackwell: Oxford UK & Cambridge USA.

Webster's New Dictionary of Synonyms. (1978). G & C Merriam Company Publishers.

Webster's Third New International Dictionary of the English Language Unabridged. (1961). Springfield, Mass.: Merriam-Webster.

Weinstein, C. E. and Mayer, R. E. (1986). The Teaching of Learning Strategies. In M. C. Wittrock (ed.) *Hand-book of Research on Teaching, 3rd edition* (pp. 315–327). New York: Macmillan.

Wierzbicka, A. (1985). *Lexicography and Conceptual Analysis*. Ann Arbor: Karoma.

Wilkins, D. A. (1972). *Linguistics in Language Teaching*. London: Edward Arnold.

Wilson, D. (2004). Relevance, Word Meaning and Communication: The Past, Present and Future of Lexical Pragmatics. *Modern Foreign Languages*, 27(1), 1–13.

Woolard, G. (2000). Collocation: Encourages Learner Independence. In M. Lewis (ed.) *Teaching Collocation: Further Development in the Lexical Approach* (pp. 28–46). Oxford: Oxford University Press.

Yang, Y. and Hendricks, A. (2004). Collocation Awareness in the Writing Process. *Reflections of English Language Teaching*, 3, 51–78.

Yule, G. (1996). *Pragmatics*. Cambridge: Cambridge University Press.

21世纪英语教育周刊. 2009–5–18. 中国日报社.

董燕萍. 2005. 心理语言学与外语教学. 北京: 外语教学与研究出版社.

桂诗春. 2000. 新编心理语言学. 上海: 上海外语教育出版社.

桂诗春. 1991. 认知和语言. 外语教学与研究, 06.

何平安. 2004. 语料库语言学与英语教学. 北京: 外语教学与研究出版社.

何兆熊. 2000. 新编语用学概要. 上海: 上海外语教育出版社.

何自然. 2004. 当代语用学. 北京: 外语教学与研究出版社.

胡壮麟. 2004. 认知隐喻学. 北京: 北京大学出版社.

黄建华. 1992. 英俄德法西日语文词典研究. 北京: 商务印书馆.

蓝纯. 2005. 认知语言学与隐喻研究. 北京: 外语教学与研究出版社.

朗文当代英语词典(最新修订版). 1993. 北京: 朗文出版公司、世界图书出版公司.

陆谷孙. 1991/2007. 英汉大词典. 上海: 上海译文出版社.

牛津英语搭配词典. 2003. 北京: 外语教学与研究出版社.

牛津英语大词典(简编本). 2004. 上海: 上海外语教育出版社.

束定芳. 2000. 现代语义学. 上海: 上海外语教育出版社.

束定芳. 2000. 隐喻学研究. 上海: 上海外语教育出版社.

汪榕培. 2002. 英语词汇学高级教程. 上海: 上海外语教育出版社.

汪榕培、卢晓娟. 1997. 英语词汇学教程. 上海: 上海外语教育出版社.

汪榕培、王之江. 2006. 英语词汇学高级教程读本. 上海: 上海外语教育出版社.

汪榕培、王之江. 2008. 英语词汇学. 上海: 上海外语教育出版社.
汪榕培、王之江. 2008. 英语词汇学实践. 上海: 上海外语教育出版社.
汪榕培、王之江. 2008. 英语词汇学手册. 上海: 上海外语教育出版社.
汪榕培、王之江、吴晓维. 2005. 英语词汇学教程读本. 上海: 上海外语教育出版社.
王馥芳. 2004. 当代词典学与词典创新. 上海: 上海辞书出版社.
王寅. 2001. 语义理论与语言教学. 上海: 上海外语教育出版社.
网络与书编辑部. 2005. 词典的两个世界. 北京: 现代出版社.
文秋芳. 1996. 英语学习策略论. 上海: 上海外语教育出版社.
熊学亮. 1999. 认知语用学概论. 上海: 上海外语教育出版社.
杨惠中. 2002. 语料库语言学导论. 上海: 上海外语教育出版社.
英语搭配大词典. 1991. 南京: 江苏教育出版社.
英语习惯搭配词典. 2005. 北京: 北京科学技术出版社.
赵艳芳. 2001. 认知语言学概论. 上海: 上海外语教育出版社.

Key

Chapter 1

I. Match the following words to their definitions.
1. h 2. g 3. f 4. e 5. a 6. b 7. c 8. d 9. o 10. n 11. m 12. l 13. i 14. j 15. k

II. What are the Chinese for the following?
1. 首字母(组合)缩略词 2. 反义词 3. 同义词 4. 下义词 5. 词缀 6. 词素、语素 7. 词位、词汇单位 8. 习语、成语、俗语 9. 搭配词 10. 功能词 11. 实词 12. 语料库 13. 语料库语言学
14. 词块 15. 一词多义 16. 措辞、用词 17. 词类 18. 词目
19. 即 3C 产品：通讯产品（Communication）、电脑产品（Computer）和消费类电子产品（Consumer Electronics）。这三类产品互相融合，将三种数字化电子产品的功能互相渗透，从而实现信息资源的共享和互通，使人们能够在任何时间，任何地点实现信息交流与融合，达到更方便地工作和更快乐地生活的目的。
20. 5G 是 5GPP 的缩写，全称是 The 5th Generation Partnership Project，即第五代合作伙伴计划，指的是第五代移动通信技术。
21. 即 Global System for Mobile Communications 的缩写，意思是全球移动通信系统，简称"全球通"。
22. 即 SIM（Subscriber Identity Module）卡，是 GSM 提供的一种智能卡。
23. 即 Time Division Multiple Access 的缩略写法，译为"时分多址"，是一种现代移动通讯技术。
24. 即 Code Division Multiple Access 的缩略写法，译为"码分多址"，是第三代移动通讯技术的首选。第三代手机结合了无线通讯与网际网络等多媒体资讯，能够处理图象、语音、串流影音等多种媒体形式。
25. 是 liquid crystal display 的缩略写法，译为"液晶显示"，液晶电视机可以叫 a liquid crystal display TV。
26. 是 ultra mobile personal computer 的缩略写法，译为"超级移动个人电脑"。
27. 是 sport utility vehicle 的缩略写法，译为"运动型多功能车"。
28. 是 compact disc read-only memory 的缩略写法，译为"（信息容量极大的）光盘，只读存储器"。
29. 是 information technology 的缩略写法，译为"信息技术"。
30. 是 digital videodisc 或 digital versatile disc 的缩略写法，译为"数字激光视盘；数字多功能光盘"。
31. 是 hyper text markup language 的缩略写法，译为"超文本标记语言"。
32. 是 local area network 的缩略写法，译为"局域网"。
33. 是 random-access memory 的缩略写法，译为"随机存取存储器"。RAM 也可译为"随机存取存储；内存"。
34. 是 China Railway High-Speed 的缩略写法，译为"中国高速铁路"，即"动车组列车"，是中国铁道部对中国高速铁路系统建立的品牌名称，用来指时速 200km/h 以上的高速列车。

Chapter 2

I. True or False decisions.
1. F 2. F 3. F 4. T 5. T 6. T 7. F 8. F 9. F 10. T 11. F 12. T 13. T 14. F
15. T

II. Choose the best choice to answer the following questions.
1. C   2. C   3. A   4. D   5. B   6. C   7. A   8. A   9. A   10. C

Chapter 3

I. Give the British English equivalents of the following American English words.
1. flat   2. row   3. pram   4. plaster   5. loo or WC   6. tin   7. mince   8. biscuit   9. maize   10. nappy   11. lift   12. rubber   13. torch   14. chips   15. petrol   16. bloke/chap   17. motorway   18. bonnet   19. jelly   20. jam

II. Give the American English equivalents of the following British English words.
1. kerosene   2. lawyer   3. license plate   4. line   5. mail   6. motor home   7. movie theater   8. muffler   9. napkin   10. zero   11. overpass   12. pacifier   13. pants   14. parking lot   15. period   16. pharmacist   17. potato chips   18. rent   19. sausage   20. sidewalk

III. Give the American English equivalents of the following British English words, and put them into Chinese.
1. storage battery/cell 蓄电池   2. antenna 天线   3. studio apartment 一室一单元   4. custom-made 定做的   5. checkroom 衣帽间   6. crib 儿童床   7. absorbent cotton 脱脂棉   8. (potato) chips 炸土豆片   9. thumbtack 图钉   10. bathrobe 晨衣   11. elementary/grade school 小学   12. realtor 房地产经纪人   13. station wagon 客货两用车   14. flat tire 漏气车胎   15. freight car (一节)货车   16. bobby pin 发夹   17. purse 女用手提包   18. installment plan 分期付款(购货法)   19. hardware store 五金店   20. ready-made 现成的   21. filling station 汽车加油站   22. braids 辫子   23. comfort station 公共厕所   24. sideburns 鬓角   25. one-way/round-trip ticket 单程/往返(票)   26. wrench 扳钳   27. dessert 餐后甜品   28. faucet 龙头   29. long-distance call 长途电话   30. rare 煮得嫩的

IV. Choose the best choice to answer the following questions.
1. A   2. C   3. B   4. B   5. A   6. A   7. B

Chapter 4

I. Fill in the blanks by using the following new words with the appropriate forms.
1. bad hair days   2. Canyoning   3. consensualist   4. don't ask, don't tell   5. ethnic cleansing   6. Euroland   7. Gabbers   8. goodfellas   9. hot desking   10. internots   11. luvvies   12. off-message   13. personal stereo   14. pukka   15. roadkills   16. slacker   17. SoHo   18. stalked   19. twigloo   20. zorbing   21. Black Monday   22. boot   23. domains   24. Dragons   25. du jour   26. eco-friendly   27. feel good factors   28. gnarly   29. informericals   30. marketization

Chapter 5

I. Fill in the blanks with the proper forms of the words in brackets.
1. asocial   2. arranged   3. condescended   4. empowered   5. interview   6. misconduct   7. outdoor   8. telecommunication   9. unconditional   10. adjustable

II. Use *in-*(*il-*, *im-*, *ir-*), *non-*, *un-* to form new words of the following.
1. incorrect   2. unfriendly   3. unwrap   4. nonfree   5. irrational   6. inconsistent   7. unremarked   8. nonbusiness   9. nongreen   10. unexpected

III. Fill in the blanks with the proper forms of the appropriate words in the following box.
1. Homing   2. dispatched   3. light   4. sound   5. sense   6. changes   7. attributes   8. exemplify
9. mobile   10. compass

IV. True or False decisions.
1. T   2. F   3. F   4. T   5. F   6. T   7. F   8. T   9. T   10. F

Chapter 6

I. True or False decisions.
1. T   2. F   3. F   4. T   5. F

II. Fill in the blanks with proper words according to the first letters given.
1. abbreviation   2. existing   3. Instruction   4. first   5. shortening   6. acronym   7. Oriented
8. recursive   9. backronym   10. apronym

III. Read the following passage and fill in the appropriate words with the help of the first letters given.
1. root   2. affixes   3. verb   4. peas   5. adjective   6. enthusiasm   7. flabby   8. Standard
9. comic   10. Liaise

IV. Translate the following sentences from English to Chinese, paying attention to onomatopoeic words.
1. 咔嚓！棒子断为两截。
2. 只有地下室窗户上的鼓风机发出无休无止的呼呼声。
3. 沿着月牙海湾的地方，从一堆堆破碎的岩石堆中，一群羊叽嗒叽嗒地跑了过来。
4. 院子里的雄鸡已经叫头遍了。
5. 他感到简直要大喊大唱，耳际仿佛传来无数翅膀的拍击声。
6. 他们一路踏着泥水向村子去。
7. 木柴在火中哔哔剥剥烧得正旺。
8. 伊梅尔达哼了声："没家教！"
9. 接着，路尽头一所农舍附近响起狗的汪汪声。那是一声长长的痛苦的哀鸣，似乎是因恐惧而发出的。
10. 冬季傍晚，我一打开门常常听到"唿——唿——唿，唿——唿"的鸟叫声。声音很悦耳，前三个音节听起来有点像英语的"你好哇！"；有时便只是鸟叫而已。

Chapter 7

I. What are the non-denotational meanings of the italicized words in the following sentences?
1. Stylistic meaning. It is most probably used by a criminal talking about the happenings to another criminal.
2. Affective meaning. It means over-determination to achieve the aim by whatever means.
3. Collocative meaning. Handsome and pretty share common ground in the meaning "good-looking", but they are different in the nouns they collocate with.
4. Connotative meaning. Rose here has a connotation of beauty, youth and fragrance.

II. Work out the meanings of the word *way* in the following sentences and discuss what kind of trend is happening to the meanings of *way*.
1. *Way* means "route along with sth. moving".
2. *Way* means "manner of doing sth.".

3. *Way* means "distance".
4. *Way* means "neighborhood".
5. *Way* means "particular aspect of sth.".

   It shows that the meanings of *way* can be used to indicate many different things. There is the tendency in English to have some words so powerful that they can be all-embracing. For example: affair, matter, condition and thing.

III. **Many technical terms are used in daily life and get their meanings extended. Find out the general meanings of the following words by matching the pairs.**
1. h 2. c 3. b 4. a 5. f 6. d 7. g 8. i 9. j 10. e

IV. **Point out the shortening form of the following phrases in their new meanings.**
1. crescent 2. the main 3. lyric 4. correspondence 5. duties 6. a natural 7. sale 8. expecting 9. dumps 10. gate 11. concert 12. fare 13. cardinal 14. play 15. enormity

V. **Study the meanings of the italics and discuss the different functions of euphemism in our life. What do you think of the phenomenon of more and more euphemisms?**

   The italics are all used euphemistically to mean: 1) ugly or unattractive; 2) a bad driver; 3) died; 4) toilet; 5) stole.

   Some euphemisms are formal euphemisms and they are different from the slang euphemistic substitutes. In the first case they are solemn and delicately evasive, and in the second rough and somewhat cynical, reflecting an attempt to laugh off an unpleasant fact.

VI. **With the illustration of the word *expire* to describe the possible process of meaning change.**
   The possible change process:
   Word *expire* has established literal sense, S1: die.
   Some creative use of *expire* gives it a new figurative sense, S2: come to the end of a period of validity.
   S2 catches on and becomes established. S2 stands side to side with S1 and *expire* gets a new meaning.
   S1 begins to become less popular. S2 begins to be perceived as literal.

Chapter 8

I. **How can you decide which one of the pair is relatively more normal?**
   The first sentence in each pair is relatively more normal. So in deciding synonyms, a contextual approach helps to find out anything which affects the contextual normality of lexical items.

II. **Read the following paragraph from *A Tale of Two Cities* by Charles Dickens. How many contrasts can be found and what effect have they achieved?**
   They are: best/worst; wisdom/foolishness; belief/incredulity; Light/Darkness; spring/winter; hope/despair; everything/nothing; going direct to Heaven/going direct the other way; good/evil. In total, nine contrasts are presented, most of which are established antonymous pairs. The effect of the antonymy is to describe a period of confusion, contradiction and extremity.

III. **Choose the right word to fill in each sentence.**
1. bated 2. blondes 3. break 4. bridal 5. pedal 6. reigned 7. raze 8. stationary 9. complement 10. pore

IV. It is said that native speakers are generally in agreement over a fair range of examples of homonymy and polysemy. Which of the following pairs do you think are homonyms, and which are cases of polysemy?

Polysemy: barge, court, dart, stuff, watch
Homonymy: fleet, jam, pad, steep, stem

V. Find in column B the superordinates of the words in column A.
1. c   2. h   3. e   4. a   5. f   6. g   7. i   8. d   9. j   10. b

Chapter 9

I. True or False decisions.
1. T 2. F 3. T 4. T 5. F 6. T 7. F 8. T 9. T 10. F 11. F 12. T 13. T 14. F 15. F 16. T 17. T 18. T 19. F 20. F

II. Cloze.
1. A 2. B 3. D 4. A 5. D 6. D 7. A 8. B 9. C 10. D

Chapter 10

I. Try to find the idioms in the following sentences and explain them.
1. play the game: to behave in a fair and honest way
2. coin money: to earn a lot of money easily or quickly
3. drug on the market: something that can't be sold because there is too much of it available or it is out of date
4. seventh heaven: state of great happiness
5. in hot water: in trouble
6. leave at the drop of a hat: without waiting, immediately
7. spill the beans: to tell sth. that someone else wanted you to keep a secret
8. tear one's heart: to make someone feel extremely upset
9. Tom, Dick and Harry: anybody at all
10. the birds and the bees: the truth about sex, birth and life

II. Complete the following binomials with proper words.
1. pains   2. pieces   3. desist   4. baggage   5. front   6. corner   7. pine   8. pant   9. haul
10. truly   11. nonsense   12. moil   13. turns   14. means   15. good

III. Translate the following proverbs of William Shakespeare.
1. 家里成长的青年只有家里的见识。 2. 人不是天使。 3. 一口气又哭又笑,难以做得到。 4. 多讲实际,少弄玄虚。 5. 借出你的钱,失掉你的朋友。 6. 有就是有。 7. 要了什么就要付出什么。 8. 凡事必有因。 9. 每个人只该得自己的一份。 10. 把真理告诉魔鬼使他感到羞愧。 11. 忧伤无益。 12. 简洁是智慧的灵魂。 13. 真正爱情之路从来崎岖不平。 14. 女人是易碎的器皿。 15. 整个世界就是一个舞台。 16. 所有的猫都爱鱼,但又怕湿了猫爪。 17. 任何事都有个分寸。 18. 聪明的父亲才了解自己的孩子。 19. 懦夫死多次,勇士只死一次。 20. 你把老年人的头放在年轻的肩膀上。

Chapter 11

I. Among the alternative words and expressions in the brackets, select one with the closest meaning related to the word MEAN in italic type.

1. represented 2. shows 3. that is to say 4. indicate 5. stand for 6. signified 7. be specially important 8. intend 9. is well-intentioned 10. suggested

Chapter 12

I. Complete each phrase of simile with a proper word.

1. black 2. bold 3. bright 4. clear 5. cold 6. dark 7. dry 8. fat 9. greedy 10. hard
11. hot 12. like 13. mad 14. pale 15. quick 16. a Jew 17. lead 18. A, B, C 19. a mole
20. a guinea 21. a cherry 22. punch 23. grass 24. a fox 25. a rake 26. a church mouse 27. a lark 28. a bee 29. down 30. life

II. Complete each sentence of metaphorical expression with a word from the box.

1. broke 2. get 3. give 4. keep 5. ran 6. took 7. done 8. explained 9. fade 10. passed
11. thrown 12. hid 13. put 14. working 15. write 16. hide 17. work 18. throw 19. do
20. broken

Chapter 13

I. True or False decisions.
1. T 2. F 3. F 4. T 5. F

II. Choose the best choice to answer the following questions.
1. C 2. D 3. A 4. B 5. D 6. A

Chapter 14

I. Choose the best choice to answer the following questions.
1. D 2. A 3. B 4. C 5. D 6. A

II. True or False decisions.
1. T 2. T 3. F 4. T 5. T

III. (Omitted)

Chapter 15

I. Fill in the blanks with proper words according to the first letters given.
1. Memory 2. storage 3. encoding 4. retrieval 5. Short-term 6. Long-term 7. episodic
8. Semantic 9. Decay 10. Interference

II. Choose the best choice to answer the following questions.
1. D 2. C 3. A 4. B 5. D

Chapter 16

I. How many words do you know?

Level A
1. committee 2. strong 3. popular 4. success 5. government 6. house 7. head 8. true 9. office 10. let

Level B
11. ball 12. bag 13. remember 14. share 15. king 16. read 17. leg 18. receive 19. suggestion 20. camp

Level C
21. travel 22. organic 23. councilor 24. glance 25. female 26. discover 27. champion 28. employee 29. instruction 30. estimate

Level D
31. residence 32. finish 33. ladder 34. boycotting 35. canal 36. yield 37. vacuum 38. portable 39. mining 40. waiter

Level E
41. feminism 42. handicapped 43. ash 44. barrister 45. volunteer 46. vaccine 47. easy 48. manufacture 49. grill 50. spa

Gauging your vocabulary size

Now count up your score at each level and make a small mark for your total at each level, join up the crosses and see your vocabulary profile. This will tell you how many words you know at each frequency level. Usually you will get a curve going down towards the right. The size of your vocabulary is the last level at which you score above 5.

	How many words do you know? Basic Words Test				
Level	A	B	C	D	E
	→1,000	→3,000	→5,000	→10,000	→20,000
10					
9					
8					
7					
6					
5					
4					
3					
2					
1					
0					